Anti-Social Media?

The Impact on Journalism and Society

EDITED BY
JOHN MAIR, TOR CLARK,
NEIL FOWLER, RAYMOND SNODDY
and
RICHARD TAIT

Published 2018 by Abramis academic publishing

www.abramis.co.uk

ISBN 978 1 84549 729 3

Printed and bound in the United Kingdom

Typeset in Garamond

Abramis is an imprint of arima publishing.

arima publishing
ASK House, Northgate Avenue
Bury St Edmunds, Suffolk IP32 6BB
t: (+44) 01284 700321

www.arimapublishing.com

Contents

Acknowledgements

This is (probably) the 26th Abramis 'Hackademic' book.

These books are always team efforts. This one more than most. People ask us how we get them together so quickly. The answer is a good idea which drives them, a weekly conference call and good author contacts. This book emerged from discussions around our previous edited collection, Brexit, Trump and the Media (Abramis, 2017), and took six months of blood, sweat and tears. We five editors have worked together genially and effectively throughout the process as we de facto peer reviewed all the contributions along the way.

We offer a sincere thanks to all our 40 contributors who, along with the five editors, offer their wisdom and services without charge. They believe, as we do, that these big issues in media and society need the widest debate and discussion if we're going to find the best solutions. We look now for the 'impact'.

Huge thanks as well to Richard and Pete Franklin from our publisher, Abramis, and our wonderful cover designer Dean Stockton. They all turn it round in record time without a word of complaint.

Our small but effective team now offers you this volume in the hope you will find enjoyment and perhaps even a little enlightenment.

John Mair, Oxford.
Tor Clark, Leicester.
Neil Fowler, Northumberland.
Raymond Snoddy, London.
Richard Tait, London.

The editors

John Mair has taught journalism at the Universities of Coventry, Kent, Northampton, Brunel, Edinburgh Napier, Guyana and the Communication University of China. He has edited 20 'hackademic' volumes over the last eight years, on subjects ranging from trust in television, the health of investigative journalism, reporting the 'Arab Spring', to three volumes on the Leveson Inquiry. He and Richard Lance Keeble invented the sub-genre. John also created the Coventry Conversations, which attracted 350 media movers and shakers to Coventry University; the podcasts of those have been downloaded six million times worldwide. Since then, he has launched the Northampton Chronicles, Media Mondays at Napier and most recently the Harrow Conversations at Westminster University. In a previous life, he was an award-winning producer/director for the BBC, ITV and Channel 4, and a secondary school teacher.

Tor Clark is Associate Professor in Journalism and Programme Director of the BA Journalism degree at the University of Leicester, UK. After studying Politics and History at Lancaster University, he worked for the Northamptonshire Evening Telegraph, before becoming editor, first of the Harborough Mail in Leicestershire, and then of Britain's oldest newspaper, the Rutland & Stamford Mercury, where he led a successful bid to the Heritage Lottery Fund to preserve its unique 300-year-old newspaper archive. Previously he was Principal Lecturer in Journalism at De Montfort University in Leicester, where he launched two Journalism degrees, one accredited by the NCTJ. He holds an MA in Mass Communication from the University of Leicester and is now researching towards a PhD. He is reviews editor of the academic journal Journalism Education, a regular commentator on politics and media for BBC Leicester and a Senior Fellow of the Higher Education Academy.

Neil Fowler has been in journalism since graduation, starting life as trainee reporter on the Leicester Mercury. He went on to edit four regional dailies, including The Journal in the north east of England and The Western Mail in Wales. He was then publisher of The Toronto Sun in Canada before returning to the UK to edit Which? magazine. In 2010/11 he was the Guardian Research Fellow at Oxford University's Nuffield College where he investigated the decline and future of regional and local newspapers in the UK. From then until 2016 he helped organise the college's prestigious David Butler media and politics seminars. As well as being an occasional contributor to trade magazines he now acts as an adviser to organisations on their management and their external and internal communications and media policies and strategies.

Raymond Snoddy OBE, after studying at Queen's University in Belfast, worked on local and regional newspapers, before joining The Times in 1971. Five years later he moved to the Financial Times and reported on media issues before returning to The Times as media editor in 1995. At present, he is a freelance journalist writing for a range of publications. He presented NewsWatch on the BBC from its inception in 2004 until 2012. His other television work has included presenting Channel 4's award-winning series Hard News. In addition, Snoddy is the author of a biography of the media tycoon Michael Green, Greenfinger. He was awarded an OBE for his services to journalism in 2000.

Richard Tait CBE is Professor of Journalism at the School of Journalism, Media and Culture, at Cardiff University. From 2003 to 2012, he was director of the school's Centre for Journalism. He was editor of Newsnight from 1985 to 1987, editor of Channel 4 News from 1987 to 1995 and editor-in-chief of ITN from 1995 to 2002. He was a BBC governor and chair of the governors' programme complaints committee from 2004 to 2006, and a BBC Trustee and chair of the Trust's editorial standards committee from 2006 to 2010. He is a fellow of the Society of Editors and the Royal Television Society, board member of the International News Safety Institute and an independent trustee of the Disasters Emergency Committee.

Introduction

Journalism, free speech and the search and social giants

These are troubling days for journalism, says Mark Thompson. Even the primacy of fact and well-sourced, objective reporting over delusion and propaganda is under assault. Transparency is the first task for those writing the algorithms, he argues

A concert party of Russia and other repressive regimes, populists and extremists, assorted trolls and bots, not to mention the 45th President of the United States, are doing their best to convince the world of what George Orwell in Nineteen Eighty-Four called 'blackwhite': that dispassionate, accurate journalism is fake news, and conspiracy theories, gross exaggeration and outright lies the real thing.

Their aim is to level reality with their own alternative facts and, by this process of levelling, to rob serious journalism of its civic impact and value. They don't have to be believed to succeed; they merely need to sow enough doubt in enough minds that a large slice of the population no longer knows who to trust.

Some of the conventions that protect the ability of real journalists to report real news are also being flouted. In June 2018 we learned that, as part of a leak inquiry, the FBI had seized years' worth of emails and phone records belonging to New York Times reporter Ali Watkins. This may be standard operating procedure in controlled societies. In the US, it breached established precedent,

was manifestly against the spirit of the First Amendment, and was rightly condemned by the Committee to Protect Journalists as a 'fundamental threat to press freedom'.

But these threats can be seen off. The fake-newsers may have convinced some people that up is down for now. Sooner or later brute reality and common sense will settle the argument in favour of the facts. As for the state and press freedom: the safeguard enshrined in the Bill of Rights, and the tradition of self-restraint by the authorities when free speech is at stake, should prevail – at least if citizens speak out, and Congress and the courts do their job.

But the most serious threat facing journalism – the disruption of the traditional business model, and the failure of all but a handful of titles across the western world to find credible digital alternatives – is much more intractable. It presents

1

as an economic problem but its consequences, which are already playing out and, unless something changes, are likely to grow far worse over the coming years, are civic and political.

Democracies cannot remain healthy if citizens do not know what is happening in their communities; if public and private institutions are not held to account; and if elections come and go without issues being aired and candidates being scrutinised. Unfortunately, at present the local, regional and national professional journalism, which historically played such an important role in meeting these civic needs, is ailing – in some cities and regions dying – in much of America and the West.

There are exceptions, and The New York Times is one of them. We have national scale and international potential. We realised in time that high-quality journalism, a deep relationship with our most engaged readers, and an effective digital subscription model offered a far more promising path to the future than digital advertising alone. Today we have more digital news subscribers than any other news organisation in the world – and, at getting on for four million, twice as many total subscriber-relationships as at the peak of print 25 years ago.

Our revenue and operating profit have been growing, not 'failing', whatever a little bird may have told you. Most importantly, we have a newsroom and editorial department, which – at some 1,450 strong – are bigger and more formidable than they were 10 and 20 years ago. For me, that's less the result of our digital success than the single most important reason for it: The New York Times responded to digital disruption, not by disinvesting in high-quality news and opinion, but by doubling down on them. And as we've found – whatever cultural pessimists may say – a growing number of people here and around the world are willing to pay for it. But we have advantages that most news providers do not enjoy. And, even with those advantages, we find the environment for growing our digital revenue – and securing the funding of our newsroom – harder than I believe we should.

So to what extent are the major digital platforms – Google, Facebook, Apple and the others – part of the problem? And, if they are, what could they, we, and the world's policy-makers and regulators do to put things right? Two caveats first:

- One: there's no point blaming individual digital companies, no matter how big, for the fundamental attributes of the internet, or for the decline and fall of the cosy print-advertising based business model that supported journalism for so long. Neither is their fault and, in any event, there's no way of putting the clock back.

- Two: I want to proceed with a presumption of good faith on the part of the major platforms. Like many media executives, I've spent time with the leaders of Google, Facebook and Apple and I've seen no evidence that they want to destroy journalism, or are unaware of the crisis in the economics of news, or unwilling to explore ways of improving the eco-system.

Google, in particular, has taken a series of tangible steps to help news organisations build digital subscriptions, for instance allowing publishers to deploy their subscription business rules on its platform rather than imposing Google's own rules on them.

However, major unresolved issues remain. We can put them under four broad headings:

- Opacity – we do not know, beyond inevitably imperfect and incomplete empirical observation, how the algorithms of the major platforms sort and prioritise our content, nor can we reliably predict or influence changes in those algorithms, nor in any sense hold the companies to account for them.

- Impoverishment of the news experience – to appreciate and critique news sources over time, and to decide which to trust, users need to develop sophisticated relationships with news brands and individual reporters and opinion writers, but the platforms encourage atomised consumption of single stories and the jumbling of stories of different depth and quality from different sources, and they strip away essential signals – news or opinion, for instance, lead story or minor footnote – about editorial intentionality.

- Inequitable economics – although the platforms undoubtedly help publishers reach new audiences, most publishers believe that the current division of the economic benefit of the presence of news content on the platforms unfairly favours the platforms.

- Independence and plurality of editorial decision-making – this is the least-discussed issue; it is that open societies require multiple independent points of editorial control, which can compete and hold each other to account, and between which the public can choose; but that the major platforms may decide, or feel pressured, to replace this plurality with single points of essentially algorithmic editorial control.

These four categories are not mutually exclusive, but mutually reinforcing: the relative poverty of the news experience on the platforms makes it harder for publishers to monetise it; the opacity of the operation of the search and social algorithms increases the risk of a loss of plurality in editorial decision-making; and of course business model failure because of the inferior economics of the platforms will have its own impact on plurality.

Most people assume that publishers only care about the disappointing revenue they derive from their presence on the platforms. My view is that all four headings are important, and not just to publishers but to society at large. Let me offer you a few responses to these concerns:

- First, full transparency about both algorithmic and human editorial selection by the major digital platforms is an essential preliminary if we are to address any of these issues. It would be best if this were done voluntarily, but even if it requires regulation or legislation, it must be done – and done promptly.

- As a second preliminary, the major platforms must engage with the collective industry bodies of the news business to arrive at shared principles both on the presentation and choice of news content, and on its monetisation. The stakes – and the need for consistency and comparability in the treatment of news providers – mean that, though the present informal bilateral relationships between, say, The New York Times and Google, or The Washington Post and Facebook, should no doubt continue, they are not enough.

- Third, we need to do more to restore the labels and design cues that help users make sense of news in a physical newspaper, or on a TV screen, or even on a traditional web page, but which are stripped out in smartphone newsfeeds and search results. Without sufficient signposts, no wonder users confuse news and opinion and other significant editorial nuances.

- Fourth, regulators, both in the US and in Europe and other jurisdictions, should examine how well these markets are functioning. In economic terms, news provision on the major platforms consists of two barters: consumers exchange their attention and personal data for the services provided by the platform; while publishers offer the platforms valuable content in exchange for distribution, audience leads advertising opportunities. It is sometimes argued that, because the major platforms do not charge consumers money for their services, the public cannot suffer exploitative pricing. But barter implies an exchange of goods or services of real and quantifiable value in which a party can get a better or worse deal. If scale and network effects allow a search or social platform to achieve market dominance, a consumer who feels that they must use the platform may find themselves exchanging their attention and data for less in return by way of services than they would if there were effective competition. The same goes for a publisher who may conclude that they have no choice but to offer their content to a platform despite the poor economics. In other words, a market based on barter can experience market dominance, market failure and market abuse. I don't want to jump to the conclusion that such abuse is occurring, but these markets deserve close technical scrutiny and may require competition remedies.

- Lastly, the topic of independence and plurality of editorial decision-making. We face an immediate threat here, which is that Facebook's catalogue of missteps with data and extreme and hateful content will lead it into a naïve attempt to set itself up as the digital world's editor-in-chief, prioritising and presumably downgrading and rejecting content on a survey- and data-driven assessment of whether the provider of the content is broadly trusted or not.

Now you might expect The New York Times to favour such a scheme. Indeed Mark Zuckerberg, whose idea this seems to be, told us The New York Times should

4

expect to do well in such a ranking. In fact, we regard the concept of broadly trusted as a sinister one, which misunderstands the role journalism plays in an open society and is likely to lead to damage and distort, not just the news business, but democratic debate.

Democracy depends in part on unbounded competition between different journalistic perspectives and the clash of different judgements and opinions. History suggests that mainstream news organisations frequently get it right, but also that, not infrequently, it is the outliers who should be listened to.

At any given moment – think of mainstream media today in Russia, or in continental Europe in the 1920s and 1930s – a majority of the public may judge trustworthiness incorrectly. To feed transient majority sentiment about trust back into the editorial decision-making process – and to do it essentially behind closed doors – is profoundly dangerous. The process of citizens making up their own mind which news source to believe is messy, and can indeed lead to fake news, but to rob them of that ability, and to replace the straightforward accountability of editors and publishers for the news they produce with a centralised trust algorithm will not make democracy healthier but damage it further. The depth of Facebook's lack of understanding of the nature and civic purpose of news was recently revealed by their proposal – somewhat modified after representations from the news industry – to categorise and label journalism used for marketing purposes by publishers as political advocacy, given that both contained political content.

This is like arguing that an article about pornography in The New York Times is the same as pornography. Facebook admitted to us that their practical problem was that they were under immense public pressure to label political advocacy, but that their algorithm was unable to tell the difference between advocacy and journalism. This would be the same algorithm that will soon be given the new task of telling the world which news to trust.

When it comes to news, Facebook still doesn't get it. In its efforts to clear up one bad mess it seems set on joining those who want to blur the line between reality-based journalism and propaganda. But the underlying danger – of the agency of editors and public alike being usurped by centralised algorithmic control – is present with every digital platform where we do not fully understand how the processes of editorial selection and prioritisation take place. Which right now means all of them.

Thus the urgent need for transparency. The internet could still fulfill its promise as the enabler of more informed, more-empowered democracies. But it won't get there on its own. And nor will the major digital platforms.

* This chapter is taken from a presentation made by the author at the Open Markets Institute conference in June 2018 - 'Breaking the News: Free Speech & Democracy in the Age of Platform Monopoly'.

Note on the contributor

Mark Thompson is President and CEO of The New York Times Company. He was previously Director General of the BBC.

Section One

The context of social media

* * *

Despite its obvious benefits, social media needs regulating

Raymond Snoddy

Jeff Jarvis, the Leonard Tow Professor of Journalistic Innovation at the City University of New York and author of Geeks Bearing Gifts, believes technology is being blamed for the behaviour of a small number of people.

"Computers do not threaten or harass people – fraudsters, propagandists, bigots, misogynists and jerks do."

Despite that we demand technology companies cure what ails us as if technology were the disease. The internet, Jarvis argues, is not ruining humankind, humankind is still trying to figure out what the internet can and should be. Studies have produced no consensus on the definition of what the problems are, let alone the solutions. Some have even argued that we cannot agree on where to start the conversation.

But Jarvis believes good can come of the current crisis 'trumped up or not' and that there is the potential for a flight to quality on the net. Senior Google executives are now promising the platform will take responsibility for the authority, reliability and quality of sources ranking. It's only 24 years since the creation of the commercial web and it is too early to know what the web is yet. Jarvis worries about the danger of premature regulation.

He worries too about the unintended consequences of well-intentioned regulation, but mostly he is concerned we may be entering a full-blown moral panic with technology-internet platforms as the enemy. Jarvis insists publishers should now work with platforms to fulfil journalism's real job – to convene communities into civil, informed and productive conversations.

Alan Rusbridger, former editor of The Guardian, now Principal of Lady Margaret Hall, University of Oxford, argues in an extract from his latest book, Breaking News, that social media has created 'the most prodigious capability for spreading lies the world has ever seen'. And as the economic system for supporting journalism looks dangerously unstable, the stakes for truth have never been higher.

In this extract from a wide-ranging and extensive book Rusbridger examines in detail the claim by President Trump in a speech at a Florida rally that Sweden was now facing serious social problems because of the large number of migrants it had taken in. The Swedish Government was mystified but Trump explained to his 40m Twitter followers that he had got his information from a Fox News documentary. This had featured a gonzo journalist dealing in outrage and entertainment who has claimed that rape and violence had spread across Sweden because of its immigration polices.

What Rusbridger saw as the 'germ' continued to spread with former UKIP leader Nigel Farage using his radio show to call the Swedish city of Malmo 'the rape capital of Europe' and maybe the world. Matters got worse with reports a 17 year-old girl had been raped in Malmo and lighter-fuel poured into her and ignited. While there was no doubt about the rape, Malmo police eventually said the lighter-fuel story was untrue. An investigation by the Dagens Nyheter newspaper found no correlation between rape and immigration levels and Rusbridger also concludes apparent rises in Swedish rape levels may be linked to the legal criteria involved. He argues:

> *"The patient work of journalists to take time to discover what actually happened was buried in an avalanche of rumour, and then invisible except to the relatively tiny minority who still cared enough for old-fashioned facts to pay for them."*

Professor John Naughton, a Senior Research Fellow in the Centre for Research in the Arts, Social Sciences and Humanities at Cambridge University, and technology correspondent of The Observer, argues Facebook founder Mark Zuckerberg has created a monster, but unlike Frankenstein he is still enamoured of his creation. It has made him richer than Croesus and the undisputed ruler of an empire of 2.2m users. Facebook has given Zuckerberg power and the responsibilities that go with it. Naughton says:

> *"But it is increasingly clear that his creature is out of control, that he is uneasy about the power and has few good ideas about how to discharge his responsibilities."*

Problems with Facebook surrounding corporate governance and social responsibility are made more acute because Zuckerberg has the economic power of a monopolist. He also operates a business model that affects democratic processes and may perhaps have influenced the outcomes of the 2016 EU Referendum in the UK and the presidential election in the US.

The level of engagement with Facebook is truly staggering – every 60 seconds 510,000 comments are posted, 293,000 statuses are updated and 136,000 photos are uploaded.

The world has belatedly woken up to the fact we are in a perfect storm. It is made up of networks which lead to global monopolies, a form of capitalism which makes insatiable demands for user engagement using addictive apps, which lead

8

to digital echo chambers online and the weaponising of social media by political actors.

In a revealing interview Zuckerberg was asked about false news and continuing to carry Infowars even though, among many other conspiracy theories, it perpetuates the claim the Sandy Hook school massacres didn't happen. "Everybody gets things wrong," replied the Facebook founder, who added it would limit choice if everything that was wrong was taken down.

Naughton notes Infowars continues to flourish on Facebook and asks whether it was there because everybody gets things wrong, or because the website has 900,000 followers.

The problem with ruling the world is you have to govern and that apparently is not what Zuckerberg wants to do. "In which case who will?" Prof Naughton asks.

Michael Schrage, a research fellow at MIT's Sloan School of Management's Initiative on the Digital Economy, and former Washington Post journalist, believes you should ignore bots, Russians and political polarisation. It's the elites who have failed society. The problem is elites can't help being elitist and experts can't resist being experts and their combined vanity is their great vulnerability.

The New York Times, Oxford, Harvard, the BBC, the CIA and, perhaps, the NHS, have plenty to fear because their status is at stake. Social media environments are hostile environments for experts and elites – more than 70 of the top 100 Twitter accounts are celebrity, personality or pop culture orientated. One problem is the surge of 'self-indulgent self-expression' by experts communicating via social media undermines the values of institutional integrity that confer authority and credibility.

The centre of gravity shifts when social media reveals more about experts than their expertise.

President Trump has exploited this conundrum brilliantly by luring elite and expert critics into revealing their least professional selves. Schrage believed when Donald Trump became President he would be happy with all the levers of power at his disposal and give up Twitter. He admits he could not have been more wrong. Twitter gave Trump the power to define himself and disintermediate the hostile critics who would define him. His Twitter goal and role is to let others make fools of themselves. If experts and elites, whether it be over Brexit or Trump, refuse to come to terms with the new trolling reality the 'death of expertise' would in truth be a suicide.

Dr Kostas Saltzis, a lecturer in the School of Media, Communication and Sociology at the University of Leicester, stands back and looks at the history of the rise and rise of social media. From 2010 to the beginning of 2018 active social media users exploded from one billion to 2.6bn, around 42 per cent of the global population. It's not just about numbers it's the fact social media has permeated every aspect of human interaction, from information searching and sharing to professional networks and online dating. Early optimism has been replaced by more sceptical approaches although this may be because social media is still in its infancy.

The term social media is probably used too broadly and covers very different platforms and applications. A breakdown along functional lines differentiates between social networking sites aimed at personal contact such as Facebook, sites which exchange user-generated content like YouTube and Amazon-type online marketplaces. Social media has enabled people to communicate and connect in ways previously unimaginable but the phenomenon has also led to the blurring of private and public spaces. Grey spaces have also been created which are both public and private something individuals, employers, the law and the media are still struggling to adapt to. As a result previous assumptions about the role of mediated communication in society will have to be rethought.

Paul Armstrong, strategist and author of Disruptive Technologies, notes writers such as Jaron Lanier, the US computer specialist, argue it would be best if everyone were to close down their social media accounts. Yet people stick around 'for fear of missing out, laziness or because they don't see the problem'. Armstrong believes we should not jettison what we have learned about how we have been abused, and the good that social media has done, can do, and will do, deserves 'its day in the sun'. Even in problematical areas such as news and information social media should help users expand their thinking, but not at the expense of truth. Tackling misinformation is an uphill struggle when 67 per cent of Americans get their news from social media. Yet Twitter, for example, is increasingly a channel for the oppressed of the world to get the truth out to others. From lost dogs to helping people with mental illness, social media platforms have connected people with information they need at the right time.

With important issues still unresolved we are now entering a new era of the social media, one dominated by artificial intelligence (AI) and quantum computing. In fact AI will be the next great bastion of social media but ethics will still play a key role in making new platforms and technologies matter. The key will be adding the humanity back into social media and over the next ten years we may have to go through a bleak period 'to fight for what's right and what's good'. In the end Armstrong believes social media will be greater than anything we have seen so far.

Professor Christian Fuchs of the University of Westminster, where he is director of the Communication and Media Research Institute, applies a Marxist perspective to the problems of the social media and argues 'social' media companies claim they are social in order to advance the unsocial and the anti-social. Marx's theory of alienation is not just about wages, labour and property but is a critique of political systems and institutions which alienate humans from the control of, and influence on, setting the conditions which govern their lives. Under this approach Facebook is the epitome of digital capitalism in that it treats personal data as a commodity in order to sell targeted advertising and for Facebook it matters little whether the ad is about chocolate or alt-right. For Fuchs business self-regulation does not work and it can easily advance threats to democracy. Zuckerberg, for instance, has told Senate hearings the company does not 'feel like a monopoly'.

The implication is capital will not voluntarily do anything to mitigate its own negative impacts and therefore it is a political task to force basic rules of conduct on capital via the law, the state, and civil society. Banning political acts of digital socialisation would be a first step, backed up by fines. Another would be to replace algorithms with paid highly skilled human workers. The most important step would be to break up the monopolistic social media platforms and replace them with organisations dedicated to 'advance the digital commons and digital public services'. Taxing online advertising could even fund new alternative social media platforms run by public service organisations like the BBC, an idea recently taken up by Labour leader Jeremy Corbyn.

Raymond Snoddy, media journalist and co-editor of this book, traces the rising interest in, and growing antagonism to, the negative aspects of the social media – across newspapers, regulators and legislators. The pressure is on to persuade, or coerce, the social media tech giants to climb down from their insistence they are platforms not publishers and accept greater responsibility for the information they transmit. If they do not do so, there are growing signs their future will slide from self-regulation to regulation and if that does not work the logic of legislation and fines.

The benefits of the social media are self-evident from limitless search for information to unparalleled connectivity. But the negatives in the balance sheet are piling up. They range from the undermining of the economics of traditional publishers, the hollowing out of the High Street and serious concerns about the mental health of the young, to the creation of the most comprehensive monopolies the world has ever seen, inciting hatred and even genocide in the developing world, and even posing a threat to democracy itself. This cannot continue. The only question is what shape reform takes and whether it has to be imposed or not.

We have met the problem. Guess who?

Without academic and journalistic evidence of the problem and harms, Jeff Jarvis fears a moral panic against technology will result in unintended consequences

In all the urgent debate about regulating, investigating, and even breaking up internet companies, we have lost sight of the problem we are trying to confront: not technology but instead human behaviour on it, the bad acts of some (small) number of fraudsters, propagandists, bigots, misogynists, and jerks.

Computers do not threaten and harass people; people do. Hate speech is not created by algorithms but by humans. Technology did not interfere with the American election; another government did.[1] Yet we demand technology companies cure what ails us as if technology were the disease.

When before have we required corporations to monitor and mediate human behaviour? Isn't that the job – the very definition – of government: to define and enforce the limits of acceptable acts? If not government, then won't parents, schools, clergy, therapists, or society as a whole – in its process of negotiating norms – fill the role? But all that takes time. In the face of the speed and scale of the invention and dissemination not only of technology but of its manipulation, governments have no idea what to do. So in their search for someone to blame, governments outsource fault and responsibility, egged on by media (whose schadenfreude constitutes a conflict of interest, as publishers wish to witness their new competitors' comeuppance).

Why would we ever expect or want corporations to doctor us? Indeed, isn't manipulation of our speech and psyches by technologists what critics fear most? Some argue this is the platforms' problem because it's the platforms that screwed us up. I disagree. It's not as if before the net the world was a choir of angels. To argue that the internet addicts the connected masses, makes them stupid, turns them into trolls, and transforms them into agents of society's ruin is elitist and fundamentally insulting, denying people their agency, their intelligence, their goodwill or lack thereof. The internet is not ruining humankind. Humankind is still trying to figure out what the internet can and should be.

It is true that internet technology has provided bad actors with new means of manipulation and exploitation in the pursuit of money and lately political gain or demented psychology. It's also true that the technologists were too optimistic and naive about how their powerful tools could be misused – or rather, used but for bad ends. I agree that Facebook, Google, Twitter, and company must exercise more responsibility in anticipating and forestalling manipulation, in understanding the impact they have, in being transparent about that impact, and in collaborating with others to do better. There's no doubt the culture of Silicon Valley is too isolated and hubristic and must learn to listen, to value and empower diversity, to move fast but think first. Do I absolve them of responsibility? No. Do I want them to do more? Yes.

The terms of the conversation

But what precisely do we expect of them? For a project underwritten by the How Institute for Society, founded by Dov Seidman, I interviewed and convened discussions with people I respect as leaders, visionaries, and responsible voices in journalism, technology, law, and ethics. What struck me is that I heard no consensus on the definition of the problems to be solved, let alone the solutions. There is general head-shaking and tsk-tsking about the state of the internet and the platforms that now operate much of it. But dig deeper in search of an answer and you'll find yourself in a maze.

At Google's 2018 European journalism unconference, Newsgeist, I proposed a session asking, 'What could Facebook do for news?' Some journalists in the room argued Facebook must eliminate bad content and some argued Facebook must make *no* judgments about content, good or bad. Sometimes, they were the same people, not hearing themselves making opposing arguments.

In my interviews, Professor Jay Rosen of New York University told me we do not yet have the terms for the discussion about what we expect technology companies to do. Where are the norms, laws, or regulations which precisely spell out their responsibility? Professor Emily Bell of the Columbia School of Journalism said capitalism and free speech are proving to be a toxic combination. Data scientist Deb Roy of the MIT Media Lab said capitalistic enterprises are finely tuned for simple outcomes and so he doesn't believe a platform designed for one result can be fixed to produce another, but he hopes innovators will find new opportunities there.

Technologist Yonatan Zunger, formerly of Google, argued computer scientists must follow the example of engineering forebears, e.g., civil engineers, to recognise and account for the risks their work can bring. Entrepreneur John Borthwick, founder of Betaworks, proposed self-regulation to forestall government regulation. Seidman the ethicist insisted neutrality is no longer an option and technology companies must provide moral leadership. And philosopher David Weinberger argued that we are past trying to govern according to principles as society is so divided it cannot agree on those principles. I saw Weinberger proven right in the discussion at Newsgeist, in panels I convened at the International Journalism Festival,[2] and in media. As Rosen says, we cannot agree on where to start the conversation.

The limits of openness

In the web's early days, I was as much a dogmatist for openness as I am for the First Amendment. But I have come to learn, as the platforms have, that complete openness invites manipulation and breeds trolls. Google, Facebook, and Twitter, like news media themselves, argue they are merely mirrors to society, reflecting the world's ills. Technology's and media's mirrors may indeed be straight and true. But society warps and cracks itself to exploit these platforms. The difference between yesterday's manipulation via media (PR and propaganda) and today's via technology (from trolls to terrorists) is scale; the internet allows everyone who is connected to speak – which I take as a good – but that also means anyone can become a thief, a propagandist, or a tormentor at a much lower cost and with greater access than mass media permitted. The platforms have no choice but to understand, measure, reveal, and compensate for that manipulation. They are beginning to do that.

Good can come of this crisis, trumped up or not. I now see the potential for a flight to quality on the net. After the 2016 elections and the rising furore about the role of the platforms in nations' nervous breakdowns, Google's head of search engineering, Ben Gomes, said thenceforth the platform would account for the authority, reliability, and quality of sources in search ranking.[3] In a search result for a query such as 'Is climate change real?' Google now sides with science. Twitter has recognised at last that it must account for its role in the health of the public conversation and so it sought help from researchers to define good discourse.[4]

For its part, Facebook downgraded the prominence of what it broadly considered public (as opposed to social) content, which included news. Now it is trying to bring back and promote quality news. At CUNY's Tow-Knight Center, I am working on a project to aggregate signals of quality (or lack thereof) from the many disparate efforts, from the Trust Project to the Credibility Coalition and many others[5]. We will provide this data to both platforms and advertisers to inform their decisions about ranking and buying so they may stop supporting disinformation and instead support quality news. [Disclosure: This work and that of the News Integrity Initiative, which I started at CUNY, are funded in part by Facebook but operate with full independence and I receive no compensation from any platform.]

Are these acts of self-regulation by the platforms sufficient? Of course, not. But I argue we must view this change in temporal context: We are only 24 years past the introduction of the commercial web. If the net turns out to be as disruptive as movable type, then in Gutenberg terms that puts us in the year 1474, years before Luther's birth and print-sparked revolution, decades before the book took on the post-scribe structure we know now, centuries before printing and steam technology combined to create the idea of the mass.

Causes for concern

We don't know what the net is yet. That is why I worry about premature regulation of it. I fear we are operating today on vague impressions of problems rather than on journalistic and academic evidence of the scale of the problems and the harm they are causing. I challenge you to look at your Facebook feed and show me the infestation of Nazis there. Where is the data regarding real harm?

I worry, too, about the unintended consequences of well-intentioned regulation. In Europe, government moves aimed at challenging the power of the platforms have ended up giving them yet more power. The so-called right to be forgotten has put Google in the uneasy position of rewriting and erasing history, a perilous authority to hold. Germany's *Leistungsschutzrecht* (ancillary copyright) gave Google the power to set the terms of the market in links to news. Spain's more aggressive link tax led to the exit of Google News from the country. I shudder to think what a pending EU-wide version of each law will do. Germany's hate-speech law, the *Netzwerkdurchsetzungsgesetz* or NetzDG law, is all but killing satire there and requires the devotion of resources to killing crap, not rewarding quality.

The EU's General Data Protection Regulation (GDPR) will leave Google and Facebook relatively unscathed, as they have the resources to deal with its complex requirements, but some American publishers have cut off European readers, balkanising the web. Anticipated ePrivacy regulation will go even farther and I fear an extreme privacy regime will obstruct a key strategy for sustaining journalism, providing greater relevance and value to people we know as individuals and members of communities and gaining new revenue through membership and contribution as a result. Thus this regulation could artificially extend the life of outmoded mass media and the paternalistic idea of the mass.

I worry mostly that we may be entering into a full-blown moral panic, with technology – internet platforms – as the enemy. Consider Ashley Crossman's definition: "A moral panic is a widespread fear, most often an irrational one, that someone or something is a threat to the values, safety, and interests of a community or society at large. Typically, a moral panic is perpetuated by news media, fuelled by politicians, and often results in the passage of new laws or policies that target the source of the panic. In this way, moral panic can foster increased social control."[6] Sound familiar? To return to the lessons of Gutenberg's age, let us recall Erasmus feared what books would do to society. "To what corner of the world do they not fly, these swarms of new books?" he complained. "The very multitude of them is hurtful to scholarship, because it creates a glut and even in good things satiety is most harmful." But we managed.

When I was invited to contribute this chapter, I was asked to write 'in defence of Facebook'. With respect, that sets the conversation at the wrong level, at the institutional level: Journalism vs. Facebook. Thus we miss the trees for the forest, the people for the platforms. No matter what we in journalism think of Facebook, Google, or Twitter as companies, we must acknowledge the public we serve is there and we need to take our journalism to them where they are. We must take advantage of the opportunity the net provides to see the public not as a mass but as a web of communities. We cannot do any of this alone and need to work with platforms to fulfill what I now see as journalism's real job: to convene communities into civil, informed, and productive conversation. If society is a polarised world at war with itself – red vs. blue, white vs. black, insider vs. outsider, 99 per cent vs. one per cent – we perhaps should begin by asking how we in journalism led society there.

Notes

[1] I expect someone on Twitter to respond to this paragraph with a picture of the bumper sticker declaring that guns don't kill people; people do. The sentence structures may be parallel but the logic is not. Guns are created for one purpose: to kill. The internet was created for purposes yet unknown. We are negotiating its proper and improper uses and until we do — as we are learning — the improper will out.

[2] Video available on these pages:
https://www.journalismfestival.com/programme/2018/help-define-the-moral-imperatives-that-should-be-guiding-media-and-platforms-decisions
https://www.journalismfestival.com/programme/2018/what-should-facebook-et-al-do-for-news
https://www.journalismfestival.com/programme/2018/moral-panic-over-technology-is-it-all-that-bad

[3] Blog post by Google VP of engineering Ben Gomes. https://blog.google/products/search/our-latest-quality-improvements-search/

[4] Blog post by Twitter. https://blog.twitter.com/official/en_us/topics/company/2018/twitter-health-metrics-proposal-submission.html

[5] Schmidt, Christine (2018) So what is that, er, Trusted News Integrity Trust Project all about? A guide to the (many, similarly named) new efforts fighting for journalism, Niemanlab 5 April. http://www.niemanlab.org/2018/04/so-what-is-that-er-trusted-news-integrity-trust-project-all-about-a-guide-to-the-many-similarly-named-new-efforts-fighting-for-journalism/

[6] Crossman, Ashley (2018) Definition of moral panic, Thoughtco, 19 January. https://www.thoughtco.com/moral-panic-3026420

Note on the contributor

Jeff Jarvis is the Leonard Tow Professor of Journalistic Innovation in the Craig Newmark Graduate School of Journalism at the City University of New York, where he directs the Tow-Knight Center for Entrepreneurial Journalism. He is the author of Geeks Bearing Gifts, Gutenberg the Geek, Public Parts, and What Would Google Do? and cohost of the podcast This Week in Google.

Lies are free, but sacred facts can prove elusive

Alan Rusbridger, former editor of The Guardian, warns social media has created a world where lies are everywhere and the truth is increasingly difficult to access and verify

Here is just one small example of this new world of information chaos, playing out as I was writing this chapter. I could have chosen a thousand such illustrations, but this had most of the components of the unfolding problem. In February 2017 Donald Trump used a rally in Melbourne, Florida, to draw attention to disturbing events he said were happening in Sweden.

"You look at what's happening in Germany. You look at what's happening last night in Sweden." The President of the United States paused for the name to sink in and then repeated it. "Sweden. Who would believe this? Sweden. They took in large numbers and they're having problems like they never thought possible."

Sweden was puzzled. The country, like others in Europe, was not without its tensions after the recent wave of migration from North Africa and the Middle East. There had been a widespread – but by no means universal – welcome to the 163,000 asylum seekers who arrived in the country that year. But, amid a spate of really frightening terror attacks in Europe, it seemed curious to single out Sweden for a stump speech in Florida. So little of note appeared to have happened in Sweden the previous evening – apart from a national singing competition – that social media regarded the intervention as a bit of a joke. "Sweden? Terror Attack? What has he been smoking?" former Swedish prime minister Carl Bildt tweeted. There were spoof hashtags – #JeSuisIKEA and #IStandWithSweden – while other users questioned the safety of ABBA.

The following day Trump clarified his Sweden statement. He told his 40m followers on Twitter it had been 'in reference to a story that was broadcast on @FoxNews concerning immigrants & Sweden'. And so began an anatomy of how Donald Trump arrived at his version of the truth, which, given he was the most powerful man on earth, was quite important to understand. The previous Friday night's Tucker Carlson Tonight had included an interview with someone we might call a media controversialist, Ami Horowitz, about a documentary the latter was making about Sweden.

"There was an absolute surge in gun violence and rape in Sweden once they began this open-door policy," Horowitz had told Carlson. Who was Ami Horowitz? For 13 years he worked as an investment banker with Lehman Brothers before reinventing himself as a gonzo filmmaker. His website shows him engaged in a series of provocations ('Ami on the loose') where, for instance, he descends on the campus at the University of California, Berkeley, to alternate between waving an American flag and an Isis flag – and gauge the supposed difference in reaction from students. That, he says, was watched 15m times across various platforms.

In another, he retaliates at Palestinians lobbing stones at an Israeli checkpoint on the West Bank ('It was time to get stupid'). His work – inspired, he says, by Michael Moore – has been called 'docu-tainment' or 'mockumentaries'. In 2017 anyone can be a 'journalist' and anyone can transmit their work to a global audience. It helps if a huge mainstream news channel amplifies your work. Horowitz has described Rupert Murdoch's Fox News as 'a partner' ('They've done a phenomenal job of disseminating the videos and my point of view'), and they duly picked up on a YouTube video he'd published in December 2016 claiming that 'rape and violence has exploded across Sweden due it's [sic] immigration policies'. Within 15 seconds of the video, an alert viewer would see what kind of an exercise this was. Horowitz lingers on a BBC headline 'Sweden's rape rate under the spotlight'. In fact, that four-year-old, 1,200-word article – pegged to the extradition of WikiLeaks leader Julian Assange, rather than immigration – was a nuanced exploration of whether Sweden's apparently higher rates of rape were mainly down to changes in the way the police record incidents. But that was not how Horowitz used the headline. Horowitz dealt in outrage, entertainment and provocation. It was central to his Unique Selling Point that he told uncomfortable home truths the despised Mainstream Media (MSM) ignored. He was not a reliable source for the President of the United States. Or anyone else.

Following Trump's discovery of Horowitz's work the Swedish paper Aftonbladet analysed his film and found it 'contained many errors and exaggerations'. Another newspaper, Dagens Nyheter, quoted two police officers interviewed by Horowitz as saying the filmmaker had selectively edited and distorted their comments to prove his thesis. "We don't stand behind what he says," said one of them, Anders Goranzon. "He is a madman." But the truth, or otherwise, of the film appears to have been of little concern to Fox, America's most-watched cable network – described as Murdoch's 'profit machine' by Bloomberg. The programme, seen by as many as 2.5m viewers, gave further exposure and credibility to the video, which had itself had half a million views on social media.

Enter the President of the United States. It's doubtful Donald Trump had any idea of who Horowitz was, or whether he had any journalistic credentials. In general, he appears predisposed to believe Fox News tells the truth and the New York Times tells lies. So – after his stump speech in Florida – the President then broadcast the existence of Horowitz's gonzo docu-tainment to his 40m-odd followers on Twitter. Thus were half-truths blasted around the planet's new global information eco-system. This horizontal transmission of news – from person to person – is virtually unmappable. But let us suppose hundreds of millions of people around the world would by now have registered – at some level – this… germ. I use the word 'germ' in the absence of another easy label. The exercise Horowitz was engaged in, and which the President and Fox News megaphoned, was not conventional journalism. These were not 'facts'. Deeply buried in some of the assertions in a ten-minute film there may even have been some semi-truths. I will not call the rest 'lies'. The point is that most of the hundreds of millions who will have been touched by the germ will not have registered the detail. They will not have researched the origins of Trump's Swedish intervention or looked into Horowitz's techniques or motivations.

The virus is likely to have lodged itself as little more than a perception, in those ready to believe Muslim immigration leads to unspeakable things such as mass rape – and the West had better wake up. A couple of days after Trump spoke there was some rioting in the northern suburbs of the Swedish capital, Stockholm. No smoke without a fire? But which was the smoke, and which the fire? The patient analysis and denials of Swedish newspapers counted for little as the virus spread. In the UK the former UKIP leader (and friend of Donald Trump) Nigel Farage used his radio show on LBC to announce Malmo, a city in southern Sweden, was now the 'rape capital of Europe and, some argue, perhaps even the rape capital of the world. And there is a Swedish media that just don't report it.'

Months later I was browsing through my Twitter feed and saw someone I follow – Godfrey Bloom, a leading UKIP figure and former Member of the European Parliament – retweeting news of a horrific attack on a teenage girl in Malmo. Someone calling himself @PeterSweden7 tweeted about his 'blood being at boiling point… While she was being raped the rapists poured lighter fuel in her vagina and set it on fire. MSM is quiet. RETWEET.' This germ was so graphically specific and shocking that it caused understandable revulsion as it ricocheted around the internet. On the social media website Reddit there was a bitterly angry thread. The attack was said to be the fourth rape in two months. It was taken as read that the attackers were Muslim immigrants. If you let Muslims into your country – so many commenters raged – what do you expect? This was war.

But did the incident – with the obscene barbarity alleged by @PeterSweden7 – actually happen? That was a more complicated question and would take more than a day of patient digging to get near any kind of truth. A 17-year-old girl had undoubtedly been raped that evening in Malmo – and the attack had been widely reported in the press. But @PeterSweden7 was right to say that newspapers had made no mention of lighter fuel being poured into the victim's vagina and set on fire. Was this out of political correctness, or because it hadn't happened? I tweeted an appeal for help in getting some facts. A couple of Swedish journalists sent me links to reports in the so-called MSM. I tried to read both… but, in each case, hit a paywall. One wanted me to commit to £9 a month before it would allow me to read the article; the other wanted nearly twice as much. Chaotic information was free: good information was expensive. In the horizontal world of twenty-first century communications – where anyone can publish anything – the germs about rape in Malmo spread indiscriminately and freely. The virus was halfway round the world and the truth had barely even found its boots. Truth – if that's what journalism offered – was living in a gated community. But the truth mattered. The idea that immigrants would reward a society's compassion by barbarically raping its women could – if true – profoundly shape popular attitudes and political responses to immigration in Sweden and beyond. That was especially true now Donald Trump – and numerous white nationalists and their fellow travellers – were using the country as a prime exhibit of the dangers of open borders.

I did my best, as a non-Swedish speaker, to establish some facts. For a start, who was @PeterSweden7? Many of those exploiting the horrific lighter fuel story belonged to far-right extremist groups around the world. @PeterSweden7's previous tweets gave some clue to his politics: 'I don't like fascism, but i think Hitler had some good points. I am pretty certain that the holocaust actually never happened.' Or another: 'The globalists (mainly Jews) are ones bringing in the Muslims to europe. They seem to work together.'

He had 81,000 followers on Twitter, growing at a rate of 10,000 a month. I contacted @PeterSweden7, who appears in real life to be Peter Imanuelsen, a 22-year-old photographer born in Norway, but possibly living, at least some of the time, in North Yorkshire. He told a website called hopenothate.org.uk that his holocaust-denial was simply a phase brought about by realising 'mainstream media was lying about everything'. Imanuelsen described this website as 'fake news'. His own website claims to be 'real independent journalism'.

Via Twitter he repeated to me that Swedish media hadn't gone into detail 'on the horrible things the girl suffered'. I asked his source. He replied 'word has gotten around in Malmo about the details and locals in Malmo have taken to social media to say what happened'. So, a combination of local rumour and gossip, amplified instantly by horizontal transmission. He later pointed me to a Facebook posting by a 37-year-old Chicago-educated researcher, Tino Sanandaji, who is considered to be the most prominent social media critic of Sweden's immigration policies, and also of the established media.

I tracked down Sanandaji. He had, indeed, blogged about the incident to his 76,000 followers. He said he had two sources, 'one citing the police investigation and one friend of the family… the same rumour was also on social media'. He was 'fairly sure' about his information, and he thought he had a duty to warn girls in the area after three rapes in Malmo in the space of seven weeks. But here was the rub. Sanandaji claimed the detail that had caused such revulsion and sent the germ around the world was not in his Facebook posting in its original Swedish, 'underliv' – or so he claimed. He claimed to have written that a source had told him the victim's 'abdomen' had been sprayed with fuel. By the time it had been picked up and redistributed by a Canadian-based British 'journalist' working for the alt-right website Breitbart, 'abdomen' had become 'vagina'.

Whether Sanandaji's finger-pointing at Breitbart was correct; or whether there had been inadequate automatic translation or distortion by Breitbart was difficult to establish. The Breitbart writer declined to comment. In any event, it was untrue. Within days the police addressed the social media rumours and announced – while the victim had other minor physical injuries – these did not include burns to the lower abdomen. Within a few weeks police announced they had dropped another rape investigation after the woman admitted the attack had never happened. Investigations into the 'lighter fuel' case were closed a few months later, with the police saying they could not show what actually happened, let alone who the offenders were.

Now, none of this is to minimise the severity of the attack, or attacks. The women of Malmo took to the streets to show how they refused to be intimidated. At the time of writing it was not known if they were behind this, or other, rapes in Malmo. It was very difficult for an ordinary reader to reach a definitive conclusion about whether there was a link between increased immigration and increased rape reports in Sweden – though a painstaking investigation by Dagens Nyheter in May 2018 found no such correlation between them. But if the facts were elusive, the digital world had transmitted half-truths and lies at a speed and scale that would have been unimaginable even a decade earlier. The patient work of journalists to take time to discover what actually happened was buried in the avalanche of rumour – and then invisible except to the relatively tiny minority who still cared enough for old-fashioned facts to pay for them. When challenged about their own role in spreading unchecked information, most of the pollinators seemed unbothered. Godfrey Bloom told me his attitude was the same as all other users of Twitter: 'It is a lavatory wall.'

There were, if you looked hard enough, calm pieces to be found on the subject, some of them involving detailed work with available data. The BBC – freely available to all – investigated Farage's claim about Malmo being 'the rape capital of Europe' and concluded the high level of reported rape was 'mainly due to the strictness of Swedish laws and how rape is recorded in the country'. The Dagens Nyheter analysis agreed. Bad information was everywhere: good information was increasingly for smaller elites. It was harder for good information to compete on equal terms with bad. The more invisible decent journalists became, the easier it was to denigrate their work. They became part of the problem – an out of touch elite. Lamestream media. Fake news. Failing. Lies. They're all the same. Enough of experts. Drain the swamp. It caught on.

In a sense Donald Trump has done journalism a favour. In his cavalier disregard for truth he has reminded people why societies need to be able to distinguish fact from fiction. At their best, journalists do that job well. They can now harness almost infinite resources to help them. But, at the same time, we have created the most prodigious capability for spreading lies the world has ever seen. And the economic system for supporting journalism looks dangerously unstable. The stakes for truth have never been higher.

Note on the contributor
Alan Rusbridger is the Principal of Lady Margaret Hall at the University of Oxford. Previously between 1995 and 2015 he was a ground-breaking and award-winning editor of The Guardian, having first joined the paper in 1979. He is chair of the Reuters Institute for the Study of Journalism and remains a respected commentator on the present and future state of journalism. This chapter is extracted from his latest book *Breaking News: The Remaking of Journalism and Why it Matters Now* published in September 2018, by Canongate

Mark Zuckerberg's dilemma; what to do with the monster he has created?

The Facebook founder is a 21st-century Rockefeller and Hearst combined, says John Naughton, but the supply of resources he has to exploit is actually infinite. It's scary that he doesn't seem to know where it is all headding

Ponder this: in 2004 a Harvard sophomore named Zuckerberg sits in his dorm room hammering away at a computer keyboard. He's taking an idea he 'borrowed' from two nice-but-dim Harvard undergraduates and writing the computer code needed to turn it into a social-networking site. He borrows $1,000 from his friend Eduardo Saverin and puts the site onto an internet web-hosting service. He calls it 'The Facebook'.

Fourteen years later, that kid has metamorphosed into the 21st-century embodiment of John D Rockefeller and William Randolph Hearst rolled into one. In the early 20th century, Rockefeller controlled the flow of oil while Hearst controlled the flow of information. In the 21st century Zuckerberg controls the flow of the new oil (data) and the information (because people get much of their news from platform that he controls). His empire spans more than 2.2bn people, and he exercises absolute control over it — as a passage in the company's 10-K SEC filing makes clear. It reads, in part:

> "Mark Zuckerberg, our founder, Chairman, and CEO, is able to exercise voting rights with respect to a majority of the voting power of our outstanding capital stock and therefore has the ability to control the outcome of matters submitted to our stockholders for approval, including the election of directors and any merger, consolidation, or sale of all or substantially all of our assets. This concentrated control could delay, defer, or prevent a change of control, merger, consolidation, or sale of all or substantially all of our assets that our other stockholders support, or conversely this concentrated control could result in the consummation of such a transaction that our other stockholders do not support... "[1]

Such concentration of corporate control is unusual in large public corporations[2] and raises questions about corporate governance and social responsibility. These problems are particularly acute in Zuckerberg's empire because he wields not just the economic power of a monopolist (in the field of social networking, Facebook has no serious competitor) but also operates a business model that affects democratic processes and may perhaps even have influenced the outcomes of the 2016 Brexit referendum in the UK and the presidential election in the US.

This is not to assert that Zuckerberg himself pursues political objectives, at least at the moment. Rather, the claim is (a) that the computerised, targeted-advertising system Facebook has constructed can be (and has been) exploited by political actors seeking to target political or ideological messages at users whose data-profiles suggest may be receptive to those messages; and (b) that the outcomes of such 'weaponisation' of social media may be at best anti-social and at worst anti-democratic.

The most striking thing about the discovery of political exploitation of social media in 2016-17 was the initial incredulity of Zuckerberg and his executives that such a thing could have happened. This suggests some or all of the following: a very high degree of political naiveté; a serious case of wilful blindness; and/or a cynical determination to avoid public discussion of the root cause of the trouble — the business model of the corporation and the responsibilities that accompany the power that it confers upon its owner.

The business model: surveillance capitalism

The five most valuable corporations in the Western world at present — Apple, Alphabet (owner of Google), Amazon, Microsoft and Facebook — are all digital enterprises. Three of them — Apple, Amazon and Microsoft — have relatively conventional business models: they produce goods and/or services for which customers pay. The other two — Google and Facebook — provide services that are free in return for the right to extract and monetise the personal information and data-trails of their users. The data thus extracted, refined and aggregated are then deployed to enable advertisers — the actual *customers* of the companies — to target advertisements at users. This is often summarised in the adage 'if the service is free, then you are the product'.

Google and Facebook operate what economists call two-sided markets: in their cases revenue from customers on one side (advertisers) subsidise users on the other side. In recent years, the term *surveillance capitalism*[3] has been coined to describe this business model. Although Google and Facebook portray themselves as tech companies, it's sometimes more illuminating to regard them as extractive enterprises like oil or mining companies. The latter extract natural resources from the earth, which they then refine, process and sell to customers. Facebook and Google do something analogous, but the resources they extract, refine and monetise are purely digital — the data-trails generated by their users' activities on their platforms.

There is, however, one radical difference between the oil/mining enterprises and the two digital giants. Whereas reserves of natural resources are, ultimately, finite[4], reserves of the 'resources' extracted by Google and Facebook are, in principle, virtually infinite because they are created by what the industry calls user engagement — i.e. users' online activity. Such activity includes clicking on advertisements, liking and sharing, status updates, browsing web pages, writing and replying to messages, uploading, tagging and commenting upon photographs and videos, streaming live audio or video to online platforms, etc. The level and volume of this engagement is staggering; every 60 seconds on Facebook, for example, 510,000 comments are posted, 293,000 statuses are updated, and 136,000 photos are uploaded.[5]

Since user engagement is what produces monetisable data-trails, the overriding imperative of the business model is to continually increase engagement. Accordingly, the companies deploy formidable technical and design resources to persuade users to spend more time on their platforms and to engage with them more intensively.[6]

Much of this supply-side design is informed by applied psychological research on human behaviour — the same kind of research that informs the design of slot machines.[7] Some of the services are addictive by design[8] while others exploit known human fallibilities[9] (for example, by using default settings like autoplay on videos — which users can change but generally don't).[10] And the companies continually conduct thousands of A/B experiments a day in real time to determine which presentational tweaks most effectively increase user engagement. In a metaphorical sense, therefore, users of social media are unwitting rats in Skinnerian mazes created for their delectation. This is what leads some commentators to speak of social media as a 'dopamine economy'.[11]

On the demand side, human psychology and sociality play important roles in keeping the machine humming. Humans are famously subject to a wide range of cognitive biases[12], which social media exploit. Well-known examples include *confirmation bias* (the tendency to search for, interpret, focus on and remember information in a way that confirms one's preconceptions); and *hyperbolic discounting* (the tendency for people to have a stronger preference for more immediate payoffs relative to later payoffs). On the sociality side there is *homophily* — the tendency of individuals to associate and bond with similar others.

What the world has belatedly woken up to is the realisation that we are in a kind of perfect storm created by the confluence of a number of powerful forces: network effects which lead to the emergence of global monopolies; the business model of surveillance capitalism, with its insatiable demands for increased user engagement; astute deployment of applied psychology to design compulsive or addictive apps, devices and services; cognitive biases which are part of human psychology; powerful tendencies to cluster together (which are probably an inheritance of early human social groups) and which leads to digital echo chambers online; and weaponisation of social media by political actors.

User-generated content: a double-edged sword

When the internet first went mainstream in the mid-1990s it was hailed as a democratising technology that would liberate people's innate creativity. Instead of being passive consumers of content created by corporations, ordinary people would be able to bypass the editorial gatekeepers of the analogue media ecosystem. These possibilities of the 'internetworked' future were memorably celebrated in *The Wealth of Networks*, a landmark book by the Harvard scholar Yochai Benkler published in 2006.[13]

Although the technology did (and does) possess all the empowering, democratising potential celebrated by Benkler, in fact only a relatively small minority made use of it in creative ways. This changed with the arrival of Facebook and YouTube — services that made it easy for users to upload content. Much of the resulting content was unremarkable (and much of it infringed copyright), but from early on it was clear that social media platforms effectively provided a mirror to human nature and some of what appeared in that mirror was unpleasant and sometimes horrific.[14] Furthermore, it transpired that some of this extreme or otherwise problematic content increased user-engagement — which meant that it generated more monetisable data for the platforms hosting it.

Initially, Facebook's response to this was relaxed: the onus was placed on users to flag unacceptable or problematic content for possible review by the platform's owners. This casual attitude was reinforced by Section 230 of the US 1996 Communications Decency Act, which absolved internet services providers from legal liability for content hosted on their platforms.[15] But in the wake of a series of developments, including:

- the controversies about the weaponisation of social media by political actors in 2016 and 2017;

- revelations of the role that Facebook services had played in ethnic cleansing in Myanmar and Sri Lanka;

- the company's failure to remove hate-speech and conspiracy theories;

- and a raft of other scandals[16]

this relaxed posture in 2018 had become untenable and the company was now struggling — with questionable efficacy — to contain the abuses that followed from running a platform that enabled anyone to publish whatever they wanted whenever they wanted.

A window into people's souls

The surveillance capitalism companies have become very good at giving users what they want — which is one reason why some ruefully admit that they find them addictive. They are able to do this because they have garnered an astonishing amount of revealing data about those users and their likely interests, concerns and needs.

To some extent Google and Facebook have achieved this level of insight in different ways. For its part, Google has a good idea of what people are interested in because it knows what they search for. This is why Google is useful for advertisers. But it's also the case that internet searches can be very revealing in other ways — because inquiries can be exceedingly intimate: people search for stuff on Google that they would never confide to any living soul.[17]

As far as Facebook is concerned, the key insight was the discovery in 2013 of how revealing even a low level of user engagement can be. Cambridge University researchers demonstrated something that the company probably already knew, namely that Facebook likes could be used to "automatically and accurately predict a range of highly sensitive personal attributes including: sexual orientation, ethnicity, religious and political views, personality traits, intelligence, happiness, use of addictive substances, parental separation, age, and gender".[18]

Insights available from a user's behaviour on the site were eventually supplemented by (a) information gleaned from tracking Facebook's users as they traversed the wider Web and (b) data about users purchased from external sources (e.g. credit-rating agencies) to construct data-profiles which reportedly[19] came to 98 data-points per user.

In 2007, Facebook made a significant innovation that would later have major implications for both its evolution and for its role in democratic disruption. The company — which itself had been built on the software platform of the World Wide Web — suddenly offered itself as a platform on which third-party developers could run apps. "People should build an application on the Facebook platform because it provides a new kind of distribution on the internet," said a senior company executive at the time. "Really, what has been lacking in all of the other operating systems and platforms that have ever been created is the ability to really access people."[20]

But whereas the web platform was open and uncontrolled, the Facebook platform was proprietary and controlled by the company. The strategic goal for the platform move was to expand Facebook's global reach and penetration to the point where it — rather than the open web — would effectively become the internet as far as most people were concerned. From the point of developers, the attraction was that their apps could exploit the user data that Facebook had accumulated. It was the decision to allow third-party apps to run on its platform, coupled with a failure adequate to police what these apps were doing with user data that eventually led to the Cambridge Analytica scandal[21] in 2018.

The targeting engine

As we observed, Google's and Facebook's users are not their customers. That role is played by advertisers who use the automated engines developed by the companies to identify targets for their commercial messages. Consequently, the most revealing insights into how surveillance capitalism works are obtained not by being a user but by going in as a customer, i.e. an advertiser.

Both companies have constructed automated engines for enabling advertisers to identify types of audiences they wish their messages to reach. In operation and design, these engines are impressive. The Facebook one is particularly user-friendly,[22] gently nudging the customer through the various steps needed to identify what the company calls custom audiences and helpfully suggesting categories of user that one may not initially have thought about. As one critic put it:

> *"If I want to reach women between the ages of 25 and 30 in zip code 37206 who like country music and drink bourbon, Facebook can do that. Moreover, Facebook can often get friends of these women to post a 'sponsored story' on a targeted consumer's news feed, so it doesn't feel like an ad."*[23]

But one doesn't have to be a traditional firm doing commercial advertising to use the Facebook engine. The machine is at the disposal of anyone who wishes to direct almost any message at targeted audiences. What seems to have taken Facebook by surprise is that some of the entities that chose to use its system — including at least one foreign power — were in the business of sending not commercial but ideological or political messages to selected categories of users.[24]

And it looks as though the use of social media is a highly cost-effective way of doing this. According to the New York Times, Russian agents intending to sow discord among American citizens disseminated inflammatory posts that reached 126m users on Facebook, published more than 131,000 messages on Twitter and uploaded more than 1,000 videos to YouTube.[25]

A striking demonstration of the effectiveness of the Facebook targeting engine was provided by an experiment conducted by the news website ProPublica in September 2017. The researchers paid the company $30 to place three promoted posts in the news feeds of Facebook users who — according to the service's profiles of them — had expressed interest in the topics 'Jew hater', 'How to burn jews', or 'History of why jews ruin the world'. The Facebook engine approved all three ads within 15 minutes.[26]

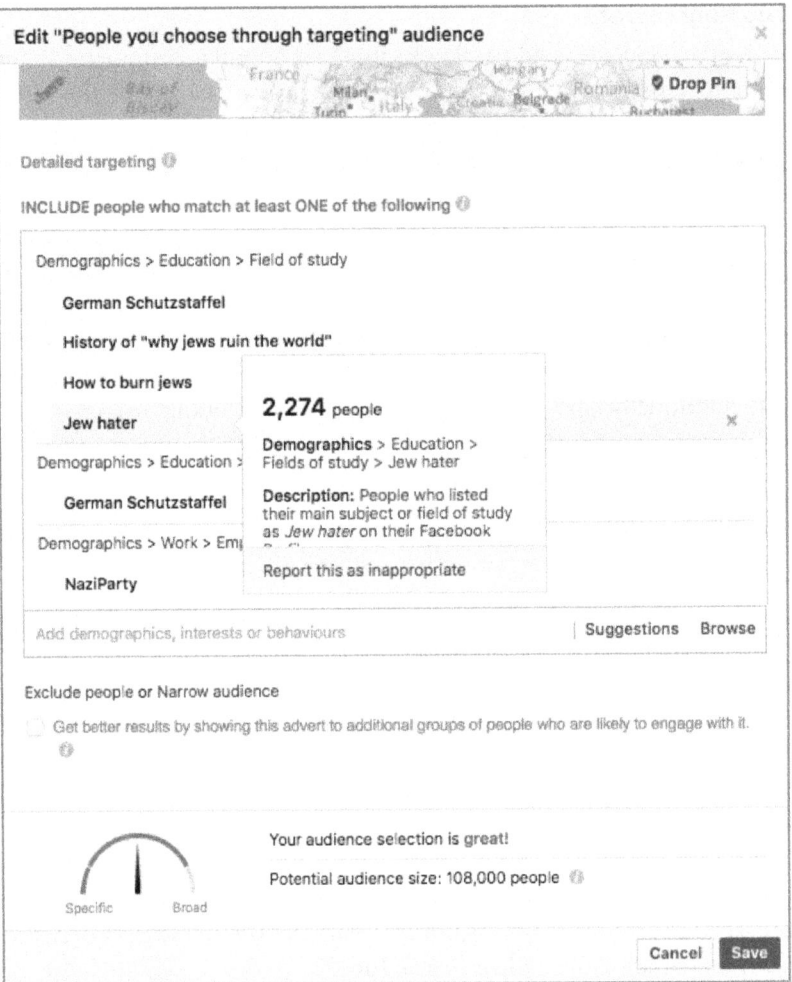

Zuckerberg's monster

The best metaphor for understanding what has happened to Facebook is provided by Mary Shelley's great 19th-century novel, Frankenstein, or, The Modern Prometheus. It tells the story of how an ingenious scientist — Dr Victor Frankenstein — creates a grotesque but sapient creature in an unorthodox scientific experiment. Repulsed by the monster he has made, Frankenstein flees, but finds that he cannot escape his creation.

Facebook is Zuckerberg's monster. Unlike Frankenstein, he is still enamoured of his creation, which has made him richer than Croesus and the undisputed ruler of an empire of 2.2bn users. It has also given him a great deal of power, together with the concomitant responsibilities that go with it. But it's becoming increasingly clear that his creature is out of control, that he's uneasy about the power and has few good ideas about how to discharge his responsibilities.

A good illustration of this was provided by a revealing interview[27] that the Facebook boss gave to the tech journalist Kara Swisher in the summer of 2018. The conversation covered a lot of ground but included a couple of exchanges, which spoke volumes about Zuckerberg's inability to grasp the scale of the problems that his creature now poses for society.

One of them – obviously – is misinformation or false news. "The approach that we've taken to false news", said Zuckerberg, "is not to say, you can't say something wrong on the internet. I think that that would be too extreme. Everyone gets things wrong, and if we were taking down people's accounts when they got a few things wrong, then that would be a hard world for giving people a voice and saying that you care about that."

Swisher then asked him about the alt-right site Infowars – whose Facebook page had more than 900,000 followers and which regularly broadcast falsehoods and conspiracy theories, including a claim that the Sandy Hook mass shootings[28] never happened. But Infowars continued to thrive on Facebook, even though Zuckerberg agreed that the Sandy Hook story was false. Was this because 'everyone gets things wrong', or because of those 900,000 followers? Swisher didn't ask, but a Channel 4 undercover investigation[29] of the Irish firm to which Facebook had outsourced content moderation suggested that objectionable content on Facebook pages with large followings could not be deleted by the traumatised serfs in Dublin; instead such decisions had to be referred up the management chain.

The most revealing part of the Swisher interview, however, concerned Holocaust denial – a topic that Zuckerberg himself brought up. "I'm Jewish," he said, "and there's a set of people who deny that the Holocaust happened. I find that deeply offensive. But at the end of the day, I don't believe that our platform should take that down because I think there are things that different people get wrong. I don't think that they're intentionally getting it wrong, but I think it's hard to impugn intent and to understand the intent."

If you think this is weird, then join the club. I can see only three explanations for it. One is that Zuckerberg is a sociopath, who wants to have as much content – objectionable or banal – available to maximise user engagement (and therefore revenues), regardless of the societal consequences. A second is that Facebook is now so large that he sees himself as a kind of governor with quasi-constitutional responsibilities for protecting free speech. This is delusional: Facebook is a company, not a democracy. Or thirdly, and most probably, he is scared of being accused of being biased in the polarised hysteria that now grips American (and indeed British) politics.

It's as if he's suddenly become aware of the power that his monster has bestowed upon him. As the New York Times journalist, Kevin Roose, put it on The Daily podcast[30], Zuckerberg's increasingly erratic behaviour could be a symptom of something bigger. "He built a company that swallowed communication and media for much of the world," observed Roose. "And now we're seeing him back away from that... The problem with ruling the world is that you then have to govern and that's not what it seems he wants to do." In which case, who will?

Notes

1 https://d18rn0p25nwr6d.cloudfront.net/CIK-0001326801/80a179c9-2dea-49a7-a710-2f3e0f45663a.pdf. The relevant passage continues: "In addition, Mr. Zuckerberg has the ability to control the management and major strategic investments of our company as a result of his position as our CEO and his ability to control the election or replacement of our directors. … As a stockholder, even a controlling stockholder, Mr. Zuckerberg s entitled to vote his shares, and shares over which he has voting control as governed by a voting agreement, in his own interests, which may not always be in the interests of our stockholders generally."

2 Though not unknown in Silicon Valley where charismatic founders use multi-tier shareholding arrangements to ensure that they retain overall control of their creations. This was the case with Google (now Alphabet), for example, and is motivated at least partly to insulate founders from the short-term pressures of Wall Street and enable them to take longer-term strategic views of their enterprises.

3 Shosana Zuboff, "The Secrets of Surveillance Capitalism", *Frankfurter Allgemeine Zeitung, 5 March, 2016. http://www.faz.net/aktuell/feuilleton/debatten/the-digital-debate/shoshana-zuboff-secrets-of-surveillance-capitalism-14103616.html*

4 Pedantic point: the key word is 'ultimately'. The level of available reserves of natural resources is a function of market-price, location and other factors. Thus the level of oil reserves depends on global oil prices. If the price is high, then it will be economically feasible to extract oil from fields which are relatively harder to work.

5 https://zephoria.com/top-15-valuable-facebook-statistics/

6 Current estimates put the time the average Facebook user spends on the platform at 20 minutes per day. (https://zephoria.com/top-15-valuable-facebook-statistics/) Some estimates are higher.

7 Natasha Dow Schüll, *Addiction by Design: Machine Gambling in Las Vegas*, Princeton, 2012.

8 See Nir Yal, *Hooked: How to Build Habit-Forming Products*, Penguin/Portfolio, 2014. Hilary Anderson, "Social media apps are 'deliberately' addictive to users", BBC News, 4 July, 2018, https://www.bbc.co.uk/news/technology-44640959

9 Mallory Locklear, "Sean Parker says Facebook 'exploits' human psychology", *Engadget*, 11 September 2017. https://www.engadget.com/2017/11/09/sean-parker-facebook-exploits-human-psychology/

10 John Naughton, "More choice on privacy just means more chances to do what's best for big tech", *Observer*, 8 July, 2018. https://www.theguardian.com/commentisfree/2018/jul/08/more-choice-privacy-gdpr-facebook-google-microsoft

11 https://eand.co/the-dopamine-economy-336b239272ef

12 https://en.wikipedia.org/wiki/List_of_cognitive_biases

13 http://benkler.org/Benkler_Wealth_Of_Networks.pdf

[14] John Naughton, "How Facebook became a home to psychopaths", *Observer*, 23 April, 2017. https://www.theguardian.com/commentisfree/2017/apr/23/how-facebook-became-home-to-psychopaths-facebook-live

[15] John Naughton, "How two congressmen created the internet's biggest names", *Observer*, 8 January, 2017. https://www.theguardian.com/commentisfree/2017/jan/08/how-two-congressmen-created-the-internets-biggest-names

[16] For example the use of Facebook Live to stream horrific acts of violence, bullying and worse. See John Naughton, "How Facebook became a home to psychopaths", *Observer*, 23 April, 2017. https://www.theguardian.com/commentisfree/2017/apr/23/how-facebook-became-home-to-psychopaths-facebook-live

[17] *See Seth Stephens-Davidowitz, Everybody Lies: What the Internet Can Tell Us about Who We Really are, Bloomsbury, 2017.*

[18] Michal Kosinski, David Stillwell, and Thore Graepel, "Private traits and attributes are predictable from digital records of human behavior", *PNAS*, April 9, 2013. 110 (15) 5802-5805; https://doi.org/10.1073/pnas.1218772110

[19] https://www.washingtonpost.com/news/the-intersect/wp/2016/08/19/98-personal-data-points-that-facebook-uses-to-target-ads-to-you/?tid=sm_tw

[20] https://betanews.com/2007/05/25/facebook-becomes-a-software-company-with-platform-rollout/

[21] https://www.theguardian.com/news/series/cambridge-analytica-files

See also Kevin Roose, "How Facebook's Data Sharing Went From Feature to Bug", *New York Times*, 19 March, 2018. https://www.nytimes.com/2018/03/19/technology/facebook-data-sharing.html

[22] https://www.facebook.com/business/a/custom-audiences

[23] Jonathan Taplin, *Move fast and Break Things: How Facebook, Google and Amazon Have Cornered Culture, and What it Means for All of Us,* Macmillan, 2017, p.143.

[24] Dipayan Ghosh and Ben Scott, "Russia's Election Interference Is Digital Marketing 101", *The Atlantic*, 19 February, 2018, https://www.theatlantic.com/international/archive/2018/02/russia-trump-election-facebook-twitter-advertising/553676/

[25] Mike Isaac and Daisuke Wakabayashi, "Russian Influence Reached 126 Million Through Facebook Alone", *New York Times*, 30 October, 2017. https://www.nytimes.com/2017/10/30/technology/facebook-google-russia.html

[26] Julia Angwin, Madeleine Varner and Ariana Tobin, "Facebook Enabled Advertisers to Reach 'Jew Haters'", *ProPublica*, 14 September, 2017. https://www.propublica.org/article/facebook-enabled-advertisers-to-reach-jew-haters

[27] https://www.recode.net/2018/7/18/17575156/mark-zuckerberg-interview-facebook-recode-kara-swisher

[28] https://en.wikipedia.org/wiki/Sandy_Hook_Elementary_School_shooting

[29] http://uk.businessinsider.com/channel-4-finds-facebook-not-deleting-child-abuse-and-racism-2018-7

[30] https://www.nytimes.com/2018/07/20/podcasts/the-daily/facebook-mark-zuckerberg-misinformation.html

Note on the contributor

Professor John Naughton is a Senior Research Fellow in the Centre for Research in the Arts, Social Sciences and Humanities at Cambridge University, Director of the Press Fellowship Programme at Wolfson College, Cambridge, and the technology columnist of The Observer.

Uncomprehending but still condescending experts and elites

Michael Schrage observes that Twitter and other social media platforms created not just new rivals to establishment elites but have brought out the worst aspects and elements of elite behaviours. They better smarten up sharp and behave themselves, he argues, or else their professional credibility and influence will continue to decline

With a tongue-in-cheek apology to American president Franklin Roosevelt, May 4, 2009 is a day that will live in infamy forever. On that day, @realDonaldTrump emitted his very first tweet (promoting his upcoming appearance on a late night chat show). Whoever would have guessed…?

Make no mistake: without Twitter, Donald Trump would never have been elected President of the United States. The medium and his method were essential to the man's success. No Pinterest, Facebook, Instagram, Snapchat or – pace the collusionists – Vkontakte would have paved his triumphant path to the presidency. Maybe next time….

Vivisecting the 'Trumpification of Twitter' or 'Twitterfication of Trump', however, misses the larger point. To grasp the power and purpose of so-called social media platforms – and the egomaniacs who love them – requires revisiting simple but unhappy fundamentals. These explain why and how so many people seem to find fake news both more appealing and more believable than experts.

Ignore tired tropes blaming bots, Russians and political polarization – they're rubbish. The technologies haven't failed; credentialed elites have. That provocative, even insulting, Trumpian discourse is ascendant even as confidence in expert and establishment credibility erodes is natural and inevitable. Why? Human nature. Elites can't help being elitist and experts can't resist being expert. Their vanity is their great vulnerability. Read their tweets; review their posts. Take them as seriously as they take themselves. Social media successfully seduce the self-declared smart into demonstrating – over and over again – just how clever they really are.

Discretion is not the better part of valour here. Subtlety, humility and empathy undermine efforts to simultaneously prove points and signal superiority. As Descartes would surely have tweeted, 'I think therefore I troll'.

Recall Brexiteer Michael Gove's – no populist troll he! – tart 2016 remark that 'people in this country have had enough of experts'. Although disingenuously interpreted as an assault on expertise, Gove's true target was the intellectual presumptuousness and pretention of an aspiring epistocracy. After all, experts know what's best; that's what makes them experts. But look how thoughtfully, dispassionately and respectfully their social media musings characterise those who (dare) disagree. Observe their calm response to criticism. Track how often their expert contributions enrich and elevate discussion. One doesn't need sophisticated, 'sentiment analysis' algorithms to quickly come to unflattering conclusions.

These conclusions have ominous implications for elite Western establishments and institutions – particularly the news media, the intelligence community and public policy – those experts ostensibly represent. The New York Times, Oxford, Harvard, the BBC, the CIA and, perhaps, the NHS have plenty to fear. Their status is at stake. Social media will likely continue to help the world's Trumps at the expense of his far better educated, far better informed expert critics. The only outstanding question is, by how much?

The disrespect of the masses

'I told-you-so' claims of expert omniscience or infallibility are not the issue. (If they were, humility and circumspection would dominate internet discourse). No, experts and elites reputationally suffer as social media expand because ordinary people dislike being disrespected. They further resent how the intelligence and credentials of experts and elites are publicly used to demean their own. Why should this surprise? All too often, the tweet tweet tweets of expertise and elite opinion devolve into streams of credentialed condescension.

Their essential message: "You are less educated and wrong. But because I am a professional expert, I shall give you the benefit of my expertise. My tone is irrelevant. [Please] defer to my superior intellect, knowledge and status".

That sentiment may be technically true but is not culturally sustainable in countries ruled by the consent – not the obeisance – of the governed. Consequently, the most important thing to understand about social media is that they're not really social. Social media is a misnomer, as any serious review of dictionary definition or real-world behavior affirms. Yes, Twitter, Facebook, Instagram et al possess social aspects and elements. But these are incidental, not central, to actual use – more spice than ingredient. To mix metaphors, social media are to social engagement much as Impressionism is to pigments and paintbrushes. Without real talent and vision, the result is a colourful mess.

Yet because they believe so strongly in their own talent, virtue and vision, experts and elites willingly create colorful messes. Twitter, Facebook and Instagram offer up temptingly large canvases to show off their brilliance. That's why social media are best understood not as engagement, interaction and/or news platforms but as means and mechanisms for self-expression and self-promotion. In Norman Mailer's prescient phrasing, they're advertisements for myself.

Community and comity matter far less than effectively projecting one's self. Celebrity and notoriety, not credibility or prudence, are the coins of these digital realms. Self-image aspires to become a branded self – a public intellectual; a proud pundit. Sociability here means relentless posts, pictures and poses – aka selfies – from the egoist, exhibitionist, and/or narcissist. Does this sound like anyone we know…or follow…or friend?

Look at Twitter global rankings. Even after its 2016 rebranding as a 'news app', it's no accident that – at the time of this writing – performers Katy Perry and Justin Bieber enjoy the largest followings. Barack Obama is #3 followed by Rihanna, Taylor Swift and Lady Gaga. The seemingly unavoidable Kim Kardashian West ranks #11 and Twitter itself comes #16. The first news organisation appearance is CNN Breaking News at #17 followed by The New York Times at #25. President Donald Trump appears at #18, commanding roughly 10x more followers than in 2015. Perhaps his numbers will surpass Barack's during a second term.

In fact, more than 70 of the top 100 Twitter accounts may fairly be described as celebrity, personality and/or pop culture oriented. Instagram's rankings are comparable. Let's be clear: there's nothing wrong or inappropriate about this. But social media ecosystems rooted in celebrity and popularity aren't likely to inspire users to sacrifice 'attention getting' for accuracy or privilege thoughtfulness over immediacy. As Trump's remarkably effective use of his favorite news app affirms, the incentives don't line up that way.

That makes these platforms poor – even hostile – environments for experts and elites striving to honour professional standards of competence and excellence. Indeed, everyday evidence overwhelmingly suggests few such strivers. Social media success demands less serious – even unserious – embrace of elite values and norms.

When you put a cucumber in brine, you don't purify the water – you get a pickle. Similarly, when experts and elites dive into Twitter streams, you don't get wittier or more thoughtful tweets – one gets celebrity experts and cleverer self-promotion. To paraphrase the US Navy Seals training aphorism, "You don't rise to the challenge of persuasively sharing your knowledge; you sink to the surest way of calling attention to yourself".

So calibrating where provocative insights end and viral insults begin isn't worth the effort. If less self-restraint means more retweetability, go for it. Better to ask forgiveness than ask permission. The internet may be forever but the time to comment is now. Instant gratification isn't soon enough. Self-expression and self-promotion slithers, slips and slops into self-indulgence. All that's missing is self-awareness. Indeed, doesn't Facebook's once-vaunted 'Move fast and break things' enterprise motto now sound foolishly self-destructive?

When expertise died

Consider, for example, the Twitter account of a well-credentialed public intellectual who literally wrote the book on 'The Death of Expertise'. Thoughtful, thorough and well-reviewed, his text deplores the anti-intellectual/anti-institutional behaviours of a broader public: "…what I find so striking today is not that people dismiss expertise, but that they do so with such frequency, and on so many issues, with such *anger*. [emphasis in original]."

As much as I like and admire both the book and its author, I can't help but note the man (an inveterate #NeverTrumper) often sounds as angry as the people he critiques when he tweets:

- Remember: you cannot reason with people this stupid….

- No. I refuse to make arguments – things that take my time and energy – to engage people who have no interest in actual learning or discussion. I'd rather just skip the foreplay and call them idiots and be done with it.

- It's not that I disagree about policy with Trump supporters. It's that I know they don't give a shit about policy. There's no way to have a policy argument with people whose eyes are always looking up to the television for a cue from Dear Leader about what to say next.

No prizes for guessing how much these tweets improved the quality of discourse on their respective threads.

Is this sampling unfair? Of course it is….but, trust me, it's not atypical or misleading. There are far better and far, far worse tweets to be found. That said, the viral nature of social media and their audiences assures that the most controversial/caustic/passionate/provocative/insulting tweets are most likely to be retweeted and shared. Only a naïf doesn't recognize this.

Professor Death of Expertise is no naïf. Just ask him. The savant who crafted an Oxford University Press book about the cultural obstacles experts face in an internet age deliberately chooses to be as dismissive and obnoxious online as the ignorant masses he deplores. This eyebrow-arching double standard has become a new normal for social media experts and experts on social media. Who deserves greater respect in public policy debate – the expert hypocrite or the hypocritical expert? (If you feel that question silly or trite, you are – without doubt – an expert in your chosen field….)

Yet it captures the duality, the schizophrenia and Jekyll-and-Hyde dysfunction social media platforms unavoidably inspire. Social media make deliberately – or impulsively – dissolving the distinctions between one's personal, political, professional and expert self remarkably easy. Easy invites lazy.

Once-meaningful separations between individual and institutional identity vanish. Confusion and conflict around personal and professional accountability can't be avoided. Is that Harvard University expert sharing her expert knowledge?

Or is she yet another bloviator who happens to be an expert based at Harvard? Are institutional affiliations central or peripheral to the public attention experts seek and/or the arguments they make? If that elite credential or affiliation went missing, would the expert vanish without trace from social media view?

Infectious bad behaviour

For sociologists, social psychologists and ethicists, questions around institutional selves and role conflict are cliché. More than 60 years ago, sociologist Erving Goffman anticipated that presentation of self in everyday life grows richer and more complicated in multimedia environments.

But even the Greeks grasped that bad behaviour in one role could infect the reputation of the whole. How many bad tweets or vitriolic insults do experts and elites get before their professional reputations are better defined by their social media antics than their credentials? Look no further than the successful Twitter mob takedown – Disney's 'Guardians of The Galaxy' director James Gunn for decade's-old offensive posts. The episode foreshadows sobering professional futures for experts in a 'no platform' academic world.

The surge of self-indulgent self-expression undermines the values of institutional integrity that confer authority and credibility. Despite what many credentialed elitists privately believe and publicly post, people aren't stupid – they can tell when egocentric experts are trying too hard to be too clever. But what deference is due when expert invective and insight become harder to distinguish? It's both foolish and arrogant to believe people will ignore bad behavior by their 'betters.' As elites offer less principled, less professional, more self-absorbed attention-seeking online comment, just how seriously do they deserve – or expect – to be taken? Are they kidding themselves? Their followers? Or the elite communities they represent? The deepest wounds are self-inflicted. Epistocrats become their own worst enemy.

Shifting reputations

The centre of reputational gravity shifts when social media reveal more about experts than their expertise. The questions switch from, 'Who do I trust or believe?' to 'Who would I rather trust or believe?' Tainted tweets poison expectations. Most experts understand that calling people stupid or idiots is not likely to change minds.

This, not fake news or 'political polarisation' is at the heart of the social media conundrum bedeviling global elites. Indeed, fake news feeds off the pre-existing credibility of institutional norms. This conundrum is what Trump has so brilliantly, ruthlessly and relentlessly exploited to his great benefit. The man is a genius troll. He weaponises social media in ways that lure elite and expert critics into revealing their least professional and unprofessional selves. As partners, Trump and social media do astonishingly well at bringing out the worst in people. His followers revel in this.

Yet because they are smarter and better than he is, the best and brightest insist on rising to his tweeted bait. Trump's apparent lack of self-restraint is exceeded only by their own. With that choice, they 'social media signal' that their personal anger and disgust trumps the professional principles they once promised to honor. These behaviors discredit the very institutions – news, intelligence, academe, think tanks, etc. – from which their expert legitimacy is derived.

To be sure, this conundrum existed before Trump's candidacy was a gleam in Barack Obama's eye. But no one on earth has so effectively provoked so many individuals at so many institutions into actively betraying their public professed professional values online. Rather than even appear to hold fast to institutional standards that once elevated them, elite communities allowed Trump's trolling to disrupt and corrupt ethical norms. The worst of both worlds result: elite communities appear less credible and competent as the expert individuals who represent them give into self-justification and self-righteousness. What, exactly, do they now stand for? How can one tell?

Stupidly self-serving tweets, posts and YouTube videos from partisan politicians are to be expected. But it remains shocking that ostensibly non-partisan and professional establishments can so thoroughly humiliate themselves through the social media self-mutilation by staff.

In America (and, to a lesser extent, the UK), the news media, intelligence agencies and education are the most obvious elite institutions where social media have facilitated individual self-expression that undermines hard-won institutional reputation. Books have already been written about how the internet and social media behemoths like Facebook, Google, Twitter and (increasingly) Instagram have transformed news coverage. But surely the conflicts created between the enterprise – and egos – of individual journalists seeking to build their own branded followings online and the editors they ostensibly report to deserve a chapter or three.

The ethics of tweeting

In 'Journalists, You Are What You Tweet,' America's Poynter Institute reviewed difficulties most news operations confronted as they struggled to ethically balance individual initiative with imperative. "Broadcasting one's hot takes and personal opinions used to be reserved for drinks with friends; on Twitter, it can be a career-ender," Poynter's reporter observed. "…In many newsrooms, even those that have some guidelines, the lines between what's acceptable and what's not are pretty fuzzy and subjective, and it's easy to see where confusion creeps in."

At ESPN, for example, a female African-American Sports Center anchor tweeted – on 9/11, no less – that 'Donald Trump is a white supremacist who has largely surrounded himself w/other white supremacists'.

Jemele Hill, who apologised to the network and her colleagues (but not to Trump!), was not disciplined for that tweet. She was suspended for a fortnight later that year when she tweeted that people should consider boycotting the Dallas Cowboys football team. She ultimately left the network.

While Hill's high-profile departure was exceptional, the 2017 Poynter report noted that Twitter-driven employment clashes are not uncommon. "Managers across the country tell me they frequently have to put out fires from tweets that reflect badly on the news organisation, and routinely rule out job candidates if their Twitter feeds raise concerns."

In one two-week span in 2017, the story observes, journalists from CNN, Breitbart, the Denver Post and LBC were let go for tweets their employers determined to be incendiary or offensive. In July 2018, a New York Times White House correspondent, arguably one of the most prestigious positions in elite American journalism, announced she was abandoning Twitter – in no small part because of how her Twitter persona subverted her perceived professionalism.

"After nearly nine years and 187,000 tweets, I have used Twitter enough to know that it no longer works well for me," declared the Times' Maggie Haberman. "Twitter has stopped being a place where I could learn things I didn't know, glean information that was free from errors about a breaking news story or engage in a discussion and be reasonably confident that people's criticisms were in good faith… The viciousness, toxic partisan anger, intellectual dishonesty, motive-questioning and sexism are at all-time highs, with no end in sight… Twitter is not where a nuanced or thoughtful discussion can happen."

Indeed. It's worth noting that embattled Twitter chief executive Jack Dorsey largely agreed with Ms. Haberman's comments. But what the correspondent left out of her departure note was just as revealing: a medium that had initially been seen as a way to extend institutional reach and influence measurably hurt the reputation of the paper and several key journalists. In scarcely five years, Twitter mutated from helpful symbiont to harmful parasite. The New York Times, in fact, didn't have a coherent and comprehensive Twitter policy for its newsroom until the end of 2017. The policy's first declared principle focused on the digital reality that individual social media excess risks institutional integrity.

> *'In social media posts, our journalists must not express partisan opinions, promote political views, endorse candidates, make offensive comments or do anything else that undercuts The Times's journalistic reputation.'*

The Times' episodes here simply illustrate the social media challenges confronting virtually every elite news media operation in the West. Recent polls – which overwhelmingly indicate that news organisations are seen as less credible and more biased than ever by their audiences – suggest that reputational issues run far deeper than mere competition from Facebook, Google and Amazon.

But there is now explicit acknowledgement by top journalists at The NY Times that, institutionally and individually, the risks of social media engagement outweigh the rewards. Could this be a new beginning for more measured, more temperate and less self-indulgent journalistic initiative online? Speaking as a former journalist, I would say that is a bad bet.

The intelligence elite joins in

The great irony here is that even as The New York Times institutionally restrains its social media enthusiasm and restricts its journalists, America's intelligence elite have apparently gone rogue:

— *Donald Trump's press conference performance in Helsinki rises to & exceeds the threshold of "high crimes & misdemeanors." It was nothing short of treasonous. Not only were Trump's comments imbecilic, he is wholly in the pocket of Putin. Republican Patriots: Where are you???*

— *[To Trump] You are to governance & politics what Bernie Madoff was to the stock market & investment advice. The two of you share a remarkably unethical ability to deceive & manipulate others, building Ponzi schemes to aggrandize yourselves. Truth & justice ultimately caught up with Bernie.*

— *Today, Donald Trump simultaneously lied about the Iranian nuclear deal, undermined global confidence in US commitments, alienated our closest allies, strengthened Iranian hawks, & gave North Korea more reason to keep its nukes. This madness is a danger to our national security.*

Tweets from a partisan political extremist who loathes Donald Trump? Not exactly – John Brennan was a lifelong intelligence operative and CIA Director from 2013 to January 2017 – the beginning of the Trump Administration. He helped coordinate the intelligence community's investigation of Russian interference in the 2016 presidential election and played a direct role in assessing the new president's personal involvement in any possible collusion.

America's Central Intelligence Agency – like Britain's GCHQ - is, of course, supposed to be non-partisan and apolitical. Both by statute and by custom, agency leadership focuses on issues on intelligence, analysis and operations – not policy or domestic politics. Yet the frequency, ferocity and fervor of his public post-directorship tweets have irreparably broken with tradition. More profoundly, the intense and accusatory nature of Brennan's social media communications – he literally accused the President of the United States of treason – has called into question his professionalism and open-mindedness when serving as CIA director.

Could a man so readily provoked into public vehemence online truly behave objectively and dispassionately on the job? Even #NeverTrumpers have been taken aback by Brennan's unbridled, undocumented and – many critics say – unhinged – accusations. What was the tone at the top during Brennan's CIA tenure? Is it possible – even probable – that the CIA's leadership behaved in secret then much the way its leader has chosen to behave in public now? Needless to say, Donald Trump's tweets make clear his disdain and distrust of Brennan:

"John Brennan is panicking. He has disgraced himself, he has disgraced the Country, he has disgraced the entire intelligence community. He is the one man who is largely responsible for the destruction of American's faith in the intelligence community."

But wait! There's even more 'intelligence.' Former Director of National Intelligence James Clapper offered comparably indiscreet comments about Trump that created a global Tweetstorm:

Former Dir of Natl Intelligence James Clapper on CNN: Russia considers and treats @realDonaldTrump as an intelligence asset. In other words, they think Trump works for them.

The President, as usual, was uninhibited in tweeted response:

'James Clapper, who famously got caught lying to Congress, is now an authority on Donald Trump. Will he show you his beautiful letter to me?'

Between his testimony, book and Twitter, former FBI Director James Comey had multiple networked run-ins with the president who fired him.

Mr. President, the American people will hear my story very soon. And they can judge for themselves who is honorable and who is not.

Trump fired a tweet after Comey's book was published declaring him an

….untruthful slime ball who was, as time has proven, a terrible Director of the FBI. His handling of the Crooked Hillary Clinton case, and the events surrounding it, will go down as one of the worst "botch jobs" of history. It was my great honor to fire James Comey!

While breathing new life into 'truth is stranger than fiction' clichés, this Twitter war – it's too big to be a battle – between Trump and the former leaders of America's intelligence communities starkly illuminate the individual/institutional themes discussed.

In no small part due to Trump's tweets, these former national security and law enforcement officers were selectively – and surprisingly – indiscreet. Again, their social media responses fly in the face of virtually all the institutional norms and values their agencies held dear. In the turbulent wake of these ongoing disclosures, the credibility and reputations of these men and the intelligence community were badly wounded. Their personal and professional trustworthiness are in question. Could this – would this – have happened without the Trump/Twitter force multiplier? That seems utterly unlikely. Is it fair to say that the institutions are ambivalent to the point of schizophrenic about the deliberate social media provocations of their former leaders? Absolutely.

Crazy psychiatrists

Perhaps on a more amusing note, Trump's tweet-fetish has apparently driven America's psychiatrists crazy. So crazy, in fact, that a vociferous and superbly credentialed minority has sought to fundamentally revise an important ethical rule that has served the discipline well for half a century.

The Goldwater rule, Section 7.3 of the American Psychiatric Association's ethical code, was enacted in the wake of Republican Barry Goldwater's failed 1964 run for the American presidency. An unprecedented feature of that campaign were public declarations by several high-profile members of the psychiatric community that, in truth, the Republican candidate was crazy.

According to the APA itself, members asserted that "I believe Goldwater to be suffering from a chronic psychosis" and "A megalomaniacal, grandiose omnipotence appears to pervade Mr. Goldwater's personality giving further evidence of his denial and lack of recognition of his own feelings of insecurity and ineffectiveness" and even "I believe Goldwater has the same pathological makeup as Hitler, Castro, Stalin, and other known schizophrenic leaders." (These would have been great tweets had Twitter then existed)

These unsolicited diagnoses – made without any direct examination of the subject – were deemed outrageous at the time and led directly to ethical rules to forbid public speculation and psychoanalysis by members.

The Goldwater Rule was officially born in 1973. Needless to say, the unexpected election of Donald Trump provoked a high-profile professional clamor for its revision. Goldwater-driven twitter storms and social media postings swept the discipline. Or, as a collaborative comment written by both a Harvard and Yale psychiatrist – as elite as elite can be – observed, 'We're psychiatrists. It's our duty to question the president's mental state'. The President's obsessive-compulsive twitter habit has apparently intensified the psychiatric lust for ethical overhaul.

As with the intelligence and news media establishments, social media enabled heretofore innovative wedges between the ambitions of individual actors and more traditional values of existing establishments. In each case, the individuals thought themselves bold and brave for taking the social media plunge. In each case, their institutions struggle to strike a balance between the preservation of credible norms and the promotion of individual expression. The successes of the latter seem to destroy the aspirations of the former. And, of course, in each case, Donald Trump used Twitter to tactically and strategically troll individual and institutional critics alike.

In this, he is a special case who illustrates a general principle. Unlike those he criticises online, Trump is not bound by institutional norms. To the contrary, he violates norms with abandon and is sui generis. The most readily discernible Twitter-norm is that of near-instant response and retaliation to perceived criticism. Professionalism is incidental to his digital persona. His id is his identity.

As a former Washington Post reporter and Los Angeles Times columnist, I had thought that – once elected – a President Trump would cut back on Twitter on enjoy the levers of power he now possessed. I was completely, utterly and stupidly wrong. Twitter gave Trump the power to both define himself and disintermediate the hostile critics who would define him. He would have been a fool to give up the medium that made the White House possible. He is not that kind of fool. His Twitter goal and role is letting others make fools of themselves.

"He has redefined everything about American politics," observed public opinion guru Frank Luntz. "He has redefined political loyalty. He has redefined political language. He has redefined polling. Nothing is as it was. And it will never be the same."

But Trump's Twitter is also redefining the expectations of and engagements with experts and elites. His trolling has both shocked the public conscience and created new self-consciousness around elite behavior and expert arrogance. This is not limited to the institutions described above but will surely extend to many others. The NFL/National Anthem protest kerfuffle offers but one other example. A second Trump term would bring even starker institutional confrontations and expert trolling.

Trump, of course, is not the only force of nature challenging elites and experts – the original Brexit shock was a harbinger of disruption to come. But if experts and elites refuse to come to grips with both the meaning and manipulation of Trump's expert trolling, it will not be unfair to observe that 'The Death of Expertise' was, in truth, a suicide.

References

https://www.theguardian.com/uk/2009/jul/27/twitter-socialnetworking

https://www.psychologytoday.com/us/blog/psychiatry-in-society/201806/mental-health-experts-urge-revision-the-goldwater-rule

https://www.poynter.org/news/twitter-dustups-are-reminder-journalists-you-are-what-you-tweet

https://www.politico.com/magazine/story/2018/01/10/were-psychiatrists-its-perfectly-healthy-to-question-the-presidents-mental-state-216266

Note on the contributor

Michael Schrage is a research fellow at MIT's Sloan School of Management's Initiative on the Digital Economy. He has advised several digital media platform players – including Microsoft, Facebook, Amazon and Google – on matters both technical and political. He was previously a Washington Post reporter and columnist for the Los Angeles Times and Fortune magazine.

The rise and rise of a 21st-century phenomenon

Kostas Saltzis examines the key points in the history of social media and reflects on some of main opportunities and challenges that have been associated with its remarkable growth

It is hard to imagine that social media barely existed two decades ago, given that it is now such an inextricable part of our daily lives. The rise in the popularity of platforms such as Facebook, Twitter, Instagram and Snapchat has been so sharp that in a period of eight years the number of active social media users has increased from one billion in 2010 to 2.6bn in January 2018, which is around 42 per cent of the global population (Statista, 2018; Kemp, 2018). These figures include of course a wide range of uses and social media platforms, and they are predicted to keep on rising for the foreseeable future (Statista, 2018).

But it is not just this rapid growth that makes mapping down the development of social media over the years important. It is also that it has permeated all aspects of human interaction, from information searching and sharing, to professional networks and online dating.

A variety of terms have been used to describe social media conversations: crowd sourcing, wisdom of crowds, peer production, wikinomics and collective intelligence are examples. What these terms suggest is the collective strength of social connections that are facilitated and enabled by social media (Malone et al. 2009).

On the other hand, more recent experience has highlighted a negative side of this phenomenon with expressions of anger, insults, lack of meaningful conversation, or short attention spans, which suggest that social media may still be in its infancy period. As with any new medium, here as well the early optimism has been followed by more sceptical approaches, but there is no denying that social media has become an important part of our digital lives.

First online communities

It would be wrong to assume that social media has invented online communities as the latter existed since the early stages of the internet, in the form of bulletin board systems (e.g. the WELL) in the 1980s and later MUDs (multi user domains) and

IRC (internet relay chat) where users could connect and form communities and online groups across the world. In fact, according to Fuchs (2014) most social media platforms integrate and combine pre-existing information and communications technologies such as webpages, mail, digital images and videos, discussion groups, connection lists and search engines etc.

The invention of the World Wide Web in 1991 by Tim Berners-Lee is widely hailed as a key milestone in the history of the internet. The web managed to organise and interconnect information and networks via hypertext technology in such ways that allowed the wider public to access information in unprecedented ways. As such, it led to a number of functions and applications that we would recognise in today's social media. For instance, web logs (or blogs as came to be called later) were available in the late 1990s (Allen, 2012), wiki technology appeared in 1995, while the first social networking sites (Classmates and Sixdegrees) were introduced in 1995 and 1997 (Fuchs, 2014).

Web 2.0

A significant moment in the history of social media has been the so-called 'dot-com bubble' in 2000. This was essentially a stock exchange crash of online ventures, which was fuelled by exaggerated optimism of the late 1990s and resulted in many internet companies going bankrupt. In that context, web 2.0 emerged as a new phase of the internet, which emphasised connectivity, participation, user-generated content and networking. In the years around and following the dot-com bubble a number of firms appeared – Google and Napster in 1999, Wikipedia in 2001, Myspace in 2003, and Facebook in 2004 – which fully embraced web 2.0 and allowed what has been described as networked sociality (Wittel, 2001).

This new type of online companies may have not invented new forms of online activity but they built on the interactive two-way communication tools and targeted particular activities with their coding technologies (Van Deck, 2013), such as micro blogging (Twitter), video sharing (YouTube) and video conferencing (Skype) etc.

Furthermore, the success of some of those companies has meant that they have become so embedded in our daily lives and online experiences that secondary applications and services have been built based on connected to services such as Facebook, Twitter and Google. As a result, an 'entire ecosystem of interconnected platforms and applications' (Van Deck, 2013: 8) which trade on the currency of connections and data has been created.

Types of social media

As mentioned above the term social media is probably used too broadly and includes very different types of platforms and applications. Van Dijck (2013) provides a categorisation based on the platforms' main functions: social networking sites (SNS) are aimed at interpersonal contact and include some of the most popular sites in the world: Facebook, Twitter, LinkedIn, Google+ (or QQ and Wechat in China); user-generated content (UGC) sites such as YouTube, Flickr and Wikipedia provide the platform for the exchange of amateur or professional content; trading and marketing sites (TMS) such as Ebay and Amazon are targeted as online marketplaces; and finally playing and gaming sites (PGS) such as Farmville and Angry Birds etc. are providing gaming experiences based on interconnectivity of users.

Current picture: business models and conglomeration

The explosion in popularity of social media platforms has also been accompanied by a revolution in online advertising and the emergence of new business models. The first has had a significant impact on the publishing business and more specifically on the news industry (Currah, 2009), which used to be the main way for advertisers to reach mass audiences. Thanks to the growing availability of personal data through social media and a very close monitoring of users' behaviour online, advertising (whether it is commercial or political) on social media can be much more targeted and sophisticated in reaching audiences to the extent that it becomes almost customised.

In many ways, the collection of masses of personal data has become the predominant business model for social media companies, which have turned this wealth of information into a tradable commodity (Van Dijck, 2013). The case of Cambridge Analytica in 2018 with the collection and use of personal information from Facebook profiles demonstrated the extent of such trading and highlighted some of the dangers for misuse of such data (Greenfield, 2018).

In the relatively short span of social media history, a number of companies have emerged and have gained great popularity over relatively short period of time. Whereas some of them, such as Facebook and Twitter have managed to sustain their popularity and almost monopolise their respective markets, others have faded almost as quickly as they emerged.

For example, Friendster, one of the first social networking sites that allowed users to discover friends, was founded in 2003 and by 2015 it had already collapsed, while Myspace in 2008 was the most popular SNS (ahead of Facebook) with 76m unique visitors per month (Adegoke, 2011), but by 2016 its traffic had dropped to 15m (Barr, 2016).

Another characteristic of the market has been a tendency for conglomeration, which saw the most successful upstart companies being snatched up by larger organisations. Some of the biggest acquisitions have been that of Myspace by News Corporation in 2005, which was later sold again to Specific Media (Rushe, 2011), YouTube by Google in 2006, Tumblr and Flickr by Yahoo, which was later also acquired by Verizon in 2016, and Instagram (2012) and WhatsApp (2014) by Facebook.

Impact on public communication

Although initially social media platforms promoted personal communication and connections they soon evolved into more complex networks characterised by the strength of numerous weak ties (Granovetter, 1973). Social media platforms have become more than spaces for personal exchanges as users share news and links, create content and in general use those sites for many different purposes.

It is not an understatement to say that the nature of both public and private communication has changed in the era of social media. The sheer amount of information that has been produced and shared is extraordinary and difficult to process: in 2007 it was calculated that the amount of information each person receives per day on average had increased fivefold since 1986, equalling to 174 newspapers a day, while average information output for each person equalled to six newspapers a day, a 200-fold increase (Hilbert & Lopez, 2011). More recent figures suggest that the rate of growth of data is still very high: in 2017 the average number of tweets was 656m per day, whereas 4m hours of video content is uploaded to YouTube every day (Schultz, 2017).

The new participatory culture (Jenkins, 2008), which emerged out of web 2.0 and blurred the boundaries between content producers and users (Bruns, 2008), has led to an explosion of mediated information via social media.

Rather than being just recipients of media messages, individuals now can share and co-create media content, which ranges from the mundane to more serious efforts that provided alternatives to traditional media. The latter has been a particular challenge to media/news organisations because it allowed a new relationship with the audience where citizen journalists and others could provide alternative news coverage and interpretations that in some ways complemented but also questioned the authority of traditional media producers and journalists (Allan & Thorsen, 2009).

Despite an initial period where traditional journalism treated social media with scepticism it is now embracing them more systematically as they provide new opportunities for engagement with the audience. More recently journalists have started treating social media and micro-blogging in particular, as awareness systems, providing them with more complex ways of understanding and reporting on the subtleties of public communication (Hermida, 2010).

Fake news

The general attitudes towards the impact of social media on public communication have evolved over time. The initial optimism for a democratisation of communication and information probably reached its peak at the time of the so-called Arab Spring, with commentators even suggesting that the role of social media was integral in causing a revolution in the Middle East (Shearlaw, 2016).

Although such voices greatly exaggerated the impact of social media in those movements, they were characteristic of the general euphoria that surrounded social media usage. More recently new critical questions are being asked about the role of social media conversations on public debates, journalism and information sharing. For instance, concerns have been raised about the spreading of rumours and inaccuracies on social media platforms where information can be shared and disseminated instantly without any checks and filters that we would normally expect in traditional media (Newman, 2009).

This rather fragmented news experience appears to have received more attention recently in case of fake news, which has been described by many as a great threat to democracy due to its spread of misinformation (Titcomb & Carson, 2018). It is worth highlighting here that, despite the appearance of seamless information and interconnections social media have been providing a structured experience where ever-evolving algorithms have been responsible for recommendations, news item pushes etc.

A greater focus on how certain types of information have been promoted on sites such as Facebook (or even other applications linked to it) has followed revelations that Russia have been sending targeted messages and advertisements on users to influence the 2016 American presidential elections (Solon & Siddiqui, 2017).

Homophily

Another related phenomenon which seems to go against earlier predictions for more open and pluralistic public communication is homophily: in other words, the tendency of individuals to connect with others who validate their core beliefs rather than be exposed to opposing viewpoints (McPherson et al., 2001).

The role of social media in that respect has been the focus of a number of studies: whereas some suggested a complex picture by observing both homophily and heterogeneity in social media (Yardi & Boyd, 2010), others have highlighted their role in creating echo chambers and increased polarisation (Pfeffer et al, 2014).

Conclusion: blurring of public & private spaces

The relatively short history of social media has shown that the new ways of communication and connectivity have had an impact on many aspects of our daily lives enabling people to connect and share information in ways previously unimaginable. At the same time new challenges have emerged, such as the blurring of private and public spaces. Social media has created grey spaces that are both public and private where individuals, employers, the law and the media are still struggling to adapt to. Numerous cases where people's private messages have become public highlight the kind of new challenges that we face in the era of social media and that require us to rethink previous assumptions about the role of mediated communication in society.

References

Adegoke, Yinka (2011) *How News Corp Got Lost in Myspace*, Reuters Special Report, available online at: http://graphics.thomsonreuters.com/11/03/MySpace.pdf, 7 April, accessed on July25, 2018

Allan, Stuart & Thorsen, Einar (eds) (2009) *Citizen journalism: global perspectives. Global Crises and the media*, Vol.1 New York: Peter Lang

Allen Matthew (2012) 'What was web 2.0? Versions and the politics of Internet history', *New media & Society*, 15 (2): 260-275

Barr, Jeremy (2016) *Does MySpace Have Any Distribution Juice Left for Publishers?*, AdAge, 28 April, available online at: http://adage.com/article/media/myspace-juice-left-publishers/303781/, accessed on July 27, 2018

Bruns, Axel (2008) *Blogs, Wikipedia, Second Life, and beyond: From production to produsage*, New York: Peter Lang

Currah, A., (2009) *What's Happening to Our News: An investigation into the likely impact of the digital revolution on the economics of news publishing in the UK*. Reuters Institute for the Study of Journalism, Challenges Series. Available online on: http://reutersinstitute. politics.ox.ac.uk/fileadmin/documents/Publications/What_s_Happening_to_Our_News. pdf, accessed on July 27, 2018

Fuchs, Christian (2014) *Social Media: A critical Introduction*, SAGE: London

Granovetter, Mark (1973) The Strength of Weak Ties, American Journal of Sociology, Vol. 78, No. 6, pp. 1360-1380

Greenfield, Patrick (2018) The Cambridge Analytica files: The Story So Far, The Guardian, Available online at: https://www.theguardian.com/news/2018/mar/26/the-cambridge-analytica-files-the-story-so-far, March 26, accessed on July 15, 2018

Hermida, A. (2010) Twittering the news. The emergence of ambient journalism. *Journalism Practice* 4 (3) 297-308.

Hilbert, Martin & Lopez Priscila (2011) 'The World's Technological Capacity to Store, Communicate, and Compute Information', *Science*, Vol 332, Issue 6025, pp60-65

Jenkins, Henry (2008) Convergence Culture: Where Old and New Media Collide. New York University Press.

Kemp Simon (2018) *Digital in 2018: Essential Insights into Internet, Social Media, Mobile and Ecommerce Use Around the World*, Wearesocial & Hootsuite, Available online at: https://wearesocial.com/uk/blog/2018/01/global-digital-report-2018, accessed on July 15, 2018

Malone, Thomas, Laubacher, Robert and Dellarocas, Chrysanthos (2009) Harnessing Crowds: Mapping the Genome of Collective Intelligence, MIT Sloan Research Paper No 4732-09, available online at: https://papers.ssrn.com/sol3/papers.cfm?abstract_id=1381502 accessed on July 27, 2018

McPherson, M., L. Smith-Lovin, and J. M. Cook. (2001) 'Birds of a Feather: Homophily in Social Networks.' *Annual Review of Sociology*, 27: 415–444

Newman, N. (2009), *The rise of social media and its impact on mainstream journalism*, Reuters Institute for the Study of Journalism, Working Paper. Available online at: https://reutersinstitute.politics.ox.ac.uk/sites/default/files/2017-11/The per cent20rise per cent20of per cent20social per cent20media per cent20and per cent20its per cent20impact per cent20on per cent20mainstream per cent20journalism.pdf, accessed on July 27, 2018

Pfeffer, J, Zorbach, T & Carley K (2014). 'Understanding online firestorms: Negative word-of-mouth dynamics in social media networks'. Journal of Marketing Communications, 20 (1-2): 117-128

Rushe, Dominic (2011) Myspace sold for $35m in spectacular fall from $12bn heyday, The Guardian, Available online at: https://www.theguardian.com/technology/2011/jun/30/myspace-sold-35-million-news, June 30, accessed on July 15, 2018

Schultz, Jeff (2017) *How Much Data is Created on the Internet Each Day?*, Micro Focus Blog, October 10, Available online at: https://blog.microfocus.com/how-much-data-is-created-on-the-internet-each-day/, accessed on July 27, 2018

Shearlaw, Maeve (2016) 'Egypt five years on: was it ever a 'social media revolution'?', *The Guardian*, Available online at: https://www.theguardian.com/world/2016/jan/25/egypt-5-years-on-was-it-ever-a-social-media-revolution, January 25,, accessed on July 10, 2018

Solon, Olivia & Siddiqui, Sabrina (2017) 'Russia-backed Facebook posts 'reached 126m Americans' during US election', *The Guardian*, Available online at: https://www.theguardian.com/technology/2017/oct/30/facebook-russia-fake-accounts-126-million, October 30, accessed on July 27, 2018

Statista (2018) *Number of social media users worldwide from 2010 to 2021*, Available online at: https://www.statista.com/statistics/278414/number-of-worldwide-social-network-users/, accessed on July 27, 2018

Titcomb, James & Carson, James (2018) 'Fake news: What exactly is it – and how can you spot it?', *The Telegraph*, Available online at: https://www.telegraph.co.uk/technology/0/fake-news-exactly-has-really-had-influence/, July 25, accessed on July 27, 2018

Van Dijck, Jose (2013) *The Culture of Connectivity: A critical history of social media*, Oxford University Press

Wittel, Andreas (2001) 'Toward a Network Sociality', *Theory Culture & Society*, Vol 18 (6), pp: 51-76

Yardi, Sarita and Boyd, Danah (2010) 'Dynamic Debates: an analysis of group polarization over time on Twitter'. *Bulletin of Science, Technology & Society*, 30(5): 316–25

Note on the contributor

Dr Kostas Saltzis is a Lecturer in the School of Media, Communication and Sociology at the University of Leicester. His main research and teaching interests include the study of journalism, digital media and the impact of technology on news production. Prior to that he has worked as a Lecturer at De Montfort University, and as a journalist in Greece.

Going wrong may be the necessary route to getting it right

The current climate around social media is unfriendly. But, argues Paul Armstrong, that is no reason to clamp down on it; if we persevere, he says, good will prevail

Back in the early 2000s, having 500m monthly users was just unheard of, and many said Myspace (even with its faults) was unstoppable. Fast-forward to today and Facebook gets the same accolades with more than 2bn users. The climate, however, is not so rosy. Racist algorithms, artificial intelligence, faked video, bot armies and insidious governmental abuses now feel like daily occurrences and are almost normalised. Time to the pull the plug, right? The answer to that is not an easy one – although it may appear to be.

The easy answer is 'yes' and Jaron Lanier, the American computer philosophy writer, agrees. Lanier should know: he helped to build VR and early computer systems at Microsoft and Atari. Oh, and he also has no social media accounts and is a big proponent of you deleting yours.

In his recent book, Ten Arguments for Deleting Your Social Media Accounts Right Now, Lanier likens quitting social media almost to a civic duty: "If you have the latitude to quit and don't, you are not supporting the less fortunate; you are only reinforcing the system in which many people are trapped." Strong words no doubt but switching off is hard. The systems and platforms have been built to be addictive – the root of much of many of the issues the platforms face today – and so people stick around for fear of missing out, laziness or because they don't see the problem.

Lanier is right of course; we continue to be used by the big blue misery machine that is Facebook and co. However, do we throw away all we have learned in the process of being abused? Doesn't the good that social media has done, can do and will do deserve its day in the sun? Lanier argues no, but many rely on social media for a wage, granted not billions, but there are real positive and negative consequences.

The news is another area where loss has both positive and negative effects. Not all news on platforms like Facebook and Twitter is factually correct and unbiased but then neither is the news printed by traditional news outlets. Each news outlet has biases, political leanings, affiliations and owners who have stakeholders. As a species, we have to reject prejudice and learn to think more critically about everything. Social media should help us to expand our thinking, see more sides but not at the cost of the truth.

The issue of misinformation

Platforms are tackling the issue of misinformation in various forms, but it's an uphill battle and one that is unlikely ever to be won. When 67 per cent of a country, the US, gets their news from social media (according to Pew Research Centre: http://www.journalism.org/2017/09/07/news-use-across-social-media-platforms-2017/) winning the battle isn't a nice to have, it is a must achieve or you risk changing whole societies.

Social media connects people; it can connect good people to good people, good people to bad people and bad people to bad people. While this is a lot of bad, the good to good ratio seems to be getting lost or ignored in the Western world during this current climate. In Western countries, we get a skewed perspective. Gone are the stories of the cute Facebook group that was set up to make a park by locals. Instead, we seem to be moving towards something that no-one expected nor wants. The result is a by-product of misspent attention and inaction. Disturbing and true, this is, however, not the full picture.

Social media has done some vital good for the world. It is important to remind ourselves that while we may see one side of something, others may see something (or use something) entirely differently.

It's the one man's terrorist is another man's freedom fighter adage or the difference between a wave and signalling you are drowning. Perspective and context are key and increasingly important. Looking ahead (and back), it is essential not to lay the issues we see at one platform or another – each have caused, contributed to or been the vessel through which malice has occurred. Equally, good things spring from these networks, from increasing political discourse to enabling full-blown coverage of Egyptian regime changes.

For example, Twitter is increasingly a channel for oppressed members of the world to get the truth out to others. The world would be poorer without Twitter even though the platform is far from perfect. Community action groups have formed in difficult neighbourhoods, and councils are alerted to issues in record time thanks to such pages. Residents can meet, arrange events and fix things for themselves – empowering people is crucial and an argument that many forget when discussing social platforms.

From lost dogs to helping people with mental illness find the help they need, social media platforms have connected people with the information they need at the right time. People reunite, fall in love, learn skills and forge new careers. All important things but when a tweet can travel faster than an earthquake, social media also has the potential to save lives.

From social services like Waze to the ALS 'ice bucket challenge' that raised millions of dollars overnight, social media is a mighty beast that undoubtedly has a softer and more forgiving side. An essential element when uncertain times hit.

When people turn to social media

The Argentinian people turned to Facebook groups when unemployment and inflation grew to arrange goods trades in barter clubs before exchanging them in person. Equally, the issues with Myanmar and how Facebook handled that market offers a stark look into how wrong things can go when problems go ignored, and impacts get underestimated.

No-one can argue that we do not live in times where light needs to be shone longer in places where issues arise, and obfuscation occurs. The 2018 furore over Cambridge Analytica data and allegations of outside forces' involvements in politics shows that transparency is needed now more than ever.

The issue with clarity is that it will not come voluntarily. There's no business reason, save threat of regulation, that these vastly successful money-making and attention-sucking machines make money from ads that require your attention and your data which it gets one way or another. Until we find better business models things are unlikely to change. How this could happen is a matter for another day although it'll need to involve the regulation mentioned above or en mass non-use sanctions. People will, as always, eventually need to vote with their wallets and their feet.

Is there hope for the future? Yes and no. While device makers and employees at the large companies do seem to be thinking in right way (mirroring back our usage to us and declining to work on unsavoury projects) the psychologist in me reminds me we are obsessive, stimuli-driven and forgetful beasts.

Dark pattern design (the tricks that get people to click on and sign up to things) is tragically less of an art and more of a science now. The technologies we now have at our fingertips are powerful ones and mixed with the ability to reach anyone around the world makes them as persuasive as they are pervasive.

Bullying, sleep-deprivation, fomo (Fear Of Missing Out), depression and stress are all negative areas that social media exacerbates in one way or another. Perhaps we just got too addicted to the fomo, with the changes the handset, politicians and app developers are making we might be on our way to jomo...the joy of missing out.

Dark pattern design and ethics (while significant issues) skirt around the central issue social media faces as it moves through its teen years. The economics of the ecosystem drive these decisions and until this is fixed or alternatives are offered, issues will undoubtedly remain. Any real change in the way these platforms grow and behave starts with removing the economic incentive systems under which most if not all the platforms currently operate.

The start of a new era

We are entering a new era when it comes to social media – the age of artificial intelligence and quantum computing. Super powerful computers and algorithms that will make what we see today look childlike in their complexity. Before now we have witnessed dumb machines make dumb mistakes because humans made stupid decisions. Moving into a time when humans let computers run things unsupervised based on stupid decisions and not learning from our previous mistakes is rightly concerning.

Whether we like it or not, AI is the next great bastion of social media. Ethics will play a key role in making it and serving it but how we form new technologies and platforms matter as much as the why. Google has now mastered convincing a human it is not talking to a robot thanks to ums and ahs – its next job is to convince us that it is a good thing.

A quote that Lanier ends his book with is core to the idea of where social media is going. A fundamental which, if left unchecked, has the power to continue dismantling democracy but also the fabric of society: "We cannot have a society in which, if two people wish to communicate, the only way that can happen is if it's financed by a third person who wishes to manipulate them."

The key is adding the humanity back into social media. Whether it is an instapod on Instagram that fluff engagement rates or a paid reviewer that doesn't disclose his or her affiliation – the intention behind the action matters. The person whom the intention is for matters. Humanity isn't about clicks now, and it never was or will be. Humans will always be about shared connections, experiences and stories – mainly thanks to the rise of artificial intelligence and sentient computers.

Social platforms like Facebook, LinkedIn, Pinterest and others all claim to connect, but in reality naturally became data sinkholes thanks to the models that surround them. Diminishing value to the user and lack of better options mean systems need to be gamed (dark patterns, engagement bait) to remain viable and grow bigger and bigger. The future may include regulation, user revolts, and self-correction but until the fundamental economics become resolved, little will change. This scenario doesn't mean social media is useless, far from it.

The role of employees

Instead of sticking with poor platforms there is hope from several sources. The first is employees at the companies themselves; both Google and Facebook employees have shown ethical stances that have not just challenged the corporate position but forced change. The second is the media; Cambridge Analytica and other issues would not have come to light without the media's help. Third, and possibly the most important source, is the role of various governments around the world. Without regulation the platforms will keep dealing in clicks and time spent without a care for the wellbeing of the users. The metaphor of a drug dealer with too much knowledge is apt and not one of which the government is unaware. The question is not if but when things will be changed. The current system cannot continue as it stands. Whether this means more obfuscation by platforms or a softening of edges is all that remains to be seen.

Social media won't look the same in ten years' time as it does today. Increasingly developers, users and platforms are bringing the adage 'it's not what you use, it's how you use it' back into play. Perhaps we have to go through a period where everything feels and goes wrong to fight for what's right and what's good?

From the current state of messaging apps in Asia to new services and the way smartphones are being built, new possibilities are storming through; crowd banking and micro-loans through messenger apps to dialling a specialist doctor through Skype from your wrist or using mobile users to react or respond better to disasters. Social media is great at the moment – it's not perfect – but it can still be greater than we have seen

Note on the contributor

Paul Armstrong is a leading strategist, author and speaker on the future of technology, disruption, retail innovation, media industry, social technologies, consumer technology, mobile innovation, IoT, Martech/Adtech, start-ups and the start-up ecosystem. Paul runs the technology advisory HERE/FORTH (www.hereforth.com) where he helps clients including PwC, Coca-Cola, O2, P&G, jkrGlobal and MEC understand trends and how to sensibly apply emerging technologies strategically.

His first book, Disruptive Technologies, offers organisations a distinct response to emerging technologies including blockchain (Bitcoin), artificial intelligence, graphene and nanotechnology and other external factors – such as the sharing economy, mobile penetration, millennial workforce, ageing populations – that impact on their business, client service and product model.

Socialising Anti-Social Social Media

Social media has become a key part of digital capitalism, with troubling consequences, says Professor Christian Fuchs, but a more public service-orientated approach is possible and should be tried

'Social' Media

Twitter says it is about 'what people are talking about right now'[1]. Facebook argues its 'mission is to give people the power to build community and bring the world closer together. People use Facebook to stay connected with friends and family, to discover what's going on in the world, and to share and express what matters to them'[2].

So according to social media corporations' self-description, 'social' media is about expression, sharing, communication, and community. This understanding is in line with bourgeois social theory's notion of the social: For the French sociologist Émile Durkheim (1982: 59), the social means social facts which exercise 'an external constraint' on the individual. As a consequence, every expression is seen as social because it enters into others' thoughts and behaviour. So in a Durkheimian understanding, every posting on Facebook and Twitter – even if nobody responds – is social because it has the potential to enter others' thoughts and behaviour. For the German sociologist Max Weber (1978: 26), action is social if it 'takes account of the behaviour of others and is thereby oriented in its course'. So, for Weber, Facebook and Twitter are social insofar as users respond to and comment on others' tweets, Facebook postings, etc. The Durkheimian and Weberian understandings of the social fit well into social media corporations' worldview that presents these companies' technologies as the essence of the social: Facebook CEO Mark Zuckerberg said in an interview in 2011 that Facebook is 'true' sociality because it fosters the 'ability to stay connected to more people'[3]. Facebook's COO Sheryl Sandberg claimed in the same interview Facebook is the 'social technology people use' and Facebook wants 'everything to be more social for everyone else'.

Anti-Social Social Media

I have argued on another occasion that commercial social media's corporate strategies advance the engaging/connection/sharing-ideology (Fuchs 2017: 122-128, 273-277). That something is an ideology points towards a darker reality:

Someone advancing an ideology makes a claim that does not correspond to reality and that distracts from the actual state of reality in order to hide power structures. 'Social' media companies claim they are social in order to advance the unsocial and the anti-social.

The Cambridge Analytica scandal has evidenced the anti-social character of 'social media': In 2013, University of Cambridge-neuroscientist Aleksandr Kogan started using Facebook's developer platform for running a personality quiz on Facebook, by which he collected personal data of almost 90m users that was sold to Cambridge Analytica, whose vice-president was right-wing ideologue Steve Bannon. Bannon later became Donald Trump's White House chief strategist. Cambridge Analytica used the data for personalising political advertisements in election campaigns. This practice has widely been considered as the attempt to manipulate democracy. As a consequence, commentators started speaking of Facebook's anti-social and unsocial character. So for example, the *Financial Times* (2018) suddenly spoke of the 'anti-social network'.

The problem of the mainstream public sphere's sudden discovery of anti-social media is that the same commentators, pundits and media for years celebrated corporate social media as the newest big thing that would transform everything and would make everything better. They overlooked that anti-sociality is immanent to and built into digital capitalism.

2018 is not just the year the Cambridge Analytica/Facebook-scandal broke, but happens to also be the year we celebrate Karl Marx's bicentenary. And it is Karl Marx, whose theory is the most powerful tool for unveiling the unsocial and anti-social character of corporate 'social' media and digital capitalism (Fuchs 2017).

The *Economic and Philosophic Manuscripts of 1844* are an early philosophical work of Marx (1844), in which he most powerfully formulates the critique of capitalism as anti-social system by coining the notion of alienation.

For Marx, humans are social beings because they produce social life and society together. So for Marx, social production constitutes the social character of human beings: "Not only is the material of my activity given to me as a social product (as is even the language in which the thinker is active): my *own* existence *is* social activity, and therefore that which I make of myself, I make of myself for society and with the consciousness of myself as a social being" (Marx 1844: 298). "The individual *is the social being*. His manifestations of life – even if they may not appear in the direct form of *communal* manifestations of life carried out in association with others – *are* therefore an expression and confirmation of *social life*. Man's individual and species-life are not *different,* however much – and this is inevitable – the mode of existence of the individual is a more *particular* or more *general* mode of the life of the species, or the life of the species is a more *particular* or more *general* individual life" (Marx 1844: 299). In order to stress humans' social character, Marx also speaks of the human being as the species-being (*Gattungswesen*).

Marx interprets Hegel materialistically for arguing that domination and class structures result in a gap between the existence of humans in contemporary society and their social essence. Capitalism constitutes the non-identity of humans' essence and existence. Capitalism *alienates* humans from their social nature. Alienation constitutes capitalism's unsocial and anti-social character. Marx (1844: 321) argues that the division of labour, class structures and commodity exchange result in the domination of society by 'unsocial, particular interests'. As a consequence, there are four kinds of alienation (Marx 1844: 276-277): 1) Humans are alienated from nature; 2) Humans are alienated from their bodies and minds, their subjectivity; 3) The human is alienated from the 'product of his labour, from his life activity' (Marx 1844: 276-277) and also from other humans and society. In alienated structures and societies, humans do not control the things, structures, resources and social relations they produce and that they produce with.

Marx's concept of alienation is not just a critique of wage-labour and private property of the means of production that estrange humans economically from ownership of what they together produce in the economy and that is privately owned by capital. It is also a critique of political systems and institutions which alienate humans from the control of and influence on setting the conditions which govern their lives. The critique of alienation is a critique of economic and political domination and the demand for political democracy and economic democracy.

The Cambridge Analytica scandal is not simply a story about fake news, fake attention, fake accounts, fake personality tests and fake advertising on social media. It is a story about the intersection of right-wing digital ideology, digital capitalism and digital neoliberalism: Far-right ideologues and movements will do whatever it takes to achieve their goals, including using digital media in all ways necessary for spreading propaganda and defeating political enemies. The political culture of fake news is an expression of the friend-enemy-scheme in a highly polarised political world dominated by new nationalism and right-wing authoritarianism (Fuchs 2018a). Facebook is the epitome of digital capitalism: It treats personal data as a commodity in order to sell targeted advertisements. In 2017, Facebook's profits amounted to US$15.9bn in 2017. Targeted advertising is driven by algorithms that are blind for the content of what is being advertised. For Facebook, it does not matter if the ad is about chocolate cookies or alt-right – it only cares about selling targeted ads for the sake of profit. It is therefore no surprise that Facebook has tolerated highly problematic data practices. Its logic is that the more online activity, data and meta-data is generated, the more potential profit emerges. But as a consequence, profitability and capitalism's economic freedom come into contradiction with political freedom (democracy) and social freedom (fairness, quality). Capitalism is based on generalised commodity production by workers who do not own the commodities they create. Commodities are capital that yield profits for capitalists. Users' unremunerated digital labour produces big data that

Facebook commodifies and turns into profit. The users of advertising-based social media platforms are digital workers, the 21st century's digital proletariat (Fuchs 2017). Because of the mistaken ideology that what is good for capitalist businesses' profits must be good for society, neoliberal politics and politicians are lax on privacy protection and regulating digital corporations. Business self-regulation does not work. It has become evident that it can easily advance threats to democracy.

The Cambridge Analytica scandal is just the tip of the iceberg of digital alienation: Digital corporations alienate users from data and platforms. Users are not in control of privacy. Neoliberalism alienates citizens from access to common goods necessary for leading a decent life. Far-right demagogues alienate society from democracy.

In the Congressional hearings on Facebook conducted by the Senate Committee on the Judiciary and Senate Committee on Commerce, Science, and Transportation on April 10, 2018, and the House Committee on Energy and Commerce on April 11, Mark Zuckerberg acted as the unknowing CEO. His most frequent answer to the hundreds of questions posed to him in the two hearings followed the styles 'I don't know' and 'I don't know off the top of my head, but we can follow up with you' (see US Congress 2018a, 2018b).

Zuckerberg acted as the great Donald Rumsfeld-impersonator. The then-US Secretary of Defense famously justified the US war in Iraq with the following words: "There are known unknowns. That is to say, there are things that we now know we don't know. But there are also unknown unknowns. There are things we do not know we don't know." Zuckerberg responded to questions about Facebook's dataveillance and digital capitalism predominantly with the logic of the known unknowns and unknown unknowns.

Slavoj Žižek (2004) argues that Rumsfeld deliberately overlooked that 'the main dangers lie in the unknown knowns', 'the things we don't know that we know', 'the disavowed beliefs, suppositions and obscene practices we pretend not to know about, even though they form the background of our public values'. In a public hearing, Zuckerberg disavowed knowledge of the hidden knowledge and values that underpin digital capitalism and therefore form the background knowledge of his and Facebook's everyday practices. In the Senate hearing, Zuckerberg said Facebook 'doesn't feel like' a monopoly (US Congress 2018a). Zuckerberg certainly 'feels' and senses the growing amounts of money on his bank accounts, so is knowledgeable of it. But he says he does not feel monopoly structures. He does not want to think of the broader implications of the monopolist practices of capital accumulation on society, which shows that capital is blind for its own negative features and impacts on society. The implication, however, is that capital will not voluntarily do anything to mitigate its own negative impacts. It is therefore a political task to force basic rules of conduct on capital via the law, the state, and civil society.

Socialising Anti-Social Social Media

Liberals now call for more privacy regulation and data protection. But there is no simple fix to digital capitalism's structural problems. What can be done? We need to socialise unsocial social media. Political acts of digital socialisation entail different measures (see Fuchs 2018a): Banning targeted political online advertising reduces the dangers of advertising to democracy. It can only be effective if high fines for disregarding the ban are introduced and executed. Such a measure can as a starting point be introduced in single national jurisdiction. Another measure is to substitute algorithmic activity by paid human work of highly skilled and well-paid fact-checkers and knowledge professionals. The most important measure is to challenge and break up the monopolies of corporate social media platforms. We require new types of online platforms which advance the digital commons and digital public services. Public service broadcasters should be encouraged and legally enabled to build and operate their own social media platforms, e.g. a public service YouTube run by a network of PSBs, including BBC, ARD, France Télévisions, RAI, PBS, etc. Taxing online advertising and other digital profits would create a finance base for funding alternative social media and solve the problem that digital corporations avoid paying taxes (Fuchs 2018b). A participatory media fee could thereby be enabled which gives an annual public sphere cheque to citizens, who donate the received money to non-profit media projects. Facebook, Twitter, Google could be turned into non-profit platform co-operatives not owned and controlled by shareholders, but by the users themselves. Overcoming the threats posed to society and democracy by unsocial social media requires us to advance the digital commons as alternatives to digital capitalism.

Notes

[1] https://about.twitter.com, accessed on April 24, 2018.

[2] https://newsroom.fb.com/company-info/, accessed on April 24, 2018.

[3] http://sreetips.tumblr.com/post/12476985572/facebook-charlie-rose-interviews-mark-zuckerberg

References

Durkheim, Émile (1982) *Rules of Sociological Method*, New York: Free Press.

Financial Times. 2018. The Anti-Social Network. Facebook Bids to Rebuild Trust After Toughest Week. *Financial Times Online*, March 23, 2018.

Fuchs, Christian (2018a) *Digital Demagogue: Authoritarian Capitalism in the Age of Trump and Twitter*, London: Pluto.

Fuchs, Christian (2018b) *The Online Advertising Tax as the Foundation of a Public Service Internet*. London: University of Westminster Press, https://www.uwestminsterpress.co.uk/site/books/10.16997/book23/

Fuchs, Christian (2017) *Social Media: A Critical Introduction*, London: Sage. Second edition.

Marx, Karl (1844) Economic and Philosophic Manuscripts of 1844. In *MECW Volume 3*, London: Lawrence & Wishart., pp. 229-346.

US Congress (2018a) Transcript of Mark Zuckerberg's Senate Hearing, *The Washington Post Online*, April 10, 2018. Available online at https://www.washingtonpost.com/news/the-switch/wp/2018/04/10/transcript-of-mark-zuckerbergs-senate-hearing/?utm_term=.d3e94119e9ef

US Congress (2018b) Transcript of Zuckerberg's Appearance before House Committee, *The Washington Post Online*, April 11, 2018. Available online at https://www.washingtonpost.com/news/the-switch/wp/2018/04/11/transcript-of-zuckerbergs-appearance-before-house-committee/?noredirect=on&utm_term=.a8a47da06e61

Weber, Max (1978) *Economy and Society*. Berkeley, CA: University of California Press.

Žižek, Slavoj (2004) What Rumsfeld Doesn't Know That He Knows About Abu Ghraib, *In These Times*, May 21, 2004. Available online at http://inthesetimes.com/article/747/what_rumsfeld_doesn_know_that_he_knows_about_abu_ghraib/

Note on the contributor

Christian Fuchs is a professor at the University of Westminster, where he is director of the Communciation and Media Research Institute (CAMRI) and the Westminster Institute of Advanced Studies (WIAS). He is author of more than 400 publications, including the books Digital Demagogue: Authoritarian Capitalism in the Age of Trump and Twitter (Pluto 2018) and Social Media: A Critical Introduction (Sage 2017, 2nd edition) @ fuchschristian http://fuchs.uti.at.

The empire strikes back?

Traditional media is beginning to fight back in the battle for advertising pounds. But, as Raymond Snoddy writes, the love affair with social media from both advertising agencies and consumers will be difficult to shake

Thursday July 5, 2018 was like any another other day in a crazy, news-laden summer for a newspaper like The Times. The splash was devoted to the couple accidentally poisoned by the nerve-agent novichok, Dawn Sturgess, who subsequently died, and her partner Charlie Rowley.

There was an article about how the longest British heat wave since 1976 wasn't all that special geographically, as record highs 'leave the world baking.'

As it was right in the middle of the World Cup there was a banner promoting a World Cup pullout on: 'What England must do to beat Sweden' and 'The Secrets behind that penalty shootout' that defeated Columbia. Away from the noise of the front page there was an unmistakable scatter of stories on the social media – about the need for a tough internet regulator to tackle the problems of the tech giants, an apparent volte face by Facebook on whether it is a publisher or not, and further evidence of the advertising lifeblood of a national newspaper group bleeding away in the face of competition from the social media.

For good measure in a leading article The Times supported the need for online regulation. The day, and the newspaper, were chosen almost at random, and nothing scientific can be deduced, other than that they are fragments of evidence of rapidly changing attitudes to the multi-billion social media operators and the often unwitting harm they do.

The most prominent story was an appeal by Jeremy Darroch, chief executive of the Sky television group, urging the UK government to create a regulator 'with sharp teeth' to rein in Facebook, Google and the others. Darroch had written to the then Culture Secretary Matt Hancock asking the Government to create a watchdog with robust powers to ensure that the online giants take responsibility for the content on their platforms.

"We as a society must find effective ways to stem the flow of hate, abuse, and offensive, illegitimate, and even dangerous content online, and we must act fast," argued Darroch, who also warned that society now faced "a tsunami of harms" on the internet.

By chance as the Sky executive wrote, Hancock was appearing at a political event in London where the politician ridiculed suggestions that no individual nation was powerful enough to stand up to the internet billionaires. "By God, if the UK as a society, represented legitimately through Parliament and from Parliament in government, wants to do something, then that is what we do," Hancock insisted, speaking before his promotion as a result of the Brexit Cabinet resignations.

Television enters the fray

A few days earlier another senior British television executive, Dame Carolyn McCall, chief executive of ITV, had entered the social media fray on issues of both tax and regulation. ITV, unlike newspapers, she conceded, was not a serious victim of social media, though Netflix and Apple were obvious new video competitors. The British commercial broadcaster still wanted a more even playing field.

Dame Carolyn argued that the small amount of tax paid by Facebook in the UK compared with its revenues was 'quite odd'. Some have used more forceful terms. She added that Facebook might have 20,000 moderators, but they were self-moderating and "they are not independently moderating."

She also argued that Google and Facebook should be treated as publishers rather than platform operators. "They have to be responsible for content, taking responsibility for their content, because that is what they make their money out of," Dame Carolyn insisted.

The second of The Times social media stories of July 5 carried news of what seemed to be a dramatic U-turn by Facebook, as it appeared to admit for the first time that it was indeed a publisher, something often denied in the past.

The social media giants had been gradually edging towards taking greater responsibility for removing posts on everything from jihadi propaganda to hate speech and fake news. The official line, however, had remained that social media did not create content, were platform owners and mere distributors with the discretion to decide what was acceptable or not. Crucially they had argued they could not be held legally liable, certainly in the US, for what was distributed. Apart from the first amendment they had been helped by a section of the US Communications Decency Act of 1996, which protects web companies from liability over third-party content posted on their sites.

As recently as April, 2018 Facebook founder Mark Zuckerberg was asked by senators investigating the Cambridge Analytica data scandal to explain whether Facebook was a tech company or a publisher. Zuckerberg replied that it was a tech company 'because the primary thing we do is build technology and products'.

Now in a court case in California Facebook had to defend a claim that Zuckerberg had deliberately created a loophole enabling developers to access the data of users' friends. It was the 'loophole', subsequently closed, that enabled Cambridge Analytica to obtain the personal data of more than 80m Facebook users without their agreement. The data may also have been misused in both the Trump election campaign and the Brexit referendum.

Sonhal Metha, a lawyer for Facebook argued that the company's decisions about data acquisition were 'quintessential publisher function' and as such were covered by the first amendment. Metha went on to compare the issue to those faced in the traditional print media. "Publisher discretion is a free speech right irrespective of what technological means is used," she said.

These arguments have enormous potential implications for all of the social media and their relations with traditional publishers, their responsibility for content and the push for regulation.

It was not immediately clear whether Zuckerberg had signed up to such a fundamental change in stance, or whether it was a lawyer acting in isolation to boost a legal case in a specific set of circumstances.

Print's ongoing troubles

On July 5th, in the business section of The Times, there was also a hint of the troubles facing the newspaper industry with the news that annual profits at the Telegraph Group fell to £13.7m in 2017/18 compared with £27.1m in the previous year. The reason given was the continued slump in newspaper print advertising.

While social media was not implicated directly, the results, in line with many other newspaper groups, reflected the impact of the industrial-scale vacuuming up of online advertising by social media and Facebook and Google-owned YouTube in particular.

The disappearance of classified advertising online, combined with changing social habits, is posing an existential threat to some regional newspapers, so great a threat that in February the Government launched a review of 'press sustainability' in the UK.

In its final July 5 piece The Times argued in a leading article for the need for an independent online regulator to protect internet users from harmful content and the monopolistic behaviour of the biggest online names. Facebook and Google might argue that they should be left to regulate themselves but, according to The Times, they had tried half-heartedly and failed. In practice, The Times believed, "it is almost as hard to force the internet giants of Silicon Valley to take responsibility for what they publish as it is to bring the law to bear on the creators of that content."

And anyway by the time police and prosecutors are involved the damage has long since been done.

The handful of Times articles published on a single day are unrelated. Together, though, they hint at a single truth, that there is a growing sense of unease about the enormity of the impact of the Silicon Valley giants on almost every aspect of society and even the operation of democracy itself, and an equally growing feeling that something now needs to be done.

No definitive balance sheet

It is impossible to draw up any definitive balance sheet on the contributions of social media groups to society. The huge positives are well known – everything from the limitless shopping choice and convenience of Amazon and the equally limitless sources of information and search on Google to the most powerful engine for breaking news the world has ever seen in Twitter, and the barely imaginable connectivity and creation of communities of interest among Facebook's two billion subscribers.

Unfortunately the items in the negative column are piling up. In no particular order they include:

- The destruction of thousands of jobs in retail and the danger of the hollowing out of the High Street although Amazon is hardly the single cause.

- The creation of the most comprehensive monopolies the world has ever seen, and with it the arrival of the imminent arrival of the trillion dollar company, monopolies that put the steel and railway barons of the 19th century into the shade.

- Serious concerns about the mental health and capabilities of the young with researchers from Revealing Reality finding that some teenagers are spending up to 12 hours a days 'mindlessly swiping' through social media without lingering on much for more than two seconds.

- Serious negative effects in the developing world where in some countries Facebook is the dominant means of communication. In Myanmar UN investigator Yanghee Lee found that ultra-nationalist Buddhists used Facebook to incite hatred and violence against the Rohingya and other ethnic minorities that led to genocide "I'm afraid that Facebook has now turned into a beast, and not what it originally intended," Lee said.

- There is also an ultimate threat to democracy. However, according to political journalist Philip Collins the threat to democracy will not be a repeat of the 1930s or from tanks in the square. Apart from the stagnation of real wages, the threat Collins believes comes from the fact that "the public realm is slowly being dominated by over-powerful corporate digital behemoths whose power we do not yet comprehend. Democracy is being undermined invisibly online, not by tanks in the square."

- If there is a threat to democracy then one of its central constituents is the threat to journalism and flows of trustworthy information without which democracy cannot function. It takes the form of threats from fake news, alternative facts, manipulations of political campaigns and ultimately the undermining of the financial base that funds teams of independent journalists, largely through falling print circulations and social media dominance of digital advertising.

There are few simple causal relationships involved and the preferences and choices of consumers have been crucial to the rise of the social media giants. They could not have done it unaided or without striking a chord with hundreds of millions of people. As a result behaviour has been transformed, probably permanently, but the burden of unintended consequences is growing, not least on the social media giants themselves.

Facebook's ultimate irony
Facebook felt the need to hire those 20,000 moderators to oversee content and in common with Google has been working continuously on new algorithms to weed out fake news or unacceptable content. Despite the apparently endless acquisitions of dozens of AI (artificial intelligence) start-ups by the social media giants automated editing clearly remains an inexact science.

In July 2018 Facebook had to apologise for perhaps the ultimate irony as it blocked parts of the US Declaration of Independence as hate speech. It again ran into heavy weather when it tried to do something to prevent its advertising being manipulated during elections and instead, in the words of New York Times chief executive Mark Thompson ended up unintentionally 'supporting the enemies of quality journalism'.

Facebook banned an ad promoting a news article about President Trump's summit with Kim Jong-un by labelling it unacceptable political content. Another ad for the New York Times cooking site was banned for unexplained reasons.

Other media executives, such as Robert Thomson, chief executive of Rupert Murdoch's News Corp and Jonah Peretti of Buzzfeed have been pushing for years for higher payments from the likes of Facebook and Google for their content. Never mind being properly paid for their journalism, traditional publishers have often wondered why they appeared to garner so little from their online advertising.

Last year The Guardian's chief revenue officer, Hamish Nicklin, experimented by buying his own ad inventory to assess where the money was spent across the supply chain and found that only 30 pence in the pound made it back to the publisher.

"There are so many different players taking a little cut here, a little cut there – and sometimes a very big cut. A lot of the money that (advertisers) think they are giving to premium publishers is not actually getting to us," Nicklin told a London conference.

Major advertisers have also been voicing their disquiet at both the lack of transparency of social media's numbers and the environment in which their online ads can appear. Keith Weed, chief marketing officer of Unilever, the Anglo-Dutch consumer goods company, has warned the social media groups that they need to take 'urgent action now to rebuild trust before it's gone forever'.

The action Weed said he was seeking was control over bad practice in the online space ranging from fake followers and fraud to robot viewers – bots – and what he called dishonest business models.

Weed was talking in June 2018 about the relatively new field of influencer marketing when companies pay for influencers to mention their brands – sometimes as much as £75,000 for a single post by a famous name. The concern of companies like Unilever is that as many as 15 per cent of Twitter users may be fake, while up to 60m Facebook accounts could be automated or bot accounts.

Earlier in that year Weed warned that Unilever, one of the world's largest advertisers, would stop buying advertising on social networks such as Facebook and Google unless they stopped helping people to spread hate speech. "Unilever will not invest in platforms or environments that do not protect our children or which create divisions in society, and promote anger and hate," Weed told an industry gathering in California, the backyard of the tech giants.

Weed's remarks came two weeks after it became clear that Procter & Gamble, Unilever's great rival, has already taken action and cut $200m in digital advertising spending from areas where there was concern about bots and brand safety. The money had been spent in areas where there was proven media reach including television, radio and ecommerce. The action followed publicly stated concerns by Marc Pritchard, P&G's chief marketing officer about fraud, a lack of proper measurement and murky contracts in the digital advertising supply chain.

A wish to reform?

Many industry observers suggested that while governments and regulators might pose future threats to the social media giants it would be the major international advertisers who could command their more immediate attention by refusing to advertise.

For whatever reason, including a wish to do the right thing, combined with commercial self-interest, there is some evidence of a wish to reform, or at least to do something about growing reputational damage and the financial implications that could follow.

One of the most visible manifestations of a new mood was the extensive advertising campaign in the British press by Facebook. The whole page ads concentrated on a single message: "Fake news is not our friend."

The ads went on: "We're committed to reducing its spread; so we're working with more fact-checkers globally, improving our technology, and giving you background information on the articles in your News Feed." Undoubtedly a step forward but the difficulty remains in defining what is a fact, and what to do when one person's fact equals another's fake news?

In July Twitter announced that it had begun the process of removing tens of millions of fake accounts from user's followers. The purge was designed to tackle social media fraud in which users buy followers, who are often automated bots to artificially magnify their influence, and possibly to sell on to advertisers.

The behaviour of social media in the Irish referendum on abortion reform was another indication of the sector changing its behaviour. Google and Twitter decided it would not accept campaign advertising on either side of the argument, which ended in an overwhelming victory for reform. Facebook merely banned all foreign sourced and financed advertising.

In July Facebook was also warned that the UK's Information Commissioner's Office (ICO) intention to impose the maximum fine available under existing legislation, £400,000 on the company because of the huge data leak to Cambridge Analytica. The ICO found that the personal data of about one million UK users had been leaked out of a total of 87m.

Damian Collins, the MP chairing the UK's Digital, Culture, Media and Sport committee, which was investigating Facebook and Cambridge Analytica, at the time, raised further questions for Facebook to answer.

"Given that the ICO is saying that Facebook broke the law, it is essential that we now know which other apps ran in their platform may have scraped data in a similar way. This cannot be left to a secret internal investigation by Facebook," Collins said.

The ICO would have even greater impact in future if a Facebook or other social media group breached legislation. A UK change of law allows the ICO to fine data transgressors up to four per cent of revenue taking potential fines into the billions.

The ICO decision on Facebook and Cambridge Analytica was being closely watched in the US where the Securities and Exchange Commission, the FBI, the Justice Department and the Federal Trade Commission were all believed to be taking an interest.

Meanwhile apart from the journalist kickback against fake news and what many publishers believe are unfair terms of trade, the traditional newspaper industry is finally, some would argue very belatedly, starting to set usual rivalries aside and uniting against the common Silicon Valley 'enemy'.

Print gets it together

After more than four years of effort the publishing industry at last produced what advertisers have long asked for – accurate, non-duplicated figures for real readers across all platforms, print, tablet, desktop and phone.

Publishers had long claimed the extent of their reach in the modern world was greater than usually acknowledged but did not have the numbers to prove it. Pamco, the successor to the National Readership Survey, combined the latest passive measurement technology with 35,000 face-to-face interviews, to produce a more reliable trading currency reflecting the changes in how readers consumed media.

The first figures, which should help in the advertising battle with social media, showed that the UK's newsbrands have a total monthly reach of 46.07m with the highest achieved by print on 31.6m a month followed by phone, desktop and tablet.

At the same time Newsworks, the national industry marketing body and WPP's GroupM agency released research (see also chapter xxx, pxx) showing that ads appearing in quality online environments provided by publishers were 42 per cent more cost-effective for advertisers based on levels of engagement, viewability and dwell time. A premium exposure was 58 per cent more likely to be 100 per cent in view for at least five seconds – GroupM's global viewability standard.

In the world of fragile attention spans the online industry standard is 50 per cent in view for at least one second. In contrast the study found that 48 per cent of measurable ads on the open exchange were never actually seen. The research should help traditional publishers in the battle with social media, which took more than 90 per cent of the increase in global online advertising last year.

At the same time the self-help continued when three of the largest British national newspaper groups, News UK, publishers of The Times and The Sun, and the Guardian and Daily Telegraph finally got together to create The Ozone Project. This offers advertisers and agencies direct access from a single point to an audience of nearly 40m unique users in 'brand safe, fraud-free, premium environments'.

As I write, it's difficult to say whether all the research in the world will be enough to wean advertising agencies away from what many see as the easy, even lazy, choice – programmatic, computer-driven online advertising despite growing evidence that it can be associated with bots, fraud and low engagement and dwell times.

Even more problematical, will the public love affair with social media start to cool in the face of serious, unintended, negative consequences? There is little evidence of it.

A study by consultants Deloitte found that following the implementation of GDPR – General Digital Protection Regulation – 72 per cent of respondents were aware that companies they interact with online used their personal data 'most' or 'all' of the time. But it did not seem to affect behaviour negatively. Usage of social networks continued to rise.

But there are signs that rising costs of doing business for the social networks is starting to have an impact on revenues and share prices. In July 2018 Facebook lost nearly 19 per cent of its capital value, or $150bn, when its second quarter results failed to hit forecasts with founder Mark Zuckerberg blaming, in part, the cost of investing heavily in security and safety. For the social media giants it could be the shape of things to come.

Note on the contributor

Raymond Snoddy has been a journalist all his working life on local and regional newspapers and on the Financial Times and The Times, for many years specialising in the media. He has also presented a number of television series including Hard News for Channel 4 and the accountability programme News Watch for the BBC.

Section Two

The death of journalism as we know it?

* * *

Can there be life without (not too much) social media – or is traditional reporting a fad of the past?

Neil Fowler

Can traditional journalism survive without the overbearing intrusion of Twitter, WhatsApp and co? There might be a chance if some of the UK's more doughty print publications, in particular, have anything to do with it.

Prince among those who hang on to the good old days is the fortnightly Private Eye, which steadfastly refuses to have too much to do with digital. It has a basic website; it publishes a little online of what is in the current magazine; it has a regular podcast; but in essence to read it you have to dip in to your pocket and purchase its content on old-fashioned dead trees and ink.

In 2018 its sales were as good as they have ever been, at well over 250,000, and with some 57 per cent through regular subscription. Occasionally editor Ian Hislop will print a letter from a reader complaining about the magazine's digital presence, but they are given short but practical advice about what to do, generally built around the phrase 'Buy it – Ed'.

Private Eye is not alone among magazines, especially, in being aggressive when it comes to print and payment for content. The Economist, The Spectator and the New Statesman are among those that from the start have maintained strong pay-for-what-you-read policies. It is true they have been more open to generous discounts such as £12-for-twelve-weeks offers, but in the end there is little of what you can read of them that is free.

The Eye has never been known to sell openly at a cut price – though at the time of writing in the late summer of 2018 it was offering a year's direct-debit subscription of 26 issues for £30, which with three bonus issues made for an opening deal of £1.03 per copy vs a cover price of £2. When first-class postage is included (it is printed on a Tuesday and lands on most readers' doormats on Wednesday mornings. Even without the bonus copies it is still only £1.15 a time.

Not only is that a remarkably good deal, but also the magazine's ad team must be selling at a very good yield. Which brings it down to the centuries-old way of doing news – an attractive cover price which brings in 'quality' readers for whom advertisers are willing to pay a premium. 'Simples', in modern parlance.

Clearly one of the reasons why the Eye has done so well is it has remarkably strong and loyal relationship with its readers and offers a feast of unique content, both serious and satirical. The same can be said for other current affairs magazines such as The Economist, The Spectator and the New Statesman. They all have first-class writers, often with unique standpoints, and, in the case of The Economist especially, enjoy news editing of the highest calibre. Bluntly you'll have to pay to read them – and they seem to be having the nerve to hang on to that demand. And they've supported their content message through all acting aggressively in the 2010s on cover price.

In the case of general news it is all a different story, in the main. UK regional and local newspapers have tended to follow the let's-give-it-away model with the unfortunate – putting it mildly – result that the sector is in freefall, in terms of overall revenue, sales and, in many cases, quality.

National papers, through having the legacy of very much higher circulations and thus critical mass, have been able to hang on for much longer. Most had hoped giving news away free online would bring in sufficient replacement support advertising revenues. It clearly hasn't worked.

But there are exceptions: The Times follows a Private Eye-type route, though producing a twice-daily updated version of itself online which only subscribers can access; the Financial Times puts news online first and has a feature-led newspaper as support for subscribers only; The Guardian asks for donations but is still free for anyone to read; the Daily Telegraph has a meter system aimed at encouraging digital readers to subscribe. The jury is out on all of them. Even with The Times, which in 2018 was probably in the best financial health in its 233-year history, it was unclear whether all its traditional (and ageing) readers would be replaced as they died by younger customers, used to reading their content for free.

So in this section we ask if this is the death of journalism as we know it? Can it hang on? Can even Private Eye still remain afloat with its business model? Or has too much changed already?

Jim Chisholm, for long one of the UK's, and indeed one of the world's, leading forensic analysts of news business statistics, says it may a familiar story. Media through the centuries has always adapted, He writes:

> *"History shows the media has a Darwinian way of turning adversity into advantage through adaptability. Records (vinyl) suffered from the launch of radio in the1920s but musicians soon realised radio was their best form of promotion. More recently musicians have turned the disruption of Spotify and YouTube to their advantage, bypassing the middlemen to attract new fans and buyers."*

Though this time it may all be different, he argues. The overwhelming dominance of the Big Five, as he calls them – Alphabet (Google), Amazon, Apple, Facebook, Microsoft – means the rules have all changed. He wants traditional publishers to fight back more. And he sees more control of the Big Five as essential.

Many commentators see younger minds as providing hope for the future, but he looks to a slightly older demographic in paving a new route through a group who he calls the 'new newsers'. He spotlights Edinburgh as a location for a thriving news industry – often driven by journalists made redundant from long-established media businesses – but not as we have known it in the past.

However, they don't always look for the money, he says:

> *"With no disrespect to these often brilliant, pioneering writers, I observe a lack of commercial expertise and in many conversations, I would suggest there is also commercial naivety. There has always been a healthy conflict between the content creators and the moneymakers, but today realism must prevail."*

And this brings optimism, he says. "But to succeed, these excellent publishers need to adopt the entrepreneurial skills as they demonstrate in editorial." This is the challenge.

Alan Geere, another globetrotter with multi-national experience, takes a close look at how a traditional news producer in the north-east of England (where he and I both worked in the 1990s) has evolved over the years.

He finds the world of newspapers in 2018 a much-changed place, from even finding the front door. But some things haven't been lost – like the news conference:

> *"Strangely for such a state-of-the-art operation the conference guest list is largely unchanged from time immemorial with representatives from news, production, business, sport and entertainment all sharing the table to sing for their supper."*

However, in this digital-first era, there is a new overseer:

> *"Behind them the league table of story hits, as compiled by Chartbeat, flickers and burps its way through real-time consumption showing how many people are engaged with a particular story and how long they spend looking at it. It is incessant and relentless and impossible not keep glancing at it."*

Overall he is impressed: "In an era when the template rules and many regional newspapers are a lack-lustre reflection of former glories the titles produced from Newcastle still exude flair and authority..." He finds "committed, capable people confidently handling all the channels of delivery with a dexterity that can only be marvelled at." But will it work in the long term? As with Jim Chisholm the jury is out.

Professor Richard Sambrook, formerly a stalwart of BBC news for many years, asks for a rethinking of the marriage between broadcast news and social media: 'It's complicated,' he says. Back in the noughties, he writes, he used to be a social media evangelist. Then the infant social media held such promise for broadcasters and audiences alike, he believed. There was talk about the promise of interactivity, empowering the audience, real connection and insight into their thoughts and ideas – and free distribution! Such innocence, he now says.

> *"With the benefit of hindsight, it's clear how the promise of reach, access to the younger demographic and granular feedback through user data seduced broadcasters to allow intermediaries to come between them and the audience."*

But he adds:

> *"We can't even say it was a strategic mistake – for where was the alternative? The platforms grew so rapidly on the back of extraordinary technology and offered services which inevitably had broader customised appeal than anything a single broadcaster could offer. The elusive under-30s audience were hanging out online, not in front of their TVs."*

He now sees the two sides as having different agendas:

> *"Social media encourages opinion over fact, it is increasingly fed by outrage and emotion which as a consequence feeds division. Emotional triggers encourage greater use, more data, bigger profits. Broadcasting, on the other hand, is committed to bringing audiences together for common experiences, a constructive public debate and building rather than dividing communities."*

So is there an answer? "Content regulation online," he says, "would be hugely complex and likely to have damaging collateral consequences. Who chooses what we should see or share? And what about the impact on free expression?"

But he believes the pendulum, now seemingly having swung irrevocably to the side of the social media providers, may be on its way back:

> *"They (the broadcasters) have strong brands loved by audiences...they have decades of experience in handling content and complex ethical issues...they continue to produce great and much loved content. (Social media) may need the broadcasters more than they realise."*

Dr David Nolan, of the University of Melbourne, takes a specific news story and analyses in depth how it was reported both in the traditional news media and via social media to illustrate how journalism has changed in recent years.

The story was the speech of then Australian prime minister Julia Gillard in October 2012, when she launched a ferocious and personal attack on the opposition leader Tony Abbott. Her words were part of a debate on a vote of no confidence in the speaker of the Australian parliament Peter Slipper after a texting indiscretion.

The speech, which Nolan says contained one of the most famous lines in Australian political history, was so strong and targeted on Abbott's alleged misogyny that it led to a massive global debate digitally and in print. And it was the difference in the debate on social media to the more traditional outlets that Nolan believes was a landmark in journalism.

"The reaction among Australian political journalists…appeared cynical," he writes. "Gillard's speech was not only described as defending the indefensible, but derided as opportunistic… Australian media coverage worked to substantively undermine the substance of Gillard's speech, presenting it as hypocritical, delegitimising it as a valid challenge to misogyny."

But "simultaneously, however, the speech went viral, with a YouTube posting of the speech receiving 1.5m views within a week, not least thanks to positive coverage from websites Salon and Jezebel (who labelled it 'the best thing you'll see all day!'), a positive write-up in The New Yorker's 'Ladylike' column (Lester 2012), and further coverage in the UK, Canada, South Africa and India."

So major differences in interpretation and major differences in what readers of specific branches of the media were seeing. Nolan sees this as good reason to celebrate as "…social media have offered new capacities for self-organisation for social movements to amplify a range of voices." But he also acknowledges print journalists were merely acting in the way they believed was correct, adding:

"The Canberra press gallery journalists viewed Gillard's speech through the prism of their normal professional practices. That is, they saw their job as political journalists, reporting on a specific political situation, not to declare a moment of historical significance in gender relations, but to interpret and communicate to their audience their interpretation of this speech in the context of electoral politics."

But overall he says the Gillard story and reaction may well prove to be significant as the ways in which journalism and debate operate have shifted, with the powers of the new providers and their algorithms much enhanced. "It is important to neither mourn nor celebrate the passing of previous boundaries," Nolan says, "but to seriously consider the problem of how new boundaries supporting democratic journalism can be reimagined, sustained and debated in the present and future."

While the business of journalism has been changing, what has been happening to its ethics? The concept of fake news is now widespread – and the term has become a pejorative phrase of its own, used with abandon by many who don't like what they read or hear.

Professor Chris Frost looks at how the ethics of journalism have developed with the rise of social media. He believes while there are new ethical challenges, the basic philosophy remains unchanged when it comes to telling the truth and holding power to account. He writes:

"Accuracy and truth remain at the heart of good journalism, whilst concern for privacy, minors, the vulnerable and a policy of non-harassment, non-intrusion, non-discrimination and using straightforward means to gather stories unless there is a strong public interest continue to underpin the ethical demand to do no harm that is central to many journalism codes."

The tools of journalism have changed with access to many more sources made so much easier with digital storage and transparency. And the ability to transmit news and comment has never been as fast. But it means traps and other ways of making mistakes have opened up – and greater vigilance is needed now, not less. He concludes:

> *"Thirty years ago, journalism ethics were important but now they are vital. Media which seek to profit from informing the public needs to ensure its public gets its money's worth."*

Which is probably a good place to end. Journalism as a whole isn't dying, that's for sure – but is certainly changing, as is all that surrounds it. Is journalism as we know it dying? Possibly, but there remains a huge amount of life left in it. The basics remain the same: journalism is still telling someone somewhere something they needed to know (whether they acknowledged that need or not!). That foundation of journalism will stay for many generations to come, but it's how we adapt to the new environment that counts.

Musician Frank Zappa once said: "Jazz isn't dead, it just smells funny." The same might be said of journalism – and might have been said for many years when it was just in the hands of print and broadcasters. The entry of social media hasn't changed it, and arguably has added to the unpleasant aroma around it. It's in desperate need of some air freshener.

A familiar story – but will the outcome be any different?

In a media world where the Big Five digital players are calling the shots, Jim Chisholm sees hope emerging from a growing breed of new newsers

It's 60 years since Francis Williams[1], forebodingly noted in 1957, the closure 'of at least 225 weeklies and 21 out of 41 regional morning dailies'. Since then countless others from Bill Gates to The Economist[2] have anticipated the newspaper's extinction.

Figure 1. The Economist front cover, March 6, 2003

I've got some bad news for those harbingers of doom. To borrow The New York Times' misquote (ha ha) of Mark Twain: 'The reports of our death are greatly exaggerated'.

There is nothing we newspaper folks report more enthusiastically than our own demise! As I've written before[3], the news is flourishing but just not as we knew it.

Some harsh realities….

- In Europe the average print newspaper has about five years of viability[4];
- Bar some exceptions, digital revenues (and critically gross profit) are not growing as fast as print revenues are declining;
- The notion of paywalls paying – with some notable exceptions – is unlikely. News media have always depended on advertising, and here lies our core challenge/opportunity;
- The reason that news media – and other aspects of life – are under threat, is in large part because of the unfettered control and revenue extraction of the Big Five digital giants: Alphabet, Apple, Amazon, Facebook and Microsoft.
- The belief that young people simply do not connect with traditional news media. They turn to Facebook and Twitter for their news. That our youth somehow adopt news media as they get older couldn't be more wrong as this chart of cohort behaviour over time shows:

Figure 2. Cohort model of readership trends[5] drawing from the past

The old reader myth (UK)

Readership penetration of UK national daily newspapers by age over time.

%	1972	1980	1990	2000	2010	Var %
15-24	77.5	74.8	63.5	49.6	30.2	-61.1
25-34	74.4	72.2	60.5	47.1	30.9	-58.4
35-44	75.8	73.2	63.1	50.8	34.1	-55.0
45-54	78.5	74.6	69	56.1	37.9	-51.7
55-64	75.3	73.8	67.1	59.9	47.8	-36.6
65+	66.1	64.2	62.9	58.5	53.5	-19.0
	-6.2	-12.5	-15.8	-23.2	-28	

History shows the media has a Darwinian way of turning adversity into advantage through adaptability. Records (vinyl) suffered from the launch of radio in the 1920s but musicians soon realised that radio was their best form of promotion. More recently musicians have turned the disruption of Spotify and YouTube to their advantage, bypassing the middlemen to attract new fans and buyers.

Digital audience broadcasting (DAB) has rejuvenated the radio industry, with a long way to go, for example linking location and personalisation tools to deliver new services during drive time.

Cinema was ravaged in the 1960s and 1970s by the arrival of television. Then first the DVD, and more recently the likes of Netflix, have not only rejuvenated film-making, but also cinema attendance. Now the BBC, ITV, and Channel 4 are having to gang up to take on the increasing threat of Netflix[6].

I first anticipated the rejuvenative opportunity of mobile in 2004[7], but it wasn't until 2012 that mobile was measured as an advertising platform and then it was only in 2016 its audience was measured. Today, mobile accounts for two thirds of all digital and approaching a third of all advertising expenditure[8]. And it accounts for around half of all newspaper readers[9]. All this in 18 years.

Media evolve in waves with long periods of little evolution, interspersed with short periods – five to tens years – of frenetic disruption.

From the invention of paper in the seventh century[10], to Gutenberg's invention of the printing press around 1439, to the world's first newspaper in 1605 took around 700 years.

Some 170 years later, we had:

- Telephony in 1876;
- The phonograph in 1877;
- Photography in 1888;
- Radio around 1894;
- The first movies emerged in 1895[11].

TV broadcasting began in 1936[12]. And while the computer's first rudimentary form was an arithmetic machine by Blaise Pascal in 1642[13] and the first mechanical computer appeared in 1833, digital computing only emerged in 1936.

The revolution in personal computers and the internet occurred in the late 1990s[14]. Around 20 years. Does it sound familiar?

Mobile followed a very similar trajectory. The internet's evolution over 25 years, has now reached the inevitable point where a few major players – Alphabet, Amazon, Apple, Facebook, Microsoft (the Big Five) – completely dominate the digital world, and increasingly other aspects of society.

Figure 3. Market domination of major digital players

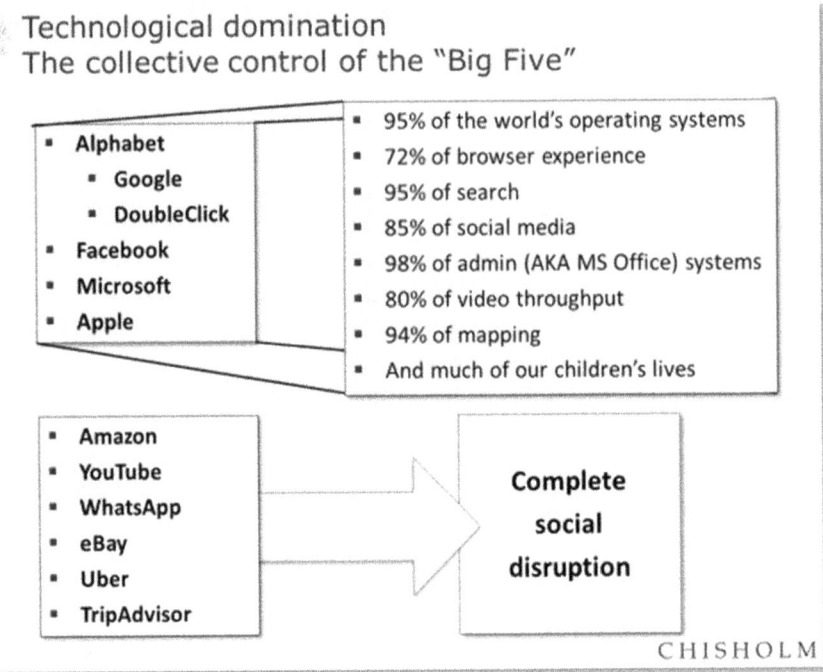

This domination must be questioned. And in some cases the question should be asked as to whether all or some of the Big Five should follow the 1984 breakup of the mighty Bell Corporation.[15] However, the big question is why have other forms of media adapted and exploited technological disruption, but news media continues to struggle?

Strategic framework

There are two frameworks that will define the future viability of news media: The first reflects media consumption in terms of:

- The forces of demand and supply; what do news consumers want/need and what are news providers offering;
- The roles of the established, legacy players versus emergent media;
- Demography, be it age, wealth, education or ethnicity. Binary political beliefs – right and left – are now a thing of the past.

Figure 4. Mapping of Media consumption and evolution

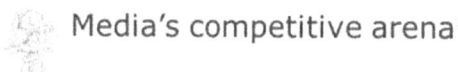

Media's competitive arena*

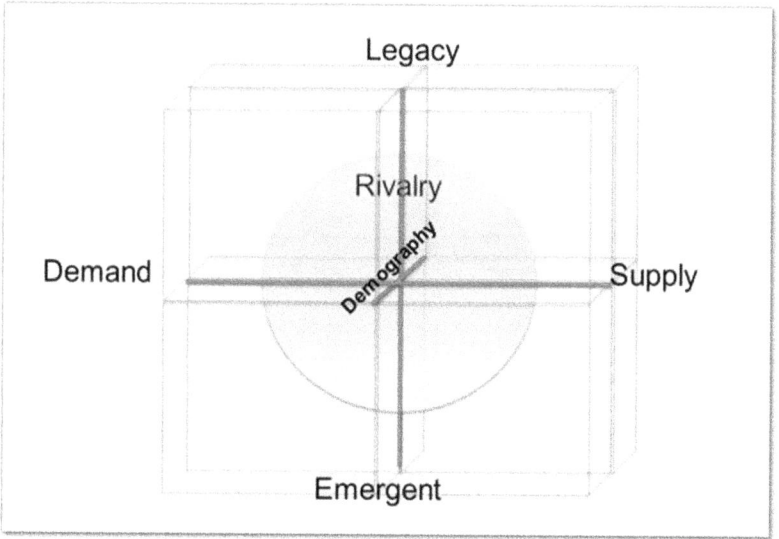

* Acknowledging Michael Porter's Five Forces   CHISHOLM

The second is the definition of the digital news revenue value chain. Once it looked like this:

Figure 5. The original digital value chain

In this version of the digital value chain, generally 10 per cent to 15 per cent of the advertisers' spending, is taken by the media-buying agency (plus creative costs).

Today it's more like this:

Figure 6. The complexity of the digital media transaction process[16]

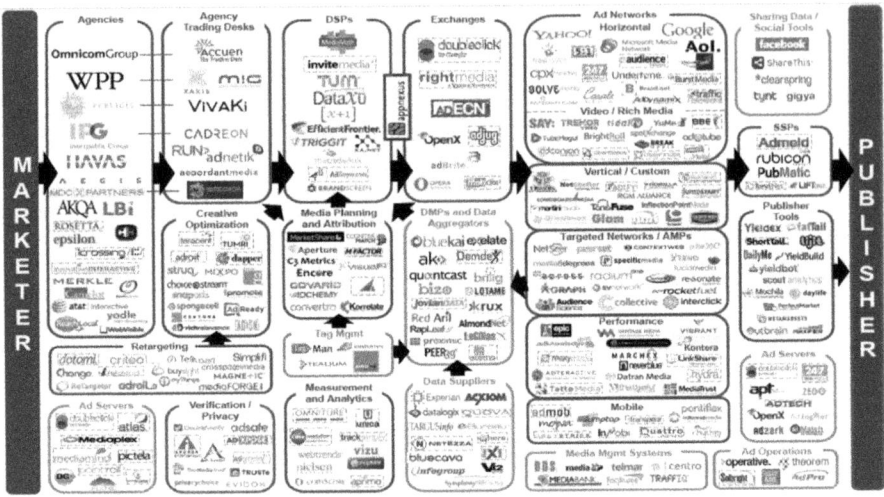

Source: LUMA, www.digitaladblog.com, and others

The econometric impact of this on publishers is stark.

Figure 7. The dilutive effect of intermediaries on the digital value chain[17]

Where has all the money gone?

| 100 | 10 | 5 | 15 | 12 | 15 | 14 | 29 |

Money spent on ad tech intermediaries

| Advertiser | Agency | Trading Desk | Data management platform | Demand side platform | Ad Exchange | Supply side platform | Publisher |

Source: AEMII Future Media Lab. Chisholm submission to House of Lords' inquiry into advertising.

In this version of the value chain, for every £100 that an advertiser spends, only 29 per cent ends up in the hands of publisher.

However, a number of independent intermediaries that allow publishers and advertisers to bypass the dilutive effect of the Big Five's value-chain grab, are reporting considerably higher returns while also removing the maelstrom of complications surrounding GDPR and how it is being interpreted/manipulated by the media agencies and Big Five.

Such an approach can more than double the share of ad spend that the publisher receives. But it will also increase the typical advertiser's return on investment (ROI) by up to five-fold, because of more effective targeting, and end-to-end visibility, without wastage[18].

Publishers are scratching around looking for paywall models, simply because such a high proportion of advertiser spend is being lost to the Big Five. And historically and looking forward news media have relied on advertising to deliver the majority of their gross profit[19].

Looking forward, what will the news media landscape look like in, say, five years' time? It was Donald Rumsfeld who infamously said: "There are known knowns, known unknowns, and unknown unknowns"[20]. And it was 111 years previously that Oscar Wilde wrote: "The public have an insatiable curiosity to know everything......except what is worth knowing..... journalism.... supplies their demands."[21]

Today quality journalism is torn between society's insatiable thirst for trivia, and President Trump's and others' attempts to present news as fake. The only consistency is tumultuous change, affecting every element of society, for better or worse.

After the boom years from 1950 to 1990 we must assume that economic growth rates will return to the historical norms of one per cent to 1.5 per cent[22]. The erosion of fair wealth distribution means that today's young people are the first generation to earn less than their parents and also the first to anticipate a shorter life expectancy. No wonder they ignore 'reputable' media in favour of social media.

We will continue to see the demise of the High Street (and now malls), with major retailers announcing closures or consolidation on an almost daily basis, as the Big Five grab this turf as well. In the last year (2017-18) 6,000 shops have closed.[23]

Meanwhile, technology itself is evolving rapidly:

- The digital environment is increasingly dominated by mobiles and tablets. By 2020 more than a third of all advertising – and two-thirds of all digital – will be on mobile platforms[24].

- Mobile networks will continue to develop, with expanded bandwidth, and availability, and also advances in micro-payments, linked to the phone subscription, enabling more automated payments; think PayPal meets Vodafone.

- We read more and more about artificial intelligence, robots, data journalism, virtual reality, etc – but my view is that while these may enhance content provision, they are secondary to the need to identify viable business models given the disruption in the value chain.

In 2018, as I write, governments, at least in Western Europe, have recognised the importance but plight of the news industry[25]. In the UK, the Prime Minister instigated the Cairncross Inquiry[26] into the future of the press. In France and Germany there are already government initiatives to control the influence and impact of the Big Five. In Brussels the European Commission is proving forceful in cracking down on the Big Five's excesses. But what we must not assume, in the UK at least is any helpful intervention from government, anytime soon.

The implications of this in terms of product development and most critically our crucial role as the fourth estate in society require significant consideration.

From lessons to directions
So, putting all this together, what are the lessons, directions and ideas that might reinvigorate the news industry?

At long last publishers are realising that they must escape their Stockholm Syndrome relationship with the Big Five, which has strangled revenues, stakeholder relationships and the reputation of news. There is an urgent need to redefine the respective roles of all stakeholders and intermediaries in the value chain to address the punitive effect that the Big Five and other intermediaries are having on content creation.

And I would include in this the increasingly redundant agencies and media buyers, as advertisers claw back control of the advertising value chain[27].

Unquestionably the likes of Alphabet, Amazon and Facebook can contribute greatly to the distribution of news, but not at the expense of revenue and stakeholders' rights. In the future the Big Five should be our recruiters, not distributors. No more taking our content and audience control to their advantage, from now on they should simply divert visitors to get their content directly from the publishers' sites.

Figure 8. News media's strategic framework

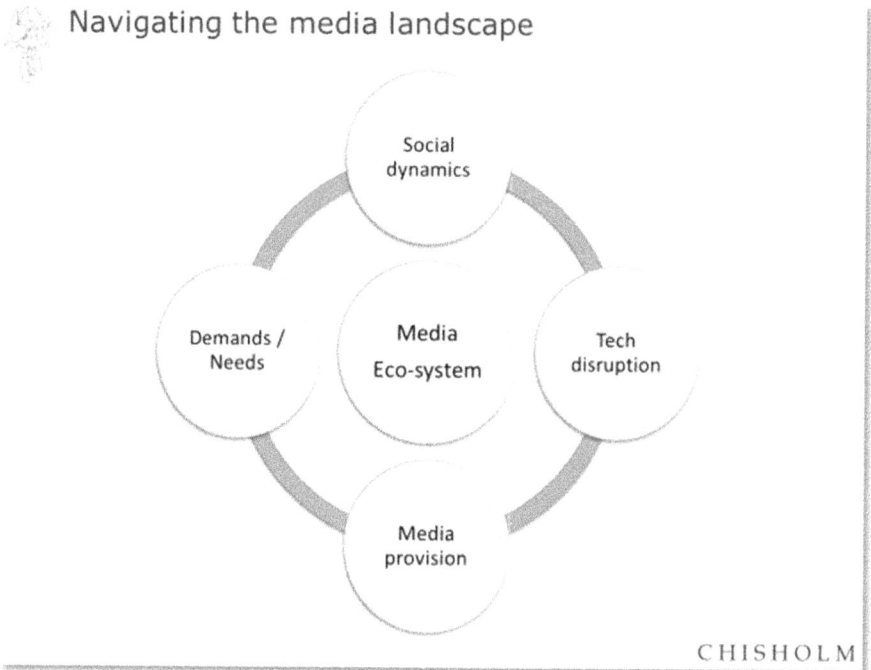

Navigating the media landscape

Social dynamics

Demands / Needs

Media Eco-system

Tech disruption

Media provision

CHISHOLM

The new news and what is happening

CP Scott, editor of The Guardian famously said: 'Comment is free. Facts are sacred.' So news media must reinforce its reputation. New approaches to news that appeal to the young and disillusioned are part of this evolution.

But to demonstrate how the news industry is thriving, let me first focus on my birthplace Edinburgh, a population of 500,000. It's very sad that the area's flagship newspaper, The Scotsman has seen its circulation fall over the last 40 years from 100,000 to 20,000, of which half are full price. Some of this is due to the growth of The (London) Times, which has seen circulation rise from 16,000 to 25,000 in the last five years, driven by investment in content. Established evening and local weekly papers have seen significant falls – but the consequence – not cause – of this is a raft of new initiatives:

First, community newspapers:

- South of Edinburgh, the Hawick News was a dominant local newspaper until its parent company made its senior editorial staff redundant. One of them launched the Hawick Paper in competition. After two years, the Hawick Paper outsells the News by more than two to one[28]. Same people. Same market.

- In a tiny district of Edinburgh, the Broughton Spurtle[29], produced and distributed by a group of up to 70 volunteers enjoys a circulation of 2,500 and a monthly online base of 12,000-15,000, (in a community of less than 10,000) based in a local florists[30]. Subscriptions are '£15 or whatever you can afford'.

- Across the city there are 44 defined communities[31], whose community councils each produce a newsletter of varying quality, mostly online, but in many areas a printed publication, funded by local advertising.

Then there are the more serious digital news media:

- Daily Business[32], founded by a previous business editor of The Scotsman, and now described by one of Scotland's leading entrepreneurs as 'My first go-to read of the day', a sentiment echoed by many. It is funded by advertising, sponsorship, paid-for-content, a range of business-to-business services, and voluntary payments.

- The Ferret[33] is an award-winning, not-for-profit consortium of experienced, independent investigative journalists. Their stories are regularly republished in the national and international press. It is funded through voluntary subscriptions, and contribution fees.

- Holyrood Magazine[34] covers the activities of the Scottish Parliament every fortnight in print and digital formats. It is funded by subscriptions, advertising and sponsored content.

- Humans of Edinburgh[35] is a Facebook site created by a young Edinburgh photographer that every day interviews someone on the streets of the city. It was the first medium to report that film producer Danny Boyle would be making a sequel to Trainspotting[36]. The scoop attracted more than a million visitors and was picked up by dozens of news-media around the world.

Then there are innumerable niche publications covering entertainment, sport, lifestyle, and tourism, and the inevitable student newspapers, which are distributed free of charge across the city, each with accompanying websites.

Without access to detailed figures, it would be reasonable to assume that this myriad of 'new news' media collectively create a local media economy at least equal in size to the established media.

Alternative thinking on revenue

What is evident is the increasing reliance on voluntary subscriptions. The Guardian is the most significant example[37]. It now boasts over 800,000 'supporters' globally, of whom 500,000 make recurring monthly payments (as subscribers, members or recurring contributors), and 300,000 who are one-off donors. This may be a tiny fraction of the medium's 150m visitors worldwide, but their impact on the publisher's future viability has been dramatic.

This, combined with significant, largely operational cost savings, has resulted in The Guardian halving its losses to £18.6m on a turnover up one per cent to

£217m, at a time when most publishers are reporting revenue declines.

Today in 2018 more than 50 per cent of turnover comes from digital, up 15 per cent year on year; reader revenues from donations and print circulation now outweigh advertising sales. The group is on course to break even on an operating basis in the new financial year,' it says.

Who are the new newsers?

One observation I would make is that, with notable exceptions, most of these new news media are produced by talented, seasoned journalists, who have become either disillusioned or deemed dispensable by the corporate publishers. Here is firm evidence that the decline of the traditional press is not a fault of its ever-declining number of employees. Many of the new news success stories across the UK have been created by staff well into their 50s, and beyond.

However, with the exception of the thriving student press, very few new products are being produced by the under 35s. In addition, very few women appear among these new news players.

If established publishers want to survive, they must seriously focus on the needs of millennials, whose needs, interests and views are never going to be satisfied by their current offerings.

Where's the money?

Not surprisingly, most new initiatives are lead by journalists. With no disrespect to these often brilliant, pioneering writers, I observe a lack of commercial expertise and in many conversations, I would suggest there is also commercial naivety. There has always been a healthy conflict between the content creators and the moneymakers, but today realism must prevail. At one time newspaper organisations employed as many commercial staff as editorial. Now the ratio is around two journalists to every one revenue generator[38]. In the new news world the emphasis is strongly on content with often little regard to the realism of revenue.

This problem is exacerbated by the fact that these are small operations fighting for funds from fewer, ever-larger, media-buying houses. This need is reflected in the many attempts by the national press to work together in their selling activities, the latest being the joint-venture between The Guardian, Telegraph and News UK[39].

The same is true of technical systems, where smaller publishers are at a disadvantage in terms of acquiring top-drawer scalable content management and commercial software. Referring to Berkshire Hathaway's decision in the USA to outsource the management of its small network of newspapers, Rick Edmunds of the Poynter Institute noted: "It's harder for smaller companies to keep up with technology needs and centralize operations like larger media companies have.[40]"

However, time has shown even the biggest publishers are struggling to make headway against the dominance of the Big Five. To this end I have long advocated the creation of an Association of Independent Publishers, that provides a platform for mutual support, idea exchanges, cross-market networks, but as importantly, a collective approach to commerce, technology, training, legal services, etc.

And in the end…

For many printed newspapers extinction awaits. The question is how many of them will survive the point of inflection from print to digital profitability. Some undoubtedly will. But others will succumb to the Big Five and their own mismanagement.

The good news is the flourishing new news. But to succeed, these excellent publishers need to adopt the entrepreneurial skills as they demonstrate in editorial. The new news has a bright future in tomorrow's society, but unless the Big Five are reigned in, who knows what will happen?

Notes

[1] Dangerous Estate ISBN: 12502346, 1957. https://www.theguardian.com/media/organgrinder/2009/aug/21/death-of-newspapers-1910

[2] The Economist: https://www.economist.com/britain/2003/03/06/fading

[3] Last Words?: How can journalism survive the decline of print? ISBN: 9781845496968

[4] Jim Chisholm report: Future of printed news http://www.jimchisholm.net/

[5] Source: UK National Readership Survey

[6] Source: The Guardian. https://www.theguardian.com/film/2018/may/07/bbc-itv-and-channel-4-in-talks-to-create-uk-streaming-service-combat-netflix-amazon

[7] Source: WAN's Shaping the Future of the Newspaper Report 3.1 The Mobile Opportunity

[8] Source Zenith Optimedia

[9] Source: PAMCO, https://pamco.co.uk. Note these figures relate to visitors and not engagement, ie times visited, time spent, pages read.

[10] https://dovetonpress.co.uk/history-of-print/ And many others

[11] https://en.wikipedia.org/wiki/History_of_film

[12] Source: Wikipedia. https://en.wikipedia.org/wiki/History_of_television

[13] Blaise Pascal. https://en.wikipedia.org/wiki/Blaise_Pascal

[14] Source: Wikipedia. https://en.wikipedia.org/wiki/Computer

[15] Break of the Bell Corporation. https://en.wikipedia.org/wiki/Bell_System#Pre-1984_breakup

[16] Source: LUMA, www.digitaladblog.com, and others

[17] Source: AEMII Future Media Lab. CHISHOLM submission to House of Lord's Enquiry into advertising. http://data.parliament.uk/writtenevidence/committeeevidence.svc/evidencedocument/communications-committee/the-advertising-industry/written/76536.html

[18] Source: AdAppTive: http://www.adapptive.eu/

[19] "Gross profit = Revenue - Cost of Goods Sold." https://www.investopedia.com/terms/g/grossprofit.asp

[20] Source: https://www.youtube.com/watch?v=GiPe1OiKQuk

[21] Oscar Wilde: The Soul of Man under Socialism". 1891. ISBN: 9780140433876

[22] Thomas Pickety. Capital. ISBN 978-1-912302-30-7

[23] https://www.theguardian.com/business/2018/apr/11/tough-year-high-street-internet-shopping-weak-pound

[24] Source: Zenith Optimedia

[25] http://www.newsmediauk.org/News/ofcom-newspapers-play-vital-role-in-democratic-society

[26] Cairncross Enquiry: https://www.pressgazette.co.uk/culture-secretary-matt-hancock-confident-cairncross-review-into-future-of-uk-press-will-find-solutions-to-help-news-industry/

[27] https://www.marketingtechnews.net/news/2017/nov/06/changing-role-media-agencies-advertising-food-chain/

[28] Local Publisher figures, confirmed with independent calls to local outlets.

[29] Broughton Spurtle – A "Spurtle" is a Scottish word describing a spoon, aka "stirring": http://www.broughtonspurtle.org.uk/about-us

[30] Broughton Spurtle: Publisher's figures

[31] Edinburgh communities: http://www.edinburgh.gov.uk/directory/28/community_councils?page=2

[32] Daily Business https://dailybusinessgroup.co.uk/

[33] The Ferret: https://theferret.scot/?s=Glenrothes

[34] Holyrood Magazine: https://www.holyrood.com/

[35] Humans of Edinburgh: https://www.facebook.com/officialhumansofedinburgh/

[36] Trainspotting 2 Scoop: https://www.dailyrecord.co.uk/news/scottish-news/trainspotting-2-filming-underway-director-7531382

[37] https://www.campaignlive.co.uk/article/guardian-chief-pemsel-arent-complacent-halving-losses-186m/1488698

[38] Review of company reports

[39] https://www.theguardian.com/media/2018/jun/20/guardian-news-uk-telegraph-launch-advertising-business-ozone-project

[40] https://www.mail.com/business/economy/8577692-lee-enterprises-to-manage-berkshire-hathaway-newsp.html

Note on the contributor

Jim Chisholm is an international media consultant and analyst.

http://www.jimchisholm.net/mediatrix/about-chisholm/

Welcome to The World of Newspapers, 2018-style

Big offices full of big personalities may be a thing of the past, but just what is happening now inside the modern regional newspaper newsroom? In Newcastle, still one of the biggest in the country, Alan Geere sees journalists marching to a different beat…

It's 10.30 on an ordinary June Thursday morning and, in a scenario repeated in newsrooms throughout the country, morning conference is about to start.

I am back on home territory, in Newcastle-upon-Tyne where 25 years ago I helped The Journal convert from a traditional broadsheet to a bright, modern tabloid heralding similar moves throughout the country.

But I am not at Thomson House, the brutally unattractive yet strangely beguiling office building which once housed four floors of newspaper workers, a giant clattering press and even its own pub just yards from the Bigg Market, once, like the newspaper office, the beating heart of this raucous city.

I am in the altogether more genteel surroundings of the Eldon Square shopping centre, just a few hundred yards but a million miles from Thomson House. "Up escalator, take a right, along past Levi's and then left between Costa and Ann Summers," the uniformed helper tells me when I ask for 'Eldon Court, second floor'.

I arrive at an unprepossessing locked door telling me the hours the police are in attendance. I think I'm at the wrong place until I spy a small notice asking me to call a Newcastle phone number if I am visiting the Chronicle & Journal.

Just grateful that I have a mobile on me – what happens to people who don't? – the door opens with someone coming out and I dart in. Press 2 on the lift, but nothing happens; it's out of order. Up the stairs, along a corridor, buzzed through a door and I'm in…to be greeted by a man with a clipboard who gives me a thorough Health and Safety workout.

Then, suddenly I'm in the newsroom. A bright, orderly space full of bright, orderly people doing what is required for a modern media business. Welcome to The World of Newspapers, 2018-style.

Chartbeat: Incessant and relentless

I am welcomed by Helen Dalby, 'Senior Editor and Head of Digital North East' aka the person in charge. There is no-one called just 'editor' any more since editor-in-chief Darren Thwaites hopped over the Pennines to edit Reach's (née Trinity Mirror) flagship daily, the Manchester Evening News. The current editor-in-chief is now based in Hull, 130 miles away.

As well as still home to the three Newcastle-based newspapers – Chronicle, Journal and Sunday Sun – the office marches to the beat of ChronicleLive, one of the biggest regional digital media operations in the country providing news, views, video and audio to an audience of millions every month.

Strangely for such a state-of-the-art operation the conference guest list is largely unchanged from time immemorial with representatives from news, production, business, sport and entertainment all sharing the table to sing for their supper.

But behind them the league table of story hits, as compiled by Chartbeat, flickers and burps its way through real-time consumption showing how many people are engaged with a particular story and how long they spend looking at it. It is incessant and relentless and impossible not keep glancing at it.

There is a news list, a complex matrix of who's doing what and when, which continually evolves during the day and gives an at-a-glance view of what is available for digital and what is coming up for the printed papers.

Flying the flag for sport is Newcastle United editor Mark Douglas. There is no longer simply a sports editor, a reflection that the Toon (plus Sunderland AFC to a certain extent) are the biggest games in town. By the close of conference, the top three stories in the all-seeing chart behind him are all Newcastle United – and this on a day when nothing has really happened.

Clickbait? Explaining the way

Douglas cuts a relaxed figure for the man who daily chaperones the hopes and fears of thousands of Newcastle United fans through the minefield of comings and goings, financial affairs and personality clashes at St James's Park.

Premiership football is obviously big business. As well as the zillions in broadcast revenue there's also the small matter of 50,000 people going through the turnstiles every two weeks at an average of £40 each. You do the math.

No wonder the club has a well-groomed media team, providing only limited access to the movers and shakers, but Douglas and his team still manage to turn out a steady stream of viable stories – all of which head straight to the top of the readership charts.

Douglas has also put his pen where his mouth is to explain to how ChronicleLive covers Newcastle United in the transfer window and beyond. In a published column he acknowledges how NUFC coverage can be a subject of fierce debate during the summer – and responds to clickbait jibes.

"It's June, it's Newcastle United and the transfer window is open. It isn't just the weather that gets heated as the combination of annual uncertainty over the club's direction, a seemingly never-ending conveyer belt of transfers rumours and a lack of tangible movement make for a spiky few months when it comes to reporting on the Magpies," writes Douglas.

"People talk about a golden era of football journalism when every reporter knew the players, managers and chairmen and had a hotline to the club. Maybe that was the case, but that's just not possible in 2018. Clubs have their own media departments and the players have a bit more distance these days."

Football's 'critical friends'

Douglas is quickly on the attack to defend ChronicleLive – whether it be via the app, Twitter, Facebook or website – from accusations that they publish anything that is misleading.

"When people call us out at the Chronicle, it's usually criticising us for writing 'clickbait'. So, here's a confession: yes, we are looking to get as many page views as we can. We need to keep growing our online audience and want to do it by innovating with the way Newcastle is being covered.

"So yes, we write about things that we think people will be interested in and get into the middle of debates that are engaging people on social media and – we reckon – in the living rooms, pubs, classrooms and offices of Newcastle.

"Clickbait implies that it's misleading but we try not to oversell or over-promise. If it's a rumour or report, we'll clearly state that. And yes, in a crowded online space we have to try and sell it in a way that stands out. But if we oversell it, we know people will stop reading. So, we've worked hard to try not to do that.'"

Calling themselves 'critical friends' of the club Douglas put himself out there with these comments and readers weren't shy to come back with their own responses.

> *"My complaints are that there are stories repeated day after day, with very ham fisted tweaking of the headline or [sic] verbage."*

> *"My advice is to separate out the drivel so people can laugh as they read it, but if you want us to take you seriously you should stop pushing this drivel as genuine news."*

But some were on a more positive note.

> *"Apart from the innumerable ads which I understand to a point, I think you do a decent job. I always read what you say. Some of it is regurgitated, some speculation and others comment. As you say you are trying to grow and compete in an ever-decreasing market - good luck."*

Competition, rather than co-operation

Back in the day, Thomson House – named after the Canadian media dynasty that acquired so many UK regional titles – was home to three independent newsrooms all with their own reporters, photographers and production teams. The Evening Chronicle printed multiple editions during the day, The Journal printed during the night for morning delivery and the Sunday Sun was its own adrenaline-fuelled version of Saturday Night and Sunday Morning.

The system thrived on competition, rather than co-operation. Sometimes three reporters from the same building were at the same event chasing the same people. With the advent of computers skills were acquired at the dark arts of hacking into a 'rival' database to look at their stories.

But for a modern media business this was a bonkers way to run the operation and, in 2009, the newsrooms were combined into a single entity and, in 2012, Thwaites was appointed to run the show. There is still a sizeable number of journalists – 100 in all – involved from hunter gatherer reporters to 'story editors', the latest incarnation of the endangered species of sub-editor.

Dalby has made it to the top through a digital route rather than traditional journalism, but that doesn't stop her getting caught up in the thrill of it all. "The job consumes me," she admits "and I find it difficult to imagine not being in the thick of news publishing. The buzz in a newsroom when everyone is pulling together on a developing story is quite intoxicating.

> "It's a cliché, but no two days are the same and that's hugely exciting. I'm proud of the content we publish, and it's gratifying to have at our disposal analytics which prove that we're answering the questions local people are asking, and doing so responsibly, ethically and with strong brand values at our core."

Dalby and regional head of print Matt McKenzie both exude authority and friendliness and take great satisfaction from the people they have brought on and the systems in place to make it happen. Dalby leads most of the monthly skills workshops that staff attend and every reporter has a quarterly one-to-one to look at their own individual progress.

"I get a lot of job satisfaction from seeing the training I've delivered helping both experienced and new reporters to reach the biggest possible audiences," she says.

The set-up, though, is far from traditional. Apart from Dalby, there are two 'digital publishing editors', working shifts to cover the bulk of the day and a 'head of print' who looks after the paper and ink side of things. There's still a news desk, but there's also an 'advance content editor'.

Live from court

One dramatic development is covering court 'live' from the Press bench. Updates come in via mobile phone from the reporter but are still checked by the digital publishing editor for grammar, accuracy, spelling and legal issues before going out via the app and social media. There is no 'self-publishing', either by staff or contributors (i.e. readers), a bumpy road much travelled in the early days of digital.

It calls for a different style of reporting. In one notorious murder trial readers were treated to updates like *'People are coming back into court for the judge to pass sentence'* and *'McFall [defendant] then looks over to the Press bench and says: "Put that in your report tonight free men".'*

It's immediate, engaging and dramatic. But not at the expense of full court report and backgrounders which are filed with similar speed and appear both online and in the printed paper.

But what about the print?

Interestingly, and some may even say perversely, for a business that is so clearly digital first they still put a lot of effort and resource into the printed product.

Matt McKenzie is a senior editor and Regional Head of Print for The Chronicle, The Journal and Sunday Sun as well as The Gazette from neighbouring Teesside, which are all produced from one production desk. Working with him is the print team, which comprises print publishing editors and story editors, who can all design pages, via templates or using the shapes in the design libraries.

These editors not only have the pick of all that content created for digital but also the input of the Print Content Unit, a new development which deals with the print-only content like readers' letters and columnists, most of which only go in print, and some specially commissioned news stories and features. Most of the work from veteran environment editor Tony Henderson, for instance, will appear in print first and usually in The Journal, his spiritual home.

Three writers produce articles exclusively for the papers, which might go online too. "A good example of this would be the recently-introduced Tyneside Revealed series which appears in The Chronicle each Monday," explains McKenzie. "It's written for the paper but may go online after discussion with the content desk if they think it'll work well on the website."

The print team also includes content curators who will gather user-generated content, which will go in print, but often also finds its way online. But who decides what goes where and what play to give it? Formerly the province of the editor reigning supreme at afternoon conference it is now a job for those print publishing editors.

"In terms of placing stories, the print publishing editors manage the flatplans for each title," explains McKenzie. "They will attend conference and review the publishing schedule – a constantly-updated googledoc with each department's content lists – news, sport, advance and business – and they'll place the stories from there. Occasionally, The Chronicle and The Journal might go with the same front page story, but more often it's different!"

In an era when the template rules and many regional newspapers are a lack-lustre reflection of former glories the titles produced from Newcastle still exude flair and authority, a testament to investing in design skills and management time – helped along by having one of the busiest news patches in the country.

How far has journalism come?

So what would the perennial naysayers ('Wasn't like that in my day...') and armchair editors make of the modern newsroom? They would find committed, capable people confidently handling all the channels of delivery with a dexterity that can only be marvelled at.

Much has changed from my harem scarem days at Thomson House. All those up-to-the- minute – no, second – blinking screens telling you what's hot and what's not are a far cry from the 'I know what my readers like' finger in the wind editor of not that long ago.

But much is the same too. The excitement when a big story breaks, the leadership needed to steer it in the right direction and the boots on ground skills of talking to people and delivering what you find out quickly and succinctly.

It has a been, to use Dalby's words a 'thrilling and intoxicating day' for me too. To see the daily dramas unfold first hand under the all-seeing eye of the metric counter reminds me how far journalism has come.

But I don't want to leave the Toon without two trips down memory lane. First to the Printers Pie pub built into the ground floor of the old NCJ building where many a newsroom experience has been shared over the years. But, now renamed, it is dark, dingy and locked shut.

So, on to Northumberland Street, Newcastle's main shopping thoroughfare where I am searching for the street vendor joyfully singing out the charms of that day's Chronicle.

Unsuccessful, I ask a patrolling police officer. "Oh, I don't think they do that sort of thing any more."

Maybe not, but they do a lot more instead....

Note on the contributor

Alan Geere is a journalist, academic and international media consultant. Latterly he was head of news journalism at Southampton Solent University and editorial director of Northcliffe Newspapers (South-East). He also edited newspapers in the UK, US, Canada and the Caribbean and led media development programmes in Afghanistan, China and the Far East. As an academic he taught at Worcester, Westminster and City universities and is currently researching a PhD looking into the changing role of editorial leadership.
E: alan@alan-geere.com T: @alangeere

Rethinking the marriage of broadcast news and social media: 'It's complicated'

Like all news organisations, broadcasters have invested heavily in social media for its huge reach and younger demographic. But has allowing the big tech companies to come between broadcasters and their audiences been a strategic mistake? Richard Sambrook argues it's time to re-assess

My name is Richard and I used to be a social media evangelist. Yes, I know – shameful and hard to believe. But back in the noughties the infant social media held such promise for broadcasters and audiences alike. In those sun-dappled days we used to talk about the promise of interactivity, empowering the audience, real connection and insight into their thoughts and ideas – and free distribution! Such innocence. As Noah Kulwin recently wrote in New York magazine[1], we failed to foresee "how the Silicon Valley dream of building a networked utopia would turn into a globalized strip-mall casino overrun by pop-up ads and cyberbullies and Vladimir Putin."

It's an age-old story. It started simply enough with a few likes and shares which provided a harmless buzz of connection to the audience. But soon that wasn't enough. We started to crave more complex analytics and greater reach; we heard people talk of 'engagement' – a state of deep meaningful connection with our viewers – and before we knew it, we were strung out, sweating in fear of an unannounced overnight tweak in the newsfeed algorithm.

Those who cared about us started to worry about the company we kept, saying they could no longer tell the difference between us and the clickbait and lies we hung around with…

And all the time we were spending more and more money to provide free content to the platforms as they seemed to play fast and loose with revenue and metrics in return. As one leading TV commissioner recently told yet another fake news seminar: "I feel like a woman who has been mugged for her handbag by a man in a Rolls Royce."

That may be taking it a little far, but we do need a serious conversation about broadcasting and social media. With the benefit of hindsight, it's clear how the promise of reach, access to the younger demographic and granular feedback through user data seduced broadcasters to allow intermediaries to come between them and the audience.

We can't even say it was a strategic mistake – for where was the alternative? The platforms grew so rapidly on the back of extraordinary technology and offered services which inevitably had broader customised appeal than anything a single broadcaster could offer. The elusive under-30s audience were hanging out online, not in front of their TVs.

Core social media strategies

There have been three core strategies for broadcasters on social media:

Direct – the hope users will click through to a broadcaster's own site providing direct user value.

Distributed – the reach value of those who see content in their news feed serendipitously,

And – a variation of the last one – pure marketing.

And to some extent, it works. One major UK broadcaster told me they have seen a direct increase in TV viewing when they invest more in social media. Hard figures of course are closely guarded and difficult to find.

The online metrics themselves, have sometimes been less robust. Automatic play or three seconds of viewing contributes to the figures, but hardly registers with the user.

We took comfort from the big technology platforms saying they weren't publishers – just distributors – before realising the algorithms determining who saw what were not neutral or transparent. Someone was making decisions about who saw our content without much discussion, agreement or openness. But those potentially huge reach numbers still seemed to justify being there. The problem has been that the platforms sacrificed quality for scale and sales – and broadcasters have not gained sufficiently from either.

Research from the Reuters Institute at Oxford University[2] shows many users fail to recognise media brands in their social feeds. Broadcasters face a huge challenge in trying to differentiate their content online or on mobile. A square video, played silently for perhaps 10 seconds may register as a metric – but does not provide a quality experience and too rarely attracts loyalty back to the provider.

Conflict of purpose

At heart, there is a conflict between the purposes of a regulated public broadcaster in the UK and the purposes and methods of social media. Jonah Peretti, founder of Buzzfeed, has explained how 'sharing' is the key metric online[3] and his and other sites are designed to encourage and enable sharing as much as possible. But sharing may be a good indicator of consumer interest – but it is no indication of citizen value (a crucial responsibility for public service media)

Social media encourages opinion over fact, it is increasingly fed by outrage and emotion which as a consequence feeds division. Emotional triggers encourage greater use, more data, bigger profits. Broadcasting, on the other hand, is committed to bringing audiences together for common experiences, a constructive public debate and building rather than dividing communities.

And the technology companies continue to exacerbate their problems through their misunderstanding – or lack of care – over journalism. For example categorising political journalism alongside propaganda in their archive of political advertising. As Mark Thompson of The New York Times put it: "In its effort to clear up one bad mess, (Facebook) seems to be joining those who want to blur the line between reality-based journalism and propaganda."[4]

Social media has been driven by engineers and brilliant technology with little experience or interest in social or political policy or anything qualitative that can't be measured and coded. A mix of naivety and hubris has meant until recently they have been dismissive of social science or editorial judgement. As a consequence, a series of scandals and misjudgements has left them in what digital pioneer Jaron Lanier calls their current 'profitable crisis state'.[5] Because for all the inquiries, committee hearings, campaigning and debate – they remain hugely profitable and continue to see their user-base grow as traditional media audiences continue to decline.

None of this is to deny the many benefits and extraordinary achievements of social media. But we can't any longer pretend there is a healthy relationship between traditional media and the newer tech behemoths. Nor, in the light of the misuse of data to politically target ads, can social media automatically be assumed to be a social good.

Reforming social media

The tech companies know they have to clean-up their act and the hubris (or some might say arrogance) they have previously displayed towards national institutions and media competitors has to change. So is it time to reassess the relationship between broadcasters and the so-called FAANGs (Facebook, Amazon, Apple, Netflix and Google)? And if so, how could things be re-set?

There is currently much talk of regulation – but less clarity about what form this might take. Even Facebook's Mark Zuckerberg is said to believe social media regulation is inevitable and may even be helpful. This is to recognise the place social media now occupies in society – more akin to a utility than a commercial service, with commensurate responsibilities which the companies themselves have previously demonstrated they don't entirely understand or respect.

Content regulation online would be hugely complex and likely to have damaging collateral consequences. Who chooses what we should see or share? And what about the impact on free expression?

Questions of scale, and control of data, seem more fruitful areas to consider for intervention. The big tech companies have bought up others – so Facebook is also WhatsApp and Instagram and more. Plurality (or absence of it) is a problem when a handful of companies have such market dominance. And with user data proving so profitable for their shareholders, content partners complain they don't get a fair share of the cake – in data or revenue. But is anyone really going to break up Google or Facebook? It seems unlikely.

The Germans are regulating against hate speech, the French against 'fake news' during election campaigns (who decides?), the European Commission is looking at what can be done short of further regulation. GDPR (The General Data Protection Regulation) is largely seen to have been successful in enshrining data protection as a human right and shifting the balance of advantage away from opaque companies towards the individual. But there is less clarity about how to deal with content. A recent EU report on online disinformation called for greater media literacy in schools and more collaboration between fact-checking organisations. But the EU is also keen to boost transparency, traceability and accountability of platforms without falling into the trap of censorship.[6]

The UK has proposed a sensible, if so far broad brush, digital charter to encourage best practise and 'set new online standards for years to come… agree norms and rules for the online world and put them into practice'.[7] It's an overdue extension of UK media policy – but slow moving in a highly dynamic environment. And politicians often have a weak understanding of the issues (as anyone watching the recent Congressional committees in the USA can testify) and motivations which may not always be pure.

The social media companies can be encouraged to self-regulate or reform – and are doing so. Where once Facebook believed artificial intelligence could manage all content they are now committed to employing 20,000 moderators to do what an algorithm can't. AI will develop and help further – it has largely removed pornography from the major platforms, and can doubtless address hate speech and violence too. (Although they often get judgements wrong, such as when YouTube reportedly removed evidence of war crimes posted by Syrian activists).[8]

Some argue Facebook and Google should offer more money to content providers. But beware the handout trap – a couple of hundred million in a fund may feel good but does little to address the structural problems. Better might be proper payment for the content they offer their users – or perhaps licensing of some form as we have for music use or under the Newspaper Licensing Agency.

The digital environment means social media – whatever our reservations – is a key part of the future for broadcasters. But now is the moment to re-set the relationship. Broadcasters may not have the global scale or resources of Facebook or Google which has led some to conclude they must accept a secondary role. But broadcasters have many strengths and benefits that the FAANGs lack – and currently need. They have strong brands loved by audiences, they enjoy strong levels of public trust, they offer clear accountability through regulation and more directly, they have decades of experience in handling content and complex ethical issues, they have high levels of editorial judgement and above all they continue to produce great and much loved content. The FAANGs may need the broadcasters more than they realise.

(This article was originally published in the Royal Television Society magazine Television in May 2018)

Notes

[1] Kulwin, Noah (2018) An Apology for the internet, New York Magazine, April 13 http://nymag.com/selectall/2018/04/an-apology-for-the-internet-from-the-people-who-built-it.html

[2] Kalogeropoulos, Antonis & Newman, Nic, (2017) I saw the news on facebook, Reuters Institute for the study of journalism, September 2017 https://reutersinstitute.politics.ox.ac.uk/our-research/i-saw-news-facebook-brand-attribution-when-accessing-news-distributed-environments

[3] Ingram, Matthew (2016) Buzzfeed's CEO on the future of media, Fortune Magazine, December 20 http://fortune.com/2016/12/20/peretti-future-media/

[4] Bell, Emily (2018) Facebook creates Orwellian headache as news is labelled politics, The Guardian, June 24th https://www.theguardian.com/media/media-blog/2018/jun/24/facebook-journalism-publishers?CMP=Share_iOSApp_Other

[5] Lanier, Jaron (2018) We blew it, The American Conservative, April 25 http://www.theamericanconservative.com/dreher/jaron-lanier-silicon-valley-we-blew-it/comment-page-1/

[6] Rankin, Jennifer (2018) Tech firms could face new EU regulations over fake news, The Guardian, April 24 https://www.theguardian.com/media/2018/apr/24/eu-to-warn-social-media-firms-over-fake-news-and-data-mining

[7] UK Government, (2018) Digital Charter January 25 https://www.gov.uk/government/publications/digital-charter

[8] CBS News, (2017) Activists worry Youtube erasing proof of Syria atrocities, CBS News, September 13 https://www.cbsnews.com/news/youtube-videos-syria-war-activists-human-rights-violations-war-crimes/

All accessed June 28th 2018

Note on the contributor

Richard Sambrook is Professor of Journalism at Cardiff University where he oversees taught postgraduate courses and vocational training. Previously he was a BBC journalist for 30 years across national radio and TV programmes, culminating with ten years on the board of management as Director of Sport, Director of News and Director of Global News and the World Service. His research interests include international newsgathering, the future of TV news, disinformation and objectivity in the digital age. Contact: sambrookrj@cardiff.ac.uk Twitter: @sambrook

Beyond Web 2.0: Reimagining journalism in the wake of change

While celebrations of 'participatory journalism' are not unwarranted, they may put us at risk of fiddling while Rome burns, says Dr David Nolan

Julia Gillard's 'misogyny speech' and its reception

On October 9, 2012, Australia's first female Prime Minister, Julia Gillard, delivered an historic speech in the Australian Federal Parliament. The context was a debate on a proposed vote of no confidence in the speaker of the house, Peter Slipper, from then opposition leader Tony Abbott, in the wake of revelations Slipper had sent a text message making offensive remarks about female genitalia and referred to a female MP as an 'ignorant botch' (sic). Abbott put the case that Slipper's misogyny made him an unfit candidate for high office. Prime Minister Gillard rose and gave a blistering response, which included what have become some the most famous lines in Australian political history:

> "I will not be lectured about sexism and misogyny by this man, I will not... If he wants to know what misogyny looks like in modern Australia, he does not need a motion in the House of Representatives, he needs a mirror."

The very personal nature of this response had a context. As Gillard pointed out, Abbott had allowed himself to be photographed with protestors outside parliament in front of protestors holding placards saying 'ditch the witch' and referring to Gillard as a male politician's 'bitch'. Her speech also provided an account of numerous other examples of Abbott's own misogyny. She told how, referring to the unmarried Prime Minister in parliament, Abbott had said she should 'make an honest woman of herself'. She recounted how he had questioned whether women having less power than men was a 'bad thing' and had raised the question 'what if men are by physiology or temperament more adapted to exercise authority or to issue command?' Aside from Abbott's personal record, the broader context for this speech was the remarkable level of aggressively misogynistic vitriol that had been directed at Gillard as Prime Minister, from media commentators and messages sent to her via email and social media, many of which were accompanied by pornographic imagery (Summers 2012).

For many, this was a landmark moment, where a woman in public life drew a very forceful line in the sand, and it is remembered as such – the speech has since been set to music by an Australian composer, and a performance posted on YouTube has been widely circulated.

The reaction among Australian political journalists, however, appeared cynical. Gillard's speech was not only described as defending the indefensible, but derided as opportunistic, as merely motivated by base political self-interest, and as 'playing the gender card'. Australian political journalists treated Slipper's resignation later that day, rather than Gillard's speech, as the real story (Collins 2012). Furthermore, Australian media coverage worked to substantively undermine the substance of Gillard's speech, presenting it as hypocritical, delegitimising it as a valid challenge to misogyny. Subsequent analyses of this coverage argued that, by framing the speech as inauthentic, calculated and tactical, coverage worked to undermine its potential to promote reflection on misogyny in Australian public life as a public concern (Wright and Holland 2014, Donoghue 2015).

Simultaneously, however, the speech went viral, with a YouTube posting of the speech receiving 1.5m views within a week, not least thanks to positive coverage from websites Salon and Jezebel (who labelled it 'the best thing you'll see all day!'), a positive write-up in The New Yorker's 'Ladylike' column (Lester 2012), and further coverage in the UK, Canada, South Africa and India.

Web 2.0: 'The gatekeepers of news have lost their keys'

Locally, some noted the striking disjunct between the reception of Gillard's speech by legacy media, routinely disposed to read political rhetoric as motivated by a struggle for electoral power, and the way in which women were responding to the speech on social media. One account, in not-for-profit multimedia site The Global Mail, suggested 'at no point in the life of Web 2.0 has the divide between the people who write the news and the people who consume it been as sharply defined as this week' (Collins 2012). Another, written by blogger Tim Dunlop (on an opinion site hosted by the public service Australian Broadcasting Corporation) presented it as an object example of how the 'gatekeepers of news have lost their keys', since audiences can now watch events live, respond and post in real-time, and are now no longer constrained by the limited interpretive terms of professional journalists:

> "The bottom line is this: we no longer trust the media to tell us the story of our lives. We no longer have to settle for the narrative they impose on events. We are no longer passive observers, but active participants in the way our news is shaped. In a world where we can watch things unfold in real-time and then chat about them among ourselves, we simply don't need them to explain or analyse them for us. This is not to say that journalists have become redundant – far from it. Just that they have to figure out a new role for

themselves in the media-saturated world in which we live and in which they hope to make a living." (Dunlop 2012)

The moral of this story, for Dunlop, was in a new era where audiences are empowered and media gatekeepers no longer exercise control over what people see and hear, journalists now must move to move to work with rather than against their audience.

Undoubtedly, there are good reasons to celebrate many aspects of this case study. Social media have offered new capacities for self-organisation for social movements to amplify a range of voices which call attention to and demand the redress of inequalities, and to demand institutional change, a trend illustrated internationally by examples such as #blacklivesmatters and #metoo.

In relation to journalism, this capacity has been recognised in the concept of the 'fifth estate', wherein media users can hold journalism accountable, and such practices of accountability now appear as a permanent aspect of hybrid media ecologies (Newman et al 2010, Chadwick 2013). Insofar as practices of journalism continue to reproduce gender inequality through their practices of representation, it should brook no argument that such practices can legitimately be called out. The degree to which digital technologies have enabled a contestation and transformation of news frames has been positioned as a shift toward a form of 'participatory journalism', wherein 'web 2.0 technologies form an architecture of participation that signal a move from a one-way, asymmetric model of communication to a more participatory and collective media ecosystem, where jurisdiction for the news is shared between journalists and audiences' (Hermida 2012: 312).

Reconsidering Web 2.0: Framing change

At this moment, however, it may be important to take pause, rather than to simply accept the idea that a turn to the audience can be generalised as both an overall good and as an imperative for journalism. Indeed, rather than simply accepting a reading of such examples as emblematic of a positive shift toward a new and enhanced 'participatory era', it may be important to consider these arguments as frames for understanding, rather than simply descriptions of, the present. In doing so, we might seek to historicise them as products of a particular moment, and consider what aspects of what is happening they might exclude, as well as what they capture. The idea that journalists should seek to renew their connection to their audience, rather than view the world from the insular bubble of journalistic interpretation, appears unarguable, particularly as it reiterates a basic understanding of the role of journalism in democracy: to represent the public. Nevertheless, it is worth unpicking and contextualising this argument.

For their part, rightly or (probably) wrongly, the Canberra press gallery journalists viewed Gillard's speech through the prism of their normal professional practices. That is, they saw their job as political journalists, reporting on a specific political situation, not to declare a moment of historical significance in gender relations, but to interpret and communicate to their audience their interpretation of this speech in the context of electoral politics. Indeed, in defending their practices, this was exactly the argument they put forward (Taylor 2012). While such a defence is undoubtedly questionable, it can be argued the problem lies not with individual journalists' judgment, but with the general tendency of political journalism to frame the significance of particular events as part of an overall struggle for power, a frame that tends by nature to dispose political journalists to view actions as the product of ulterior motives (though this does not invalidate feminist criticisms of how news stories systematically tend to invalidate female politicians' complaints about being targeted on the basis of gender). Whether a 'turn to the audience' offers a panacea to such cynicism, however, is hardly self-evident, given widespread findings of a decline of trust in politicians and government (Edelman 2018).

It is also noteworthy that the framing of web 2.0 as an 'architecture of participation' tends to reproduce a framing of social media as mere 'platforms' which provide a neutral vehicle of representation for the concerns and activities of users. In this light, a turn toward the audience appears self-evidently democratic, and the 'disruption' of traditional modes of social organisation an inherently liberating development.

A view of technology as an independent, disruptive force, rather than as objects shaped by wider social, economic and political relations is, however, questionable (Owens 2015). The idea of social media as neutral 'platforms' has, in recent years, been particularly questioned in relation to news, where the degree of control exercised by technology companies, particularly Facebook and Google, alongside their increasingly overwhelming dominance in advertising markets, has both contributed to the economic difficulties facing news organisations and has forced the latter to adopt approaches to news-making driven by metrics oriented towards platform algorithms (Bell and Owens 2017, Caplan and Boyd 2018). Indeed, studies from this period had already noted an overwhelming tendency in news organisations to both adopt a view of audiences as newly empowered *and* to engage in increasingly detailed processes of audience quantification, and in so doing to adopt a view of democratic representation as an aggregated composite of individual consumer choices (Anderson 2011: 541).

The context of this 'turn to the audience', of course, is also the institutional struggles news organisations have been confronted with in seeking to sustain viable models of journalism. It is both notable and unfortunate, however, that accounts of 'participatory journalism' and 'journalism crisis' have tended to be presented as alternative, rather than mutually constitutive, frames for engaging with journalism's present, with the former presenting a democratic vision of empowerment and the latter suggesting a threatened if not already substantively diminished role for journalism in contemporary democracy. It is important to acknowledge that questions of 'jurisdiction for the news' refer not only to an assertion of professional authority, but to the boundaries through which journalism's economic viability, professional identity and public standing rest. Rasmus Kleis Nielsen (2016), in a detailed and thoughtful comparative analysis of journalistic crisis across different media systems has usefully suggested crisis can involve different dimensions: 'economic crisis', 'professional crisis' and a 'crisis of confidence'. Such crises, he suggests, involve different causes and durations, such that they are prompted by new developments in some respects, and longer term trends in others. He notes, for example, a decline of confidence in the news is not a recent development but follows a trend which predates the internet. Likewise, we might also note that shifts toward the incorporation of more quantitative and market-based modes of news production are not simply caused by the emergence of digital economies, though they have undoubtedly been accelerated by them. Such trends have been driven by longer-term processes of cultural, economic and political transformation (see Hallin 2008).

Beyond Web 2.0

Since 2012, efforts among news organisations to 'connect with audiences' in Australia have unquestionably continued to govern the production of news content and practices of journalism. While 'clickbait' forms part of this picture, experiments in participatory news and forms of content which support increased experiences of user identity have also been prominent, alongside continued 'fifth estate' phenomena whereby news framings are challenged by campaign and user initiatives. At the same time, analyses which have documented the shifting news environment have shown substantial losses of capacity and experience in newsrooms, with estimates of over 3000 job losses and substantial declines in capacity in areas significance, such as local news provision, court reporting and local and state government coverage (Commonwealth of Australia 2018).

In this light, Gillard's speech and its reception can be read as an historical moment which was significant not only because of what it indicated about the shifting relations within which journalism operated, but also how that moment was culturally framed as indicative of a shift towards an increasingly empowering and democratic news environment. The argument presented in this essay is not that such claims were entirely wrong, but that they tended to rest on a limited frame for understanding the significance of change and the problem of how to respond to it.

Images of Web 2.0 as an 'architecture of participation' tend, by implication, to celebrate the empowering potentials of digital technologies while de-emphasising the role of institutions and the problem of how a journalism that supports a viable public life can be supported and extended. It is undoubtedly true that, in today's hybrid media environment, the relations between news institutions, news users and technology companies have been substantially realigned, and this is far from all bad news (see Schudson 2016). Nevertheless, given the historical reliance of journalism upon boundaries through which its economic viability, professional identity and public trust were sustained, the problem of how to respond to such realignment remains an issue of public significance, requiring regulatory responses, particularly around the issue of algorithmic power and the issue of how journalism can be supported. In addressing these problems, it is important to neither mourn nor celebrate the passing of previous boundaries, but to seriously consider the problem of how new boundaries supporting democratic journalism can be reimagined, sustained and debated in the present and future.

References

Anderson, Christopher W. (2011) Between creative and quantified audiences: Web metrics and changing patterns of newswork in local US newsrooms. Journalism, Vol. 12, No.5 pp 550-566

Commonwealth of Australia (2018) Report of the Senate Select Committee on the Future of Public Interest Journalism. Available online at https://www.aph.gov.au/Parliamentary_Business/Committees/Senate/Future_of_Public_Interest_Journalism/PublicInterestJournalism/Report, accessed on 18 June 2018.

Bell, Emily and Taylor Owen (2017) The Platform Press: How Silicon Valley reengineered journalism, New York: Tow Center for Digital Journalism.

Caplan, Robyn & Danah Boyd (2018) Isomorphism through algorithms: Institutional dependencies in the case of Facebook, Big Data & Society, Vol. 5, No.1 pp 1-12

Chadwick, Andrew (2017). The hybrid media system: Politics and power, Oxford: Oxford University Press.

Collins, Sarah-Jane (2012). Old Media: Lessons In missing the point. The Global Mail, October 11. Available online at http://www.abc.net.au/mediawatch/transcripts/1237_tgm.pdf, accessed on 18 June 2018

Donaghue, Ngaire (2015) Who gets played by 'the gender card'? A critical discourse analysis of coverage of Prime Minister Julia Gillard's sexism and misogyny speech in the Australian print media, Australian Feminist Studies, Vol 30, No.84 pp 161-178.

Dunlop, Tim (2012). The Gatekeepers of News Have Lost Their Keys. ABC The Drum, 10 October. Available online at http://www.abc.net.au/mediawatch/transcripts/1237_drum.pdf, accessed on 18 June 2018

Edelman (2018) 2018 Edelman Trust Barometer. Available online at https://www.edelman.com/trust-barometer, accessed on 24 July 2018

Hallin, Daniel C. (2008). Neoliberalism, social movements and change in media systems in the late twentieth century. Hesmondhalgh, David and Toynbee, Jason (eds) The Media and Social Theory, London: Routledge, pp 43-58

Hermida, Alfred (2012) Social journalism: Exploring how social media is shaping journalism, Siapera, Eugenia and Veglis, Andrea (eds) The Handbook of Global Online Journalism, Chichester, UK: Wiley-Blackwell, pp 309-328

Lester, Amelia (2012). Ladylike: Julia Gillard's Misogyny Speech. *The New Yorker,* October 9. Available online at http://www.abc.net.au/mediawatch/transcripts/1237_tgm.pdf, accessed 18 June 2018

Newman, Nic, Dutton, William H., & Blank, Grant (2012). Social Media in the Changing Ecology of News: The Fourth and Fifth Estates in Britain. International Journal of Internet Science, Vol. 7, No.1, pp 6-22

Nielsen, Rasmus Kleis (2016). The many crises of Western journalism: A comparative analysis of economic, professional, and symbolic crises, Alexander, Jeffrey C., Butler Breese, Elizabeth and Luengo, Maria A. (eds), *The Crisis of Journalism Reconsidered* New York: Cambridge University Press, pp 77-97

Owen, Taylor (2015). Disruptive Power: The crisis of the state in the digital age, Oxford, UK: Oxford University Press.

Schudson, Michael (2016). The crisis in news: Can you whistle a happy tune?, Alexander, Jeffrey Butler Breese, Elizabeth and Luengo, Maria (eds), The Crisis of Journalism Reconsidered: Democratic Culture, Professional Codes, Digital Future, New York: Cambridge University Press, pp 98-115

Summers, Anne (2012) Her rights at work: The political persecution of Australia's first female prime minister, The Economic and Labour Relations Review, Vol. 23, No. 4 pp 115-126

Taylor, Lenore (2012), Speech did stir hearts but remember the context, The Sydney Morning Herald, 13 October. Available on https://www.smh.com.au/politics/federal/pms-speech-did-stir-hearts-but-remember-the-context-20121012-27i1h.html, accessed 18 June

Wright, Kate A., & Holland, Jack (2014). Leadership and the media: Gendered framings of Julia Gillard's 'sexism and misogyny'speech. Australian Journal of Political Science, Vol. 49, No. 3, pp 455-468

Note on the contributor

Dr David Nolan is Deputy Director of the Centre for Advancing Journalism and Senior Lecturer in Media and Communication at the University of Melbourne. His research, focusing on change in journalism and its social, political and public impact, is published in leading journals including Journalism, Journalism Studies, Media, Culture & Society and Journal of Intercultural Studies. He recently co-edited Australian Media and the Politics of Belonging (Anthem Press, 2018).

Ethics for social media journalism

Has social media and the internet changed journalists' ethical practice? Not according to Professor Chris Frost, who argues whilst social media presents new ethical challenges to achieving good journalism, the basic philosophy remains unchanged when it comes to telling the truth and holding power to account

Changes in the way journalists work over the past 20 years have caused many to ask whether publishing on the internet or social media should change the way journalists approach their craft both practically and ethically. The simple answer is that while the practice may have changed considerably, the underlying ethos of journalism and the ethics of its practice have remained fundamentally unchanged.

Of course that does not mean there are not new ethical problems and challenges; more ethical tripwires of which the good journalist needs to be aware and avoid. However the basic ethical underpinnings of journalism as outlined by codes around the world have not changed. Accuracy and truth remain at the heart of good journalism whilst concern for privacy, minors, the vulnerable and a policy of non-harassment, non-intrusion, non-discrimination and using straightforward means to gather stories unless there is a strong public interest continue to underpin the ethical demand to do no harm that is central to many journalism codes.

Internet publishing and researching is now too old and deeply embedded in journalism practice to be called new technology and did not in any case throw up, of itself, too many new ethical problems. The ability to use the technology to hack into people's private affairs has been illegal since the serious introduction of desktop computers, not that that has always prevented unethical hacking of computers and phones as LJ Leveson heard at his 2011 inquiry.

It is the introduction of the smart phone and its access to the internet and the social media which sprung up in various forms over the past ten years which really allows journalists to expand their activities using social media. It has brought journalists closer to their audience allowing a two-way conversation and a real connection. It is a great way of contacting people, to help the journalist see what's trending and also to use as a publication method either in support of a more traditional publication or as a sole method. Facebook, Twitter, Instagram and all the others each have their own pros and cons. This means today's journalist relies heavily on social media to find out what is going on and to tell others about it. But, although the ethics have not really changed, the fast pace of social media and the direct contact with sources means journalists need to take extra care and be fully aware of potential pitfalls.

Social media as a source

Social media is a great source of news and features, both providing new and interesting contacts, showing trends of public interest and identifying possible stories. However, it also adds new concerns in order to adhere to standard practice as identified in the various codes in the UK such as the National Union of Journalists, the BBC, Ofcom, the Independent Press Standards Organisation and Impress. Anyone publishing on Twitter should understand it is a public forum and it is therefore perfectly acceptable to follow anyone who fits into your field of journalism whether they are celebrities, sports people, local councillors, trade unionists, campaigners, charity workers or just noisy know-it-alls. However, to ensure the story is suitably accurate, it needs to be confirmed elsewhere. This is usually easy to do with an authority source or even by sending out a general call for confirmation on social media.

Journalists also need to be careful about privacy. The recent scandal involving Cambridge Analytica and Facebook shows just how significant privacy can be. Mark Zuckerberg, CEO and co-founder of Facebook, told the Cruncie Awards in San Francisco in 2010: "People have really gotten comfortable not only sharing more information and different kinds, but more openly and with more people." Following his 2018 appearances before a House of Representatives hearing in the US, Zuckerberg seems less confident about this.

Scraping data from Facebook pages is widely practised but its ethics are more complicated. People put information about themselves on Facebook and other social media, on the assumption that only those who know them can access it and that certainly only those who know them would want to access it. We can liken it to a group of friends gossiping around a table in a public place who do not expect eavesdroppers and certainly do not expect to see their views repeated later in a news story. Of course they are wrong. A person dying in bizarre circumstances on holiday or involved in a major disaster may suddenly become very newsworthy and accessing their Facebook page will bring pictures, data and potential contacts to further the story. Is it appropriate to access such intrusive pages despite high privacy settings or because the subject did not fully understand how to set high privacy settings?

The Independent Press Standards Organisation has dealt with a number of such complaints. The Herne Bay Gazette carried a story about a young woman jailed for causing death by dangerous driving and drink driving. They used a photograph from her Facebook page showing her holding up a full wine glass toasting a 'booze-fuelled Christmas trip just days before she was jailed'. In fact the picture was taken on a family outing and the glass contained cola. She said that her Facebook page was set to family and friends but the newspaper said it was publicly accessible. The Ipso upheld the complaint (ipso.co.uk).

Twitter can also get you into problems. A woman complained to Ipso after a photo of her daughter was published on the front page of the Daily Star identifying her as one of the people missing or dead following the terror attack in Manchester Arena; the caption identified her as 'missing' and referred to her by a false name. Ipso upheld the complaint and required the publication of an adjudication after hearing that the complainant's daughter's details had been appropriated and used by a hoax Twitter account. The newspaper had taken no further steps to establish the accuracy of the claims on the Twitter account.

If journalists access social media for publication, they should confirm privacy settings and accuracy. Fully private settings should only be breached if there is a significant public interest.

Other issues to consider are:

- Is the subject a minor? If so the public interest needs to be overwhelming.
- Think about the nature of all the material. Just because a road accident concerning the subject is in the public interest, it does not mean that other details of the subject are appropriate to publish. Health (including injuries) requires a much higher level of public interest.
- Take a screenshot of the page with privacy settings to confirm what was there.
- Who placed the material on the page and is it therefore still appropriate to use it?
- When was the picture or item published by the user? Is it still current and appropriate to use?
- Is the material likely to intrude on anyone's private life, grief or distress without an over-riding consideration of the public interest?

Ipso also offers guidance on social media use (https://www.ipso.co.uk/press-standards/guidance-for-journalists-and-editors/social-media-guidance/ accessed June 21, 2018).

Some stories on social media could be hoaxes. Much material comes from unofficial or commercial sources and needs to be treated with suspicion. The rise in conspiracy theories can probably be laid at the door of social media as anyone with a campaign, no matter how ridiculous, can not only find an audience of potentially millions but also sufficient people to take the idea seriously to give it some authority. Credibility and balance is difficult to measure on the internet without seeking additional sources. Try googling 'Flat Earth Society' (320m hits) to find just one group that is apparently growing its membership by 200 a year.

There are plenty of other conspiracy theories or hoaxes that continue to circulate on social media, some of them decades old and even some that have been recently updated (see Frost 2000 and 2002).

Social media for publication

Social media is a useful publishing medium either to promote publication elsewhere or as the sole publication. However the limited nature of publication on sites such as Twitter can lead to problems, especially with automation starting to be more widely used to provide links and support.

In one recent case, a dodgy curry house in south London was prosecuted after a rat appeared during an environmental health inspection. The report put out by a magazine was safe but the website automatically generated a libel when a pop-up headed 'Similar stories' flagged up a meal review about another restaurant in the same area. The stories weren't similar at all. The review was very complimentary, and the restaurant was in no way 'similar' to the one with the rat.

In another example a 'similar stories' tool picked up a link to a story that named a woman who had since been given anonymity as a rape victim.

Other problems specific to social media include ensuring stories can stand on their own. Reporting from court, for instance, can lead to contempt if care is not taken or if you forget to number link several tweets. Since one of the advantages of publishing on social media is speed, it is also important to remember to correct any false information as soon as possible.

On professional social media

Wherever a journalist is working, it is important to remember personal views and those of any employer should never be confused. This may mean keeping personal views private – journalists do not always have the same option of parading personal views on social media that is open to many others for fear of damaging the accuracy and neutrality of their professional work.

For instance, the BBC says:

> "…when someone clearly identifies their association with the BBC and/or discusses their work, they are expected to behave appropriately when on the Internet, and in ways that are consistent with the BBC's editorial values and policies…

> "Our audiences need to be confident that the outside activities of our presenters, programme-makers and other staff do not undermine the BBC's impartiality or reputation and that editorial decisions are not perceived to be influenced by any commercial or personal interests."

> (http://www.bbc.co.uk/editorialguidelines/guidance/social-networking-personal/guidance-full accessed 8/5/18)

The BBC has plenty of other good advice about social media in particular about appearing impartial on websites. Whilst this is important to a public service broadcaster controlled by the Broadcasting Act it may not apply to newspapers or other websites that are happy to take a partial view. However, most publications do expect their staff to largely adhere to the ethos of the organisation.

Personal ethics

Journalists use social media both to gather information and to publish it in a way that means they need to be more careful about personal social media outings. Details of personal lives conflicting with professional lives have always been a problem with some journalists deciding they should have no personal life at all – not something many of us are prepared to stomach. For those of us who live in the real world where we can have beliefs and concerns it has always been wise to let your news editor know if your hobbies, beliefs or pastimes risk coming into conflict with your work. That has become even more important as more of our lives become public record on various social media. When we start Tweeting and social networking as a person, not a reporter we can easily run into problems with our readers or our employers.

Journalists around the world have faced reprimand or even dismissal for a thoughtless tweet or Facebook comment. Octavia Nasr lost her job as CNN's senior editor for Middle Eastern affairs for a tweet that caused a furore among some Israeli supporters. Brian Pedersen was fired by the Arizona Daily Star for 'inappropriate and unprofessional' tweeting. Gavin Miller, the Australian radio announcer, was dismissed for 'a severe breach of the station's social media policy'. The list goes on.

Copyright

It is important to remember material on the internet and social media is somebody's copyright although it's not always easy to work out whose. The pictures may well be the copyright of corporations, the subject's family members, friends or even professional photographers. Whilst plenty of material is placed on the web and social media by organisations in the hope of attracting other publishers, journalists always need to ensure copyright permission has been granted before publishing. This also applies to stories in other publications. Plagiarism is difficult to prove, especially in the area of news, but lifting quotes and other details from stories published elsewhere, risks copyright infringement and also risks spreading inaccurate or false stories that have not been properly checked.

Archive

Another issue which has grown in significance over the past few years and will only become more important is archive material on the web, including social media. Stories on the web form a superb archive of material published by news providers. While it has always been possible to research newspaper archives, this is cumbersome and time consuming, and so such research is normally only carried out for very good reason. Now archive searches are quick and easy so any error in the archive, or any invasion of privacy will easily be discovered and publishers are having to reconsider their policies about archive material. For instance, imagine a person was arrested in connection with a series of serious crimes and a report appears in social media and on a website but a few weeks later the charges are withdrawn as the person arrested is found to have no involvement at all. Every time someone searches that person's name, the arrests will come up. This makes it more important than ever to ensure the end story is published at the very least in a tag on the website. Newspapers and broadcasters are being increasingly bombarded with requests to 'unpublish', to remove references to people according to Kathy English, public editor of the Toronto Star. (2009: 6). This is not about errors, the main concern now is legitimate, accurate stories that may make life very difficult for a person in an age when searching is so easy. The GDPR and the UK's Data Protection Act now lay down stringent guidance on the right to erase or amend data – the so-called right to be forgotten. Whilst publications' archives are not normally affected, search engines can be.

Harm and offence

A previous Director of Public Prosecutions, Sir Keir Starmer, in guidelines on harm and offence, identified two broad categories: messages that contain credible threats that would be prosecuted robustly and messages that are offensive, insulting or controversial but should attract free speech protection. The main difference between harm and offence is harmful messages will contain credible threats whist offensive messages will not. While few journalists look to be offensive, it is a mark of free speech that messages which could be considered offensive attract the protection of free speech, otherwise what does free speech mean (Frost 2016: 197-209)?

The enduring importance of journalism ethics

Whilst web publishing and social media have been developing, the ethics of journalism have been developing as well. The rise of propaganda, rumour and fake news on social media means more than ever, if journalism is to be taken seriously – and it needs to be if we expect people to pay for it – it also needs to be ethical. News should be gathered from trusted sources or be supported by other trusted sources. Journalists need to be careful about gathering information unethically and ensure what they are publishing is the truth. Thirty years ago, journalism ethics were important but now they are vital. Media which seek to profit from informing the public, needs to ensure its public gets its money's worth

References

English, Kathy (2009) *The Longtail of News: To unpublish or Not To Unpublish* APME, Toronto

Frost, Chris (2016) *Journalism Ethics and Regulation* (4th Edtn) London: Routledge 978-1-138-79658-4

Frost, Chris (2002) *Source credibility: Do we really believe everything we read?* Aslib Proceedings Vol 54, 4 pp222-228 London: AIM (July 2002) ISSN 0001-253X

Frost, Chris (2000) *Rumours on the Internet: making it up as you go along* Aslib Proceedings vol 52, 1 January 2000 pp5-10 London: AIM ISSN 0001-253X

IPSO.co.uk

Note on the contributor

Chris Frost is Emeritus Professor of Journalism at Liverpool John Moores University and has been a journalist, editor and journalism educator for more than 40 years.

He is a former Chair of the Association for Journalism Education in UK and Chair of the National Union of Journalists' Ethics Committee. He is a former President of the Union and a former member of the UK Press Council. He has authored several books, including Journalism Ethics and Regulation 4th edtn (2016) and Reporting for Journalists 2nd edtn (2010), as well as many book chapters and academic papers.

Section Three

Social media, mainstream media and advertising

* * *

Tech giants hoover up advertising revenue, but is their dominance finally under threat?

Raymond Snoddy

Sir Peter Bazalgette, who chairs ITV, the UK's leading commercial broadcaster, believes absolutely public service broadcasting can survive the onslaught of 'the unregulated internet'. For comfort he draws on the sayings of Wolfgang Riepl, a German newspaper editor in the early 20th century, who argued each time a new medium of communication appeared it added to earlier forms rather than replacing them. The internet may have its benefits but it has become a latter day Tower of Babel, home to rumour, gossip and paranoia.

Sir Peter believes peddling pervasive lies is cheap but verifying and reporting facts, as in the PSB model, is expensive. According to communications regulator Ofcom more than three-quarters of those who watched PSB channels regarded its news as trustworthy and in future 'that trust is the gold reserve of our democracy'. To survive previous rivals such as the BBC, BT and Channel 4 will have to become ITV's new friends. These very necessary new alliances will be a very important part of ensuring that PSB remains accessible and well-funded. Definitions of commercial success will have to include share of video or even display advertising rather than traditional television advertising as in the past. But according to Sir Peter, public service broadcasting can be redefined as 'a medium of the future' if the PSB map can be redrawn, nurtured with new ideas, fresh regulations and novel alliances.

Alex Connock, former independent production executive, now associate fellow at the Said Business School, University of Oxford, has a more radical, and for some, alarming, vision of the future. According to Connock, even after the dramatic changes of the past five years, you haven't seen anything yet. Digital marketing is racing forward again and heading to a new world of millions of pieces of content which are untrackable, anarchically distributed and hyper-personalised.

117

It will apply both to commerce and politically influencing. One aspect of the future of the global digital advertising market – worth an estimated €268bn by 2021 – will be a multi-faceted stream of customer interactions rather than any single channel, influential post or adwords purchase. In another facet of the future, the next wave of digital marketing, and political marketing, will be made up of bulk individualised video messaging to individuals. According to one UK digital executive, the skill will be to make an infinite number of targeted videos carved out of a limited number of creative assets. If you can infinitely reduce the cost of creation, such as endless edits of Peppa Pig on YouTube, you can win the search battle. Advertisers will be able to go straight to individual consumers with videos using customer-specific targeting. Add a bit of artificial intelligence (AI) and each viewer will get their own, perfectly customised 'butterfly landing on their wrist' at the perfect time in any campaign.

Yet all is not negative or selfish – research shows positive inspirational messaging works best in charity advertising and the same might even be true of political messaging. Long-term City media analyst Alex DeGroote argues the City has been slow to embrace social media but is getting better at using it for distribution and marketing channels. The London Stock Exchange has not however been involved in many successful or large-scale initial public offerings (IPOs) in social media. This is partly because social media investing has largely been an overseas affair, but also because attitudes were coloured by the dot com boom and bust era of 1999-2001 and the rise and fall of Friends Reunited.

The parable of Friends Reunited was an important lesson – that established media companies were not to be trusted to make acquisitions in the social media space, and risk aversion and low valuations for the traditional media, set in as a result. Such views became entrenched by the failures of the likes of Myspace and Bebo, which seemed to underline the short-lived competitive advantage social networks might have. Since then through video display on the internet, the personalisation of ads via data, the ubiquity of 4G, enabled smart phones and sheer scale of the likes of Facebook and Google appear to be 'unstoppable forces', something reflected in their share prices.

Will GDPR (General Directive on Data Protection) and other regulations and legislation halt them in their tracks? It's too early to say, DeGroote believes.

> *"Investors acknowledge the concerns over consumer data privacy, and the potential misuse of personal data, but ultimately if a company is delivering earnings upgrades, that will be at the fore."*

Advertising industry specialist Torin Douglas supports the verdict of the House of Lords Select Committee on Communications that both the UK Government and the Competition and Markets Authority (CMA) should investigate the digital advertising market and its use of data. The delivery of digital advertising to consumers is a notoriously 'murky' business in which advertising services don't know how their money is being spent, whether their advertising is being displayed next to obscene or terrorist material, or even whether it is being viewed by humans at all. Consumers are also bombarded with 'clickbait' or their personal data may be exploited without their knowledge. The concern of advertisers is shared by consumer groups and a critical report by Which? increased the likelihood of a full CMA inquiry, something that is under active consideration.

Despite all of that, senior advertising executives, speaking in confidence, explain how Facebook and Google have been able to take such a large share of the advertising market. The explanations range from the sophistication of their technology, enormous public support and global reach, to the appeal of the 'long tail' of small businesses and the automation of selling millions of slots through programmatic advertising. There is growing anger in the advertising community that some of the claims made by some of the tech companies to advertisers were untrue or wildly exaggerated. Google caused particular anger in the television industry when it advised advertisers to shift 24 per cent of their TV advertising budgets to YouTube if they wanted to reach 16-34 year-olds. The appeal was denounced as laughable by the industry which countered with the fact that at the time YouTube accounted for 7.5 per cent of the video time of the young demographic compared with TV on 65 per cent.

Since there has been little sign of such controversies permanently denting either the share price or the profits of Facebook or Google there seems little financial incentive to change. "It seems that regulation may be the only answer," Torin Douglas believes.

Unlike Sir Peter Bazalgette, Bill Dunlop, president and chief executive of Eurovision Americas, predicts much greater challenges for Europe's public service broadcasters and their news provision in particular. In spite of a proud history and reputation, the challenges come not just from politicians but from the viewing public itself. As the media environment continues to fragment, the audience for news gets older and older. The average age of a BBC1 viewer is 61 and the news audience skews older still.

To add to the problem across Europe a growing number are disillusioned with the news output of their PSBs. The BBC failed to pick up the Brexit vote and similar forces are at work in Germany, Denmark, Sweden and elsewhere. PSBs tend to report the established order and promote liberal democracy and find themselves out of touch with many viewers as a result.

Finnish network YLE was one of the first to take an honest look at itself and try to widen its appeal – making sure news was relevant to eight people deemed to be a cross-section. Examples include a female student, an executive in a suit and an unemployed man in a rural setting. YLE started a TV programme for young adults but had to ditch it through lack of interest. The potential viewers were all on Facebook, Instagram and YouTube.

So, is going after the missing young viewers via the social media the answer? Alas it's not simple. The 'firehose of content' on Twitter means most individual posts are never seen at all by most users and young passionate users of SnapChat are not there for news. Perhaps Facebook is the solution and the decision by Channel 4 News to concentrate its online presence on Facebook has been successful. Now, however, Facebook in answer to criticism has returned to basics and is emphasising 'meaningful social interactions' rather than 'relevant content' such as news. For public service broadcasters, constant innovation, ceaseless experimentation and a willingness to fail and move on is a pressing necessity, something that will not come easily for such traditional organisations.

Tom George, chief executive of advertising agency GroupM UK, emphasises Google and Facebook are the 'locomotives' that have grown, and continue to grow, the global digital advertising market worth, according to GroupM estimates, $198bn in 2017. Facebook's share grew from 16 per cent in 2015 to 30 per cent in 2017, excluding China where Facebook is banned, while Google's ex-China take rose from 48 per cent to 52 per cent. As a result the advertising coffers of many smaller long-established digital publishers and media vendors have been depleted. However, the fact Facebook encourages large advertisers to replace big single campaigns with many shorter, smaller ones leads to inadequate research and short-termism.

Yet well-publicised problems have barely affected digital's growth trajectory and the social media sector is on track to capture £3.3bn revenues in the UK in 2018 – representing 24 per cent year-on-year growth. George argues digital advertisers have become more concerned about audience delivery and less about environment or quality of content, and this has gone hand-in-hand with the rise of blind programmatic buying. But last year GroupM began a collaboration with Newsworks, the marketing body for the national newspaper industry, to see if there was a positive correlation between the quality of the environment in which ads are delivered and the impact on brand metrics. There was, and it was significant. Ads in a premium environment stood out better, were more likely to be viewed for longer and gave uplifts in brand awareness and recall levels. Tom George argues:

> *"Advertisers would attach no value to a poster with half missing or a 30-second TV spot played out for only two seconds. Yet these pass for billable impressions in digital. It's a status quo which suits tech firms and discriminates against premium environments in which users have greater engagement with content. Buyer beware."*

Agnes Nairn, Professor of Marketing in the School of Management at the University of Bristol, was specialist adviser to the House of Lords Communications Committee's investigation into the advertising industry. She takes a dim view of the current state of digital advertising where content, in the worst-case scenario, is simply clickbait used to lure the largest possible audience. And as host websites are paid per click the advertising ecosystem has attracted widespread fraudulent activity. Even when fraud is not involved, all the new actors and intermediaries involved syphon off as much as 70 per cent of ad revenues whereas publishers used to get 90 per cent with 10 per cent commission going to the advertising agencies.

Prof. Nairn also highlights the fact that viewability of ads counts when 50 per cent of the ad is in view for two consecutive seconds – and that's before concerns about ad misplacement alongside unacceptable material. She believes no-one wins from the current opaque supply chain and trust in brands, adverts, news and journalism is fast being eroded. "We need regulation and we need it quickly," she argues.

The industry has responded by creating Jicweb – Joint Industry Committee for Web Standards – but membership is voluntary and neither Google nor Facebook have joined. The Lords inquiry decided the large tech company players should sign up and Jicwebs should be given greater power to create and enforce standards. If they fail to do this, the Lords Committee recommended, the Government should propose legislation.

We must cherish and protect our public service broadcasting

As we agonise over the power of the tech giants and whether the internet could or should be regulated, Peter Bazalgette, Chair of ITV, reminds us we already have regulated media which we'd do well to sustain

Wolfgang Riepl, a German newspaper editor in the early 20th century, observed that innovations in media tended to add to earlier forms rather than replace them. Thus, despite all the predictions each time a new medium appeared, film did not replace the theatre, radio did not replace newspapers, television did not replace radio. Sure, the established media were affected and had to adapt, but they survived – more the car and the train than the car and the horse.

Riepl's Law, as it's known, applies just as neatly today, as we negotiate the typhoon of digital disruption. YouTube 'snacks' have not replaced our desire to see an enthralling long-form television drama. And, again contrary to the soothsayers, 21st century media consumers do not expect everything free. Subscription is now a big growth area for content creators (ask everyone from the FT to Netflix). So can our tradition of public service broadcasting survive the onslaught of the unregulated internet? With Riepl's simple insight to nourish our thinking, the answer is, yes. Let me apply three lenses to the debate: democratic, cultural and economic.

The democratic lens

Only one country has worked out how to regulate the internet. It's China, a country to which our liberal notions of expression and democracy are anathema. Totalitarian countries don't have independent news services. Independent news is the lifeblood of democracy, without which citizens are disempowered to take informed decisions. But if it merely means choosing between the Daily Mail and The Guardian, or BuzzFeed and Vice News, then we're still under-served. What public service television news has brought to this is a gold standard of impartial news. We have a compulsory tax, the BBC licence fee, which funds a news service whose accepted role includes scrutinising the Government. And we have the public regulator, Ofcom, requiring the same standards from ITV's national and regional news. Can there be any better evidence of a genuine democracy?

The internet, extraordinary and beneficial as it may be, is also a latter day Tower of Babel – the home of rumour, gossip and paranoia. We know from all the fake news controversies that we're facing nothing less than a crisis of trust in the public sphere. Peddling pervasive lies is cheap. Verifying and reporting facts is expensive.

We knew the World Wide Web broadened our horizons, but we didn't realise it would also narrow them. You know those people we try to avoid in pubs… the ones with a glassy-eyed look, the conviction that Elvis is still alive and the moon landings were definitely faked? Well, now they can find all their fellow believers online and confirm their mutual prejudices, in a one-to-one narrowcast.

And an age of populist politics from central Europe to the US uses this amoral echo chamber to launch conspiracy and prejudice as an accepted currency. This is all fuelled by Facebook's algorithms and Google's search. For all their many advantages, they only offer us what they think we'd like, all too often narrowcasting leads to narrow minds.

Conversely, public service broadcast news broadens the mind. One of the fundamental requirements of a functioning democracy is that we hear points of view other than our own, and that they're filtered by agencies we can trust. These are not 'alternative facts', in the deathless phrase of the Trump adviser, but genuine investigation, honest reporting, and impartial presentation. It's instructive that Ofcom's most recent research reveals that the public think the most important PSB purpose is informing our understanding of the world. More than three quarters of those who watched any of the PSB channels also regarded the news as trustworthy. That trust is the gold reserve of our democracy.

I was trained as a BBC news journalist in the last century. Television has had to modernise drastically since those days, when pipe-smoking blokes never reported anything unless it was spoon-fed to them and corroborated via three wire services. Now it has to modernise again. All the PSB services have their online iterations. But how effectively are they promulgating their valuable stories in the new, digital 'Wild West'?

A cursory look at other successful news sites reveals perhaps a different tone of voice is required. A recent Vice News headline went: 'What's dumb about today's fake news'. Or Buzzfeed: '27 Things You'll Understand If You Went To A Crap British School'. We need PSB news to stay true to its philosophy but find a new audience. It should be the nutrition in the digital soup. And when was the last time you heard a news service explain or promote its principles? In future it's going to be crucial that viewers, listeners and surfers understand the exacting standards of impartiality and sourcing that PSB adheres to. Contrast that with the frankly unsustainable position of the unregulated tech giants, that they are not 'publishers'. PSB providers are proud publishers and will always take responsibility for what they distribute.

The cultural lens

What do I mean by culture? I'm referring to our way of life, our national conversation, our identity. In this sense, culture defines civic society, to which we subscribe or fail as a state. And that shared conversation is also what helps us debate and develop the sort of country we want to live in in the future. The key contribution PSB makes to our culture is original content – programmes made by us, for us and about us. Public service broadcasters currently invest about £2.5bn a year in originations. As competition hots up and funding comes under pressure this has declined a little recently. But compare it to the primetime schedule of old, when imports Friends and Frasier dominated the Channel 4 schedule, Dallas and Dynasty held sway on BBC1 and The A Team kicked off Saturday evenings on ITV.

Documentaries are an important part of the mix, but drama is the thing that moves us, captures our emotions and gains the biggest audiences, the telling of human stories that holds a mirror up to our lives. There's more money than ever flowing into drama with the important commissions of Sky and the extraordinary intervention of Netflix and Amazon, beneficially adding to consumer choice. Many of their series are aimed at the international market and have more than a Yankee flavour. Very enjoyable they are too. But they don't routinely explore sexual grooming, miscarriage, Muslim homosexuality, gay adoption, multiple sclerosis and recreational drugs – all recent, domestic story lines in ITV'S Coronation Street. Or dementia, breast cancer, child abuse in the family, post-natal depression, acid attacks and heroin addiction – all included in Emmerdale in the past year.

I've mentioned Netflix and Amazon. We now hear that Google (through YouTube), Apple and Facebook are also beginning to commission long form content. Good for them. But as we increasingly enjoy stories of dead bodies on Scandinavian bridges or crystal meth manufacture in New Mexico, let's also nurture the shows that are about us and the system which produces them.

I'd argue, as I do with PSB news, that British originations are more important today, as we graze internationally, than they were in the past. But our public service broadcasters will need to update their technological relationship with the next generation of viewers. Much more sophisticated and flexible video-on-demand delivery is essential. Have you watched a three-year-old swiping an iPad?

The economic lens

PSB has economic benefits too. The UK has created an enviable creative TV economy, perhaps the most vibrant in the world for the size of our population. We're strong exporters of content, with a rising positive balance of trade. Extraordinarily we account for around half the international trade in entertainment formats. Why are we selling so much? The English language is an obvious advantage. But also, for our number of people, we have more channels demanding more original ideas than anywhere else. Companies such as Sky make a very serious contribution to this ecology, but at its heart lie the public service broadcasters. Post-Brexit, exports matter more than ever before. But TV shows and formats are added value – they're cultural exports which harness so-called 'soft power'. We know where British culture goes, wider commerce follows.

Advertising can remain an important source of funding for PSB, even as subscription revenues grow. Television advertising remains the most cost-effective commercial medium. And in TV an impact is watching the whole commercial, not a second and a half with the sound down and the picture half off the screen. The impacts are all real, not generated by bots in far off countries. And you won't find your brand next to extreme porn or radical videos. Welcome, if that's the word, to the world of internet advertising.

In 2017 I wrote a review of the creative industries, feeding growth and investment ideas into the Government's industrial strategy. I emphasised how important this sector was to our future, growing as it is around three times faster than the economy in general. At this rate it will create a million jobs by 2030. Meanwhile artificial intelligence will replace millions of jobs elsewhere, from surgeons to traffic wardens. This makes our industry more important than ever before.

Whatever else automation subsumes we'll still need people to write soap operas, shoot documentaries and report the news. My key review proposal was that the Government back Key Creative Clusters (now accepted in their more recent Sector Deal). ITV in Salford and Leeds and the BBC – in their case in Cardiff, Bristol, Glasgow and again Salford – can ensure PSB makes its own contribution to clusters. As will Channel 4 as it decides where to relocate.

The future

I recently had an illuminating encounter with Amazon's Alexa. My hosts were playing some pop music, which I tired of. So I said, "Alexa, play some Chopin." She instantly replied, "I'm sorry, I can't find a shopping channel." It certainly is a brave new world, and one in which the platforms and the portals are the gatekeepers.

If we want to cherish PSB then viewers need to be able to find its channels and its video-on-demand services. This is why digital terrestrial television (DTT) and Freeview are still very important to ensuring the BBC, ITV, Channel 4 and 5 remain free, unmediated, universal services. We need long-term certainty for the DTT platform. It's spectrum others covet but which guarantees access to precious public service content. And we need PSB channels to be given reasonable prominence and fair value by distribution platforms. After all, they profit from this popular programmimg.

At ITV we may criticise the BBC sometimes and argue it should be held more tightly to its remit. We may compete hard with Channel 4 for talent and advertising. And we may negotiate hard with Virgin, Sky and BT about the value of our content. But in the future I think our old adversaries will also be our new friends, in order to sustain public service broadcasting in the 21st century. We've partnered with the BBC to offer the best of British content on subscription video on demand (SVOD) abroad. The service – Britbox – is already up and running in the US and Canada.

Along with Channel 4, Sky, Virgin and BT can also be our critical partners, with their subscriber data, in developing best-of-both-worlds television advertising: the benefits of both a mass audience and targeting. As we update Barb to measure viewing on mobiles and game consoles, we'll need to co-operate around a common data currency for all online audiences, ensuring commercial TV continues to be an effective competitor in the global market.

All these necessary alliances will be a very important part of making sure PSB remains accessible, well-funded and thus a deliverer of public good. But the market definitions we currently work under will have to be refreshed. We'll be talking, at the very least, about share of video or even display advertising, not television advertising. And maybe in markets no longer confined just to the UK.

The PSB map needs to be redrawn, nurtured with new ideas, fresh regulations and novel alliances. We can redefine PSB as a medium of the future. Showing us the way is the contemporary band called, encouragingly, Public Service Broadcasting. And their first album, which actually entered the charts, was called 'Inform – Educate – Entertain'. You can't get much trendier than that.

Note on the contributor
Sir Peter Bazalgette is Chair of ITV. He was elected President of the Royal Television Society in 2010 and is an Honorary Fellow of the National Film School. He was Chair of Arts Council England from 2012 until 2016 and before that on the board of Channel 4 while an independent TV producer. He began his career as a BBC news journalist in the 1970s and was knighted in the New Year Honours for 2012 for services to broadcasting. His latest book is The Empathy Instinct (John Murray).

Bad Actors 2 – another smash-hit in the making?

Facebook's Mark Zuckerberg described the political operators who manipulated social and digital media in 2016-17 as 'bad actors'. Now even more high-tech misbehaviour is on the way, says Alex Connock. It could ensnare a whole new audience

Get ready for the follow up to the controversial, 2016 digital, global blockbuster hit: Bad Actors. The next instalment in this populist franchise will draw in hundreds of millions more. And like every other product in the streaming economy from Netflix to Spotify, this time it will sign them up one by one.

Mark Zuckerberg claimed those who manipulated Facebook's social and digital media to such effect in the democratic cataclysms of 2016 and 2017 were 'bad actors'. An un-heralded cast, they got eye-popping results, including the Brexit and Trump votes. And however nefarious these groups were – from the dubiously legal if murkily financed, through to full-scale state-funded espionage – they weren't always acting on innovative tradecraft. Many of the tools they used were just off-the-shelf digital marketing.

It's troubling but unavoidable that much of what fundamentally disrupted political campaigns in 2016-17 actually came from the popular, day-to-day practice of glitzy Instagram industries like fast fashion, and that is only set to continue. The same technology that is disrupting the High Street is doing it to politics as well.

Ask a standard, millennial digital marketeer working a product line in an e-commerce company, and they will tell you the much-critiqued behavioural profiling, along with the targeting, re-targeting and real-time approach to digital media buying, which lay at the heart of the effective digital media operations of (say) Brexit, was bog standard. I've had several conversations with blasé e-commerce professionals about Cambridge Analytica's techniques, which took pretty much the opposite editorial trajectory as Channel 4 News. They went along the lines of: 'Yeah, whatever'.

The consumer industries that are shaking up the consumer world, and bulldozing high streets worldwide with real-time digital marketing, have also ended up helping to revolutionise politics. Which means that if you want a preview of Bad Actors 2 – i.e. what's going to happen in the next political cycle, 2018-22, legitimate or not

– don't expect a regulator-driven return to the comfortable dialectic of identifiable, transparently-sourced and regulated party materials. Take a moment instead to look at how digital marketing is racing forwards again – then read across to a new world of (now) millions of pieces of content – untrackable, anarchically distributed and hyper-personalised.

Here are two previews of how next season's blockbuster politics will be affected by the changing dimensions of digital marketing – in ways as different from the party political broadcast, leaders' debate, The Sun front page, or for that matter intra-bubble Twitter spats between Westminster pundits, as Mission Impossible: Fallout is from The Maltese Falcon.

Messaging to go multi-channel?

The first preview is that across digital marketing, messaging is going much more multichannel, and more predictive. The global digital advertising market – expected to reach €268bn by 2021 – is becoming a multi-faceted stream of customer interactions, rather than any single-channel, any influential post or adwords purchase. As New York University digital marketing commentator Scott Galloway writes[1]: "The ability to leverage multiple data points to provide a contextual view of consumers will drive the evolution of predictive analytics, giving retailers models that will help them determine consumers' likely future actions and needs. This will not be a perfect process by 2026, but it will certainly be instrumental in reducing the risk in R&D for new product development."

For new product development, read political campaign. For multiple data points, read finding the hot buttons in each person's echo bubble, and then slamming your fist down on them all simultaneously.

Enhanced user data will now drive integration between marketing and transactions, whether those transactions are e-commerce purchases – or votes. UK fashion brand boohoo.com had 7.8m video views in July 2018 – a number for which the Conservatives would have bitten your arm off in their feckless, Edwardian-era June 2017 campaign a year before.

Like fast-fashion brands, parties will now need to open this omni-channel, real-time communication with their users. Start a conversation with a customer or voter on one channel, 'drop a pixel on them' (industry parlance for digitally watermarking a customer so that you can tell henceforth where they go on the internet and what they like) and you can pick that conversation up a month later on a completely different channel, as if neither of you had ever been away.

Anyone for AI?

The second preview sees the next wave of digital marketing, and therefore political marketing, made up of bulk individualised messaging to individuals, based on videos.

Eighty per cent of the world's internet traffic will be video by 2019. The ecology of personalised and individually served video content is growing fast. One UK digital advertising executive describes it like this:

> *"The skill is to make an infinite number of targeted videos out of a limited number of creative assets. If you can infinitely reduce the cost of creation you can win search. There are an infinite number of Peppa Pig edits on YouTube made in real time by an AI (artificial intelligence) that is hooked into inbound search that is trained to win searches for Peppa Pig. You could do that for any video and any product. One agency invented the library-based approach to dynamic ad serving. We would serve up an ad with the right product at the right time for the right person with dynamic pricing within set parameters. Where are you based? What are your characteristics? There is nothing new in dynamic ad serving. What is new is the ability for the machine to learn at scale and at pace what people will respond to, and adjust itself."*

Video lengths and styles will be optimised to you and will vary depending on your sex, where you are and whether you've browsed the site before, and a hundred other factors. If you spent an hour on the site looking at a specific topic weeks ago, you don't need to see the general film today. You will more likely to be served up a topic-specific video advert now to convert you into a buyer. The very content of the video itself will be custom-made for you based on your interaction history – from the colour of the fonts, to the position it offers on the NHS.

As these methodologies of e-commerce become applied to political messaging, the level of content to fact-check will reach an exponential level compared to 2016 – when mimes and videos were already out of control. With artificial intelligence, there will be uncheckable millions of different political commercials running simultaneously, offering diametrically different policy messages even from the same party to voters in the same street.

In the consumer world, startup agencies working for global household brands are taking a set of basic visual assets, then using automated creativity to almost instantly create thousands of creative variables and test them on the audience.

Not only can the machine learning work out the most effective variant of any given advert (which is the kind of iterative testing effectively used in the 2016 Trump and Brexit campaigns). But it can also create potentially fundamentally contradictory versions of the same advert, each for a different individual. In the consumer world, there are plenty of legitimate agencies doing this stuff already – like Refuel[2] have deployed AI technology to update underperforming adverts. Persado[3] offers AI-generated headlines, images and language. And Jivox[4] offers dynamic video advert selection according to whether, for instance, men or women are viewing the content.

What does this mean for politics? It means implementing real time personalisation and adjustment like e-commerce does it. It means taking that Napoleon strategy -

'On s'engage, et puis on voit' – and applying it not across a battlefield as a whole, but to every single voter interaction individually. Keep changing your offer until they bite.

Dystopia is not the only possible future

Not all digital marketing has to end like an episode of Black Mirror. If the mainstream political class, gunned down like cavalry at the Somme in 2016-17 by the populist movements' next-generation use of social media and digital, can catch up next time around and embrace it, there is plenty on the app menu for them to play with.

In fact, parties have no choice but to embrace digital marketing, because the market is fundamentally moving against all the traditional communication channels. Getting the editor of News At Ten onside is less and less important. UK TV advertising dropped 2.9 per cent in 2017, while pure-play internet was 13.3 per cent up, according to media agency Group M figures. It was worse among the TV-shy young: among 16-24 year olds, linear TV viewing will fall by 12 per cent in 2018 while 16-34 year olds will be 8 per cent down, Group M predicts. For the under 25s, press is all but dead as a channel.

Advertisers – including political advertisers, candidates and parties – can go straight to individual consumers with videos using customer-specific targeting of digital marketing. They can do this right down the conversion funnel of awareness, consideration, conversion and retention. And they can flex their messages as subtly as they choose, with AI to tweak every message so that each viewer gets their own, perfectly customised butterfly landing on their wrist, at the perfect time in the campaign.

The attention economy is now measured in the flick, Facebook's new unit of time. Snapchat – the chosen platform of the under 20s – advises advertisers to put their branding in the first two seconds of a video because view time is so short. Any longer and it will be lost. Did you ever see a conventional party political broadcast that came anywhere close to achieving that?

But don't confuse the medium with the message. Colleagues of mine at Oxford's Said Business School have shown in research that positive, inspirational messaging can be more powerful than negative propositions in charity advertising. Could the same be true in political messaging? Maybe if liberal politics embraced the new digital marketing medium as aggressively as the outriders did in 2016 and 2017, but put the positive messages in, Bad Actors 2 could be the glorious flop at the box office that we'd all love to see.

Notes

[1] The Four: The hidden DNA of Amazon, Apple, Facebook and Google, published by Portfolio Penguin 2017 pp.

[2] https://www.refuel4.com/

[3] https://persado.com

[4] https://www.jivox.com/showcase/

Note on the contributor

Alex Connock is Associate Fellow at the Said Business School, University of Oxford, visiting professor at Salford and Sunderland Universities, and entrepreneur-in-residence at Insead. He has just delivered a PhD titled Optimising video content for e-commerce.

It's all about the earnings, stupid…

It has taken some time for the financial markets to fully understand where social media companies fit in. But they get it now – and Alex DeGroote says there are some potentially unstoppable forces in play

The City has a complicated and, at times, slightly forlorn relationship with social media. This relationship however operates on many levels, as we shall see, and a one size fits all characterisation is not quite appropriate.

In terms of a working environment, the City itself has been slow to embrace social media, but in some cases now uses it well as a distribution and marketing channel for clients. Ever tightening regulation in the City, and how best to police content in a record keeping environment, is a challenge. This also reflects the very nature of engaging in social media across platforms, e.g. liking, sharing, retweeting and hyperlinking.

A word then on geography. What is the City? Well let's agree on the following, at least to begin with. We mean that London-centric financial community, which encompasses investors in all asset classes and the full spectrum of financial advisors. Where corporate fund raising takes place to undertake the sort of M&A that makes or breaks reputations.

The London angle here is important because, of course, almost all the major social media stocks are listed on Wall Street, not on the London Stock Exchange (LSE) or Aim. Facebook, Alphabet, Twitter and Snap are all listed on the major US exchanges. The likes of Renren, Weibo and Sina are also US listed, even though they are Chinese social media platforms. And so, for London-based or domestic investors, there is little direct exposure to the largest, publicly quoted social media stocks.

Tech and media in the LSE

The market capitalisation of the LSE is c$4trn, across its five main indices. So it ranks behind the NYSE, Nasdaq, Japan and Shanghai. Taking the FTSE 100 as a barometer of UK-only investing, there is modest technology and media sector exposure for investors, let alone social media. In this basket, we could name WPP, Sky, Rightmove, Pearson, Micro Focus, and ITV as FTSE 100 listed stocks, but none has a pure social media dimension. Nor has the City funded many successful or large-scale initial public offerings (IPOs) in social media.

Social media *investing* is therefore largely an overseas experience, almost entirely in the US. This is a cause of frustration amongst many UK or European large-cap investors, or stock pickers. After all, they are chasing growth and capital appreciation. And the dramatic rise of the FAANG (FAANG comprises Facebook, Apple, Amazon, Netflix and Google (or Alphabet) stocks on the S&P 500 has not gone unnoticed. The aggregate market value of FAANG at the time of writing is now c$3trn, which comprises c11 per cent of the entire S&P 500.

There are ETFs (exchange traded funds) now dedicated to social media, and we would expect more to originate as investor demand continues to grow. Meanwhile, closer to home, one of the more delightful oddities of the social media investing explosion has been the rise of the Scottish Mortgage Investment Trust. Only the fourth investment trust to ever make it into the FTSE 100, this curiously named global fund has long been one of the most insightful investors in social media, or ecommerce. Amazon and Baidu are currently top holdings, and have greatly buoyed the fund performance of late. Interestingly, Facebook is a stock they have been selling down.

The parable of Friends Reunited

Was the City's social media investing experience ever thus? No, for those who lived through it, the dotcom era of 1999-2001 was a memorably high-charged boom and bust. All media companies, by default, became internet growth stocks, on high valuations, albeit briefly. Fund raising was straightforward.

Perhaps the parable of Friends Reunited is then also worth remembering briefly. In 2005 ITV spent £120m upfront on Friends Reunited. The site, of course, predated Facebook, and was one of the earlier UK social networks, based around reconnecting former school classmates. At the time of acquisition, the site had in excess of 1m paying UK subscribers. Friends Reunited was to be at the core of ITV's online and consumer strategy.

By 2009, ITV had sold Friends Reunited to DC Thomson for £25m, salvaging some value as the financial crisis bit hard. By 2011, DC Thomson had written down the value of Friends Reunited to £5m. By 2016, the site was fully closed down.

What had gone wrong? Friends Reunited was subscription-driven and domestic, at a time when online advertising, 'free-to-use' and international were becoming the hallmarks of successful social network upstarts like Facebook. We now also know that the newsfeed launch was the UX (user experience) tool that transformed Facebook in 2006, from a derivative profiles-based platform.

For the City, the failure of Friends Reunited under ITV was an important learning. Respected media companies were not to be trusted to make acquisitions in this space. Precious capital could be wasted on assets with only intangible value, and no apparent barriers to entry. This was capital that could be used for dividend payments, or debt reduction.

Elsewhere in the UK, the likes of DMGT and Trinity Mirror had undertaken similar M&A in the 2005-10 period, albeit lower profile and in the classifieds space, with equally poor outcomes. More broadly, the failure of the likes of Myspace and Bebo seemed to underline the short-lived competitive advantage that social networks might have.

Traditional media and low valuations

UK Media Plc was thus not seen at time as being well placed to benefit from the rise of social media. Far from it, investors were worried about cannibalisation from the new entrants. I recall well the very low valuations on traditional media stocks around the time of the financial crisis, as risk aversion set in and investors fretted that all advertising revenue would migrate to new entrants. At the 2009 nadir, ITV delivered just £70m of post-tax profit and had £612m of net debt.

In fact, there was a quiet revolution already underway a decade ago that would successfully reshape the media sector and the media industry, both in the UK and overseas. However, few of the plcs that dominated the sector at the start of the 2000s would prosper through this new digital industrial revolution. Social media was at the heart of this change, but there were other factors too.

First, the economy started to recover, helped of course by quantitative easing (QE). And advertising followed suit, almost without anyone noticing. Between 2009-2017, the UK advertising market almost doubled in value from £11bn to > £20bn. Advertising has always been the bellwether revenue stream of media. So it was a good time to be in media.

'A rising tide floats all boats'? Well not quite. TV recovered. But classified advertising, so long the preserve of newspapers, and such a lucrative revenue stream, started to migrate to dedicated, free-to-use UK platforms such as Rightmove, Autotrader and Zoopla. These online-only companies became very profitable, with operating margins of more than 50 per cent. Newspapers could not (and cannot) compete against these near monopolies. Print has never recovered.

Second, price comparison websites likewise emerged as similar aggregator platforms, enabling consumers again to search online seamlessly, and at no cost. Paid search, mainly the preserve of Google, also compounded throughout the 2009-17 period. Paid search is now 20 per cent of the entire UK advertising market.

Social media advertising itself is now around 15 per cent of the UK advertising market, or £3bn. Whilst the near-term growth prospects for the overall UK advertising market are muted due to Brexit and a soft economy, most industry forecasters expect further strong market share gains by social in the coming years, mainly at the expense of traditional media such as TV and newspapers. Latterly, it is the growth of video sharing in social media that has been the undoing of TV ad spend, for so long a quite resilient sector.

Third, social media changed the marketing industry beyond recognition. And this has created some opportunities for the agencies, which operate in it. However, disruption to media buying, like in lucrative classifieds, has had calamitous consequences for some marketing services groups.

The Duopoly

In the new world, Google and Facebook are now known as the Duopoly. Amazon is an outside bet to disturb this in the future, with its presence in retail. But for the time being, what underpins this Duopoly?

Where Google has bossed search advertising since day one, Facebook has been increasingly successful with online display advertising. And the advertising virtues of Facebook, or other scale social platforms, are simple to highlight:

1. The internet as an alternative display medium (video);

2. Data-backed targeting of ads to audiences (personalisation);

3. Globalisation of content;

4. Ubiquity of 4G-enabled smartphones;

5. Scale of Facebook (c75 per cent of all adults use it). In this context, advertisers are behaving logically, and with an eye of measurable return on investment.

These seemingly unstoppable forces are also why Facebook's share price has recovered so sharply from the dip, which occurred around the time of the Cambridge Analytica scandal in March 2018.

At a current share price of c$203, the Facebook stock has rallied > 30 per cent from its March 2018 lows. As a reminder, its IPO back in May 2012 was at $38 per share. It has been a highly successful investment for its shareholders.

There is a creeping sense of the need for regulation around social media and the digital behemoths, however it feels ill formed in our view. For some time, other media companies – mainly in the newspaper sector – have lobbied intensively, but to date unsuccessfully, for tighter controls and 'a fairer playing field'.

The impact of the Facebook newsfeed cannot be underestimated, and underlines the importance of the social platforms to many professional publishers. In January 2018 Facebook altered its newsfeed algorithm, to upgrade user-generated news, at the expense of newspapers. This reduced the amount of newspaper articles used by around 20 per cent. This of course has had revenue implications for many publishers.

Will GDPR – or other related legislation, outside of Europe – yet halt social media in its tracks? It is probably too early to say, at this stage. Investors acknowledge the concerns over consumer data privacy, and the potential misuse of personal data, but ultimately if the company is delivering earnings upgrades, that will be at the fore.

There is also an argument that it is the bigger social platforms will in fact thrive in an era, in which compliance costs are higher. Consumers are more likely to default to known networks, than give explicit tick-box consent to obscure ad tech vendors.

Note on the contributor

Alex DeGroote is an independent media analyst, and owner/founder of DeGroote Consulting. Alex worked in the City for 20 years as a media analyst for a number of investment banks and securities firms. In this role, he advised investors on sector trends and stock picking, and corporates on strategy and financial matters. Amongst others, he has worked closely with the likes of Trinity Mirror (now Reach), Johnston Press and STV.

How Google and Facebook hoovered up the advertising

Since Google revolutionised the advertising business with its AdWords system in 2000, computers, algorithms and the internet have delivered audience segmentation and targeting far more efficiently than traditional media. Google and Facebook now have billions of users and take 60-90 per cent of digital advertising revenue, the biggest sector of the market. But many of their audience claims have proved misleading and advertisers have woken up to concerns about fraud, data privacy and the advertising of their reputable brands on disreputable websites. There are growing calls for the market to be regulated and for competition law to be updated, writes media commentator Torin Douglas

The market for delivering digital advertising is notoriously 'murky'

In April 2018, a House of Lords committee recommended that the UK Government and the Competitions and Markets Authority (CMA) should both investigate the digital advertising market and its use of data.

"Digital advertising has quickly become the most significant form of advertising by spending," wrote the committee chairman, Lord Gilbert of Panteg, in his foreword. "But the market for delivering digital advertising to consumers is notoriously 'murky': businesses which buy advertising services don't know how their money is being spent, whether their advertising is being displayed next to content which is obscene or which supports terrorism, or whether their ads are being viewed by a human being at all.

"The consumer's experience is also poor as they may be bombarded with 'clickbait', or their personal data may be exploited without their knowledge. To restore the public's trust in advertising as a whole, the industry must commit to adhering to proper standards." (House of Lords Select Committee on Communications, 2018, UK advertising in a digital age)

The report recommended the CMA should carry out a market study of the digital advertising market, to ensure it was working fairly both for businesses and consumers, and that the Government should review whether competition law was appropriate for the 21st century digital economy, when two global companies hold 60 to 90 per cent of the total market.

The report's summary didn't mention Google or Facebook – but it didn't need to. In the spring of 2018, those companies were already in the media spotlight in a way that neither of them relished. In April, Facebook's founder Mark Zuckerberg was called to give evidence before the US Congress after a wave of controversial disclosures about his business and its use of data.

The scale of the duopoly's market dominance was highlighted by the author and New Yorker columnist Ken Auletta: "Google and Facebook each has a market value exceeding the combined value of the six largest advertising and marketing holding companies," he wrote. "Together, they claim six out of every ten dollars spent on digital advertising, and nine out of ten new digital ad dollars. They have become more dominant in what is estimated to be an up to two-trillion-dollar annual global advertising and marketing business. Facebook alone generates more ad dollars than all of America's newspapers, and Google has twice the ad revenues of Facebook." (Auletta, 2018, The New Yorker)

Facebook overestimated the time spent watching video by up to 80 per cent
Since advertisers and ad agencies give so much revenue to Google and Facebook, you might think they must be delighted with the two companies' performance and effectiveness. Not so, wrote Auletta:

"Ad agencies and advertisers have long been uneasy not just with the 'walled gardens' of Facebook and Google but with their unwillingness to allow an independent company to monitor their results, as Nielsen does for TV and com. Score does online. This mistrust escalated in 2016, when it emerged that Facebook and Google charged advertisers for ads that tricked other machines to believe an ad message was seen by humans when it was not. (Auletta, 2018)

"Advertiser confidence in Facebook was further jolted later in 2016, when it was revealed that the Math Men at Facebook overestimated the average time viewers spent watching video by up to 80 per cent. And in 2017, Math Men took another beating when news broke that Google's YouTube and Facebook's machines were inserting friendly ads on unfriendly platforms, including racist sites and porn sites." (Auletta, 2018)

In 2018, the Sunday Times reported Facebook was still overclaiming the size of its audience: "Mark Zuckerberg often waxes philosophical about the 'magic' of technology. The Facebook founder's best trick, however, may be conjuring up millions of non-existent users, and then using them to convince companies to plough billions of pounds in advertising into his ever-growing empire." (The Sunday Times, 2018)

'It is far from clear we can trust Google and Facebook to act as responsible custodians of our data'

The advertisers' concern is shared by consumer groups. A critical report by Which? in June 2018, following the House of Lords report, increased the likelihood of a full CMA investigation.

The Times reported: "The Competition and Markets Authority (CMA) said it was 'actively considering' launching an inquiry after a report from Which? warned the technology companies were 'taking advantage' of public and governmental ignorance to collect and profit from the personal data of Britons on an unprecedented scale. (The Times, 2018)

"Alex Neill, of Which?, said: "It is far from clear we can trust Google, Facebook and other companies to act as responsible custodians of our data. We believe the competition regulator must urgently examine how targeted ads affect consumers and whether Facebook and Google's substantial power in the digital ad market in particular could have knock-on effects on advertisers that lead to consumers paying more." (The Times, ibid)

It's a far cry from the situation 40 years ago, when Which?'s forerunner, the Consumers' Association, praised advertising for bringing prices DOWN. In 1978, I was one of the founders of Marketing Week magazine and this year, in the magazine's 40th anniversary edition, I wrote:

"Viewed from the digital-dominated perspective of 2018, when Google and Facebook hoover up the ad revenue and advertising is seen as sinister, the 1970s and 1980s could be seen as a golden age for advertising and marketing. Directors such as Alan Parker, Hugh Hudson and Ridley Scott were cutting their teeth in the commercial break and the ads were widely regarded as better than the programmes.

"There was a clear demarcation between the ads and the content (and no sponsored programming for fear of blurring the lines). Regulators and the Consumers' Association lauded advertising for promoting competition and bringing down prices. And the arrival of Channel 4 in 1982 and breakfast TV in 1983, and the breaking of print union power in 1986, unleashed a wave of new programmes, newspapers, magazines and media creativity, all funded or underpinned by advertising." (Douglas, 2018, Marketing Week)

40 years on, the ad-funded business models for newspapers, magazines and investigative journalism have been broken by the digital disrupters, while television, though still strong, is assaulted by misleading claims from Google, Facebook and other digital operators that "TV is dead" and the internet is a more effective advertising medium.

Facebook is winning because it has amazing advertising products which work incredibly well

So how did Google and Facebook become so dominant? And why did it take advertisers, agencies and opinion-formers so long to realise the two companies weren't as effective as they claimed to be?

Senior executives, speaking in confidence, gave me various explanations as to how Facebook and Google have built such a huge share of the advertising market:

- They have very sophisticated technology, harnessing data to help users search for items and get in touch with each other, and to provide advertisers with precise targeting;

- They have enormous public appeal – what they do is highly valued by billions of users all over the world;

- Their technology is universal and global and extremely scalable, and there is no single regulator to limit their growth;

- As global businesses, they can strike global deals with global advertisers in return for bulk discounts.

- But they're also easily accessible for the long tail of small businesses looking for highly targeted advertising, whether geographic, demographic or psychographic.

- They offer perceived accountability, using analytic models which attribute sales to the last 'click' or to any online exposure, without taking into account existing sales patterns or the impact of offline media.

- They have been hyped by the media and are businesses which generate excitement and are seen to be 'new'. Nobody ever got fired for increasing 'digital' investment.

- Advertising agencies get more money from placing their clients' ads in digital media than in most offline media such as newspapers and television, and 'programmatic' advertising systems have automated the business of buying millions of slots.

"Facebook is winning because it has amazing advertising products that work incredibly well," said Will Haywood, Buzzfeed's former VP for Europe, at a Newsbrands debate in London. (Pidgeon, MediaTel Newsline, 19 September 2016)

The same is true for Google, which revolutionised the advertising process when it launched AdWords, linked to its world-beating search engine, in the year 2000.

"When you use Google to search for anything from financial information to local weather, you're given a list of search results generated by Google's algorithm," explained Eric Rosenberg, in Investopaedia. "The algorithm attempts to provide the most relevant results for your query and, along with these results, you may find related suggested pages from an AdWords advertiser. Any recommended websites you see when logged into Gmail, YouTube, Google Maps, and other Google sites are generated through the AdWords platform.

"To gain the top spot in Google advertisements, advertisers have to outbid each other. Advertisers pay Google each time a visitor clicks on an advertisement. A click may be worth anywhere from a few cents to over \$50 for highly competitive search terms, including insurance, loans and other financial services." (Rosenberg, Eric, 2016, Investopaedia)

Through a second advertising programme, AdSense, "Google served as a matchmaker, marrying advertisers with Web destinations," wrote Ken Auletta. "If Intel wanted to advertise on technology blogs or a hotel in London wanted to promote itself on travel sites, Google put them together via a similar automated auction system." (Auletta, 2016, Googled: The End of the World As We Know It.)

"Unlike the ads traditional media had sold for more than a century, based on the estimated number of people reading a newspaper or watching a program, Google's system ensured advertisers were charged only when the user clicked on an ad. And unlike traditional analog media companies, which can't measure the effectiveness of their advertising, Google offered each advertiser a free tool: Google Analytics, which allowed the advertiser to track hour by hour, the number of clicks and sales, the traffic produced by the keywords, the conversion rate from click to sale." (Auletta, Googled.)

'Marking their own homework'

Further innovations, such as DoubleClick search management, enhanced Google's offering to advertisers, while its huge scale, and that of Facebook, made their algorithms even more effective and attractive.

Unfortunately, it turned out that many of the claims the tech companies made to advertisers were untrue or wildly exaggerated. Rejecting independent auditing (the accepted practice in the ad industry) – and thus 'marking their own homework', in the words of former WPP boss Sir Martin Sorrell – they boosted their audience claims with clicks generated by robots; overestimated the time viewers spent watching video by up to 80 per cent; and inserted advertisements for reputable advertisers into disreputable sites, including those which showed porn and terrorist videos.

Google caused particular anger among UK commercial TV companies in 2015 when it advised advertisers to shift 24 per cent of their TV budgets to YouTube if they wanted to reach an audience of 16 to 34-year-olds. Lindsey Clay, chief executive of Thinkbox, the commercial TV marketing body, called Google's advice 'laughable', 'self-serving', 'irresponsible', 'flaky' and 'biased'. In an article in Inside Business, she set out some of her reasons:

- Official industry sources including comScore showed that YouTube then accounted for 7.5 per cent of 16 to 24-year-olds' video time, with TV at 65 per cent. The numbers for the whole population were 3.5 per cent and 81 per cent.

- Internet 'impacts' were (and still are) much less rigorously defined than those of TV. A view on YouTube required merely that the ad was served and that 50 per cent of the pixels were seen for one second. A TV impact (measured by BARB, the official ratings survey) is based on the average viewing across a minute of continuous TV viewing and the ad must be seen in its entirety at normal speed.

- Google refused to share its research for inspection but Thinkbox learned the TV elements were based around a panel of Google users which did not measure all TV, while the YouTube element was provided by Google itself.

- Thinkbox asked whether the research took account of the 50 per cent of online ads that were not seen by humans? (Clay, 2015, Inside Business)

A wake-up call came in a speech by Marc Pritchard, chief brand officer at Procter & Gamble, one of the world's biggest and most respected advertisers. Speaking at the Internet Advertising Bureau's leadership conference in Florida in January 2017, he said: "We have a media supply chain that is murky at best and fraudulent at worst. We need to clean it up and invest the time and money we save into better advertising to drive growth." (Pritchard, 2017, Marketing Week)

He said P&G would be taking four steps: Adopting one viewability standard; implementing accredited third-party measurement verification; getting transparent agency contracts; and collaborating with the Trustworthy Accountability Group, a self-regulatory body aimed at eliminating ad fraud. (Pritchard, 2017, Marketing Week). Its global rival Unilever quickly took similar action, together with advertisers who had already removed campaigns which had been placed on porn and terrorist sites.

In the UK, the Incorporated Society of British Advertisers and the Institute of Practitioners in Advertising, which represents agencies, also demanded action. In September 2017, the IPA director-general Paul Bainsfair wrote an open letter to Google and Facebook accusing them of being too slow to tackle the problems and demanding 'urgent action'. (Spanier, 2017, Campaign)

A Facebook spokesman responded: "We've announced an extra 3,000 content reviewers to nearly double our existing team, as well as new buying options and controls for advertisers that give choice and transparency over how and where ads appear on the platform. We have also updated our metrics to give more clarity and confidence about the insights we provide, including our work with 24 third-party measurement partners who can verify the value we drive for advertisers."

Despite the damage to some tech companies' reputations, little damage has been done to their profits

The IPA said: "While we acknowledge that small steps towards addressing recent concerns have been taken, our advertisers and agencies are increasingly telling us that this progress is neither fast, nor significant, enough." (Spanier, 2017, Campaign)

The following month, The Economist made a powerful case for more government regulation of the five digital giants – Facebook, Google, Amazon, Apple and Microsoft – saying data were 'the oil of the digital era': "Old ways of thinking about competition, devised in the era of oil, look outdated in what has come to be called the 'data economy' ". (The Economist, 2017)

Since then more damaging revelations about data misuse have tarnished the tech companies' reputations, but though major advertisers withdrew their campaigns and cut their budgets it has caused little damage to Facebook and Google's profits.

Fortune reported in April 2018: "Facebook's recent data privacy missteps and closely watched Congressional hearings about the topic do not appear to have significantly impacted the company's latest quarterly earnings. The social networking giant said first quarter revenue jumped 49 per cent year-over-year to $12 billion versus an expected $11.4 billion and earnings per share of $1.69, easily beating analyst estimates of $1.35." (Fortune, 2018)

Google has emerged similarly unscathed. The Guardian reported: "Google owner Alphabet shrugged off mounting concerns over privacy on Monday to report an 84 per cent rise in profits for the last quarter." (The Guardian, 2018)

Since Facebook and Google have little financial incentive to mend their ways, it seems that regulation may be the only answer.

References

House of Lords Select Committee on Communications (2018), report: UK advertising in a digital age. Available online at: https://publications.parliament.uk/pa/ld201719/ldselect/ldcomuni/116/11602.htm

Auletta, Ken (2018), The New Yorker, How the Math Men overthrew the Mad Men, from his book Frenemies: The Epic Disruption of the Ad Business (and Everything Else). Available online at: https://www.newyorker.com/news/annals-of-communications/how-the-math-men-overthrew-the-mad-men

The Sunday Times (2018) Zuckerberg's missing millions on Facebook. Available online at: https://www.thetimes.co.uk/article/zuckerbergs-missing-millions-on-facebook-7tpqvg2c9

The Times (2018) Facebook and Google exploit ignorance to rake in profits. Available online at: https://www.thetimes.co.uk/article/facebook-and-google-exploit-ignorance-to-rake-in-profits-099lhxfj6

Douglas, Torin (2018) Marketing Week's first five years: An era of change, Marketing Week, June 2018

Pidgeon, David (2016) Newsbrands debate strategies as they square up to Facebook and Google, MediaTel Newsline, 19 September 2016

Rosenberg, Eric (2016) How Google Makes Money, Investopaedia. Available online at: http://www.investopedia.com/articles/investing/020515/business-google.asp

Auletta, Ken (2009) Googled: The End of the World As We Know It, Virgin Books

Clay, Lindsey (2015) Inside Business, Why Google is wrong to say advertisers should shift 24% of their TV budgets to YouTube. Available online at: http://uk.businessinsider.com/thinkbox-ceo-lindsey-clay-on-youtube-versus-tv-2015-10

Pritchard, Marc (2017) P&G issues call to arms to ad industry, Marketing Week, 30 January 2017. Available online at: https://www.marketingweek.com/2017/01/30/pg-media-buying/

Spanier, Gideon (2017) IPA: Google and Facebook are not moving fast enough to tackle ad problems, Campaign. Available online at: https://www.campaignlive.co.uk/article/ipa-google-facebook-not-moving-fast-enough-tackle-ad-problems/1441916

The Economist (2017) The world's most valuable resource is no longer oil, but data, 5 May 2017. Available online at: https://www.economist.com/leaders/2017/05/06/the-worlds-most-valuable-resource-is-no-longer-oil-but-data

Fortune (2018) Facebook Escapes Recent Data Privacy Scandals with Big Profit Gain, 25 April 2018). Available online at: http://fortune.com/2018/04/25/facebook-quarter-earnings-data-privacy/

The Guardian (2018) Google owner Alphabet reports 84% rise in profits despite privacy concerns, 23 April 2018). Available online at: https://www.theguardian.com/technology/2018/apr/23/google-owner-alphabet-reports-earnings?CMP=Share_iOSApp_Other

Note on the contributor

Torin Douglas has been writing about advertising and the media for more than 40 years. He worked for Campaign and the Independent Broadcasting Authority before joining the team that launched Marketing Week in 1978. From 1982, he wrote a weekly column about advertising and the media, first for The Times and then for The Independent. He presented Advertising World for LBC Radio from 1984-89 and was then media correspondent for BBC News for 24 years. He is the author of The Complete Guide to Advertising (1985). He was visiting professor in media at the University of Bedfordshire and holds an honorary doctorate from the University of West London.

The battle for relevance: public service broadcasting's social media dilemmas

Life was once straightforward for public broadcasters: they got money from every household in the country and used it as they liked. Then, as Bill Dunlop explains, their audience began to desert them

Public service broadcasting is a European tradition with a proud history and reputation. Far from the admirable but underfunded notion that passes for a public network in the United States, across Europe the main television channels with a public service remit – the BBC, ITV and Channel 4 in the UK, France Télévisions, ARD and ZDF in Germany, RAI in Italy and more than 50 others – have historically been well-funded, independent and fiercely protective of the quality of their journalism.

Today, however, the outlook for these storied networks is as challenging as it's ever been. In Poland, Hungary and Turkey authoritarian regimes have quashed the independence of national broadcasters. Spain and Italy haven't suffered to the same extent, but their networks' senior managements tend to be uncomfortably close to the political parties in power at the time.

In the Nordic countries, right-wing movements have decried public broadcasters as liberal and out of touch. Even the broad scope and remit of the BBC was threatened by a Conservative Culture Minister who had little time for the notion of publicly funded broadcasting – until a massive backlash from members of said public forced him to reconsider and leave the Corporation largely intact.

Even so, neither the BBC nor any other public broadcaster in Europe has any room for complacency because challenges from politicians are one thing: but today's reality is that the greater challenge comes not from the corridors of power, but from the viewing public itself.

As the media environment fragments and thousands of new sources of information become available, the audience watching TV news today has become older and older. When you consider that the average age of a viewer of BBC1 is 61 – and that's for all programming, the news audience skews older still – you can see the problem.[1]

Add to that the growing number of people all over Europe who have become disillusioned with the news output of their public service broadcasters and the problem gets worse.

Some BBC managers admit privately that, ensconced in their vast newsroom in London W1, they were completely taken aback by the result of the Brexit vote. Up and down the country, as a mix of austerity and globalisation has hit the non-metropolitan economy hard, the Westminster shenanigans which dominate traditional TV news have come to be regarded as an irrelevance.

It's the same in Germany, in Denmark, in Sweden and many more countries: public service broadcasters, with their natural inclination to report on the established order and promote liberal values such as equality and non-discrimination, find themselves out of touch with people whose jobs have gone to the Far East, whose towns are full of boarded-up shops…and who have decided that the blame lies, one way or another, with people from another country.

This has two important consequences for public broadcasters. Firstly, if you're watched only by a dwindling number of ageing people, how can you justify demanding a compulsory licence fee from every household in the country?

And secondly, if your output is not adequately reporting the real-life concerns of a substantial proportion of the population, they're going to look for output from other sources that does. The websites and social media platforms they feel more in tune with may or may not have a factual basis for their content – but you can be sure that their tone will not be conducive to accepting things the way they are and just getting along in peace and harmony.

How does a public broadcaster compete with that when it must refuse as a matter of principle to pander to people's basest instincts and maintain its commitment, both legal and moral, to detached, quality journalism?

Facing up to the problem

The first thing it must do is accept that there's a problem. The Finnish network YLE was one of the earliest to take an honest look at itself and realise that if it was to maintain its relevance in a fragmenting landscape, it had to broaden its outlook. Now all over the newsroom walls in Helsinki there are posters featuring a grid that every journalist is expected to glance at from time to time.

Along the top of the grid are pictures of eight people deemed to represent a cross-section of Finnish society, among them a young female student, an executive in a suit, a parent and an unemployed man in a rural setting. Down the left are hours of the day: 06.00, 09.00 and so on, all the way to 21.00. The question producers are constantly required to ask themselves is, 'What are we doing to serve THIS person at THIS time of day?'

Danish public television reviewed its output with such brutal honesty that it ended up cancelling the entire breakfast programme on the main DR network.

Senior management deployed the 'U' model of strategic decision making attributed to Cardiff journalism professor Richard Sambrook.

At the top right of a large letter 'U', they wrote 'Update'; at the top left they wrote 'In depth'. Two-thirds of the way down the letter, they cut it with a horizontal line and shaded the area below. Then every piece of news output generated by DR was tested against the U model: either it provided fast updates to running stories, or it provided depth and context to important stories. If it provided neither, it fell to the bottom of the U and was axed. And thus came to an abrupt end DR's breakfast programme.

Building on the need to broaden the audience, the Finns have taken a decisive stand on a question that has exercised many public broadcasters: whether to launch a completely separate brand aimed at the youth market.

YLE has gone all in with its brand for young people, Kioski, which features factual content aimed at 16-24 year olds. It started as a TV programme, website and social media apps; but in a sign of the times, the TV programme was quickly discarded due to lack of interest and the web presence was diluted as it became clear that Facebook, Instagram and YouTube were the places to find the elusive young audience.

It's important to note that a key principle of the rebranding was that the content should remain worthy of a public service broadcaster. There is no showbiz and no celebrities; rather, the aim is to tackle significant issues in a way that's engaging for the youth audience. With Finland as divided as other European countries over the migration issue, Kioski placed a young man who looked stereotypically Muslim on the street holding a placard saying, 'Hug me.' Then they filmed the public reaction, positive and negative, which led to a lively online discussion among young people about attitudes towards immigration and religious minorities.

Choosing effective platforms

The choice of platform on which to place content is important not just for finding young people, but for engaging all age groups and social classes. Unfortunately, the bigger the platform becomes, the more trouble it tends to bring with it.

Firstly, a reality check for many newsrooms: forget about Twitter as an audience driver. The social media app most commonly associated with breaking news actually has the lowest engagement per post, per user of all major platforms.[2] The sheer number of tweets constantly rolling through, sometimes described as 'a firehose of content', means most individual posts are never seen at all by most users.

Twitter is regarded in many countries, especially in the non-English speaking world, as an incestuous tool of the industry: a way of competing with a news provider's peers and maintaining a profile with politicians, but with little evidence of widespread public engagement with the constant diet of breaking news tweets.

Secondly, SnapChat is not the solution to a broadcaster's youth problem. However popular it is with teens and twenty-somethings, they're not there looking for news. The BBC goes to the considerable trouble of editing items to make them work in SnapChat's quirky format, but after a presence of more than two years, they've amassed just a few thousand followers on the platform.

Which leads to the big two: in ascending order of importance, Instagram and Facebook.

The growth in Instagram subscribers over the last couple of years has been breathtaking, from 700m at the end of 2016 to 1bn in June 2018.[3] But Instagram is about more than just numbers. It offers news providers a unique combination of relatively youthful consumers – mostly under 35 – on a platform whose whole reputation is built around quality and high aesthetic value – the very features a public broadcaster wants to be associated with. Uniquely among mainstream social media outlets, the Instagram community is majority female, an important factor when a news provider wants to contribute to the discussion over issues central to today's society, such as the gender awareness #MeToo movement.[4]

And these socially diverse consumers are engaged: one major survey showed that interactions such as likes, comments and shares per media-related post on Instagram were about 14 times higher than the same kind of post on Facebook, and no fewer than 82 times higher than media-related posts on Twitter.[5]

Again, it's partly about volume: people post less material to Instagram and what they put there are their best photos and videos accompanied by sparse but intelligent commentary. Broadcasters can do the same: ARD in Germany spends a great deal of effort producing news videos which are polished enough for Instagram, knowing that they can get added value by reposting them to Facebook, because once you've made an item good enough for the platform with the highest aesthetic values, it can also cascade down to other outlets.

Dealing with Facebook

Which brings us to the colossus of all social media outlets: the platform which is so big and dominant that no newsroom can avoid it, no matter how much trouble it might cause them.

With 2.2bn monthly active users[6] and little sign of recent controversies significantly stemming its growth, Facebook provides opportunities to reach audiences right across the social spectrum. It's sometimes painted as a middle-aged platform which became uncool for younger consumers long ago – but the sheer numbers involved mean that even if the user base nowadays skews towards people in their 40s and 50s, there is still very significant penetration into younger - and older - age groups. Since Facebook owns Instagram, there is also a large volume of traffic that is posted on one site that makes its way automatically on to the other.

Channel 4 News in the UK is the most prominent example of a relatively small news operation with limited resources that decided to concentrate on Facebook – and made a massive success of it. Deploying a team of digitally-aware journalists, they applied all the rules for making video work on the platform: the most engaging shot had to be right at the top to instantly hook users flicking through their news feeds; video was cropped to square format so it worked both horizontally and vertically on a mobile phone; and captions large and simple enough for a five-inch screen were added, nodding to the remarkable statistic that 85 per cent of Facebook video is watched without sound.[7]

Coupled with powerful editorial content – most notably a series of disturbing reports about life inside the city of Aleppo as it was besieged by the Syrian army – Channel 4 News saw its Facebook views grow from 80m in 2014, to 600m in 2015, and no fewer than 2bn in 2016.[8] A heavyweight news programme with a small audience, which had been virtually unheard of outside of the UK, suddenly had a global profile.

But Channel 4 News, along with every other media outlet that has a Facebook presence, would soon experience the downside of being on the platform.

It's hard to believe in retrospect how completely caught out Facebook's senior management was by the rapid encroachment of fake news. Two days after the November 2016 US Presidential election, CEO Mark Zuckerberg told the Technonomy conference in California, "Personally I think the idea that fake news on Facebook, which is a very small amount of the content, influenced the election in any way, I think is a pretty crazy idea." Such was the derision poured on him for that statement that within weeks there was a scramble to implement a raft of counter measures.

An alliance was formed with ABC, the Associated Press and others to fact check stories; but such a measure could only hope to deal with a fraction of the content posted on Facebook every minute of every day. Measures were introduced to delete spoof domains linked to 'ad farms' where people clicked continuously on a made-up story to generate revenue; but this missed the point about fake news posted for political, not financial, reasons.

Changes were made to Facebook's algorithm in an attempt to promote content based on user interaction; but those backfired badly following the Las Vegas mass shooting in October 2017, when the algorithm relegated valid news sources and promoted reports which falsely identified the gunman, stating that he was an anti-Trump liberal and linking him to the anti-racist group Antifa, which had been accused of violent conduct.[9]

Seven months later, as if nothing had been learned, virtually the same thing happened with the school shooting in Santa Fe, Texas: the algorithm promoted a picture of the gunman doctored to show him in a 'Hillary 2016' hat, alongside an allegation that he, too, was a member of Antifa.[10]

Following the Parkland school shooting in Florida in February 2018, a rash of items published on Facebook – as well as on Instagram and YouTube – alleged that the students who launched a heartfelt campaign for gun control were not students at all, but 'crisis actors'. When one user started to type the name of the student David Hogg into the Facebook search box, the algorithm intervened and auto-completed it as 'David Hogg actor', then the site listed links to a whole series of conspiracy theory articles.[11]

The crux of the matter is this: relying on artificial intelligence to get it right in such a massive, complex and nuanced environment as Facebook is not good enough; but employing enough humans to bring subjective judgement to every post in what amounts to a global game of 'whack-a-mole', is simply impossible.

Facebook attempts to reform

In January 2018, having finally come to terms with the scale of the issues that were overwhelming his platform, Mark Zuckerberg announced a major policy shift in which Facebook would prioritise 'meaningful social interactions' over 'relevant content'.

Essentially, Facebook would go back to basics and re-emphasise the idea of socialising among friends. The problem was that as well as giving less prominence to fake news and the sea of dubious political ads which were doing so much damage to Facebook's reputation, the new policy also led to the de-emphasising of valid journalism from reputable suppliers. In the months that followed, every worthwhile contributor, from quality news providers to non-profits promoting important causes, found it more difficult to get eyes on their content.

In a sense, the problem for public service broadcasters had come full circle. They went on social media sites such as Facebook to broaden their audience, and now they were finding that the very consumers they were looking for were being shielded from them by the social media platform itself.

The obvious way forward is to play the Facebook game: if 'meaningful social interaction' is what counts, then stories which newsrooms post on Facebook must encourage that; to use the fashionable term, they must be 'discussable'. The more users who find content from organisations like the BBC and ARD and like, share or comment on it, the bigger its audience becomes.

But this has serious implications for public service newsrooms when creating content for Facebook. For example, it would be potentially suicidal to post a story about an active court trial, no matter how big or significant the case. The last thing a news provider wants with a court story is a sea of ill-informed or prejudiced public discussion attached to it, lest they end up in court themselves facing a contempt charge.

On the other hand, if there's been a morning of train disruption or a bad snowstorm or a motorway pile-up, these are perfect stories for the new criterion of being discussable, and are therefore likely to succeed on the reformed Facebook: but what happened to the public service remit of covering serious and consequential issues whether they're necessarily popular or not?

There's no reason why the broadcaster can't still post these stories, but there's far less chance that they'll ever be seen - and not being seen is exactly the problem they came to social media to overcome.

In the end, a public broadcaster must use the extensive metrics which are available to constantly monitor the popularity and user profile of the major platforms – well-established ones and new players – and regularly revise its strategy to reach the broad audience it needs. If Facebook becomes the home of discussable stories, maybe another platform like YouTube will be where more heavyweight content grows in prominence. News executives can argue that there's nothing inherently wrong with that because story selection has always been part of the job: the running order for the 8am bulletin on Radio 4 bears little resemblance to the running order of Newsbeat on Radio 1, and assigning different content to different social media platforms is no different.

Most public broadcasters are still lucky enough to benefit from a guaranteed source of income; but using it effectively presents a challenge involving constant innovation, ceaseless experimentation and a willingness to fail and move on. These are not qualities which necessarily come easily to public service journalists, but in adopting social media as a way of keeping up with their fast-moving audience, they have entered a world where there is no settled solution – not now and not ever.

Notes

[1] BBC Trust report, March 2017

[2] Rival IQ 2018 Social Media Industry Benchmark Report, April 2018

[3] Statista quoting Instagram, TechCrunch, June 2018

[4] Instagram Demographics, Salman Aslam/Omnicore, January 2018

[5] Rival IQ 2018 Social Media Industry Benchmark Report, April 2018

[6] Statista quoting Facebook

[7] VideoUniversity.com, '85% of Facebook video is viewed without sound', June 2017

[8] Channel 4 News/ITN

[9] The Guardian, 'Facebook and Google promote politicized fake news about Las Vegas shooter', October 2, 2017

[10] Washington Post, 'Fake Facebook accounts and online lies multiply in hours after Santa Fe school shooting', May 18, 2018

[11] Quartz, 'This is how quickly fake news that exploits tragedy spreads on Facebook', February 21, 2018

Note on the contributor

Bill Dunlop is President and CEO of Eurovision Americas, Inc. He is a former Senior Programme Editor of ITN's Channel 4 News and Editorial Director of Euronews. He has served as a judge at the Royal Television Society Journalism Awards and the International Emmy Journalism Awards in New York. In 2017, he authored the European Broadcasting Union report 'Perfect Storm: the multiple challenges facing public service news, and why tackling them is vital for democracy'. He contributed the chapter 'How the mainstream media created President Trump – and President Trump saved the mainstream media' to the book 'Brexit, Trump and the Media', Abramis, 2017.

The murky world of digital advertising

How important is online marketing? How vital are quality media and brand safety to advertisers? What does it all mean? Tom George guides us through this opaque new world

For better or worse, media agencies use advertising revenue as a proxy for advertiser demand. Thus global digital advertising spend was $198bn in 2017 and we expect this to have grown 12 per cent in 2018 to reach $221bn, and by another 10 per cent in 2019 to reach $243bn. This would bring digital's share of global ad investment to 39 per cent in 2018, then 42 per cent in 2019. Digital advertising will account for 95 per cent of net new global advertising growth in 2018 and 99 per cent in 2019.

Arguably the most impressive recent digital superlative has been the growth in Facebook's market share. Using our own estimates of global digital ad investment excluding China, where it is banned, Facebook's share grew from 16 per cent in 2015 to 30 per cent in 2017 – and in 2017 it accounted for more market growth than Google. Google's ex-China share rose from 48 per cent to 55 per cent. These two are 'locomotives' which grow the market, but also deplete many smaller long-established digital publishers/media vendors.

We estimate the big agencies handle about a quarter of digital ad investment. Large advertisers buying without agencies – mostly e-commerce 'endemics' – might account for another five-10 per cent. The remainder is the long tail of self-serve advertisers too small to use agencies.

Digital media made advertising possible for many, and indeed brought many into existence. The long tail accounts for more than its share of new demand for digital advertising. This becomes more evident as larger advertisers are more likely to baulk at the rising risk, price and clutter inherent to a saturating market.

The digital advertising market has several characteristics likely to reinforce price inflation. Privacy and brand safety restrict ethical inventory. Header bidding and sellers moving from second- to first-price auction tend to realise higher prices. Having fewer points of external reference, the long tail is less price-sensitive.

Self-service, especially Facebook's, encourages large advertisers to replace big single campaigns with many shorter, smaller ones, making it less likely they will attract sufficient research support to measure branding intangibles. This encourages a focus on tangibles, and thus short-termism.

From this it is a short step to running one's whole business on the basis of the advertising cost of sales, disregarding the net present value of brand investment. This pathology may be rational, but proof of this is surprisingly scarce. It certainly suits the vendors, because it means the market runs on their rules.

A damaged advertising medium?

Well-publicised problems have barely affected digital's growth trajectory. In the UK, social media platforms such as Facebook, Instagram, Twitter, Snap and Google's YouTube were on track to capture about £3.3bn, or 25 per cent, of all digital media budgets in 2018, of which Facebook was expected to take about half. This represented growth of 24 per cent year-on-year.

Social networks offer advertisers impressive technical reach. In the UK, 40m, or 60 per cent of the population, are active on social media. Advertisers worry about the young turning away from traditional media, and social media is a ready replacement. Facebook itself is hardly immune to the changing habits and preferences of the young. Advertisers monitor the ageing profile of the Facebook brand, which Facebook Inc cleverly anticipated by acquiring Instagram and aping Snapchat.

We do not know as much about the quality of digital reach as we are used to in other media. 'Walled gardens' do not disclose their natural usage patterns, perhaps fearing this would reveal, for example, 20 per cent of users account for 80 per cent of usage. Then there is dwell time: for example, you will be charged if only a single pixel of your Facebook video loads. And by definition, these walled gardens generally resist third-party verification unless they control it.

YouTube faced considerable obstacles in 2016-2018, mainly adjacency issues of brand advertising placed around inappropriate or illegal content. Automatic filters are not perfect, whether missing harmful context, or blocking good context such as journalism dealing with unsavoury subjects. Many larger advertisers paused their YouTube investment, but we think YouTube revenues continued growing throughout, despite that. Advertisers using YouTube for paid search avoid adjacency problems because they are bidding on keywords. Search comprises the majority of our own business with YouTube.

It is said about one in 20 Britons deleted their Facebook accounts after the Cambridge Analytica scandal, but it's likely many have since returned. Users arrange much of their digital worlds within Facebook's walled garden, from consuming news content to buying clothes, like a portal in the 'olden days'.

Facebook and YouTube still have work to do. Trust between them across consumers and advertisers has been damaged, but not irrevocably. Users of social media are now more aware they are party to a value exchange, responsible for setting their own limits, and entitled to expect that any data harvested is handled responsibly and openly.

The introduction of GDPR in 2018 underlined that year as the year consumers were encouraged to become conscious that the trails they leave in the digital represent both risk and reward. The ability to reach an audience with high levels of intelligence and targeting is hugely valuable to advertisers. Facebook has the unique ability to connect usage on different devices to individual profiles, offering advertisers credible cross-device activation.

Facebook allows advertisers to analyse post-impression audience behaviour on Facebook-defined audiences in the Facebook domain, and allows advertisers to build new audience profiles from this. It does not however allow detailed information to leave its walls to be analysed or 'ingested' elsewhere. All it allows is aggregations, which may not reveal as much as the advertiser hoped.

The affects of brand safety considerations

Digital advertisers have become more concerned about audience delivery and less about environment or quality of content, hand-in-hand with the rise of blind programmatic buying, complicated supply chains and less and less transparency. We have seen intermediaries adding little or no value to transactions, but extracting huge undisclosed fees for their trouble. Advertisers should only invest where digital advertising has a real opportunity to be seen, by a person, within the right target audience, in compliance with data protection regulations, and in an appropriate editorial environment – noting neither premium nor quality guarantees brand safety.

We help advertisers assess their risk appetite and from this devise strategy and mitigation.

Executing brand safety entails all elements of digital media quality (ad blocking, ad fraud, contextual placement and viewability) and data protection (both client and consumer), using technology, tools and buying models.

There is never a 100 per cent safe solution, and any promises of such merit scrutiny. Strategy must therefore include cures and countermeasures for brand safety emergencies. Brand safety is but one risk attending digital media. Less obvious others are that over-specialisation impairs objectivity, or that the chain of command lacks capacity for or otherwise discourages critical scrutiny of such as objective setting, opportunity cost or cost/benefit analysis.

The importance of quality media environments

In mid-2017, GroupM began a collaboration with Newsworks, the marketing body for the UK's national newspaper brands, to see if there was a positive correlation between the quality of the environment in which ads are delivered and the impact on brand metrics. The research took in more than 400m exposures to 84 digital advertising campaigns across nine months in all categories, generating more than 80,000 survey responses. Metrics and Cint (an online insight marketplace researcher) independently tracked evidence including brand awareness, ad recall, brand perception and recommendation intent. The aim was to identify the most positive impacts on digital ad campaigns and demonstrate the effect of premium inventory, delivered in a quality environment, against a control of inventory acquired from blind networks.

Eighty two per cent of ads in the premium inventory bought directly from media owners were seen compared with 52 per cent from networks, or 33 per cent if one insisted on third-party validation. Premium environments make ads stand out much better too: 42 per cent more likely to be delivered fully in view, 63 per cent more likely to be delivered better than 50 per cent in view, 58 per cent more likely to be in view for more than five seconds, 98 per cent more likely to be delivered above the fold and if not, then 165 per cent more likely to be brought into view by the user.

Advertisers would attach no value to a poster with half missing or a 30-second TV spot played out for only two seconds. Yet these pass for billable impressions in digital. It's a status quo, which suits tech platforms and discriminates against premium environments in which users have greater engagement with content. Buyer, beware.

Does viewability matter?

Some companies claim two seconds of a video ad delivers half of the impact of an ad viewed in full. Two seconds is an arbitrary cut-off validated by spurious, if well-intentioned, industry standards. It is no surprise to learn that research cannot back this up, convenient though it would be for tech and social platforms and for user-generated content and for environments where users are not fully engaged, in which users scroll through huge columns of content that barely detains them. It is said these columns can be the height of Big Ben, or even the Empire State Building, but in any case, they are filled with ads, hardly any of which are actually seen, but for which advertisers have often paid.

Our Newsworks research revealed that fully in-view ads delivered a seven per cent uplift in brand awareness and eight per cent on recall compared to ads not fully in view. If an ad was in view for at least five seconds, the uplift was six per cent and eight per cent respectively. Above-the-fold vs. below-the-fold supplied an uplift of five per cent on brand awareness and 14 per cent on ad recall. The best brand tracking uplifts came from ads that were 100 per cent in view for over five seconds, and above the fold, and in view for 30 seconds or more.

GroupM and Newsworks wanted to find out whether premium inventory can provide greater value for clients in improving brand metrics – and the research discovered that uplifts on premium inventory beat the control on all measured categories. They were 10 per cent better on brand awareness, nearly 20 per cent for ad recall, 10 per cent for brand perception and recommendations: double-digit uplifts for all criteria.

The future

Digital media management is surprisingly labour-intensive: to many, an optimiser still means a human rather than a machine. Workflow automation, with the goal of faster decision-making, is vital to liberate labour for higher-value tasks, and there is not nearly enough of it. The more common approach has been to look for cheaper labour.

It is fashionable to argue consumer goods brands should develop direct-to-consumer communications. It is however hard even just to tag websites. Very few advertisers can yet manage this dynamically. The technology exists, but the data is siloed. Netflix is perhaps the best example. The question whether mass personalisation is worth the effort is therefore still unanswered, but its value is likely to rise as high-quality audience touchpoints grow more elusive or expensive.

Most people will agree that advertisers and buyers are operating in a murky world, in which long, complicated and costly supply chains marginalise publishers, the sole creators of fundamental value. GroupM is therefore calling on the premium publishers – companies that create content employing professionally trained and qualified journalists, which operate under strict regulation for what can and cannot be published – to join together and provide viable alternative ways of creating value for advertisers.

Note on the contributor

Tom George is CEO of GroupM UK

Legal, decent, honest, truthful...and trustworthy?

Agnes Nairn explains how digitisation has changed the advertising landscape forever. It is eroding trust in unexpected ways and posing potential threats not just to the £120bn advertising industry but arguably to serious journalism. What needs to happen next?

The date is January 29, 2017, the location is the Internet Advertising Bureau's annual leadership meeting in Florida. Marc Pritchard, Procter and Gamble's influential Chief Branding Officer drops a bombshell and the aftershock is still being felt. The world's top advertising spender (an estimated annual $7bn) declares to his assembled fellow advertisers that "We serve ads to consumers through a non-transparent media supply chain with spotty compliance to common standards, unreliable measurement, hidden rebates and new inventions like bot and methbot fraud," adding that "We have a media supply chain that is murky at best and fraudulent at worst." (Campaign Live, 2017). No one has argued with this conclusion in the ensuing 18 months.

This chapter examines how this has happened, what it means for advertising and journalism and what needs to happen next. Over the autumn and winter of 2017/18 the House of Lord's Select Committee on Communications investigated the 'murky supply chain' as part of a broader inquiry into the future of the advertising industry. I was the special advisor and some of what follows is drawn from the published proceedings of that inquiry (House of Lords, 2018).

Advertising pre and post digitisation

Pre digitisation, advertising followed content. If a brand sought a particular demographic, its media buyers located the content most widely read, watched or listened to by that target group, and paid for the privilege of placing an advert. The media got the money to produce good content, the advertiser got the consumers it needed for profits, and everyone was happy. Post digitisation, advertising follows people, while content – in the worst case scenario – is simply clickbait, used to lure the largest audience to be served up to advertisers. And as host websites are paid per click, the advertising ecosystem has attracted fraudulent activity in the shape of bots (automated clicking software) including large scale organised crime such as Methbot (Bornyakov, 2017) which, according to the News Media Association (2018), created 250,000 fake websites and half a million fake users to defraud advertisers of between $3m and $5m a day. The media don't get the money, the advertisers don't get access to consumers, and no one is happy.

Finding an immediate solution to this is not easy as there is little agreement over the extent of this ad fraud. Phil Smith of ISBA (the body that represents advertisers such as Procter and Gamble) told the House of Lords inquiry committee that "the estimates vary so much depending on the vested interests you ask. Some people will tell you 2 per cent and some tell you way more than 50 per cent, and that is a very big range" (Smith, 2018, pp. 376). In terms of monetary loss to the industry he reported a global estimate of $6.5bn from a study by the National Association of Advertisers in the US. However, another witness to the inquiry (Thinkbox, 2018) referred to a well-publicised WPP study (Stewart, 2017) that put the figure at $16.4bn. To understand why no one agrees we have to take a closer look at how digital has altered the advertising industry supply chain.

Digital supply chain: robots, middlemen and money

Between 2005 and 2016 digital advertising leapt from eight per cent to 48 per cent of total UK advertising spend whilst print plummeted from 39 per cent to 11 per cent (House of Lords, 2018, p10). Some estimate that digital now makes up 57.3 per cent of all advertising (Chisholm, 2018). However, a radical change in the way advertising is traded had accompanied the shift in money. Super speedy robots now sit at the heart of the process and by 2019 80-90 per cent of UK online advertising is expected to be traded programmatically usually through a process called real-time bidding (IAB UK, 2018). The transaction itself is accomplished in milliseconds inside ad exchanges, which are digital market places where trade is enacted between advertisers and media owners through automated real-time auctions.

When an individual visits a webpage, all known information on that person, from the myriad sources in the supply chain, is fed to the exchange and advertisers enter into a bidding war with the highest bidder's ad being served up to the visitor. According to James Collier (2018) of Prism, 400 or 500 advertisers may be bidding for access to a single individual as they land on a website. Because this process is fast, furious, automated and complex a host of new facilitating intermediaries have sprung up. Jim Chisholm's chapter in this book ('A familiar story – but will the outcome be any different?') includes graphics (his figures 6 and 7) that illustrate the actors and the money flow.

Thousands of organisations offer a busy new range of services: trading desks; data management platforms; demand side platforms; ad exchanges; supply side platforms; and other smaller intermediary functions such as data suppliers and data aggregators. Each business, of course, takes a cut. According to Jim Chisholm

(2018) and Guardian News and Media (2018) whereas pre digitisation the media (publisher) would have received 90 per cent of ad spend revenue – after the 10 per cent commission paid to the advertising agency – this has now reduced to 30 per cent. The remaining 60 per cent is spread across the new actors. The structure and speed of this eco-system has two consequences: advertisers and consumers/citizens can no longer see where data and money are flowing and media funding for quality content is drastically reduced.

Implications of the 'murky supply chain' for Advertisers

The new supply chain brings two problems for advertisers. First, they are unable to produce reliable ROI figures as they do not really know across how many different parties their spend has been distributed or how to measure the effectiveness of each transaction (Sky UK, 2018). Apart from the core issue of ad fraud described at the start of this chapter, advertisers are unsure if they should measure clicks, attention paid to ads, emotion generated by ads or viewability, which according to IAB means 50 per cent of the ad being in view for two consecutive seconds (Sky UK, 2018). The second implication is that advertisers have limited control over where their ads will appear meaning that they can appear next to offensive sites. This ad misplacement is of huge concern to the owners of mass family brands with wholesome reputations to protect such as Unilever (Shields, 2017).

Threat to citizen privacy

For citizens, the biggest problem with the new supply chain is the difficulty in tracking the responsible use of their personal data. The ad exchange process relies on a plethora of fine grained demographic, psychographic and behaviour data on consumers gathered from across innumerable platforms, sites and databases and brought together in the real time bidding process. GDPR has only just been implemented, but it is not clear that this really address the aggregated use of consumer data. The Cambridge Analytica scandal has lifted the lid on this issue, but this doesn't mean that we are any closer to understanding what's inside the box.

The 'duopoly' of Facebook and Google

At this point it is worth addressing the role of the two most dominant organisations in the new advertising eco-system: Facebook and Google. According to James Collier (2018) Google alone, which operates at various stages of the supply chain through Double Click, owns between 80 per cent and 85 per cent of the ad tech market. This dominance is problematic. In June 2017 the European Commission fined Google and its parent Alphabet €2.4bn for contravening EU anti-trust rules by giving illegal advantage in search results to its own shopping service (European Commission, 2017). Whilst Google remonstrated to the House of Lords inquiry that they were in competition with a wide range of other large players such as Amazon, Snap, Adobe, Oracle, News Corp and WPP (Cohen, 2018) Tobin Ireland

(2018) pointed out that while technically there is an opportunity for competition, in reality it is severely curtailed: "Facebook and Google, the duopoly, have earned their market share by providing better tools, better data and better environment, which drives higher advertising performance … It does not mean there is not an opportunity to compete with that; it means the bar is pretty high." (pp. 506). But perhaps this is a rather generous view given that in July 2018 the Commission hit Google with another fine of €4.34bn (the annual EU contribution of the Netherlands) for what it sees as "illegally locking down" Android phones (worth 74% of the mobile phone market) in what the competition commissioner referred to as "a Google controlled ecosystem" (Griffin and Stone, 2018).

It also means that gaining access to the inner workings of the supply chain can be effectively blocked by any lack of co-operation from the duopoly, leaving the use of citizen data remarkably opaque. Moreover, the privacy relationship between the duopoly and the citizen perhaps still leaves something to be desired. As Phil Smith (2018) of ISBA noted, "There is something around the way in which the platforms have struck their relationship with consumers when they go advertising-free first and then introduce advertising over time, where the contract is not quite as transparent as it has been in other media" (pp. 380).

Blurring the line between advertising and content

Google owns YouTube, which brings with it new formats of advertising as well as new supply chains. These are also somewhat murky. Take 'social influencer' advertising, which is a digital spin on celebrity endorsement (think Nike and the world's top athletes) but the celebrities are famous simply because they have amassed a YouTube following of people who are interested in what they do, where they go and what they buy.

Of course advertisers have rushed to pay the influencers to recommend their products on their YouTube channels. This is legitimate as long as (according to the Advertising Standards Authority Codes) viewers can clearly distinguish between advertising and content. The problem is that they can't. There is currently no uniform way of labelling native or social influencer advertising so that citizens become confused and ultimately annoyed (Hardy, 2018).

The Lords committee recommended that "… the Advertising Standards Authority should create a universal, mandatory logo to signify wherever online content has been sponsored by a brand. It should enforce the use of the logo next to any paid for text or video" (House of Lords, 2018, pp. 25). It remains to be seen what the ASA will do. There will certainly be industry opposition to the recommendation because it suits the advertisers not to label. The minute we are aware that a communication is advertising our scepticism is engaged; we tend to trust messages that are from 'people like us' and not from those with vested commercial interests. As influencer Beckii Cruel (2018) told the inquiry, "the audience trust what you (the influencer) are saying, they trust that you will promote only things you believe in yourself." But of course money can sway what someone 'believes in' and she admitted that many influencers just 'do it for the money.'

Implications for quality journalism

We have a situation where advertisers are unclear where their money is going or whether it is well spent; brands are fearful that their adverts will end up next to undesirable content; and consumers/citizens don't know who has got their data or whether or not they are being advertised to.

The media meanwhile are left with a mere 30 per cent of the revenue that they would expect from the previous supply chain model. This doesn't leave much to commission serious journalism and quality content.

Granted, not all media funding comes from advertising and not all advertising is digital but programmatic advertising and the likely ensuing murky supply chain may become the norm in more traditional types of advertising. According to Zenith Media (2017) an estimated $5.6bn would be spent programmatically across television, radio, cinema and outdoor in the US in 2017 representing six per cent of total ad expenditure in these media. Will this mean that only subscription-funded content will be trustworthy? And how many people will pay for their news and other content now that they are used to getting it for free (or at least, in the case of the BBC, for the cost of a licence fee)?

What happens next?

It seems to me that no one stands to win from this opaque supply chain. Our trust in brands, adverts, news and journalism is fast being eroded. We need regulation and we need it quickly. The industry has responded by creating Jicwebs (Joint Industry Committee for Web Standards) that has already agreed some principles on viewability, brand safety and ad fraud. But Google and Facebook are not members and the initiative is entirely voluntary.

The inquiry recommended that the largest players should commit to signing up and that the industry should give Jicwebs greater power to create and enforce rules. Beyond that, they recommended that if they failed to do this, that Government should propose legislation (House of Lords, 2018, pp. 20). Intriguingly, Government has responded (House of Lords, 2018a, pp. 1) that, whilst this issue will be pursued in the ongoing Digital Charter, they would produce a White Paper later in the year and that "in this context, potential areas where we might consider legislating include online advertising."

Other important recommendations included asking the Competition and Markets Authority (CMA) to conduct a market study of digital advertising to ascertain if it really is working fairly for consumers and business (pp. 23/24); and asking the Government to use its Digital Charter to gather evidence on whether, given the dominance of Google and Facebook, "current competition law is adequate to regulate the 21st century digital economy that is increasingly driven by personal data rather than money" (pp. 24). Government has committed (although without timeframe) to using the Digital Charter to this end (House of Lords, 2018a); has also lobbed the issue onto the agenda of the Cairncross Review due to report in early 2019 but, significantly, is reluctant to use its power to direct CMA to conduct a market study 'in exceptional circumstances' (pg. 2). Yet these would appear to be circumstances of a decidedly exceptional nature and I, for one, will be awaiting with interest the next steps taken by the Government, industry and regulators alike.

References

ASA Broadcast Code on recognition of advertising: https://www.asa.org.uk/asset/6E7AAA50-4828-4611-B28FF16AFA089D28.5D2425F6-1196-434E-91F364F2841DDF9D/ ASA Non Broadcast Code on recognition of advertising: https://www.asa.org.uk/asset/1DB5B325-1581-4DD0-9A1E2CE1A4D1704B/, accessed June 30, 2018.

Bornyakov, Alex (2017) Methbot: The beginning of the end for digital ad fraud, Martech Today, January 17. Available online at https://martechtoday.com/methbot-beginning-end-digital-ad-fraud-194142, accessed June 27, 2018.

Campaign Live (2017) Marc Pritchard's full speech from IAB Leadership Meeting, January 29, 2017 in Florida. Available online at https://www.campaignlive.co.uk/article/procter-gamble-chief-issues-powerful-media-transparency-rallying-cry/1422599, accessed June 27, 2018.

Chisholm, Jim (2018) Written Evidence, House of Lords Select Committee on Communications, Inquiry: UK Advertising in a Digital Age. Evidence Volume, pp 147. Available online at https://www.parliament.uk/documents/lords-committees/communications/advertising-industry/theadvertisingindustry.pdf, accessed June 28, 2018.

Cohen, Adam (2018) Oral Evidence, House of Lords Select Committee on Communications, Inquiry: UK Advertising in a Digital Age. Evidence Volume, pp 233. Available online at https://www.parliament.uk/documents/lords-committees/communications/advertising-industry/theadvertisingindustry.pdf, accessed June 28, 2018.

Collier, James (2018) Oral Evidence, House of Lords Select Committee on Communications, Inquiry: UK Advertising in a Digital Age. Evidence Volume, pp 82. Available online at https://www.parliament.uk/documents/lords-committees/communications/advertising-industry/theadvertisingindustry.pdf, accessed June 28, 2018.

Cruel, Beckii (2018) Oral Evidence, House of Lords Select Committee on Communications, Inquiry: UK Advertising in a Digital Age. Evidence Volume, pp 169. Available online at https://www.parliament.uk/documents/lords-committees/communications/advertising-industry/theadvertisingindustry.pdf, accessed June 28, 2018.

European Commission (2017) Antitrust: Commission fines Google €2.42 billion for abusing dominance as search engine by giving illegal advantage to own comparison shopping service, September 27. Available online at http://europa.eu/rapid/press-release_IP-17-1784_en.htm, accessed June 28, 2018.

Griffin, Andrew and Jon Stone (2018) Google Hit with Record-Breaking $5 Billion Fine Over Android Web Browsing and Told to Change How Phones Work, Independent, 18 July 2018. Available online at https://www.independent.co.uk/life-style/gadgets-and-tech/news/google-android-fine-latest-billion-eu-european-commission-browser-chrome-web-a8452481.html, accessed August 6, 2018.

Guardian News and Media (2018) Written Evidence, House of Lords Select Committee on Communications, Inquiry: UK Advertising in a Digital Age. Evidence Volume, pp 254. Available online at https://www.parliament.uk/documents/lords-committees/communications/advertising-industry/theadvertisingindustry.pdf, accessed June 27, 2018.

Hardy, Jonathan (2018) Oral Evidence, House of Lords Select Committee on Communications, House of Lords (2018) UK advertising in a digital age, 11 April 2018. Available online at https://publications.parliament.uk/pa/ld201719/ldselect/ldcomuni/116/11602.htm, accessed June 27, 2018.

House of Lords (2018a) UK advertising in a digital age. Government Response, 16 July 2018. Available online at https://www.parliament.uk/documents/lords-committees/communications/advertising-industry/ukadvertisinggovresponse160718.pdf accessed August 6, 2018.

Inquiry: UK Advertising in a Digital Age. Evidence Volume, pp 291. Available online at https://www.parliament.uk/documents/lords-committees/communications/advertising-industry/theadvertisingindustry.pdf, accessed June 28, 2018.

IAB UK (2018) Written Evidence, House of Lords Select Committee on Communications, Inquiry: UK Advertising in a Digital Age. Evidence Volume, pp 409. Available online at https://www.parliament.uk/documents/lords-committees/communications/advertising-industry/theadvertisingindustry.pdf, accessed June 27, 2018.

Ireland, Tobin (2018) Oral Evidence, House of Lords Select Committee on Communications, Inquiry: UK Advertising in a Digital Age. Evidence Volume, pp 506. Available online at https://www.parliament.uk/documents/lords-committees/communications/advertising-industry/theadvertisingindustry.pdf, accessed June 28, 2018.

McCarthy (2017) Programmatic usage to ascend to two thirds of global digital display market by 2019, The Drum, 20 November. Available online at http://www.thedrum.com/news/2017/11/20/programmatic-usage-ascend-two-thirds-global-digital-display-market-2019, accessed June 27. 2018.

News Media Association (2018) Written Evidence, House of Lords Select Committee on Communications, Inquiry: UK Advertising in a Digital Age. Evidence Volume, pp 447. Available online at https://www.parliament.uk/documents/lords-committees/communications/advertising-industry/theadvertisingindustry.pdf, accessed June 27, 2018

Shields, Ronan (2017) Unilever CMO: 'We've got to be able to see over the walled gardens',

The Drum, 25 September. Available online at: http://www.thedrum.com/news/2017/09/25/unilever-cmo-we-ve-got-be-able-see-over-the-walled-gardens, accessed June 28, 2018

Sky UK (2018) Written Evidence, House of Lords Select Committee on Communications, Inquiry: UK Advertising in a Digital Age. Evidence Volume, pp 476. Available online at https://www.parliament.uk/documents/lords-committees/ communications/advertising-industry/theadvertisingindustry.pdf , accessed June 27, 2018.

Smith, Phil (2018) Oral, House of Lords Select Committee on Communications, Inquiry: UK Advertising in a Digital Age. Evidence Volume, pp 376. Available online at https://www.parliament.uk/documents/lords-committees/communications/advertising-industry/theadvertisingindustry.pdf , accessed June 27, 2018.

Stewart, Rebecca (2017) Ad fraud may cost industry $16.4bn in 2017 says study as questions continue about self-governance, The Drum, March 15. Available online at http://www.thedrum.com/news/2017/03/15/ad-fraud-may-cost-industry-164bn-2017-says-study-questions-continue-about-self, accessed June 30, 2018.

Think Box (2018) Written Evidence, House of Lords Select Committee on Communications, Inquiry: UK Advertising in a Digital Age. Evidence Volume, pp 528. Available online at https://www.parliament.uk/documents/lords-committees/communications/advertising-industry/theadvertisingindustry.pdf , accessed June 27, 2018.

Zenith Media (2017) 67 per cent of digital display to be sold programmatically by 2019, November 19. Available online at https://www.zenithmedia.com/programmatic-marketing-forecasts/, accessed June 28, 2018

Note on the contributor

Agnes Nairn is Professor of Marketing in the School of Management, University of Bristol. Previously she was Dean of Hult International Business School in London after ten years pursuing a portfolio career dividing her time between policy consultancy and a post as Professor of Marketing at EMLyon Business School in France. She has worked with organisations such as UN, UNICEF, and government departments in England, Scotland, France, USA and Brazil as well as businesses such as Coca-Cola and Unilever. Work with David Cameron's Strategy Unit led directly to the banning of child peer-to-peer marketing while her 2007 work for the National Consumer Council is now used on the GCSE Home Economics curriculum. Her most recent policy work was for the Economist Intelligence Unit: a cost-benefit analysis of banning child-directed advertising in Brazil and in 2017/18 she was Specialist Adviser to the House of Lords Communication Committee's Inquiry into the Advertising Industry. www.agnesnairn.co.uk.

Section Four

Social media and politics

* * *

How has social media has transformed politics and democracy and what are the consequences across the globe?

Tor Clark

Social media has transformed politics and democracy across the world. For at least the last decade it has had a growing influence in political decision-making. The misuse of social media has been accused of playing perhaps critical parts in key electoral contests such as the election of Donald Trump to the US presidency in 2016 and the knife-edge majority for the UK to leave the EU in the Brexit Referendum in the UK that same year. But how did we get to this point and what really does it mean for democracy?

Take the conduct of politics and voting behaviour in the UK as an example. Back in the day, in post-war Britain, the old theories of political socialisation told us, most of us were politically tribal and voted according to our socio-economic background. To be brought up working class was a major predictor of Labour voting and coming from a middle class background encouraged loyalty to the Conservatives. A smaller sector of the electorate voted on principle, seemingly at odds with their social background, giving us working class Conservatives and middle class intellectual socialists.

So the most interesting group of voters was the small number who defied their class background and any firmly held principles to switch between parties at different elections. These floating voters were of course the ones who made elections interesting and gave us regular changes of government, allowing power to regularly switch between the two major political parties.

This group decided who got to rule us and, crucially, it was presumed they made their political decisions based on their knowledge of politics largely gleaned from political journalism, through newspapers and broadcast news.

Whilst much of the UK press was – and remains – politically partisan, we generally thought we could trust TV news to offer us a relatively fair view of UK politics and politicians, especially during general elections. Perhaps because of this

TV was considered the most influential journalistic medium and because it was bound by law to be fair and balanced, the way undecided voters made political choices was, theoretically, in safe hands.

But, as the influence of the partisan press has waned dramatically, so technological development has brought us a completely new medium, social media, to influence politics. And social media has emerged dramatically onto the scene as those traditional links between class and party have unravelled and the number of viable political parties has grown, which leaves an ever larger section of the electorate – perhaps now even a majority – searching new areas of digital media for material on which to make their serious political decisions.

On the negative side, much political social media is partisan, personal and polemical. Much of it does not sign up to professional journalistic norms of truth, accuracy and balance. But on the plus side, social media offers a platform to voices excluded by monopolistic ownership of traditional media, especially the press, and entry to the political conversation to voices not admitted to a traditional media dominated by professional journalists.

Social media is clearly increasingly important and influential in politics and voting choices, but is that a good or a bad development for journalism and society?

Ivor Gaber, Professor of Political Journalism at the University of Sussex, thinks the influence is generally negative. Gaber, a former political journalist, fears the rise of social media has actually taken the process of political decision-making by ordinary people backwards. He thinks Twitter's character limit:

> "…*gives Twitter its essential characteristics of simplicity, impulsivity and incivility, the characteristics which have come to form a toxic combination which, in the political sphere has, almost inevitably, led to establishing the primacy of emotion over reason.*"

Gaber notes the obvious, perhaps game-changing, use of Twitter by Donald Trump in his successful US presidential campaign of 2016, but also its impact on crucial UK political decisions, especially the EU Referendum of the same year. He says:

> "*Constant derogatory references during the Brexit referendum to 'experts', 'Brussels' and the 'metropolitan elite' certainly contained strong resonances of contempt – as has the language subsequently employed in the ongoing debate between 'Leavers' and 'Remainers', still raging two years after the vote.*"

So it is well-established social media has had a major and transformative impact on politics. Vincent Campbell is an expert on the interaction of politics, journalism and technology in political communication. His case study of the New Left Media (NLM) notes the huge and recent growth in influence of these social media platforms.

"In the wake of the EU vote and through the 2017 General Election, these sites saw typical traffic in the hundreds of thousands of readers, matching mainstream news media outlets' social media reach for leading individual stories on a regular basis… the NLM potentially represents a substantive shift in Britain's political social media landscape."

But in rejecting the aspects of traditional media which it despises, especially right-wing partisanship of much of press, NLM may have contributed to a rejection of all traditional media, including that which at least tries to be objective, impartial, balanced and fair, leaving social media-using voters with only highly partisan voices from which to choose. It is, argues Campbell, a classic example of the law of unintended consequences, and as such has perhaps damaged our political system. He concludes:

"A combination of rejecting impartiality, constant critiquing of institutions supposed to be operating according to that principle, combined with the aping of successful right-wing populist media strategies for garnering audiences suggests Britain might be beginning to move towards a landscape built around more polarised, adversarial and advocacy journalism than it has been used to for most of the post-WWII period."

Following nicely from Campbell, Sean Dodson of Leeds Beckett University has made a detailed study of The Canary, one of the best-known leftist social media political actors, and finds it maintains a strong reliance on the traditional media it claims to despise. He says:

"…as awareness of The Canary grew, two things became apparent. First, it displayed a zealous over-protectiveness of Jeremy Corbyn and the populist movement that surrounds the Labour leader. And, secondly, it distrusted the mainstream media while yet producing pages full of content taken from the very organisations it purported to 'hate'."

Dodson found despite its relative freshness, many commentators thought:

"…The Canary represented the latest example of a 'filter bubble', the intellectually isolating phenomenon of presenting only a single side to each story and that, furthermore, The Canary was free largely of traditional journalistic standards, such as balance and fairness."

Faced with worrying findings on the practice and influence of these new social media-based political actors, Australian academic Denis Muller from the University of Melbourne, suggests a remedy – Open Discourse theory. He explains:

"Open Discourse theory… requires a renewed commitment by professional mass media to certain ethical norms, in particular verification, impartiality, editorial independence, pluralism and respect for persons."

The increased influence of partisan aspects of social media, whether individual or platforms, requires traditional media to 'step-up' on behalf of the public, Muller urges:

"Open Discourse theory posits that in the face of these developments the professional mass media have a responsibility to recognise it is they who, because of long-established experience, extensive reach, market power, brand identification and privileges, are called upon to provide a reliable and respectful informational basis for a common conversation among citizens, and to exert a gatekeeping function."

If this can be done, he concludes positively, traditional media may be able to:

"...provide a shared body of reliable information necessary to democratic life, provide a platform on which a range of opinions can be expressed, and so become a means by which communities engage in a common conversation on matters of common interest and concern, countering social media's echo-chamber effect and the fragmentation of the public conversation."

And it's not just the use of social media to influence the public which is causing concern. The abusive use of social media against UK Members of Parliament has been investigated in detail by Amy Binns, journalism academic at the University of Central Lancashire. She detects worrying levels of abuse but demystifies some of the perceived trends:

"...hostility on Twitter crosses demographic and party groups; and is not a problem for only one party, sex or race. It is fed by publicity on and off Twitter, so increases for people with higher profiles. It is also notably an issue for Labour MPs who criticise Jeremy Corbyn."

And Dr Binns worries about the impact this unregulated abuse of public servants may have on their calibre in the future, asking:

"Could an online climate of hostility result in more sensitive people being reluctant to enter public life? If so, this would leave our most important institutions to the more thick-skinned or even arrogant who are least likely to care about criticism."

Social media had a huge influence on peacetime politics, but it's also a new and important weapon of war, argues Greg Rowett, Research Fellow at the Institute for Statecraft. He says:

"Where social media has had a truly revolutionary, fundamental, effect on warfare is in the realm of information warfare."

The importance of the information war has several good historical examples, argues Rowett and the use of social media has merely increased the power of this tool. He adds:

"...with these technologies, there exists a tool which can be used to sculpt the moral forces of a population in a way that bypasses all the institutionalised resistances and physical defences that the state and a military can muster. The failure to turn

their physical superiority into a moral one is why the US and the USSR could not accomplish their goals in their respective wars in Vietnam and Afghanistan."

The use of social media to influence politics in of course not just a Western phenomenon. The two final authors in this section give us a flavour of its impact in two widely differing parts of the world, Africa and China.

Tatenda Chitagu, an award-winning and respected journalist working for many years in Zimbabwe, notes the impact of social media on the July 2018 elections in post-Mugabe Zimbabwe and the similarity of that impact with other nations. He says:

"While social media has increased citizen's voices and participation in recent elections, its communicative potential has been threatened by fake news, cyber propaganda by political parties and their activists, along with the spread of hate speech and vulgarity by opponents."

The positive use of social media has exposed a digital divide in his country between the digitally-connected and generally better educated urban population and the largely unconnected majority rural communities. But even for the people who are served by social media, some of its problems are very familiar, says Chitagu:

"While social media also gave rise to citizen journalism, this has created problems because they are unethical and attack rivals. Trolls, bots, doxing and online harassment by paid cyber troops, who also attacked women candidates… also diluted the socialness of social media in the election, especially in the wake of lack of digital security by netizens. Because of structural sexism and misogyny, there was a sharp rise in technology-related violence against women and its normalisation has made the use of the internet a gender issue."

Social media use is huge in China, with major platforms such as Weibo and WeChat incredibly popular, especially among younger Chinese people. Dipsy Edmunds has a deep knowledge of the sophisticated operation of social media in his country. He explains:

"Many don't realise that censorship across the Chinese internet is not just a wall to hide information, but is a growing and blunt system designed to influence social media to achieve the government's propaganda and monitoring desires."

With censorship so important in China, Edmunds points up the major differences between Chinese and Western social media operation:

"Government has three main aims with social media: the first is to provide online services; the second is to use digital surveillance to stop potential collective action; and the third is to use it as a propaganda tool."

So whether it is direct attempts to influence democracy as a semi-journalistic communication platform to voters, the use of social media by voters to interact positively, but more often negatively, with politicians or the attempts to control social media by the state, one thing is very clear; the influence of social media on politics is growing rapidly and therefore the possibility that misuse of social media is distorting democracy and acting against the will of the people is ever more apparent and possible. It is for politicians, voters and the users of social media to decide how far the benefits of social media weigh up against the obvious problems it brings.

Why Twitter loves a bad 'un

Far from ushering in a new era of an inclusive and positive public sphere, social media, especially Twitter, have been responsible for a contemptuous tone dominating contemporary political debate, laments Professor Ivor Gaber

The dream that died

A long time ago in a galaxy far, far away, maybe even a galaxy where there was no Trump or Brexit, there existed starry-eyed dreamers who saw, in the rise of social media, the creation of the nirvana of media studies – the digital public sphere. The concept of the public sphere was first formulated by the German social philosopher Jurgen Habermas. In 1985, he looked back several hundred years to the days when, in the coffee houses of Paris, Berlin and London, wealthy merchants recreated an Athenian-type democracy as they argued about the events of the day and came to a considered view as to what their governments or rulers should do about current controversies.

Such a notion was always more 'ideal type' than reality but it became a useful theoretical concept for, at the very least, detailing just how lacking our modern democracies were in maintaining healthy public spheres. This failure was attributed to the distorting effects of capitalism, which through ownership and control of the media, so the theory went, ensured the public sphere put the interests of 'capitalists' and 'capitalism' before those of democracy and its citizenry. But Habermas did not give up hope entirely and, 20 years later, he came up with the notion of a new public sphere based on, what he called, 'communicative action'. This involved communication which was open and without intimidation in which differences were respected with the ultimate goal of finding the 'truth'. And there were some, dubbed cyber-utopians, who saw in the advent of the internet, a space where communicative action could form the basis of a revived public sphere – indeed, a digital public sphere.

Alas it was not to be. Political communication on the internet became dominated by social media, Twitter in particular, and all too soon became 'nasty, brutish and short' to misquote Thomas Hobbes. It was in 2006 that Twitter first flapped its wings in public, three years later came Angry Birds (no relation) and whilst Angry

Birds moved on, Twitter just got angrier, indeed Twitter is a far angrier place for political communications than Facebook, Instagram or all the other social media platforms. This is, according to US researcher Brian Ott, is mainly because of its 140-character (now 280) message limit. This limit gives Twitter its essential characteristics of simplicity, impulsivity and incivility, which, in the political sphere has, almost inevitably, led to establishing the primacy of emotion over reason.

Easy does it

Why should this be? First, simplicity is required because the character limitation means Twitter can never be a medium for communicating complicated, or nuanced, arguments. As Ott puts it: "A Tweet may be clever or witty, but it cannot be complex." Political messages which can be communicated in simple terms are very often just plain wrong, or so vacuous as to be meaningless: 'Take Back Control' for example, begs a hundred questions, to name but three – control from whom, to whom and for what purpose?

Second, tweeting can be, often is, an impulse activity. It is easily done from a smartphone whilst watching television or in the middle of some other activity, and it requires little or no consideration or concentration. A typical example of the perils of impulsivity on Twitter befell Lord Sugar – he of the UK 'Apprentice' fame. Whilst watching the World Cup Sugar tweeted (presumably as a joke) that the Senegalese football team reminded him of the young Africans he could see from his beach-side Marbella mansion, scratching out a living selling trinkets and contrabands. Apart from its lack of humour it was perceived to be racist and within hours he was forced to recant, delete and apologise. His impulsive Twitter activity being not dissimilar to that of his fellow Apprentice host in the US – with the one difference that the other chap never recants, deletes or apologises.

Third, and perhaps most significantly, in terms of the essential characteristics of Twitter behaviour, is its informality. This leads to what researchers describe as 'uncivil communication' – speech that is impolite, insulting, or just downright offensive. This arises because a tweet does not require the formal politeness that generally blunts any sharp rhetorical edges. It is, for example, difficult to begin a communication Dear etc. etc. and then lapse into the hostility and abuse which too often dominates political discussion in the Twittersphere. Twitter is also, a more or less, grammar-free zone. This means tweeters often write as they speak – a form of communication that tends not to lead to mature consideration as to how a tweet might be received: "It is much easier to say something nasty about someone when they are not physically present," says Ott and he quotes an American academic who tweeted: "Dear obese PhD applicants: if you didn't have the willpower to stop eating carbs, you won't have the willpower to do a dissertation #truth" – which led to the professor having to recant, delete and apologise.

Courting contempt

Turning to the 45th American President's specific use of Twitter, researcher David Redlawsk and colleagues looked at how Trump had used Twitter, not in the 2016 election against Hillary Clinton but in the primaries leading up to his nomination, specifically in the Iowa Caucus. Using sentiment analysis – software that measures the content of tweets – Redlawsk suggests Trump used Twitter largely to generate anger against his opponents, and not just anger but contempt as well. Contempt, argues Redlawsk, is an emotion arguably more powerful than simple anger. Anger is characterised by researchers as an 'attack' straightforward attacks can be rebutted and tend to have only a short-term affect. But contempt is an emotion of rejection – it is more difficult to rebut, since it is about innate qualities of a politician or party and hence normally has more long-lasting and profound affects.

In his Iowa research Redlawsk found 77 per cent of Republican voters described Trump's tweets as contemptuous; the next highest being attributed to Senator Ted Cruz, of whom 48 per cent of Republican voters described his tweets similarly. By comparison, Hillary Clinton and Bernie Sanders were each seen as expressing contempt by only 39 per cent of Democrat voters. Contempt is also a useful predictor of voting behaviour. Pollsters have long-established that anger with a particular candidate, or party, is a good measure of a negative voting intention but this latest research suggests contempt is an equally powerful indicator, and perhaps has a longer lasting effect too, since it reflects on the candidate or party's ongoing character, rather than their particular position on any transient policy issues.

In the US election the use of contempt by Trump was plain for all to see by his continued use of the 'crooked Hillary' line, which he tweeted almost continually and repeated in his platform speeches. Once a politician finds him or herself labelled 'crooked', other than saying 'I'm not', there is a precious little that he or she can do in terms of rebuttal, other than offering some variant of 'I'm not, but you are' – a response which is likely to evoke a yawn and/or a smile. The one way not to rebut was the one chosen by Clinton, when she rebutted by demonstrating her contempt not for Trump but for his supporters whom she labelled as the 'disreputables' – not an ideal way to win friends and influence voters. This generalised growth in contempt, fostered by one politician against another, is one explanation for the increasing polarisation of American politics we have witnessed since the rise of Twitter, though that is not to suggest a direct causal relationship – although perhaps Twitter might not have grown into such a potent political force in a less contemptuous climate.

Twist and Shout

Whilst there is no comparable research on the role of 'contempt' in British politics, and perhaps it is less of a factor, nonetheless constant derogatory references during the Brexit referendum to 'experts', 'Brussels' and the 'metropolitan liberal elite' certainly contained strong resonances of contempt – as has the language subsequently employed in the ongoing debate between 'Leavers' and 'Remainers', still raging two years after the vote.

A sentiment analysis on the language used on Twitter by the two sides during the Brexit referendum was undertaken by researchers at the London School of Economics. They discovered 'Leave' tweeters used language that was more negative, more proactive but that also offered more 'rewards' for voting their way than did the Remain camp whose language was found to be more tentative, passive and offered more qualifications than did those of Leave supporters. In other words, the Brexiteers painted their message in loud vivid colours whilst Remainers did not.

No analysis has been done as to any direct causal linkage between language on Twitter and voting behaviour but if, in the past, it was the brash Sun 'wot won it' for Mrs Thatcher and Mr Major's Conservatives, then clearly a similar brashness on Twitter seems to have worked equally as well during the Brexit referendum. Stieglitz and Dang Xuan, in a research project which analysed more than 165,000 tweets, found emotionally-charged Twitter messages tended to be retweeted more often and more quickly compared to neutral ones. Given such amplification, the conclusion reached by Brian Ott takes on an added significance. He wrote: "Twitter breeds dark, degrading, and dehumanizing discourse; it breeds vitriol and violence; in short, it breeds Donald Trump"– and, he might have added, Brexit as well.

References

Habermas, J. (1992) *The Structural Transformation of the Public Sphere: An Inquiry into a Category of Bourgeois Society* Cambridge, Polity Press

Brian L. Ott 2016 'The age of Twitter: Donald J. Trump and the politics of debasement' Critical Studies in Media Communication, 34:1, 59-68

David P. Redlawsk, Ira J. Roseman, Kyle Mattes & Steven Katz (2018) 'Donald Trump, contempt, and the 2016 GOP Iowa Caucuses' *Journal of Elections, Public Opinion and Parties*, Volume 28, 2018 - Issue 2

Stefan Stieglitz & Linh Dang-Xuan (2016) 'Emotions and Information Diffusion in Social Media—Sentiment of Microblogs and Sharing Behavior' in *Journal of Management Information Systems* Vol. 29 217-248 Published online: 08 Dec 2014

Note on the contributor

Ivor Gaber is Professor of Political Journalism at the University of Sussex and a former political journalist at the BBC, ITN, Channel Four and Sky News. He researched the impact of Twitter on the 2015 UK General Election and has just published Culture Wars: The Media and the British Left with James Curran and Julian Petley.

Social media, politics and the law of unintended consequences

Will voters' rapidly increasing use of exceptionally partisan social media instead of regulated broadcast media for political information have a corrosive effect on their attitudes to politics and democracy, asks Vincent Campbell

Although online media have been around for a couple of decades now and people have been writing about their impact on politics for the same period of time, in the British context that impact has been comparatively marginal until recently.

In the pre-social media, Web 1.0 era, use of new media in British politics, and elections in particular, were constrained by a range of factors. The 'pull' nature of traditional websites, meaning people actively had to seek out and find political material online, for instance, saw relatively small proportions of the electorate doing that. In the 2005 General Election campaign, for example, just three per cent of voters visited party websites (Ward and Lusoli 2005).

Spiralling costs of conventional political campaigning left parties initially unable to devote much time and effort to online activities, especially coupled with uncertainties about what online media could be used for, questions that still exist for parties today – are they for voter persuasion, supporter mobilisation, party membership management, and then which tools/techniques should be used to achieve these goals? (Campbell and Lee 2016). Whilst a highly partisan tabloid press has long been a point of contention both popularly and academically, high levels of trust in broadcast news media regulated by due impartiality requirements, especially during elections, also offered little impetus for the British electorate at large to seek information elsewhere. Even into the social media era thus far, the dominance of mainstream media has persisted, not only in terms of degrees of attention and trust for broadcast media (Newman et al. 2018) but also in terms of the role they play in framing and setting the agenda for elections, including setting the agenda for social media election coverage too (Chadwick et al. 2018).

Consequentially, some were asking 'whatever happened to the internet?' as recently as the 2010 General Election (Gibson, Williamson and Ward 2010) but since then an increasing role for social media has begun to emerge particularly in the wake of the polarisation of electorates in the Scottish Independence Referendum in 2014 and, at a larger scale, around the EU Referendum in 2016. A key emerging phenomenon, for instance, has been the New Left Media (NLM), a group of loosely affiliated news and politics focused online outlets, active primarily through social media platforms, and mixing individual bloggers (like *Another Angry Voice*) in with new journalism organisations like *Evolve Politics* (who joined the post-Leveson press regulator IMPRESS and has a correspondent in the Westminster Lobby). In the wake of the EU vote and through the 2017 General Election, these sites saw typical traffic in the hundreds of thousands of readers, matching mainstream news media outlets' social media reach for leading individual stories on a regular basis (Waterson 2017). Although some online outlets had achieved occasional notable interventions into the dominant political communication landscape prior to this, such as the right-wing populist blogger *Guido Fawkes*, the NLM potentially represents a substantive shift in Britain's political social media landscape.

Whose impacts? Whose values?

In many ways the rise of NLM offers a useful illustration of the problems of evaluating the impact of social media on politics. Debates in the popular mainstream have tended to be shaped by long-form commentaries making strident claims about impacts whether for good (Gillmor, 2006), or ill (Morozov, 2011). Academic research too has often found itself empirically examining claims about impacts within this overtly normative framework, with cyber 'optimists', 'pessimists' and 'realists' along a continuum of positions discussing reams of data and evidence that, at minimum, complicate, and sometimes even outright refute, some of the widely circulating popular beliefs about social media (Elvestad and Phillips, 2018). Studies of the latest popular labels around social media news and politics, such as the debate around fake news still reflect that underlying normative perspective (McNair, 2018, Fletcher et al., 2018). Indeed, this is arguably entirely to be expected when looking with a longer historical gaze at the extent to which normative values have always closely related to evaluations of new media technologies' impacts whether that be, say, television (e.g. Postman's *Amusing Ourselves to Death* in 1985), or even as far back as the telegraph which many, at the time believed would render global conflict obsolete (Standage 1998).

The value systems which underpin appraisals of the impact of social media are thus crucially important in shaping how, both popularly and academically, impacts are framed, and these value systems have deeper roots stretching back way before the technologies that are, in effect, only the proximate causes of any possible changes in the conduct of politics. Indeed, the interaction between underlying values and technologies, in how and why technologies are created and used, in turn contribute to the shaping of the impacts of those technologies. Thus, predictions or claims of impacts are essentially reflections of the values of those making the predictions/claims.

Looking at the rise of NLM in this context, they arguably constitute both a clear example of the intersection between existing values and new technological affordances on the one hand, and how the impacts of those interactions aren't necessarily predictable on the other. Their relative significance in terms of reach is a good initial illustration of how values shape perceptions of impact. Waterson's article points to how stories from these sites sometimes reach millions of readers but the recent Reuters Institute Digital News Report 2018 regards their reach as 'very low' at around two per cent of weekly usage compared to, for instance, 43 per cent for BBC news online (Newman et al. 2018: 62). This kind of differential evaluation of significance has been commented on before as a common problem of researching the impact of new media on politics (see Wright 2012). Impacts aren't necessarily about scale or reach, as what constitutes significance in that sense is value-laden, rather it's more about possible impacts on the values inherent to journalism and communication in British politics.

The New Left Media, like much alternative and citizen journalism, are informed by several critiques of mainstream media practices in their approaches (Thorsen and Allan, 2014, Wall, 2015). First, is a critique of the structures of commercial media systems that are seen to tend to produce imbalances in media partisanship in favour of the political right, a particularly prominent feature of British national newspapers. Second, is a critique of ideas around impartiality, balance and objectivity whether embodied in public service organisations like the BBC, or more generally as a set of values intrinsic to journalism in democracy. Third, and related to these, is a critique of professional journalists as typically belonging to the same political/social elites as the political classes they are reporting on. These are seen by many as combining to ensure that, at best, journalism fails to fulfil its democratic functions of informing the public, and at worst, actively contributes to the suppression of democracy. Decades of political communication and journalism studies research show that these critiques are actually well grounded at least in some regards but the interesting thing is how practices in alternative and citizen journalism have emerged, at least in part, in relation to efforts to try and properly embody the values of journalism's role in democracy (and which occupies much of the evaluative research into citizen journalism, see Abbott 2017 for an overview).

The law of unintended consequences

It is here where the concept of the law of unintended consequences comes in. Although a longstanding everyday expression, the law of unintended consequences has its roots in a more schematic consideration by social scientist Robert Merton in the 1930s of the unintended consequences of what he called 'purposive social action' (1936). Essentially, he was interested in why, when people are trying to deliberately make positive societal impacts, this sometimes goes wrong or leads to unintended consequences. Amongst the reasons he suggested could lie behind this (such as simple ignorance of what the consequences of certain actions might be) of particular interest here is what he called the problem of *basic values*, whereby the complexities of often welcomed and lauded new practices can end up contributing to compromising and undermining the very reasons for engaging in those practices in the first place. As Merton puts it 'when a system of basic values enjoins certain specific actions, adherents are not concerned with the objective consequences of these actions but only with the subjective satisfaction of duty well performed' (1936, 903). The rise of NLM might just offer an emerging instance of these kinds of unintended consequences.

From the perspective of alternative and citizen journalism critiques of the mainstream, sets of practices intrinsically oppositional to mainstream journalism practices have been engaged in. Here possible unintended consequences begin to emerge, as a perception of failure of conventional journalistic practices leads to their outright rejection albeit in the spirit of trying to realise the same underlying values. For instance, the compromised, flawed, and arguably undesirable anyway, 'objectivity' and 'impartiality' of journalistic elites as well as their newspeak affectations, are replaced by the overt partisanship (often dubbed hyper-partisanship), subjectivity and natural language of ordinary citizens. A sense of authenticity of the ordinary people behind sites like *Another Angry Voice* are held up in contrast to the perceived detached, urban, elite journalists of the mainstream media. Whilst most citizen journalism research is caught up debates about whether a site like *Another Angry Voice* is journalism or not, and then whether it's good or bad journalism, very little ever seems to critically engage with what kind of citizenship this might be or what contemporary citizenship might mean in the context of acts like citizen journalism (see Campbell 2017 for more on this).

Aside from their partisanship, the style, language, tone and framing of NLM content very much follow the same patterns of other successful online news outlets, some of which, in turn, draw on a combination of established audience-generating strategies in the popular press and those for garnering online audiences (such as clickbait-style headlines e.g. 'The SNP owns Laura Kuenssberg on Twitter and it's quite delicious', *The Canary*, 14/6/18). Interestingly, most of those techniques have come from right-wing populist media both from the tabloid press and from right-wing online sites as well, like Guido Fawkes and Breitbart UK (in turn drawing on the experience of the political blogosphere, particularly in the USA).

There's arguably something of a paradox here in a tension between rejecting some mainstream media practices and right-wing ideology whilst using many of the same techniques from mainstream and right-wing media to garner audiences. If critiques of both the ideology and style of populist right-wing media are aped or appropriated for left-wing objectives, one might meaningfully ask what the long-term consequences of this might be for the nature and quality of political discourse. Does it contribute to a genuinely more pluralist media landscape or, due to the preferred content styles that reproduce much criticised tendencies in populist journalism, merely to a more polarised media landscape?

The constant criticism of mainstream news media as part of the bread and butter of NLM arguably compounds this potential problem as well. The commonality of language across right-wing and NLM online media when referring to mainstream media – the BBC is a 'state broadcaster' according to both – is interesting here, and whilst their perspectives differ over specifics, there is broader agreement over mainstream media's failure to cover topics either at all, or in ways reflective of perspectives other than those serving political elites, and for failure to sufficiently own up to and apologise for mistakes. Constant criticism of mainstream media valorises the activities of NLM of course, both to themselves – that 'subjective satisfaction' that Merton spoke of – and to their intended audiences but what might it mean for deeper perspectives on public attitudes towards journalism and politics in general? Some research has suggested, for instance, that combative, conflict-based political coverage on television or 'in your face politics', as dubbed by one author, has a corrosive effect on public attitudes towards politics, politicians, and journalists, at least in America (Mutz 2015).

Towards a new normal of political communication?

Whether or not the rise of NLM constitutes evidence of a real shift in the British political communication landscape, and what kind of shift it might be, remains uncertain. Presumptions of positive shifts based on aims of redressing partisan imbalances evident in national newspapers, and challenging the (perceived as) flawed impartiality claims of broadcast news outlets, however, need to be tempered by the possible unintended consequences of these purposive actions to effect change in Britain's media landscape. A combination of rejecting impartiality, constant critiquing of institutions supposed to be operating according to that principle, combined with the aping of successful right-wing populist media strategies for garnering audiences suggests Britain might be beginning to move towards a landscape built around more polarised, adversarial and advocacy journalism than it has been used to for most of the post-WWII period. Perhaps that is precisely the kind of media landscape a post-Brexit Britain requires, or perhaps it will exacerbate the current period of political polarisation beyond Brexit, indicating a parallel shift in the underlying values of what the new normal of political communication in Britain will look like.

References

Abbott, J.Y. (2017) 'Tensions in the scholarship on participatory journalism and citizen journalism', *Annals of the International Communication Association*, DOI:10.1080/23808985.2017.1350927

Campbell, V. (2017) 'The Importance of 'Citizenship': Theoretical Issues in Studying Citizen Journalism in International Context' in Tong, J. and Lo, S. (eds) *Digital Technology and Journalism in an International Comparative Perspective*, Basingstoke: Palgrave Macmillan.

Campbell, V. and Lee, B. (2016) 'Party Brands in the 2015 General Election: A Case Study of Online Political Posters', in Lilleker, DG and Pack, M (eds) *Political Marketing at the 2015 UK General Election*, London: Palgrave.

Chadwick, A., Vaccari, C. and O'Loughlin, B. (2018) 'Do tabloids poison the well of social media? Explaining democratically dysfunctional news sharing', *New Media and Society*, at: DOI:10.1177/1461444818769689.

Elvestad, E. and Phillips, A. (2018) *Misunderstanding News Audiences: Seven Myths of the Social Media Era*, London: Routledge.

Fletcher, R., Cornia, A., Graves, L. and Kleis Nielsen, R.K. (2018) 'Measuring the reach of "fake news" and online disinformation in Europe', Reuters Institute Factsheet, February 2018, at: http://reutersinstitute.politics.ox.ac.uk/sites/default/files/2018-02/Measuring%20the%20reach%20of%20fake%20news%20and%20online%20distribution%20in%20Europe%20CORRECT%20FLAG.pdf

Gibson, R.K., Williamson, A. and Ward, S. (eds) (2010) 'The internet and the 2010 election putting the small 'p' back in politics?', Hansard Society, https://assets.ctfassets.net/u1rlvvbs33ri/1T8tpdVcsIkyyeuGw62mG6/a735e387b5975f47d19b7d79006266db/Publication__The-internet-and-the-2010-election-2010.pdf

Gillmor, D. (2004) We the Media: Grassroots Journalism by the People, for the People, Sebastopol, CA: O'Reilly.

McNair, B. (2018) *Fake News*, London: Routledge.

Merton, R.K. (1936) 'The Unanticipated Consequences of Purposive Social Action', *American Sociological Review*, 1(6): 894-904.

Morozov, E. (2011) The Net Delusion: The Dark Side of Internet Freedom, London: Penguin.

Mutz, D.C. (2015) In-Your-Face Politics: The Consequences of Uncivil Media, Princeton, NJ: Princeton University Press.

Newman, N. with Fletcher, R., Kalogeropoulos, K., Levy, D.A.L and Nielsen, R.K. (2018) *Reuters Institute Digital News Report 2018*, Reuters Institute for the Study of Journalism, at: http://media.digitalnewsreport.org/wp-content/uploads/2018/06/digital-news-report-2018.pdf?x89475

Postman, N. (1985) *Amusing Ourselves to Death*, London: Penguin.

Standage, T. (1998) *The Victorian Internet*, London: W&N.

Thorsen, E. and Allan, S. (eds.) (2014) *Citizen Journalism: Global Perspectives Volume 2*, New York: Peter Lang.

Ward, S. J. and Lusoli. W. (2005) 'Logging on or switching off? The public and the internet at the 2005 general election' In S. Coleman and S. Ward (eds.) *Spinning the Web*, London: The Hansard Society.

Wall, M. (2015) 'Citizen Journalism', *Digital Journalism*, 3(6): 797-813.

Waterson, J. (2017) 'The Rise Of The Alt-Left British Media', Buzzfeed UK, 6/5/17, at: https://www.buzzfeed.com/jimwaterson/the-rise-of-the-alt-left?utm_term=.laDZXrjVB#.cdRePL2kl

Wright S. (2012) 'Politics as usual? Revolution, normalization and a new agenda for online deliberation', *New Media & Society*, 14(2): 244–261.

Note on the contributor

Dr Vincent Campbell is Associate Professor in Media and Communication at the University of Leicester. Previously he worked at De Montfort University, also in Leicester, and at the Universities of Stirling and Sheffield. His main research interests are focused on the impact of digital technologies on public communication, particularly political communication and journalism, as well as science communication. His is the author of *Information Age Journalism* (2004) and *Science, Entertainment and Television Documentary* (2016). He has published on a variety of aspects of political communication in UK, US and European elections, such as Party Election Broadcasts, party advertising on social media, and the role of blogging in campaigns.

The Canary: cooking with the same ingredients

A study of one of digital news most high-profile newcomers shows that it maintains a strong reliance on the traditional media it claims to despise, Sean Dodson looks at the data

On the eve of the UK General Election of 2017 something remarkable was happening on the internet. A small website, barely two years old, put together by a handful of unknowns, was managing to gain more attention than some of the best-known titles in the land. The Canary – a nascent left-wing political blog – had managed to scale the heights of the all-important Google PageRank, which meant that more people were linking to, liking, retweeting and sharing its content than they were on more established, subscription-based titles such as The Spectator, The Economist, The New Statesman and even the old 'newspaper of record', The Times.

This ascent of the rankings raised the profile of both the site and its co-founder, Kerry-Anne Mendoza, and led to the former management consultant appearing on BBC Question Time, the UK's most popular current affairs programme, where she established herself as a vocal critic of the UK media.

Mendoza had already declared that the aspiration of The Canary was to 'disrupt the status quo' of journalism (Mendoza, 2016) by creating an alternative platform free of external investors and advertisers. But as awareness of The Canary grew, two things became apparent. First, it displayed a zealous over-protectiveness of Jeremy Corbyn and the populist movement that surrounds the Labour leader (Lewis). And, secondly, it distrusted the mainstream media while yet producing pages full of content taken from the very organisations it purported to 'hate' (Mendoza).

And so with success came criticism. The Canary's relentless left-wing stance led to accusations that it was far too partisan. Private Eye described it as a 'pisspoor Corbynite clickbait factory' (Spence), Iain Dale, while acknowledging The Canary's influence, wrote that the site had 'a distant relationship to factual reporting' (Dale); Helen Lewis (2017), deputy editor of The New Statesman, accused the site of using the BBC's political editor, Laura Kuenssberg as a 'punching bag for clicks', while even left-wing firebrand, Guardian columnist Owen Jones, expressed concern of the 'Canary-isation' of the left-wing politics in the UK and charged the site as propagating 'conspiracy' theories (James).

Moreover, what concerned other commentators (Dunt 2016; Waterson 2017; Jackson 2017), was that The Canary represented the latest example of a 'filter bubble', the intellectually isolating phenomenon of presenting only a single side to each story and that, furthermore, The Canary was free largely of traditional journalistic standards, such as balance and fairness. Such filter bubbles have long been seen as being a product of right-wing politics.

A study by the Columbia Journalism Review (2017) concluded that 'alt-right' sites such as Breitbart "developed as a distinct and insulated media system, using social media as a backbone to transmit a hyper-partisan perspective to the world." But critics of The Canary have observed that such a description fits sites on the 'alt-left' equally well (Dean, Walcott).

Alternative and partisan sites

The Canary is part of a wave of alternative, populist and partisan sites that have broken in recent years, thanks to the growth of social media. (Newman, Fletcher et al). Founded in October 2015 (Southern) as a 'counterpoint' to mainstream journalism (Scott) with a commitment to produce 'simple and elegant' prose (Mendoza), The Canary has grown into a loose team of 20+ contributors (Daly) who are paid a percentage of the company's profits (Scott). Some writers have complained that they have earned less than the minimum wage contributing to The Canary, leading to some commentators (Le Conte) to argue that the pay-per-click model sits uneasily with the site's socialist principles.

However, the business model has allowed The Canary to grow. It currently enjoys more than 150,500 'likes' on Facebook and has 61,600 followers on Twitter (by comparison The New Statesman has 152,000 and 160,000 respectively). Like Breitbart, much of its traffic comes from Facebook (Waterson). It remains respectable on the Google PageRank, although it has fallen considerably since the last General Election. The Canary has slipped out of the top 500 sites in the UK (1,980 at the time of writing), but remains influential, and was one of only four digital-only platforms cited in the annual Digital News Report by the Reuters Institute (Newman, Fletcher et al).

What does it do?

The Canary turns out on average 8.5 stories every weekday, slightly fewer over the weekend. What's more, the stories are long for blog pieces, starting at about 800 words in length and going up to 2000 words, with a typical story being about 1000 words long. By contrast, the right-wing libertarian blogger Guido Fawkes typically publishes posts of 50 -100 words long.

The Canary defies conventional forms of journalistic articles. Its style is to use the past tense of news and the conventions of the news 'intro' (Who? What? When? Where? Why? How?) (McKane). But there the similarities end. The Canary does not conform to the recognised structure of news, the so-called 'inverted pyramid'

(Scanlan), where the most important information is placed towards the top of the article, and instead Canary articles are structured more like features where significant material is held back for the latter parts of the piece and there is almost always a formal conclusion.

Furthermore, most articles carry explicit opinion, and often employ the first person narrative in the reporter's voice – both a no-no in news (Harcup). Indeed, both opinion and fact routinely chop and change like the bank holiday weather in a typical Canary piece, leaving the reader with a hybrid of news and comment.

The tone of Canary items

In 2015 Mendoza stated a commitment to produce alternative journalism expressed 'simple and elegant' prose (Mendoza) and while the style of The Canary is lively and readable, its tone is jocular if not facetious. Swearwords, for instance, are frequently used, although represented coyly behind asterisks (e.g. The right-wing press can f**k off with its cynical manipulation of anti-Semitism for its own agenda).

Despite the looseness of language, The Canary can also be conscientious and precise. It sources the information it uses meticulously. Unlike other political blogs this study uncovered no evidence of the use of rumour. The Canary does use unnamed sources, but these are always linked to a recognisable organisation, except in the rare instances that a sources identity is protected for legal reasons. It is also transparent about its mistakes. It labels any corrections or changes it has made to an article, which has been identified as industry best practice (Dodson).

The basis of this study

Between 2017 and 2018 two large studies on the sourcing of material on the pages of The Canary were conducted. The first was a pilot study in October 2017 and the second a longer study cataloging every story in The Canary across a 10-day period. The dataset analysed in this chapter refers to the latter study (although some explicit reference to the pilot will also be discussed). The dataset focused on the primary and secondary sources employed by The Canary.

Eighty-five articles were studied in total, although The Canary's satirical section 'Off the perch' and one photo gallery were discounted, as they contained no written sources. Every source – primary and secondary – was recorded. These sources ranged from full and partial quotes, embedded tweets, embedded video, tables, graphics and material that linked back to another source.

In the study The Guardian and The Observer were treated as a single entity. YouTube links were traced back to their original source (for example material originated on the BBC, was recorded as the BBC, not YouTube). Twitter was treated as a single source as it is particularly difficult to understand whether journalists on Twitter, or other media actors, are tweeting on behalf of their organisation or in a personal capacity.

All UK government departments were corralled together (gov.uk), although Parliament was treated as a separate source (all Hansard, petitions and live channels were treated as a single source). Broken links, or links that had subsequently been taken down (for example, for copyright reasons) were not counted as it was impossible to verify them as a source.

Also noted was each time The Canary documented a failure to reach a primary source (e.g. we contacted the DWP but it failed to reply), as it did on two occasions in this study. Press releases, when expressly stated as such, were treated as secondary sources. Written statements, of which the Canary uses regularly, were treated as primary sources.

What was found

In total, The Canary used 1489 items of sourceable material in the 85 articles of this study. What was apparent is that the use of secondary sources significantly outweighed those of primary. Secondary sources were found in every article in this study. The Canary used on average 17.3 secondary sources per article, one approximately every 58 words. By contrast, The Canary used a primary source only 0.21 times per article, roughly one primary source for every five articles. Or put the other way: four out of five articles in The Canary contained no primary source at all.

Primary sources

Only 18 stories in this study contained a primary source and only 11 of these used a named source. It's difficult to discern whether the unnamed sources discovered in this study –routinely referred to as spokespeople – were the result of written statements or the product of an interview (i.e. proper quotes). Only three articles of the total sample of this study contained more than one primary source and of these only two contained two sources from separate organisations. Set against the 1471 secondary sources in our sample, primary sources constitute 1.2 per cent of the Canary's source material, and named sources less than 0.6 per cent of its total output.

While it's difficult to know the political leanings of each of the primary sources that The Canary has quoted, it might be instructive to list them and allow the reader to draw their own conclusions as to the type of primary source The Canary tends to use (see list below).

The attributable sources located in the study are as follows:

1. Reynaldo Mariqueo, from UK-based non-governmental organisation Mapuche International;

2. Nafeez Ahmed, an investigative journalist;

3. Dr Daniel Ozarow, a campaigner and senior lecturer at Middlesex University;

4. Linda Allbutt, of the pressure group Period Power;

5. Peter Stefanovic, a lawyer and patron of Period Power;

6. Jon Bartley, co-leader of the Green Party;

7. Dr Jay Watts, a medical doctor;

8. Paula Peters from Disabled People Against Cuts;

9. Anna* who suffers from an autoimmune disease and;

10. Mark*, her husband;

11. Bob Ellard from campaign group Disabled People Against Cuts (DPAC).

(*The Canary changed their names for legal reasons.)

Unnamed sources uncovered in the study include four statements by spokespeople at the Department of Work and Pensions (DWP); a spokesman for the pub chain Wetherspoons; a spokesperson for Friends of Hastings Pier and a spokesperson for the housing association Poplar Harca.

The research uncovered two instances where The Canary recorded an attempt to gain interviews with its subjects – but was rebuffed. These were the DWP and the BBC. Of course, The Canary may very well have attempted to conduct interviews in all of its stories, only to be ignored, but there was no more evidence recorded in this study. Interestingly, during the pilot study (so not part of the main statistical analysis here), we did discover one instance of a journalist doorstepping the Secretary of State for Justice, David Gauke, and filming his snub. Such a brush off is surely routine for most reporters, but it made a standalone story on the pages of The Canary.

Secondary sources

It is clear that The Canary cites secondary material with the consistency and accuracy worthy of academics. On average, The Canary uses 17 secondary sources per article. A typical Guardian news story contains an average of four in an article of a similar length (although more on specialist web-pages such as liveblogs).

The most popular source of reference is Twitter. The Canary references Twitter on average 3.2 times per article, almost always via an embedded tweet. None of the tweets we recorded appeared to be answers to questions set by The Canary. There was no evidence that the site was replacing traditional interviews with conversations on social media. It was merely repurposing existing material.

The second most popular source is The Canary itself. Although, as noted above, The Canary gathers very little of its own material, it routinely self-references an average 2.4 times an article. Sometimes the amount of self-referencing became denser. For example, in a story about homelessness (Topple), The Canary referenced back to itself six times in a single paragraph: only one of the stories it linked to contained a primary source (a statement from a DWP spokesman).

Despite its mistrust of the mainstream media (MSM), The Canary was particularly reliant on newspapers and news broadcasts for source material, particularly the liberal press (Harrison). In total, the Canary used MSM content in 90.5 per cent of the articles in this study. The Canary referenced The Guardian alone in over half of its articles (55.2 per cent) taking quotes, statistics and stories from its website. Indeed, many of its articles began as Guardian articles, only to be re-written by The Canary with much of the balance and context removed to suit better the agenda of the left-wing blog. On average, The Canary used or referenced Guardian material 1.6 times per article, greater than the BBC (0.8 times), The Independent (0.5) and The Mirror (0.17).

The Guardian, The Independent and The Mirror are widely seen as left-leaning institutions, The BBC more controversially so, but such a reliance on the left-lean of the 'MSM' adds weight to the theory that The Canary is creating a filter bubble, that it presents only one side of the story. The most frequent right-wing source used regularly by The Canary was the Daily Telegraph, which The Canary used 0.13 times per article.

The most popular non-media source used frequently by The Canary was the nexus of sites used by the UK government. The study found 57 references to UK government data and information (0.67 references per article), but The Guardian was used almost two-and-a-half times more than the entirety of the UK government.

Table 1: List of secondary sources used by The Canary

Twitter	274	NHS	14
The Canary	204	Evolve Housing	12
The Guardian	138	The Telegraph	11
The BBC	67	DNS	11
Gov.uk	57	CNN	10
The Independent	43	Sky News	9
Parliament	35	Facebook	8
Reuters	18	Amnesty	7
Huffington Post	17	Leigh Day	7
The Mirror	14	Channel 4 News	6

Sign of the times

By the standards of a newspaper The Canary's contribution to first-hand reporting is paltry. But is this because its format is different? After all, an award-winning political blog such as The Guardian's Politics Live also plays host to a majority of content sourced elsewhere, especially from Twitter. The difference being, though, that Politics Live also includes source material from many of The Guardian's reports – first-hand attributable quotes gathered and tested by trained reporters – and that the Politics Live blog is part of a much wider wheel.

Other left-wing blogs, moreover, manage somehow to reach beyond the screen and interview real people and gather original source material. A recent post by Left Foot Forward (Ramiro), written at the same time as this study about the growth of an electricians' union, featured original source material from four interviews, including one from the union's general secretary.

Indeed, if The Canary has a bunkmate, it is the right-wing libertarian blog Guido Fawkes. Like The Canary Guido Fawkes comprised largely of secondary sources, re-purposed from the mainstream and social media. Guido Fawkes and The Canary might have different political convictions, but their output and tone belong around the same table. One difference though, while Guido Fawkes sits outside the media establishment, its legal basis is re-routed to the Cayman Islands, The Canary is a proud member of Impress, the independent press regulator. And while Guido Fawkes makes much of its capacity to publish 'gossip and rumour' The Canary is more anchored in fact.

Conclusion

In this sense, The Canary, like other political blogs, conforms to Habermas's (1991) ideas of an unreconstructed public sphere. The Canary, a small team not beholden to advertising, conforms to his idea of journalism as an activity conducted by 'private men of letters', operating in a similar way to the 'small handicraft business' that characterised the early journalism of the 18th century, while enjoying considerable influence.

The Canary has also given voice to many unrepresented elements of society. It champions the cause of the disabled, has harried the DWP over its policy of universal credit and has been successful in investigating the claims of electoral fraud by the Conservative Party with some skill (White).

However, this study shows that The Canary isn't quite so independent from the political-media complex (Swanson) as it characterises itself. Its failure to gather much of its own source material, in the form of on-the-record interviews, makes it dependent on others to do so.

By avoiding the interview, as this content analysis indicates, The Canary is denying itself the 'chief tool of active journalism' (Pulford) and becomes reliant only on what others have done for it. If one were to redact the material taken from the MSM in this study, then The Canary would be reduced to the odd interview with charity workers and fellow activists. This is, by extension, the opposite of the scoop journalism that has provided an aspiration for most journalists since at least Watergate.

Instead, nine out of ten of its stories are dependent on the mainstream media for its content. The Canary is like a vegan chef who cooks foie gras in order to maintain profitability in the restaurant while bragging of a conscientious lifestyle. The question is, if The Canary has so much distaste for the press, why does it keep putting so much of its fare on its menu?

References

Apple, Emily (2018) The right-wing press can f**k off with its cynical manipulation of anti-Semitism for its own agenda, The Canary, 04 April. Available online at https://www.thecanary.co/uk/2018/04/04/the-right-wing-press-can-fk-off-with-its-cynical-manipulation-of-antisemitism-for-its-own-agenda, accessed on October 1, 2016.

Benkler, Yochai (2017) Breitbart-led right-wing media ecosystem altered broader media agenda, The Columbia Journalism Review. Available online at https://www.cjr.org/analysis/breitbart-media-trump-harvard-study.php, accessed on June 12, 2018.

Burne James, Sam (2017) 'Canary-isation' of the media a concern for the left, says Owen Jones, PR Week. Available on at: https://www.prweek.com/article/1420048/canary-isation-media-concern-left-says-owen-jones, accessed on June 12, 2018.

Dale, Iain (2017) The 100 Most Influential People On The Left: Iain Dale's 2017 List, LBC, 25 September. Available at: https://www.lbc.co.uk/radio/presenters/iain-dale/100-most-influential-people-on-the-left-iain-dale, accessed on June 12, 2018.

Daly, Patrick (2017) The Canary's Bristolian editor Kerry-Anne Mendoza is going to be on Question Time - this is the story of how she got there, Bristol Post, 29 June. Available online at https://www.bristolpost.co.uk/news/bristol-news/canarys-bristolian-editor-kerry-anne-147229, accessed on June 12, 2018.

Dean, Brian (2017) I was in the original 'alt-left' and this is what we really stood for, Independent, 22 August. Available online at https://www.independent.co.uk/voices/alt-left-alt-right-trump-internet-subculture-90s-cyber-what-we-stood-for-a7906246.html, accessed on July 12, 2018

Dodson, Sean (2012) Improving integrity online: towards a code of conduct for journalism on the internet. Chapter published in The Phone Hacking Scandal: Journalism on Trial, edited by Richard Keeble and John Mair. Bury St Edmunds: Amicus

Dunt, Ian (2016) The activist left is conspiring in the demolition of the BBC, Politics. co.uk, 09 May. Available online at: http://www.politics.co.uk/blogs/2016/05/09/the-activist-left-is-conspiring-in-the-demolition-of-the-bbc, accessed on July 12, 2018

Habermas, Jurgen (1991) The Structural Transformation of the Public Sphere, pp 183-6. Cambridge: Polity

Harcup, Tony (2015) Journalism: Principles and Practice, pp 145-6. London: Sage

Jackson, Jasper (2017) Hyper-partisan Corbynite websites show how the left can beat the tabloids online, The New Statesman, June 24. Available online at: https://www.newstatesman.com/politics/media/2017/06/hyper-partisan-corbynite-websites-show-how-left-can-beat-tabloids-online, accessed on July 12, 2018

Le Conte, Marie (2016) How A Pro-Corbyn Viral Website With A Pay-Per-Click Business Model Is Taking Over Social Media, Buzzfeed. Available at https://www.buzzfeed.com/marieleconte/the-rise-of-the-canary?utm_term=.xdNm1bEQ2#.uuaVen2rD, accessed on July 12, 2018

Lewis, Helen (2017) The Canary is running a sexist hate campaign against Laura Kuenssberg for clicks, The New Statesman, September 27. Available online at https://www.newstatesman.com/politics/media/2017/09/canary-running-sexist-hate-campaign-against-laura-kuenssberg-clicks, accessed on July 12, 2018

McKane, A (2014) News Writing, pp 24-30, London: Sage

Mendoza, Kerry-Anne (2016) The Canary is a new media outlet shaking up journalism in a radical way, Free and Fearless Magazine, April. Available online at: http://hackinginquiry.org/wp-content/uploads/2016/04/HackedOff_FF1.pdf, accessed on July 12, 2018

Mendoza, Kerry-Anne (@TheMendozaWoman) MSM: The Canary is Corbynist propaganda! Us: Nope MSM: The Canary criticised Corbyn! They hate him like us now. Us: Nope. Just journalists. January 27, 2017 5.08pm. Tweet. https://twitter.com/TheMendozaWoman/status/825072918002544641

Newman, Nic (ed) (2018) Reuters Institute Digital News Report 2018, available online at: http://media.digitalnewsreport.org/wp-content/uploads/2018/06/digital-news-report-2018.pdf?x89475, accessed on July 12, 2018

Scott, Caroline (2015) How news outlet The Canary aims to 'diversify media', Journalism.co.uk, 23 October. Available online at https://www.journalism.co.uk/news/how-news-outlet-the-canary-aims-to-diversify-media-/s2/a576960, accessed on July 12, 2018

Pulford, Cedric (2001) 201 Ways to improve Journalism. Banbury: Ituri

Ramiro, Joana (2018) Electricians are joining a small union known for beating gig-economy bosses, Left Foot Forward, July 3, 2018. Available online at https://leftfootforward.org/2018/07/electricians-are-joining-a-small-union-known-for-beating-gig-economy-bosses, accessed on July 12, 2018

Scanlan, Chip (2003) Birth of the Inverted Pyramid: A Child of Technology, Commerce and History. Poynter, June 20. Available online at: https://www.poynter.org/news/birth-inverted-pyramid-child-technology-commerce-and-history, accessed on July 12, 2018

Southern, Lucinda (2018) Politics publisher The Canary is converting text articles to audio to find new audiences, Digiday UK, January 12. Available at: https://digiday.com/media/politics-publisher-canary-converting-text-articles-audio-find-new-audiences, accessed on July 12, 2018

Spence, Alex (2016) Jeremy Corbyn and the disruptive Canary, Politico, July 18, 2016. Available online at https://www.politico.eu/blogs/on-media/2016/08/jeremy-corbyn-and-the-disruptive-canary-uk-politics-labour-leader, accessed on July 12, 2018

Topple, Steve (2018) Theresa May's DWP minister just stood up in parliament and whitewashed a 'human catastrophe', The Canary, June 20. Available online at: https://www.thecanary.co/uk/2018/06/20/theresa-mays-dwp-minister-just-stood-up-in-parliament-and-whitewashed-a-human-catastrophe, accessed on July 12, 2018

Walcott, James (2017) Why the alt-left is a problem, too, Vanity Fair, March. Available online at: https://www.newstatesman.com/politics/media/2017/06/hyper-partisan-corbynite-websites-show-how-left-can-beat-tabloids-online, accessed on July 12, 2018

Waterson, Jim (2017) The Rise Of The Alt-Left British Media, Buzzfeed, May 6. Available online at https://www.buzzfeed.com/jimwaterson/the-rise-of-the-alt-left?utm_term=.lnXJa6Z8G#.jfPAZ6J4O, accessed on July 12, 2018

Note on the contributor

Sean Dodson in the postgraduate course director of journalism and public relations at Leeds Beckett University where he specialises in the subject of digital ethics. He is a regular contributor to the New European newspaper and a former judge of the Orwell Prize, the UK's leading award for political writing. Contact: @seandodson or s.dodson@leedsbeckett.ac.uk

Open Discourse: a media theory for the twenty-first century

Faced with the unreliable onslaught of social media, professional media must step up to protect and promote reliable flows of information, argues Dr Denis Muller

Western democracy stands at a moment in time when new thinking about political communication is needed. Social media, made possible by digital technology, has given rise to the echo-chamber phenomenon, in which participants are able to communicate with like-minded individuals and exclude themselves from exposure to other perspectives. There is substantial evidence (see Sunstein, 2017, for example) that this contributes to, and intensifies, political partisanship, and to a corresponding weakening of consensus politics. It also contributes to a fragmenting of public conversation. It is this common conversation that allows citizens to identify, prioritise, and propose responses to, issues of common concern and thus have a critical influence on political, economic and social life.

The professional mass media, although weakened by the flow of revenue from them to social media platforms, remains the vehicle which carries this common conversation. The provision of a common public discourse, in which a plurality of perspectives can be debated, has been made urgently necessary by social media's fragmentation effect, by the demonstrated unreliability of social media as a source of news, by its echo-chamber effect and by its consequent contribution to political polarisation. To counter these effects, Open Discourse theory is proposed. It requires a renewed commitment by professional mass media to certain ethical norms, in particular verification, impartiality, editorial independence, pluralism and respect for persons.

Democratic societies are confronted with a great challenge: how, in the digital world, might the blessings of free speech be maximized while the curses of its excesses be minimized? Libertarian notions of free speech, exemplified by the arguments of John Milton in Areopagitica and John Stuart Mill in On Liberty have been challenged on the grounds they are fundamentally elitist (see, for example, Roberts, 2004). On this reading, Millian and Miltonian concepts of free speech have limited application even to a public sphere as narrow as that conceived of by Habermas (1991, 27). The Habemasian concept was of a bourgeois public sphere in which large numbers of middle-class individuals participated in reasoned public discussion over matters of general public interest. By the standards of today's digitally networked public sphere, the Habermasian concept looks – and is – out of touch with reality. But what is not touched by digital technology is the core Habermasian idea of a public sphere as a place of mediation between individuals and the state. In democracies, this place remains essential.

Goode (2005, 28) refers to the 'classic dilemma of balancing openness with the demands of mutual respect and care for the other incumbent on an egalitarian discourse ethic'. He also refers to Habermas's distaste for the online world (2005, 106), which Habermas argues exacerbates the fragmentation of public life and the proliferation of cultural enclaves.

Fragmentation and cultural enclaves run counter to two social conditions widely identified as necessary to democratisation: the need for a rich associative life of civil society, and the need for a communicative infrastructure of the public sphere which permits the expression and diffusion of public opinion (Bohman, 2007, 60). Bohman notes the importance of having communication in the public sphere that cuts across social spheres (2007, 70). He further argues (2007, 80-81) while the internet as a tool promotes a vibrant civil society and extends the public sphere, in order to transform the public sphere, something more is needed: the use of the internet to create public spaces in which free, open and responsive dialogue occurs. Open Discourse theory is proposed as one part of the media's institutional response to this need.

Foundations of press theory

For more than 60 years, theorising about the role and function of the press has rested on the foundations laid by Fred Siebert, Theodore Peterson and Wilbur Schramm in their seminal work, Four Theories of the Press (1956, 1963). They saw each of their four theories as grounded in certain basic beliefs and assumptions held by different societies about the nature of individuals, the nature of society and the state, the relationship between individuals and the state, and the nature of knowledge and truth (1963, 10). Siebert et al also proceeded on a basic assumption which also underpins this chapter: that for journalistic purposes there is such a thing as 'truth'. Journalistic truth is contingent and usually incomplete but represents the best-verified version of the subject-matter available at the time of publication.

The oldest theory and, as Siebert observes, the most pervasive historically and geographically (1963, 9) is Authoritarian theory. This theory holds that it is for the rulers to decide what the people should know. The theory is grounded in an assumption that the most valuable knowledge and truth will come from an intellectual elite, and the masses, once properly instructed, will arrive at a unity of thought. To give effect to these assumptions, the press is a servant of the state.

Revolutionary theory adopted the premises of authoritarian theory and built on it in two main ways. Firstly, it posited that the platforms of mass communication properly belong to the state and the ruling party and not to private individuals. Secondly, as such they exist to be used for state and party purposes: to educate the masses in correct doctrine; to ensure they are not exposed to ideas incompatible with that doctrine; to promote unity of thought and purpose among the masses, and to propagandise on behalf of the state and party (1963, 121).

The foundations of Libertarian theory were grounded in the ideals of the Enlightenment. Chief among these was the ideal of Man as a rational being, eager to seek the truth through reasoned argument. To the libertarian, the individual person is the prime unit of civilisation (1963, 40), and so the fulfillment of the individual's aspirations becomes the ultimate goal of society and the prime purpose of the state. The nature of knowledge and truth, for the libertarians, is a Cartesian distillation of reason, logic and scientific experimentation liberated from religious dogma and superstition and discoverable by the contestation of ideas.

By the late nineteenth century, the press had become not only industrialised, but habituated to putting its own interests ahead of others'. It was against this background that in 1943 Henry Luce, publisher of Time magazine, initiated and largely paid for an inquiry into press functions and standards. It was called the United States Commission on the Freedom of the Press and in 1947 it produced its report, A Free and Responsible Press. From this, as well as from the associated volume by the Commission's intellectual leader, William Ernest Hocking, Freedom of the Press, came the foundations of Social Responsibility theory.

Concerning the nature of Man and the relationship between individuals and the state, it rests solidly on the foundations laid by Libertarian theory. Concerning the nature of truth and knowledge, Social Responsibility theory asserts that the first function of the press is to provide the citizenry with a bedrock of reliable information on which they can participate in political, economic and social life.

The role of the state in Social Responsibility theory is that of residual legatee entrusted to hold the ring between press freedom and accountability; of ensuring 'an adequate press performance' without intruding on press activities (1947, 182-183).

Building on these foundations

In the 62 years since the exposition of Four Theories, there has developed what Christians et al (2009) call a 'fairly rich reservoir of ideas' about how the theories might be extended, added to or improved upon (2009, 7). Among the more notable attempts are those of McQuail. Among the many theories he has reviewed and proposed are Democratic-participant theory (1983, 84-98), Functionalist theory (2010, 98-99), Social Constructionist theory (2010, 100-101) and Communication Technology Determinism (2010, 101-103).

Open Discourse theory draws on elements of Libertarian, Social Responsibility and Democratic-participant theories, but it specifies a role for the professional mass media which in the past has understandably been taken for granted: the provision of a common conversation among the citizenry on matters of public interest broadly defined, as an antidote to the fragmentation and echo-chamber effects of social media.

The effect of fragmentation and echo chambers has been the subject of considerable research, powerfully analysed by Sunstein (2017). He argues instead of an architecture of individual control over exposure to news and opinion, democracy – as well as personal well-being – needs 'an architecture of serendipity' (2017, 5): in other words, a means by which people stumble across material which would not make it through their personalised news-filtration system. Democracies, he says, may or may not be fragile, but polarisation can be a serious problem, and it is heightened if people live in different communications universes (2017, 25).

Fragmentation in news and opinion creates these different communications universes, and the evidence showing the extent of this fragmentation is strong. A powerful factor in the development of fragmentation has been the creation of hashtags. A study of two competing hashtags, #BlackLivesMatter and #AllLivesMatter, was conducted by Gallagher et al in 2016. The first sprang up as a protest after the notorious shooting of an African-American man, Michael Brown, by a white policeman in Ferguson, Missouri, in 2014, and the second as a counter-protest.

The researchers found significant differences in the way the issue of violence between African-Americans and police were framed by each hashtag. One difference was that #BlackLivesMatter carried a proportionally higher discussion of African-American deaths than did #AllLivesMatter. By contrast, within #AllLivesMatter the only other lives significantly discussed were those of law enforcement officers.

The contribution social media makes to the fragmentation and polarisation phenomenon is intensified when mass media also become politically polarised. Martin and Yurukoglu (2014) found between 2000 and 2008, Fox News Channel (FNC) and another cable news service, MSNBC, had each become more politically polarised, with Republican voters increasingly likely to watch FNC and Democrat voters increasingly likely to watch MSNBC (2014, 37). Levitsky and Ziblatt argue extreme partisan polarisation weakens democratic norms (2018, 9). They assert a necessary response to this is the reinvigoration of institutional gatekeeping, including by the media (2018, 56) and, in the 'fake news' environment created by the presidency of Donald Trump, a recommitment to truth-telling (2018, 181-203).

What Open Discourse theory proposes

Open Discourse theory posits that in the face of these developments the professional mass media have a responsibility to recognise it is they who, because of long-established experience, extensive reach, market power, brand identification and privileges, are called upon to provide a reliable and respectful informational basis for a common conversation among citizens, and to exert a gatekeeping function. Carrying this out effectively requires renewed commitment to certain norms of professional ethics.

The first is prior verification of facts. To fulfil Open Discourse theory, the professional mass media must reassert the fundamental importance of being right and prioritise it ahead of being first. The second is a recommitment to impartiality. This has six elements (Muller 2014, 73-81): factual and contextual accuracy; fairness of portrayal; balance, which follows the weight of evidence; open-mindedness, an approach to reporting which includes the full range of principal relevant perspectives on an issue; absence of conflict of interest, and decision-making based on established news values of the kind defined at various times by scholars such as Galtung and Ruge (1965), McQuail (1983) and Harcup and O'Neill (2001). Closely allied to impartiality is the requirement to promote pluralism in public discourse. Shutting out voices or viewpoints purely on the basis of prejudice has no place in a truly common conversation.

A further ethical requirement of Open Discourse theory is the reassertion of editorial independence. This has become compromised in several ways. At the commercial level, there has been a breakdown in the separation between news and advertising content. This breakdown goes under the general name of hybrid journalism (Muller, 2016). Editorial independence has also become compromised at the political level and has led to the polarisation of news outlets as shown by the work of Martin and Yurukoglu.

A further consideration is that Open Discourse theory is being developed under global political and communications circumstances where online communications exchanges are global and transcend the borders of nation states. This expands the bases on which people develop a sense of identity to include global affiliation with others of like mind, shared interests or shared belief systems. It follows that a necessary element in Open Discourse theory is respect for persons regardless of nationality, ethnicity, race, colour, sexual orientation, religion or political persuasion. The Kantian value of respect for persons is built into journalistic codes of ethics around the world (see, for example, Keeble 2001).

Open Discourse theory posits that adherence to these five ethical norms will enable the press to provide a shared body of reliable information necessary to democratic life, provide a platform on which a range of opinions can be expressed, and so become a means by which communities engage in a common conversation on matters of common interest and concern, countering social media's echo-chamber effect and the fragmentation of the public conversation.

References

Bohman, J., 2007, *Democracy across Borders: From Demos to Demoi,* MIT Press, Cambridge, Massachusetts.

Christians, C., Glasser, T., McQuail, D., Nordenstrang, K. and White, R., 2009, *Normative Theories of the Media*, University of Illinois Press, Chicago.

Crossley, N. & Roberts J. M. (eds) 2004, *After Habermas: New Perspectives on the Public Sphere*, Blackwell, Oxford.

Dewey, J, 1941, *The Living Thoughts of Thomas Jefferson*, selected from *The Writings of Thomas Jefferson*, Washington, H. A. (ed), Cassell, London.

Gallagher, Ryan J.; Reagan, Andrew J.; Danforth, Christopher M. and Sheridan Dodds, Peter, 2018, "Divergent discourse between protests and counter-protests: #BlackLivesMatter and #AllLivesMatter", https://doi.org/10.1371/journal. pone.0195644; accessed 4 June 2018.

Galtung, J. and Ruge, M., 1965 , "The Structure of Foreign News: The Presentation of the Congo, Cuba and Cyprus crises in Norwegian Newspapers", *Journal of International Peace Research* Vol 1, pp 64-91.

Goode, L., 2005, *Jurgen Habermas: Democracy and the Public Sphere*, Pluto Press, London.

Grayling, A. C., 2017, *Democracy and its Crisis*, Oneworld Publications, London.

Habermas, J. (Burger, T. & Lawrence, F. trans.) 1991, *The Structural Transformation of the Public Sphere: An Inquiry into a Category of Bourgeois Society*, MIT Press, Massachusetts.

Harcup, T. and O'Neill, D., 2001, "What is News? Galtung and Ruge Revisited", *Journalism Studies* Vol 2 No 2, pp 261-280.

Hocking, W. E., 1947, *Freedom of the Press: A Framework of Principle*, University of Chicago Press, Chicago.

Keeble, R., 2001, *Ethics for Journalists*, Routledge, London.

Levitsky, S. and Ziblatt, D., 2018, *How Democracies Die*, Viking Penguin Random House, London.

Locke, J., *Two Treatises on Government* [1728] republished in *The Works of John Locke* (twelfth edition), London, 1824.

Martin, G. and Yurukoglu, A., 2014, "Bias in Cable News: Persuasion and Polarization", Working Paper 20798 http://www.nber.org/papers/w20798 National Bureau of Economic Research, Cambridge, Mass; accessed 4 June 2018.

McQuail, D., *Mass Communication Theory*, 3rd ed, Sage, London.

Mill, J. S. 1859 [1998], *On Liberty*, Gray, J. (ed), Oxford University Press, Oxford.

Muller, D., 2014, *Journalism Ethics for the Digital Age*, Scribe Publications, Melbourne.

Muller, D., 2016, "Conflict of Interest: Hybrid Journalism's Central Ethical Challenge", *Ethical Space* Vol 13 No 2/3, pp 95-109.

Negroponte, N., 1995, *Being Digital*, Vintage Books, New York.

Roberts, J. M., 2004, "From Populism to Political Dialogue in the Public Sphere: A Bakhtinian Approach to Understanding a Place for Radical Utterances, 1684-1812", *Cultural Studies*, 18(6), pp 882-908.

Siebert, F., Peterson, T. and Schramm, W., 1956 [1963] *Four Theories of the Press*, University of Illinois Press, Chicago.

Sunstein, C., 2017, *#republic: Divided Democracy in the Age of Social Media*, Princeton University Press, Princeton.

The Age Charter of Editorial Independence https://www.smh.com.au/national/fairfax-media-charter-of-editorial-independence-20120619-20l4t.html; accessed 27 June 2018.

United States Commission on the Freedom of the Press, 1947, *A Free and Responsible Press*, University of Chicago Press, Chicago.

Ward, S. J. A., 2004, *The Invention of Journalism Ethics*, McGill-Queens University Press, Montreal.

Note on the contributor

Dr Denis Muller is a Senior Research Fellow in the Centre for Advancing Journalism at the University of Melbourne. He is a former journalist, and author of Journalism Ethics for the Digital Age (Scribe Publications, 2014) and Media Ethics and Disasters: Lessons from the Black Saturday Bushfires (Melbourne University Press, 2011).

What makes a target: politicians and abuse on social media

Politicians are known to be targets for some of the worst abuse on social media, including rape and death threats. But exactly how bad is it? Who gets it worst? And where is this onslaught of negativity taking us, asks Dr Amy Binns and Dr Martin Bateman

Although often at odds, journalists and politicians share many of the same problems on social media. Both are obliged to maintain a public profile, and to remain cheerful and polite no matter how gross the provocation. Both struggle with the competing demands of professionalism and likeability – often a zero-sum game. Both seek trust and respect on platforms notorious for dishonesty and no-holds-barred disdain.

And both may be seen as authority figures, part of the Establishment, and thus fair game for cutting down to size (Binns, 2017).

Pugnacious criticism of politicians has always been a part of the system. Lord Bew chaired a Government report on intimidation of MPs, partly in response to the increase of abuse on social media, but said at its launch: "Politics is a rough old game, and it should be a rough game."

Nobody's policies should get a free pass, and MPs' postbags have always contained anger and abuse; but social media has allowed this to reach a level of personal hostility that has shocked and disturbed politicians and commentators.

It has also removed the traditional filters that protected politicians. Secretaries used to discard the most vicious letters from the 'green-ink brigade', so called because the unhinged seemed to favour that colour, but now every insult pops up on their phones.

The hatred and even threats aimed at politicians, particularly on Twitter, had been an issue for some time but the death of Jo Cox MP threw it into sharp focus. She had been subject to abuse on Twitter in relation to her Remainer stance. Although her killer had not sent threats himself, he researched right wing groups online and repeatedly shouted "Britain First" as he stabbed her.

The links were summed up by a tweet by Beth Murray, a social media activist: "Female MPs get daily death and rape threats: 'It's just online, why can't you ignore it?'. Female MP is murdered: 'An unexpected tragedy.'"

How can we measure hostility?

We have stored millions of tweets sent to MPs from the end of 2016 in a database. We are still capturing data, but the results below relate to tweets sent between 18th March 2017 and 11th June, three days after the general election.[1]

We then categorised the tweets using sentiment analysis software. In order to focus on tweets seen by the MPs themselves, we have only categorised tweets sent as mentions using the MP's @username. These are tweets that will appear in the MP's stream (unless the sender has already been blocked). This excludes messages which may use the MP's name but will not necessarily be seen by the person such as "Dress himself?! Have you seen Boris Johnson? He's a complete tramp."

We only categorised tweets which mentioned a single MP. This removes confusing tweets sent to multiple accounts, such as: "@theresa_may you are a disgrace, vote @jeremycorbyn #labour #hero". It also removes tweets in which the MP may not be the target of the emotion, but has been copied in, such as: "@southernrail you are ruining my life @theresa_may @jeremycorbyn".

These @messages were then categorised as positive, neutral, disagree, hostile or threat using bespoke machine learning software, trained using this dataset, to measure the emotion behind the messages people send to politicians. This is a far more reliable method than simply searching for keywords, such as profanities. We defined hostility as insults aimed at the person rather than the action or policy.

Who is hated the most?

The results were surprising. Firstly, although Twitter is seen as an unremittingly hostile place, threats were a very small part of the overall dataset. We initially intended to create a separate category of threats but found these were too rare to train the software (we require a dataset of at least 500 examples).

Based on the numbers we found during manual categorising, we estimate threatening tweets at roughly 0.1% of all tweets sent to MPs. This is not to downplay their significance. This may still be a significant number for higher-profile MPs receiving hundreds of messages a day. Also, although rare, they are likely to make a much greater impact on the MP than the hundreds of other tweets received.

Secondly, although hostile behaviour directed at women receives most press coverage, our data shows little difference between the sexes after removing Jeremy Corbyn and Theresa May from the database (due to the disproportionate number of tweets they receive).

Jewish and white male MPs receive marginally more negativity than their female counterparts, by percentage of total messages received. Asian men receive significantly more abuse than Asian women MPs, while black women receive more than black men. However, there is a relatively small number of non-white MPs, and these figures may be disproportionately affected by high profile MPs, particularly Chuka Umunna and Diane Abbott.

Differences by race and gender

	White		Asian		Black		Jewish	
Classification	female	male	female	male	female	male	female	male
Hostile	13%	16%	13%	22%	19%	14%	13%	14%
Disagree	23%	25%	23%	24%	20%	21%	20%	24%
Others	64%	59%	64%	53%	61%	64%	66%	62%

Differences by party:

	Party			
Classification	Con	Labour	Lib Dem	SNP
Hostile	15%	13%	18%	13%
Disagree	26%	21%	28%	21%
Others	59%	66%	53%	66%

Although this may seem counter-intuitive given the much greater publicity regarding abuse of female MPs, it's actually in line with other smaller studies (Phillips, 2017); while some studies have only focussed on women, so cannot offer comparisons (Amnesty International, 2017).

The major drivers of hostility become clearer when we look at the people who receive the greatest percentage of hate as a proportion of their feed: high profile jobs and criticising Corbyn resulted in long term hostility. Incautious public appearances or tweets resulted in major spikes.

Scottish politics also proved more aggressive, with both of the sole elected representatives of Labour and the Conservatives acting as lightning conductors for online hatred. Greater numbers of non-SNP representatives could have dissipated some of this hatred.

We ranked the top 100 most messaged MPs [2]. The ten receiving the greatest *percentage* of hostility were:

Chris Leslie (32%), Labour MP and Corbyn critic, enormous spike after a radio interview.

Boris Johnson (29%), Conservative minister and Brexit campaigner.

Jeremy Hunt (27%), Conservative minister.

Simon Danczuk (24.5%), Labour MP, Corbyn critic, columnist for right-wing newspapers.

David Mundell (24.5%), Scotland's sole Conservative MP at that time.

George Osborne (24%), Conservative MP and newspaper editor.

Neil Coyle (24%), Labour MP and Corbyn critic.

Sajid Javid (23.5%), Conservative minister.

Ian Murray (23.5), Scotland's sole Labour MP at that time.

Corri Wilson (23%) SNP MP, faced allegations of wrongly using funds to support her campaigns.

Michael Gove (22%), Conservative minister and Brexit campaigner.

A different picture emerged when looking at high numbers of hostile tweets. These were usually part of a very busy feed. Diane Abbott and Jess Phillips, who are known to receive a lot of hostility, appear high on the graph below, but mid-table when ranked by percentage. This is because, in addition to receiving a lot of hostile tweets, they also receive a lot of positive and neutral tweets and are generally high profile. Ms Phillips is also a heavy Twitter user and has a lot of long conversations with supporters. Boris Johnson, however, scored highly for both percentage and total numbers of hostile tweets.

Top 20 most messaged MPs
By single @messages

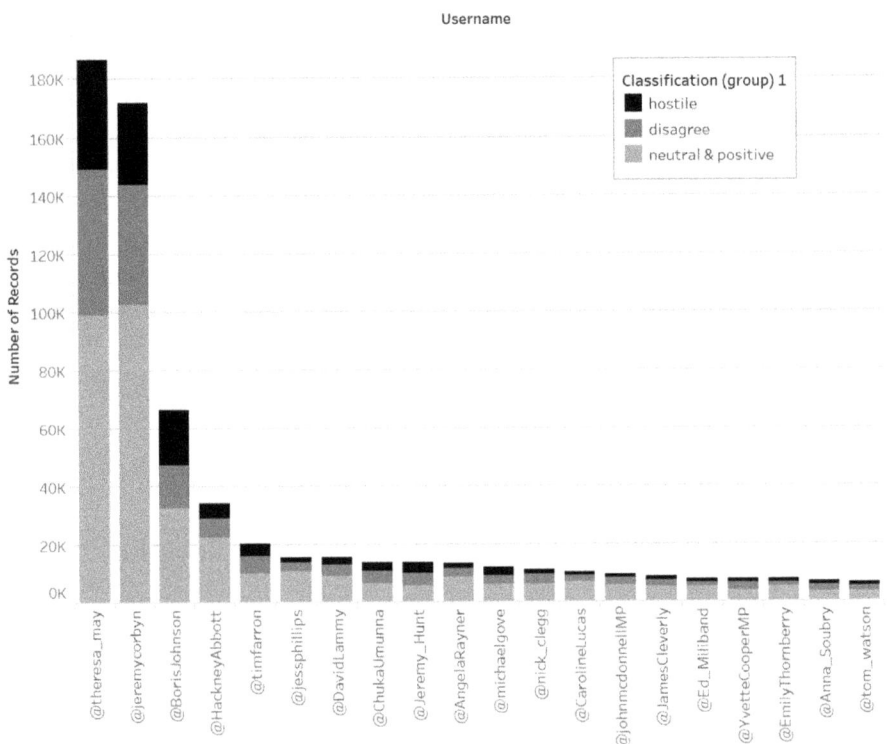

Sum of Number of Records for each Username. Color shows details about Classification (group) 1. The view is filtered on Username, which has multiple members selected.

These figures should not necessarily be read as disproving links between hostility, gender and race; as high public profiles clearly have an overwhelming effect on traffic, and front bench jobs at this time were predominantly held by white males.

In order to provide a definitive analysis, we would need a set of MPs from each of these groups who were neither frontbench or high profile, neither strongly pro- or anti-Corbyn, active on Twitter without courting publicity and who had not made an embarrassing television appearance or an incautious tweet. There are not sufficient MPs in each group to do this.

However, we can say that hostility on Twitter crosses demographic and party groups; and is not a problem for only one party, sex or race. It is fed by publicity on and off Twitter, so increases for people with higher profiles. It is also notably an issue for Labour MPs who criticise Jeremy Corbyn.

Subject or target? Our two minutes' hate

Through this research, we have examined tweets with single @usernames which will show in the MP's feed. We assume the senders are seeking to directly insult the MP; but some people use @usernames without any expectation of the MP actually seeing the thread.

In many hostile cases, the sender is discussing a major public event and tags in some of his/her own friends, along with the MP. They may then have a conversation about the MP's faults – a conversation which will appear in the MP's timeline. But the sender may have no expectation of them seeing the tweet amidst thousands of others. The sender may just be thoughtlessly using the @username as a hashtag, rather than intending a direct insult.

Such threads are essentially conversations between like-minded people. The MP is the subject of their conversation, but not the target. The real point of these conversations is not necessarily to distress the MP, but to build trust and community feeling between the other participants in the conversation. Bizarrely, abuse is being used as a form of virtue signalling.

As predicted by Orwell, hatred is used to create a sense of belonging and community-building. By including an MP of an opposing viewpoint in their abusive tweets, they prove their orthodoxy and credentials for belonging to the group. This is the 21st century's Two Minutes' Hate. This is how we prove we are goodthinkful.

The gates close

One result of the unremitting hostility online has been the quiet return of the gatekeepers. Social media was originally seen as a way for public figures to directly reach their audiences without the intermediaries of the press or broadcasters. It was also an opportunity for campaigners and constituents to circumvent the gatekeepers of secretaries and staff.

These sidedoors to power have been closing as MPs grow weary of abuse. Many MPs, such as Britain's sole Chinese origin MP Alan Mak, now state on their profile that they do not respond to enquiries via Twitter. For them, Twitter has become another one-way tool for pushing out media releases. Others are taking their conversations to the peaceful uplands of Instagram (Le Conte, 2017).

One prominent female politician told me she no longer looks at Twitter for 48 hours after a television appearance: she leaves it to her staff to monitor her feed. Others use Twitter's own tools to block hate-filled messages. Jess Phillips has said she filters her tweets for anything likely to include abuse, describing her system as "peak block, peak mute" (Elliott, 2017) and has discussed leaving the platform altogether (Press Association, 2016). Whilst these are reasonable responses to a distressing situation, this means one of the key benefits of social media has already been partially lost.

Where now?

Could an online climate of hostility result in more sensitive people being reluctant to enter public life? If so, this would leave our most important institutions to the more thick-skinned or even arrogant who are least likely to care about criticism.

This was one of the major concerns of Lord Bew's report on intimidation, which stated: "The overwhelming view of Parliamentary candidates who provided evidence… was that intimidation is already discouraging individuals from standing for public offices… If we want a diverse and experienced set of candidates for public offices, we need to address intimidation in the political arena." (Committee for Standards in Public Life, 2017)

This report recommended creating an electoral offence of intimidating Parliamentary candidates. Theresa May has endorsed this (Dearden, 2018).

It also recommended legislation to make social media companies liable for illegal content online, in the same way as newspapers are held responsible for everything they publish, even if written by readers and appearing on a letters page. Former Culture Secretary Matt Hancock made clear he was in favour of legislation (Tobitt, 2018), possibly creating a hybrid legal classification between platform and publisher.

UK politicians are not the only ones losing patience. Mark Zuckerberg's contrition tour has continued this year with appearances in front of US and EU bodies (Smith, 2018) (Rankin, 2018). Facebook and other social media companies are hurriedly hiring extra moderators and building sentiment analysis tools to try and cut back on the most offensive or criminal content.

But if politicians continue to see the worst of unregulated free speech every time they pick up their phones, we could see regulation that permanently curtails abuse.

Notes

[1] There is a natural break of a few days at this point as the set of accounts changed due to MPs winning or losing seats.

[2] We focussed on the most messaged 100 in order to discount the many MPs who are barely active on Twitter, but who may receive a small spike in hostility from half a dozen constituents angry about a local matter. This could have the result of a backbencher topping the charts due to a missed bin collection.

References

Amnesty International. (2017, September 4). *Black and Asian Women MPs Abused More Online*. Retrieved June 6, 2018, from https://www.amnesty.org.uk/online-violence-women-mps

Binns, A. (2017). Fair Game? Journalists' experiences of online abuse. *Journal of Applied Journalism & Media Studies, 6*(2), 183-206.

Committee for Standards in Public Life. (2017). Retrieved June 6, 2018, from https://www.gov.uk/government/uploads/system/uploads/attachment_data/file/666927/6.3637_CO_v6_061217_Web3.1__2_.pdf

Dearden, L. (2018, February 6). Police 'don't want' new law against intimidating politicians backed by Theresa May. *The Independent*. Retrieved June 6, 2018, from https://www.independent.co.uk/news/uk/crime/theresa-may-new-law-intimidating-politicians-mps-online-abuse-not-needed-free-speech-police-concerns-a8197856.html

Elliott, F. (2017, August 26). MP Jess Phillips forced to filter her tweets after 600 rape threats in a day. *The Times*. Retrieved June 6, 2018, from https://www.theguardian.com/technology/2016/may/31/labour-mp-jess-phillips-says-she-may-leave-twitter-over-trolls-abuse

Le Conte, M. (2017, October 17). "It's quite a relief from Twitter": the strangely gentle world of MP Instagram accounts. *New Statesman*. Retrieved June 6, 2018, from https://www.newstatesman.com/science-tech/2017/10/it-s-quite-relief-twitter-strangely-gentle-world-mp-instagram-accounts

Phillips, T. (2017, July 23). *This Is What The Twitter Abuse Of Politicians During The Election Really Looked Like*. Retrieved May 15, 2018, from Buzzfeed: https://www.buzzfeed.com/tomphillips/twitter-abuse-of-mps-during-the-election-doubled-after-the?utm_term=.milryXgmP#.br63wYXp1

Press Association. (2016, May 31). Labour MP says she may leave Twitter over trolls' rape threats. *The Guardian*. Retrieved June 6, 2018, from https://www.theguardian.com/technology/2016/may/31/labour-mp-jess-phillips-says-she-may-leave-twitter-over-trolls-abuse

Rankin, J. (2018, May 22). Complaints that Zuckerberg 'avoided questions' at European parliament. *The Guardian*. Retrieved June 6, 2018, from https://www.theguardian.com/technology/2018/may/22/no-repeat-of-data-scandal-vows-mark-zuckerberg-in-brussels-facebook

Smith, D. (2018, April 11). Mark Zuckerberg vows to fight election meddling in marathon Senate grilling. *The Guardian*. Retrieved June 6, 2018, from https://www. theguardian.com/technology/2018/apr/10/zuckerberg-facebook-testimony-latest-news-regulation-congress

Tobitt, C. (2018, March 15). Culture Secretary Matt Hancock tells MPs he would consider legislation cracking down on hate speech on social media. *Press Gazette*. Retrieved May 15, 2018

Note on the contributors

Dr Amy Binns spent ten years as a newspaper reporter before entering academia. She teaches print and digital journalism at the University of Central Lancashire. Her research is largely around finding practical solutions for difficult behaviour online, which involves working with a wide range of people including media industry professionals. She still loves a good story, and is currently working on a biography of science fiction author John Wyndham.

The sentiment analysis software used in this research was developed by Dr Martin Bateman, senior lecturer at the University of Central Lancashire. His research interests are, networks and distributed systems, network-based computer forensics, protocol analysis, video identification and cloud systems.

Social media and war

Social media has become a vital and game changing aspect of information warfare, says Greg Rowett

The moral forces are among the most important subjects in war." – Carl Von Clausewitz, *On War.*[1]

As with every aspect of human society, war and conflict have changed and adapted with the development of new technologies. Information warfare is no different. Historically, the great changes in this field were the advent of the printing press, the development of faster communication methods and mass media. The emergence of the cybersphere, and its pervasive reach into every aspect of modern life, is today's revolution.

Social media's many impacts on war and warfare are felt at all times, not only during a kinetic or 'shooting' war. The intelligence-gathering capabilities, particularly using public domain information, have flourished with social media – bored soldiers posing with pretty views that can be identified, or even just posting with the geotag on, can reveal vital information and there are many cases of serious operation security (OPSEC) breaches due to such action, as open source and unclassified information is pieced together to reveal classified intelligence. Footage and information shared on social media by those within the battlefield offers a new avenue for tactical battlefield intelligence gathering. There is also the possibility of social media – and information gathered from it – being used to facilitate security breaches of sensitive systems. But for these aspects, social media and the internet have not changed the fundamental dynamics of the game.

The game changer

Where social media has had a truly revolutionary, fundamental, effect on warfare is in the realm of *information warfare*, which is defined thus:

> *'The organised and deliberate use of communications, information and psychological operations to influence or disrupt the emotions, motives, objective reasoning, decision-making abilities and ultimately the behaviour of foreign governments, organizations, groups, and individuals in pursuit of a strategic advantage.'*

209

Information warfare, and warfare in general, on a strategic level does goes beyond what many people think of as war. War as a political activity is distinctly different, albeit related, to the general understanding of what 'war' is. Physical violence and the ability to wield it are not the only tools necessary in war. There have been many cases in recent history, such as the Vietnam War and the Soviet incursion into Afghanistan, where one side possessed supreme military, economic, and industrial power over the other, and yet was defeated. This is due to *moral forces*, a hard to conceptualise but central aspect of war. The general principle of the moral forces of war is outlined in the US Fleet Marine Force Manual – 1 (FMFM-1):

> *"The term moral as used here is not restricted to ethics, although ethics are certainly included, but pertains to those forces of psychological rather than tangible nature, to include the mental aspects of War."*[2]

FMFM-1 later elaborates on the importance of the moral forces.

> *"Moral forces are difficult to grasp and impossible to quantify. We cannot easily gauge forces like national and military resolve, national or individual conscience, emotion, fear, courage, morale, leadership, or esprit. Yet moral forces exert a greater influence on the nature and outcome of war than do physical."*[3]

This is an ancient concept, but one that has been impacted by the internet and social media more than any other technological or social change, save perhaps increasing literacy rates and the concept of nationalism. For with these technologies, there exists a tool which can be used to sculpt the moral forces of a population in a way that bypasses all the institutionalised resistances and physical defences that the state and a military can muster. The failure to turn their physical superiority into a moral one is why the US and the USSR could not accomplish their goals in their respective wars in Vietnam and Afghanistan.

The idea of directly impacting the moral forces of the enemy is not new, and historically every time there is a revolution in communications – due to social changes such as increased literacy, or technical such as the printing press, radio and television – there has been a subsequent adaption for information warfare. Social media is only the latest – though arguably the most significant – technological change that heralds a new revolution in propaganda techniques and information warfare. It is thus inevitable that social media can be, and is, used as a tool of war for its intrinsic properties.

Designed to change behaviour

Indeed, the ability to affect the behaviour of users is the central business model for many online based firms: Google, Facebook and other such companies provide free access to their users, but in exchange gather data on the users browsing habits, which is used to sell targeted advertisements[4]. Alphabet (Google's parent company)[5] and Facebook[6] have a market capitalization of $764.42bn and $544.59bn respectively, for a combined total of $1,309.1tr. Businesses such as these function by changing people's behaviour: it is downright foolish for those in the strategic sphere not to take notice and examine how that system could be turned to achieving strategic objectives, instead of advertising.

There are numerous aspects of human behaviour online which have relevance to propagandists. The cascade phenomena is one example, whereby emotions and feelings are spread through a crowd like a contagion[7]. Under these circumstances, people are much more likely to react to emotional and populist sentiments than when 'alone': this phenomenon occurs not only in physical gatherings of people, but also across social media. In effect, propaganda can be dispensed upon the target population from far away, even if it is widely dispersed[8]. Propaganda that full use of the possibilities of the platform is termed 'Computational Propaganda': *the assemblage of social media platforms, autonomous agents, and big data tasked with the manipulation of public opinion*[9].

It is this creation of a direct connection of the target population with the propagandist which is the most important aspect of the internet and social media that relates to information war. The impact of geography, and the barriers for information it creates, is massively reduced, and it is nearly impossible to intercept propaganda before it reaches the target community. Traditional information vectors – papers, pamphlets, radio, TV – are all inhibited to varying degrees by geographical distance and political boarders: for the internet, this is barely a barrier at all.

The consequences

A resultant trait, the ability to connect likeminded, but isolated, individuals is a central feature of many social media sites. There are areas of the internet dedicated to just about everything, and while most of these take the form of fan clubs, support networks, peaceful political activist groups, and niche interest sites, social media is also used as a platform by radicals and insurgents as recruiting grounds. There are many cases of terrorist and rebel organisations recruiting people through the internet, and propaganda messages can be dispersed over the internet, which would normally have been censored if traditional means were attempted.

Another factor is the functional design of social media platforms: they are not designed in a manner that facilitates informed, balanced and lengthy public debates, but rather short, snappy exchanges with a premium on time of posting and the popularity of the material. A reasoned and well sourced piece of content posted in response to an article will receive far less attention than a short, amusing or otherwise entertaining piece will, due to a variety of factors relating to deliberate design choices by the platform developers. Thus, even without the influence of propaganda machines, social media platforms are functionally insufficient to facilitate the political debates that take place upon them to a high standard. This can be easily abused by those wishing to subvert the public debate, because the criteria for a successful argument on an online debate is not about persuading the other side, but by gaming the various algorithms and social media norms to gain the maximum visibility.

This nature of social media also effects other more traditional information streams not exclusive to social media. As visibility and propagation are governed by user participation and interaction via comments and discussion, subjects that are more dramatic and eye-catching garner more attention, which in turn leads to more user participation, something that mainstream news organisations require for their revenue streams. Within the comments sections of these articles, agents – either individuals shills or botnets of large numbers of automated 'users' – can seed comments designed to angle the conversation in favour of the propagandists. This can then cause the producers of the media to cater their coverage to try and retain the interest, and the revenue, of the perceived audience. This practice of seeding comments sections is called astroturfing, and can be utilised for a number of purposes, such as marketing and PR. Within the context of social media, this takes the form of seeding favourable comments, then using botnets to use the platforms voting system (retweets, likes, upvotes, shares) to increase the visibility of the selected contents and posts. It is estimated that a majority – 59 per cent – of URL links shared on twitter are not clicked[10], indicating it is only the headlines most people view before sharing and liking, a trend that extends across most of both social media and traditional news sources. Many instead go straight to the comments and discussion areas to find a summary of the article, and by influencing these areas, the users are in turn influenced.

This practice, and others like it, are referred to as 'trolling'. The term troll itself is a term adopted from internet lingo. Traditionally a troll is an individual or group who seeks to cause discord and emotional reactions through irritation and provocation, for the troll's amusement. The mass media uses troll as a catch-all reference to any sort of online misbehaviour, encompassing everything from benign faux-idiocy, to death threats and sexual harassment. In the context of information warfare, it is a term crudely adapted to describe those who seek to manipulate and influence people via the internet for *political* aim. This distinction and disconnect in meaning – along with many other cases where articulation of the situation has been hampered by a lack of suitable vocabulary – leads to many misunderstandings of the problem.

A versatile tool of power
Information warfare of the 21st century, empowered by the technologies, and made desirable by the geopolitical circumstances, is now more central to the strategic situation than ever before. It is a tool by which the moral forces of groups can be directly reached, a means of using communication to direct the behaviour

of others. It is not as forceful or overt as the application of military force, but this subtlety is to its advantage. It is a versatile tool of power for those that choose to use it. The internet and social media are absolutely critical to this new revolution in information warfare. Information warfare is centred upon communications and as society and technology facilitates greater communications, the use of information as a weapon will undoubtedly increase, and social media platforms are already the site of information war. Like every aspect of human society, social media – despite, or perhaps because of, the huge benefits and opportunities it brings to society – has found its use in war.

Notes

[1] Clausewitz, Carl Von: *On War*. Translated by Graham, J.J., Maude, F.N. (Hare: Wordsworth Publishing Limited: 1832, republished in 1997), p. 150.

[2] USMC: FMFM-1 (Washington D.C.: Department of the Navy: 1989), P. 10

[3] Ibid, p. 13

[4] de Corni`ere, Alexandre and de Nijs, Romain: "Online advertising and privacy" in *RAND Journal of Economics*, Vol 47, No.1, 2016. pp. 48-72

[5] Investopedia: *GOOGL Stock Quote – Alphabet Inc Summary* Investopedia. *Accessed online at http://www.investopedia.com/markets/stocks/googl/ on 28/05/18. Price quoted at 15:54 GMT*

[6] *Investopedia:* FB Stock Quote – Facebook Inc Summary *Investopedia.* Accessed online at http://www.investopedia.com/markets/stocks/fb/ on 28/05/18. Price quoted at 15:55 GMT

[7] Wang, Xizhi and Zhang, Hue: "Propagation of Social Emotion in Cyber Space Based on Cognitive Social Psychology" in *IEEE Access*, Vol. 23, No. 4, pp. 225-236

[8] Ibid.

[9] Woolley, Samuel C. and Howard, Philip N.: "Political Communication, Computational Propaganda, and Autonomous Agents" in *International Journal of Communication*, Vol 10. pp. 4882-4890

[10] Gabielkov et al: Report: *Social Clicks: What and Who Gets Read on Twitter?* from ACM SIGMETRICS / IFIP Performance 2016. Antibes Juan-les-Pins, 2016.

References

Clausewitz, V. C., 1997. *On War,*. Hare: Wordsworth Editions Limited.

de Corni'ere, A. & Romain, N. d., 2016. Online Advertising and Privacy. *Rand Journal of Economics,* 47(1), pp. 48-72.

Gabielkov, M., Ramachandran, A., Chaintreau, A. & Legout, A., 2016. *Social Clicks: What and Who Gets Read on Twitter?*. Antibes Juan-les-Pins, HAL archives.

Investopedia, n.d. *FB Stock Quote - Facebook Inc Summary* Investopedia. *[Online] Available at: https://www.investopedia.com/markets/stocks/fb/[Accessed 28 05 2018].*

Investopedia, n.d. GOOGL Stock Quote - Alphabet Inc Summary Investopedia. [Online] Available at: https://www.investopedia.com/markets/stocks/googl/[Accessed 28 05 2018].

United States Marine Corps, 1989. *FMFM-1: Warfighting.* Washington, D.C.: Department of the Navy.

Wang, X. & Zhang, H., 2017. Propagation of social emotion in Syber space based on cognitive social psychology. *IEEE Access,* 23(4), pp. 225-236.

Woolley, S. C. & Howard, P. N., 2016. Political Communication, Computational Propaganda, and Autonomous Agents. *International Journal of Communication,* Volume 10, pp. 4882-4890.

Note on the contributor

Greg Rowett is a Research Fellow at the Institute for Statecraft. He is a specialist in strategic environmental issues, and information warfare. He has a special interest in the interactions of various online communities, in the use of influence operations via the internet and in information warfare theory.

Zimbabwe's 2018 elections and the role of social media

It was a case of not-so-social social media as Zimbabweans went to the polls for the first time since Robert Mugabe was ousted, says Tatenda Chitagu

Zimbabwe's July 2018 harmonised elections came in the backdrop of partially opened up political space and freedoms by the new president, Emmerson Mnangagwa, who took over power from long-time confidant and Zanu PF strongman Robert Mugabe through a soft coup in November 2017.

Interestingly, or surprisingly, a record 23 presidential aspirants were vying for the country's top job. While there were more than 120 political parties that had expressed interest in taking part in the contest, the number was whittled down after some failed to raise money to pay to the electoral management body, the Zimbabwe Electoral Commission (Zec). The plebiscite was historic, in that it was the first election in many years without Mugabe contesting, as well as his arch rival, the late leader of the mainstream opposition Movement for Democratic Change (MDC) party, Morgan Tsvangirai, who died of cancer in February 2018.

At the same time, social media was now deeply engrained in Zimbabwe's political campaign turf. Likewise, the elections were digitised (Willems 2016) because of increased social media activity and traffic – mostly WhatsApp, Facebook, Twitter and YouTube – by both the contesting candidates, their parties, supporters, the civic society and observers becoming involved.

Political parties campaigned on social media, playing numbers games by displaying pictures of their supporters, interacting with voters and also live-streaming their rallies, bringing citizen-initiated campaigns (Gibson 2015) and overcoming barriers to entry created by the partisan state media. Citizens now controlled and framed their discourses and, because they now had agency, challenged the official narrative by mainstream media as social media broadened the public sphere and civic engagement.

Background: the features of new media

Though not the deciding factor, social media political campaigns do play a bigger role in the electoral process now than before, because of the active youth and first-time voters who may be a swing constituency. The new media ecologies are generally cheap, interactive (give one to many: many-to -many communication), viral, give anonymity and transcend geographical barriers, among other advantages.

But while social media has increased citizen's voices and participation in recent elections, its communicative potential has been threatened by fake news, cyber propaganda by political parties and their activists, along with the spread of hate speech and vulgarity by opponents. Hasty (2005:7), while analysing political culture in Ghana, noted that framing of political life was 'so riven with political passions and vivid personalist narratives' that it cannot be objective.

Zimbabwe is a country that is highly polarised and dichotomous because of previous violence in elections and mistrust following rigging allegations in previous polls – so 'netizens' attack each other on social media. Instead of being complementary to democracy, social media ahead of the Zimbabwean polls had, to a greater extent, achieved just the opposite. It became instruments of misinformation through 'deepfake' videos, doctored, photo-shopped pictures of candidates and key players. People then relied on the mainstream media to find out if something trending on social media was true or not. This was because of the lack of editorial control, which pertains in the social media ecosystem.

The election itself – and the purveyors of a lot more than information

In the run up to the election, social media outlets became sites of political contestation, name calling and ridicule, and evolved into a battleground for supporters and sympathizers of the main political parties. This was worse when an assassination attempt was made on Mnangagwa in a landmine attack, and many conspiracy theories and blame games erupted even before investigations were completed.

Everything was framed from a partisan standpoint rather than on policy issues, as supporters ignored the shortcomings of their preferred party or candidates while exaggerating the weaknesses of their opponents. Politics rather became more about form and style rather than substance (Willems 2012: 96). Dyed-in-the woool supporters of Chamisa were called Nerrorists while Mnangagwa loyalists were termed Varakashi (thrashers).

Apart from being sources of information, Twitter, Facebook and Whatsapp became purveyors of a great deal of political opinion, innuendo, bias and activism. This happened before, during and after the polling, when a Constitutional Court challenge was lodged by opposition MDC Alliance leader Nelson Chamisa contesting Mnangagwa's victory. Chamisa, who received 44.3 per cent of the vote against Mnangagwa's 50.6 per cent, claimed the election was rigged after Zec revised the figure by 0.1 per cent, days after announcing the results. The middle ground of this social media content was hard to find (Zhangazha 2018).

Social media promotes echo chambers and prejudices as voters only looked for content that suited their political inclination; their political horizons were narrowed, not broadened as social media users looked for content that resonated with their opinions and beliefs. Wasswa (2013:63), commenting on Kenya's 2013 elections, noted that social media attracted those who were already interested in politics and seeking additional information, mainly reinforcing their beliefs and already existent political affiliations.

Information and communication technology (ICT), and its evolution in to social media and other online activity, has proved to be discriminatory in Zimbabwe because of its profound influence on language use. The language being used in social media contexts – dubbed Netspeak (Crystal 2011) – is not compatible with both older people and the rural population, even when they have access to social media. There is great use of extra-linguistic features like laughing (lol) or emojis.

An average social media user is not acquainted with such specialised vocabulary, which is the medium of electronic communication. New features, acronyms and abbreviations and other non-standard words and spellings have been invented in online communication. What you find today will no longer be used tomorrow – users have to stay connected or updated to be able to engage and understand online interactions. Rapid change requires constant learning to adapt one's knowledge to highly dynamic contexts (Bing (2015:180).

Instead of translating seditious mobile action into street action, ICT might actually cause citizens to be active armchair, 'cyber scarecrows', keyboard critiques online but passive offline (Ibahrine 2008: 264). Or rather, people chat on social media spaces to others far away, while ignoring those they are with physically. Some of the messages were unsolicited to an extent that a lawyer sued Zanu PF and Zec over data breaches, after he received unwanted campaign messages on his phone urging him to vote for Zanu PF despite being an apolitical person.

Moreover, the digital divide in Zimbabwe created and still creates participation inequalities for the digitally illiterate rural folk. In rural areas, mobile/broadband subscriptions are 41.3 per 100 inhabitants, while households with a computer are just 12.9 per 100, according to the International TeleCommunications Union (ITU). In these areas there are issues of availability, accessibility and affordability; they may not have handsets compatible with social media networks, or there is no network signal or power to charge the phones in remote places. But for all of Zimbabwe (rural and urban) latest statistics show that households with internet access are 22.1 per 100.

Data tariffs in Zimbabwe are also expensive for the average Zimbabwean hard hit by the decade-long economic malaise. Fixed broadband subscriptions is one per 100 inhabitants, according to the ITU latest statistics on data usage on the country.

The digital divide

Commenting on Zimbabwe's digitalised 2013 elections, Mare (2017 :1) observed that social media ambivalently created communication hierarchies and participation inequalities between the connected (mostly urbanites) and disconnected (especially rural) voters. And the digital divide ran along gender, age, income and urban-rural gaps. Universal access was not guaranteed then and still isn't. The internet-compatible minority mainly lives in urban areas, is male, and is better educated than the general populace between 25 and 34 years of age (Bing 2015). The majority of the Zimbabwean population (60 per cent) resides in rural areas, according to the last census. Most of these have no internet access. Only 10 per cent of the people in rural areas followed social media for the 2018 elections news, whilst 46 per cent got their election news from radio (Afrobarometer). The rest relied on the traditional physical interactions.

Rather than promoting transparency, politicians' visibility on Facebook engenders a new calibre of celebrity – politicians who are transiently accessible online yet very much inaccessible offline (Norris 2001).

Zimbabwe engages in subtle forms of communication surveillance, which significantly influences the nature and texture of online political discourse (Mare 2015). The country passed the Interception of Communications Act (ICA) in 2007, which empowers the spy agency, the Central Intelligence Organisation (CIO), the Commissioner of Police and the Zimbabwe Revenue Authority to snoop on citizens' mobile phones through the Monitoring of Interception of Communications Centre (MICC).

While social media also gave rise to citizen journalism, this has created problems because they are unethical and attack rivals. Trolls, bots, doxing and online harassment by paid cyber troops, who also attacked women candidates or projected female voters in regalia as sex objects and 'slay queens' in the electoral process, also diluted the socialness of social media in the election, especially in the wake of lack of digital security by netizens. Because of structural sexism and misogyny, there was a sharp rise in technology-related violence against women and its normalisation has made the use of the internet a gender issue (Majama 2018).

So rampant was the practice that the industry regulator, Postal and Telecommunications Regulatory Authority of Zimbabwe (POTRAZ), said it would start a public awareness programme calling for the responsible use of internet-based communication platforms. "We are encouraging people to use those platforms responsibly. Avoid spreading fake news and causing unnecessary grief, pain and alarm and despondency to other people, " ICT and Cyber Security Minister Supa Mandiwanzira said in June 2018.

Whether social media will change the exclusionist history in polls in Zimbabwe, and wholly complement democracy, only time will tell.

References

Afrobarometer (2018). Findings from a pre-election survey in Zimbabwe: June-July 2018: file:///home/chronos/ua0c6433ce0ec453b842583bcbef97ac3d85fd660/Downloads/afrobarometer%20zim_pre_election_survey_2018_20072018.pdf

Bing, N (2015). Kenya Decides: Kiswahili, social media and politics in Kenya's 2013 general elections, Journal of African Media Studies Volume 7 Number 2.

Crystal, D. (2011). Language and the Internet, Cambridge: Cambridge University Press.

Chuma W, (2008). Mediating the 2000 Elections in Zimbabwe: Competing Journalisms in a Society at the Crossroads: African Journalism Studies Volume 29 (1) Ecquid Novi.

Hasty, J. (2005). The press and political culture in Ghana. Bloomington: Indiana University Press.

Herman, E. W., & Chomsky, N. (1988). Manufacturing consent: The political economy of the mass media. New York: Pantheon Books.

Ibahrine, M. (2008), Mobile communication and sociopolitical change in the Arab world, in J. E. Katz (ed.), Handbook of Mobile Communication Studies, Cambridge, London: The MIT Press, pp. 258–72.

International Media Support (2018): The Professional Election Reporter: Guidelines for Journalists covering elections in Zimbabwe.

International Media Support (2018): Citizen Journalism Guidelines on Electoral Reporting in Zimbabwe.

International TeleCommunications Union (ITU) (2017): Report on Zimbabwe, accessed on www.itu.int/icteye

Majama K, 2018: Cyber violence makes internet use a gendered issue: https://koliwemajama.co.zw/cyber-violence-makes-internet-use-gendered-issue/ (accessed August 8)

Mare, A. 2015. Facebook, Youth and Political Action: A Comparative Study of Zimbabwe and South Africa. PhD diss., Rhodes University.

Mare A, (2017). Politics unusual? Facebook and political campaigning during the 2013 harmonised elections in Zimbabwe, African Journalism Studies Volume 38, Issue 2, pp. 1–22 (UNISA).

Molony, T. (2007), I don't trust the phone; It always lies: Social capital and information and communication technologies in Tanzanian micro and small enterprises, Information Technology and International Development, 3: 4, pp. 67–83.

—— (2009), Carving a Niche: ICT, social capital and trust in the shift from personal to impersonal trading in Tanzania, Information Technology for Development, 15: 4, pp. 283–301.

Norris, P. (2001). Digital Divide: Civic Engagement, Information Poverty and the Internet Worldwide. Cambridge: Cambridge University Press. https://doi.org/10.1017/CBO9781139164887

PACT: Rethinking Citizen Engagement 'Spaces' in Zimbabwe's New Dispensation: Challenges and Prospects for Civil Society Ahead of the 2018 Elections, accessed on: http://kubatana.net/2018/06/26/rethinking-citizen-engagement-spaces-zimbabwes-new-dispensation-challenges-prospects-civil-society-ahead-2018-elections/?utm_source=Kubatana.net+-+News&utm_campaign=c28995c620-EMAIL_CAMPAIGN_2018_07_03_08_30&utm_medium=email&utm_term=0_39a6c56b7a-c28995c620-132989029

Wasswa, H. W. (2013), The role of social media in the 2013 Presidential election campaigns in Kenya. A research project submitted to the School of Journalism and Mass Communication, Master thesis, Nairobi: School of Journalism and Mass Communication, University of Nairobi.

Willems W (2012): The Ballot Vote as Embedded Ritual: A Radical Critique of Liberal-Democratic Approaches to Media and Elections in Africa, African Studies, 71:1, 91-107

Willems, W. 2016. Social Media, Platform Power and (Mis)Information in Zambia's Recent Elections. Accessed January 18, 2017. http://blogs.lse.ac.uk/africaatlse/2016/08/30.

Zhangazha T, (2018), Keyboards Drawn, Perceptions Ready: Social Media and Zimbabwe's 2018 Election. Published on http://takura-zhangazha.blogspot.com/2018/06/keyboards-drawn-perceptions-ready.html Accessed on June 11, 2018.

Note on the contributor

Tatenda Chitagu is an investigative journalist from Zimbabwe with more than ten years' experience. He has been a fellow at the Reuters Institute for the Study of Journalism at the University of Oxford and holds an MSc in Media and Society Studies from the Midlands State University in Zimbabwe. He writes for the biggest privately-owned daily newspaper, The Newsday, as well as its sister weekly, The Standard. He is the current winner of the Haller Prize for Development Journalism award in sub-Saharan Africa. In 2015, he also won the Zimbabwe Human Rights Association's (ZimRights) Best Human Rights Defender Journalist of the Year award.

Few whispers go unheard in the world of Chinese social media

China ploughs its own furrow in the new digital age. The internet is a challenging alliance of private companies and government influence. Dipsy Edmunds reports on how that balance is being developed

"Chinese (are) willing to exchange their privacy for convenience or efficiency." So said Yanhong Li, the chief executive of Chinese internet giant Baidu in explaining why his nation's companies could easily collect and exploit users' data in 2018.

His statement then went viral on Chinese social media and he received thousands of negative comments. One critic said: "It's not people's willingness, but they have no other choice." Another commenter on Weibo (the Chinese microblogging site) said: "Companies collected users' data because the government first allowed them to do so."

China still has no serious law to protect personal data privacy. The government requires most social media platforms to verify the ID of users during registration (by phone), but this policy merely provides media companies with a more useful and more sophisticated database.

This is just one example that shows how the national censorship regime influences Chinese society. Academics discuss how censorship reduces access to information. However, many don't realise that censorship across the Chinese internet is not just a wall to hide information, but is a growing and blunt system designed to influence social media to achieve the government's propaganda and monitoring desires.

This chapter is based on my experience working for a state-owned media business, which helps the provincial government to develop its influences on social media and to monitor public discourse. It aims to (i) explain the market and the trends of Chinese social media; (ii) show how the government's censorship regime works with media companies and platform operators; and (iii) to detail how censorship causes 'gateway effects'.

China's social media market

With more than 911.4m active social media users, Chinese social media companies are now enjoying the juicy profits of a huge market. The administration's internet censorship and digital surveillance policies protect these companies from overseas competition. Fast-growing e-commerce, game and mobile advertisements have provided these companies with even more income.

According to a research report from CNNIC (2018), there are more than 3,000 Chinese companies providing different social media services. The structure of the Chinese social media industry is shown in figure 1:

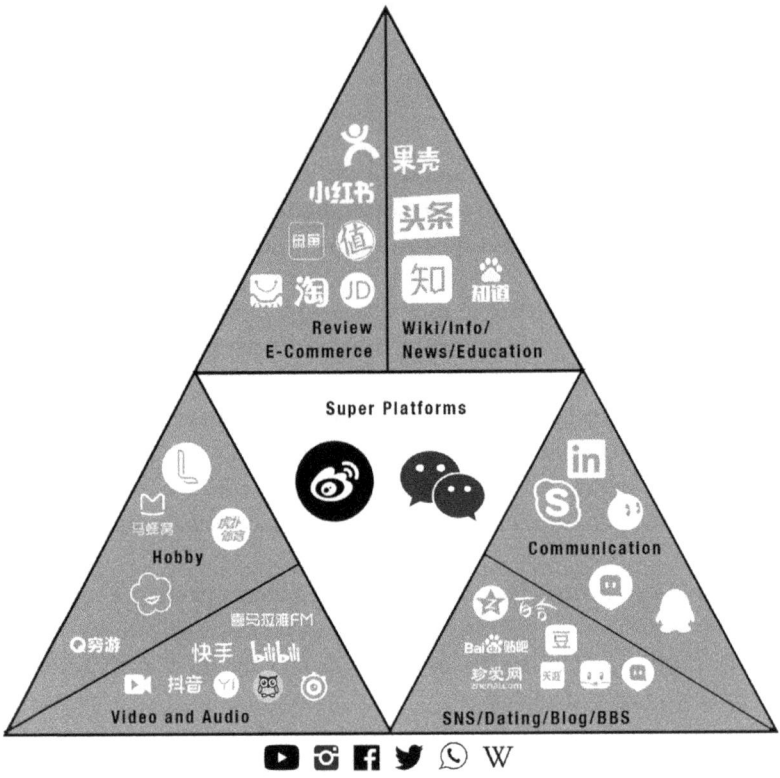

Figure 1: A brief landscape of Chinese social media platforms

The main players and their super platforms

'Bats' (Baidu, Alibaba, Tencent) are always reported as the top three Chinese internet giants. They provide the most commonly used daily services to Chinese netizens. Baidu controls the biggest search engine; Alibaba operates the biggest e-commerce platform – Taobao.com; and Tencent, the biggest game company, also runs the messaging services WeChat and QQ.

The Bats have developed from different business models, but they are now competing fiercely in social media, having invested heavily to improve their brands and to build competitive advantage. As the figure 2 shows, these three companies control or have investments in many Chinese other social media companies.

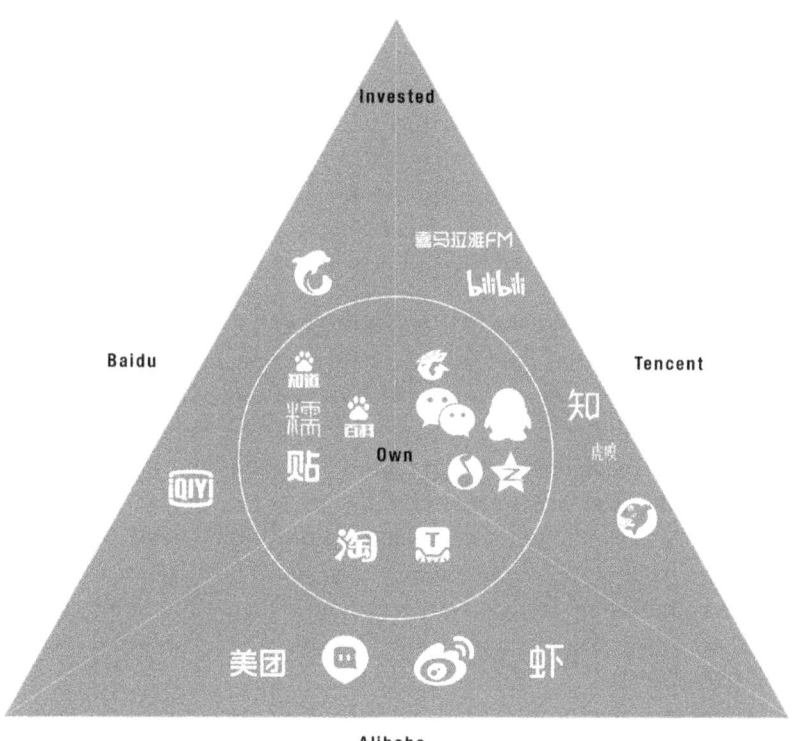

Figure 2: The social media platforms and investments of Bat companies owned and invested

Although these three companies have different focuses, they all want to extend their businesses and to defend their profits by developing their influence on social media. For this reason, the three have invested in social media platforms to help connect different services. For example, people can directly buy Taobao's goods on Weibo, and users can also write their restaurant reviews on WeChat. Those connections between the social media and services/goods help these tech giants develop their super platforms, which have multiple-functions, and where users can find almost all online services from food ordering to money transfer.

WeChat is now a dominant application in China and is found in more than 1bn devices; its Moment programme allows users to share their life; more than 3.5m businesses are using official accounts platforms to obtain data in users (Tencent, 2018).

Weibo is a leading social media, also known as the Chinese Twitter. However, it now has more functions than Twitter and is becoming a powerful super platform, especially for e-commerce, branding and advertising. According to Weibo's official report (2018), it is now in more than 411m devices, increasing at 20.7 per cent, year-on-year.

Alibaba invested in Weibo at 2013; then Weibo developed its function of online shopping with Alibaba. Weibo is now becoming the most important platform for stars, television shows and films to interact with audiences. Its revenue in the first quarter of 2018 reached $349.9m, an increase of 79 per cent, year-on-year.

Besides those super platforms, many social media platforms focus on vertical markets or specific groups; Little Red Book specialises on reviewing imported products; video platform Kuaishou focuses on young people from rural areas. These platforms are growing quickly and they attract many loyal users.

Trends in artificial intelligence (AI) technology and short-video

According to a report from the CNNIC (2018), 45 per cent of Chinese netizens purchased a product or service online in 2017. Netizens spent more than $164.22bn on fashion and beauty in 2017 and some $97.88bn on hobbies. AI technology powers social media's algorithm to promote these goods and help the customers make shopping decision, as it does around the world.

Weibo uses AI technology to help brands improve their advertising strategies. Bytedance uses its advanced AI technology to produce many popular apps such as the newsfeed application Toutiao, which has more than 120m daily active users, and the short-video sharing application Douyin, which has more than 124m monthly active users.

Douyin enjoyed significant growth in 2018. It became one of the two hottest short-video platforms of the young in China. Short-videos are now popular among Chinese millennials who use them to express their attitudes and opinions. More than 100m monthly active users post short-videos to share their stories. Platforms such as Kuaishou, Douyin, Miaopai and Huoshan are now becoming the quickest method for Chinese millennials, especially those in rural areas, to make money and become famous.

Government censorship and media companies

My previous experience in working for a state-owned media company provided me the opportunity to connect with the government. This section shows how the Chinese censorship and propaganda regime works based on my own experience, and explains how the government co-operates with media businesses and social media operators to achieve its propaganda goals.

A simple view shows this in the form of a triangle - see figure 3. But in reality it's a much more complicated process. Government has three main aims with social media: the first is to provide online services; the second is to use digital surveillance to stop potential collective action; and the third is to use it as a propaganda tool.

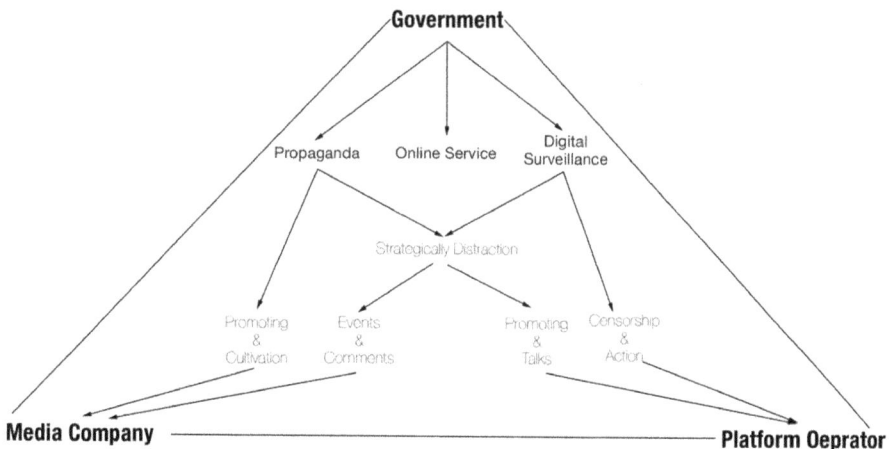

Figure 3: How the government using social media co-operates with media companies and platform operators

Using social media provides online services

In 2015 prime minister Keqiang Li ordered local government to provide quicker, easier and better services to Chinese netizen, with official accounts on platforms then becoming important conduits to make this happen. With technical support from social media businesses, many local councils set up accounts to provide services. For example, people can directly contact local offices to express their needs and complaints via Weibo; people can also make a visa appointment via the official account on WeChat. Social media is also becoming a platform for government to publicise its official announcements and reports. More than 130,000 government official accounts are providing services on Weibo (2017), and more than 100,000 government accounts are providing services on WeChat(2017). Social media is now becoming one of the most important communication channel connecting the government and Chinese citizens.

However, lacking knowledge of understanding social media and communications, many local authorities seek help from media companies. Some local councils pay for media companies to help them manage their social media accounts. Some government-owned media companies are profiting from this business, though the quality of their strategies vary enormously. Jiang Ning Police, an official Weibo account of Jiang Ning city, attracted more than 206m followers (see figure 4) and its influence is much more powerful than the provincial official account.

Figure 4: The 'dog' picture and emojis help Jiang Ning official account to attract more than 206m followers

Using social media to monitor the public discourse

The second target of government's use of social media is in monitoring public conversations and to stop any potential collective action. The cyberspace authority operates an online police force to monitor all that's happening on the internet. This digital surveillance requires social media operators to breach the privacy of users and all of their contents – even users' private chatting history is accessible. An algorithm helps the internet police to filter the content, locate the keyword and monitor related talks online.

The basic logic of this algorithm is to find out two kinds of chats or discussions: the first is the keyword that may lead to potential dangerous anti-government?) actvity; and the second is to focus on the content of in-group talks (especially those of more than 100 people). Besides the algorithm, media companies have certain technical expertise that helps local government analyse online conversations and discover potential risk areas.

For example, Weibo has a trend function to monitor localised chats in different cities; this helps the relevant local authority to weed out any so-called problems and solve them, or prepare for any potential ramifications before any issue goes viral. Government will always use two ways to stop these conversations; the first is to ban certain keywords on the main social media platforms; the second is to tell platform operators to block the key instigator of whatever the debate is.

However, the development of video sharing has made it hard to monitor online chats and a huge team is required to check video content manually. Because of this, the Chinese government requires video platforms to self-censor, with platforms being responsible for the contents uploaded on their sites.

Chinese authorities had launched several actions to control the contents on live-streaming and short-video platforms. Kuaishou had to stop its service to delete all the videos that may have 'had an extremely bad influence on society' in April 2018. The cyberspace administration also co-operates with the platform operators to develop and improve the artificial intelligence technical to ensure the content is 'matched' with 'Chinese social values'.

Using social media as the propaganda tool and government's strategically distraction

In line with its strategy on traditional media, the Chinese government is now using social media to promote its policies and values. The government requires the main social media platforms such as Weibo and Bytedance to promote its official propaganda content. For example, Weibo always puts propaganda on the top of its recommendations and research results, especially content from the state-owned media Renmin daily. Bytedance's news feed application 'Jin Ri Tou Tiao' also pushes the official content at the top of its recommendations to directly promote propaganda content.

More than directly promoting and cultivating, the Chinese government has developed a new method that guides public opinion, which ended up being the term 'strategic distraction' (King, Pan and Roberts, 2017). This strategy aims to influence online conversations to distract public attention and 'push pro-Party views through chat rooms and web forums'(Bandurski, 2008).

My previous work with government was to plan monthly events and activities to guide social media, sharing the 'beautiful life' and 'a better future' instead of discussing any problems or 'negative discussion'. The distraction strategy is always planned and implemented by government-owned media companies, which will co-operate with the platforms to advertise content and guide conversations.

It's important for the Chinese government to guide public opinion and it seems its strategy works very well. King, Pan and Roberts (2017) found that Chinese government will hire some people called '50c' (each post will paid 50 cents) to (i) taunt foreign countries; (ii) implement argumentative praise or criticism; (iii) add non-argumentative praise or suggestions, such as improving housing and public welfare: (iv) report factually about what government officials are doing; and (v) cheerlead for China. Those comments pretend to be ordinary netizens and will defend or promote the government's views and values. The active distraction and censorship tactics aim to stop discussions about people getting together to air their shared grievances, and to achieve their propaganda goals.

Censorship regime's negative effects and 'gateway effects'

Censorship has decreased access to information. However, Hobbs and Roberts (2018) found that sudden censorship *can* increase access to information. According to their theory of 'gateway effects', people trying to 'access the newly censored information provides a gateway into access to information that has long been censored or blocked', and they may receive more information than initially thought possible.

For example, the blocking of Instagram inspired millions of Chinese users to learn how to use virtual private networks (VPNs). They then become curious about other censored or blocked websites such as Facebook and Twitter. However, this censorship ethos denies access greatly, and distraction strategies aim to reduce the influence of any political discussion. Chinese netizens are now more active in the talks of stars, beauty, fashion, films and variety shows, rather than politics. The top ten topics on Weibo in 2017 were on those lighter those themes, with users enjoying 'playful interactions'. This leads to a concern about the level of the average Chinese young netizen's political awareness.

Chinese netizens have two principal ways of evading censorship to access information and express their opinion. The first is to use VPNs to visit blocked websites; the second is to use metaphors to express their opinion on Chinese social media.

For example, Chinese netizens uses 'Winnie the Pooh' instead of using 'President Xi' to evade the algorithm of censorship to discuss political topics (figure 5). Weibo had to temporary clear its search results of Winnie the Pooh to halt conversations in February and March 2018.

This didn't stop netizens using Winnie the Pooh to express their opinions when Xi changed the law to extend his presidential term. They reposted a Weibo note by a Disney official account in 2012, which said: 'Sometimes you need to take a risk to get a sweet reward'. Netizens used this quote to express their anger towards the decision. This Weibo went viral but was then quickly banned by the government, and the comment function was disabled to stop any discussion. What's more, the Disney official account couldn't be shown in any search result until May 2018.

However, as the 'cute cat theory' (Zuckerman, 2009) claimed, it's hard for authority to ban the Winnie the Pooh permanently because it may lead to Disney fans being very upset. The ban of Winnie the Pooh attracts more people to use

Winnie as the symbol of the president and express their political opinion in a metaphor way.

Figure 5: Xi and Winnie the Pooh on Chinese Social Media

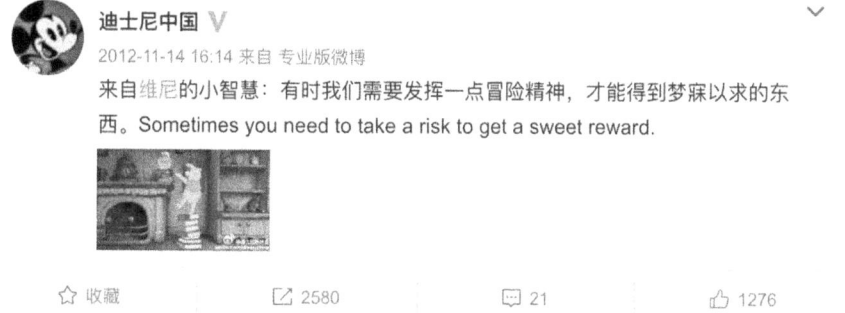

Figure 6: The Disney's Weibo reposted by thousands before banned

In the backlash against censorship, Chinese social media platforms are now seeking a safe zone for their future businesses – entertainment and e-commerce. Because of this, major Chinese social media companies are now investing in producing their own entertainment content and developing their own platforms for online shopping.

In the future, the development of AI is essential for Chinese social media. It will help the government to have better algorithms to monitor and predict public conversations; but it will also help the platforms to instigate better advertising strategies and to extend their users' online time.

The super platforms like Weibo and WeChat are growing bigger and providing more services, which may increase concerns about privacy and monopoly. The censorship regime requires co-operation with media companies and platform operators, which also inspires the development of the entertainment industry and e-commerce business.

Censorship and firewalls cannot stop the netizens seeking their own ways of accessing news and information and expressing their own opinions. But the government is also trying to improve its own online services to deal with complaints and solve the problems of citizens.

Social media itself seems like a mirror of Chinese society – the government is using its strategy to balance different groups and prevent conflicts to keep its 'China Dream' going further.

References

Bandurski, D. (2008). China's guerrilla war for the web. Far Eastern Economic Review, 171(6), 41.

CNNIC. (2018, January 31). 第41次《中国互联网络发展状况统计报告》(全文). Retrieved June 14, 2018, from http://www.cac.gov.cn/2018-01/31/c_1122347026.htm

Hobbs, W. R., & Roberts, M. E. (2018). How sudden censorship can increase access to information. American Political Science Review, 1-16.

King, Gary, Jennifer Pan and Margaret E Roberts. 2014. "Reverse-Engineering Censorship in China: Randomized Experimentation and Participant Observation." Science 345(6199):1251722–1251722.

King, G., Pan, J., & Roberts, M. E. (2017). How the Chinese government fabricates social media posts for strategic distraction, not engaged argument. American Political Science Review, 111(3), 484-501.

Lichbach, M. I., & Zuckerman, A. S. (2009). Comparative politics: Rationality, culture, and structure. Cambridge University Press.

Miller, Blake. 2017. "The Limits of Commercialized Censorship in China." Working Paper.

Tencent. (2017, November 8). The 2017 WeChat Data Report. Retrieved June 14, 2018, from http://blog.wechat.com/2017/11/09/the-2017-wechat-data-report/

Weibo. (2018, April 26). Weibo Corp - Investor Relations - Annual Reports. Retrieved June 14, 2018, from http://ir.weibo.com/phoenix.zhtml?c=253076&p=irol-reportsannual

Note on the contributor

Dipsy Edmunds is the pseudonym of a writer with a deep understanding and experiemce of how social media works in China.

Section Five

Anti-social media

* * *

Abuse, misuse and trolling

John Mair

Social media can be very destructive. The electronic town hall meeting often has no name attached to the sender of the messages. Pseudonyms rule. It is truly the Wild West. Insults and threats – 'trolling' in the jargon – are everyday. Like electronic 'knock down ginger' you go the person's front door, press the bell and run away! Irresponsibility rules. This section book examines 'trolling' in a wide variety of spheres.

Shami, Baroness Chakrabarti knows her gender and she knows her law. Years heading up Liberty and her role as Shadow Attorney General have led her to ask some pertinent questions about social media.

> *"Is it something about the brevity of the form or the blizzard of other users which encour-ages the bluntest, most shocking and sometimes cruelest expression rather than anything more reasoned, courteous or nuanced? Or is it that Twitter in particular turns communica-tion into broadcasting or even into a constant online riot that is as exhilarating to some men as an old-style bar-room brawl?"*

The solution is simple, bring in some law to the disorder.

> *"Politics and law seem slow to catch up with and respond to the new online world*
>
> *If a man might be thrown out of McDonald's for calling a woman a pig or a bitch or a dog (without going further and actually threatening her safety), why should he not be ejected or barred from Facebook or Twitter if such global corporate brands want to demonstrate their respect for half the human race? Or is it that in a world where the President of the United States is arguably an internet troll himself, the direction is towards normalising this kind of behaviour instead of tackling it?"*

Gina Miller, the Queen of the Brexit refusers, the 'Remoaners' in the derogatory jargon of nationalistic press, has become Public Enemy Number One for the Brexit trollers.

In the chapter The Remoaner Queen Under Attack: The Trolling of Gina Miller, Amy Binns of the University of Central Lancashire and I analyse the Twitter storms around Miller at the time of her court case (which she won) against the British Government in late 2016/early2017.

In her own words.

> *"I receive anonymous death threats almost every day. Strangers have informed me graphically that they want to gang rape me and slit the throats of my children, how the colour of my skin means I am nothing more than an ape, a whore, a piece of shit that deserves to be trodden into the gutter."*

A tiny flavour of the troll's tweets to her account:

> *"I despise interfering busybodies like @thatginamiller. Wonder who picked up the legal costs? Jew Alan Miller and his pet monkey try to torpedo Brexit via lawsuit. Jew judges sided with jew racial comrade."*

Her analysis of the trolling phenomena is as good as that of any academic.

> *"They no longer linger alone in their rooms or at the end of some bar in a pub; social media has amplified their destructive voices and created echo chambers that echo their views."*

Gina Miller is but one case study in the cacophony of anonymous hate that exists in not-so-dark corners of social media. The 140/280-character anonymous comments are aimed at hurting and destroying her and many others.

My fellow editor Professor Richard Tait of Cardiff University in his chapter Trolling the Messenger looks at the attacks on journalists and especially women journalists. His prognosis is not good;

> *"Although no journalist should object to criticism or challenge (it's never been a profession for the thin-skinned or over-sensitive) the abuse and threats which too many currently receive just for doing their job have got to a level where concerted effort is required by everyone involved – journalists, their employers and the social media platforms which publish this abuse – to deal with a problem which, if left unchecked, will threaten freedom of expression… the current level of online abuse of journalists has to come to an end."*

Claire Wolfe teaches Journalism students at the University of Worcester and finds them in her chapter Democracy Under Threat? entering a trade teeming with trolls partly, she says, as a by-product of media modernising.

> *"Media outlets seeking to boost audiences through titillation and controversy have effectively built troll-baiting and troll-feeding into their business models."*

Words can do some harm but sticks and stones can break bones! In their chapter Digital Weapons in a Post-conflict Society, Faith Gordon and Paul Reilly look at cyber knee-capping by the paramilitary groups on both sides of the religious/political divide in Northern Ireland;

> *"Historically, these groups would punish young people deemed to be engaging in anti-social behaviour using methods such as displaying posters in public spaces, tar-and-feathering attacks, and banning them from using local community-based services… it is clear (now) that platforms such as Facebook and Twitter are being used by loyalist and republican paramilitaries to threaten and intimidate children and young people, particularly in working-class communities in sectarian interfaces."*

On an individual/micro level, is the negative effect of social media on mental wellbeing of the young over-emphasised and just yet another moral panic? Michelle O'Reilly of the University of Leicester thinks so. In her chapter Social Media and Adolescents' Mental Health: Is the Moral Panic Justified? She talked to young people in Leicester and found they took it in their stride;

> *"…there's always going to be people like that, especially on social media where you can be like no-one will know who you are 'cos you're completely hidden." P2 Leicester yr10 (aged 14-15yrs).*

She concludes:

> *"For journalists, questions must be raised about their moral duty in reporting the 'epidemic' of mental health problems in society's youth, and positioning the role of social media at the heart of this social difficulty, against the tensions and questions this moral panic creates. We must wonder at how 'real' the problem is."*

Finally, in the nation's most popular spectator sport, football, racism has been largely driven off the terraces by Kick it Out (and others) and by the sheer number and skill of the black footballers on the field. It has found a new home John Price of Sunderland University, in his chapter Hate's Coming Home: The Rise of Football-related Abuse on Social Media, says it has now transmogrified to racism on the internet;

> *"…while overt acts of racism within and around football matches have – to some extent – been managed, these expressions of hate have found another home online. The feeling of being backstage while using social media, combined with the tribal and emotional nature of football, means people are posting hundreds of discriminatory posts each day. The vast majority of these posts go unreported and unpunished – thereby encouraging the problem to grow."*

The well of the positive side of the internet seen earlier in this book is well and truly poisoned by the trollers in all spheres. Nobody is safe from this electronic Knockdown Ginger.

Social media and the abuse of women

Though social media has created new opportunities for women, women have also been horribly abused on it, says Shami Chakrabarti

The role and use of Twitter and other forms of new media is worth examining in relation to the lot of women in general. The internet is perhaps the greatest technological innovation of my lifetime. Like the printing press, it has in so many ways been a huge force for freedom, equality and democracy, giving vital information and voice to so many previously isolated and unheard people. Human rights abuses and the revolutions they inspired have been transmitted around the world in seconds, bypassing state and oligarch-controlled conventional media. Impoverished campaigners have been able to access important research data without the archives and staff available to corporates and governments. And these campaigners have included a new generation of feminists all over the world.

The Everyday Sexism Campaign was started by the formidable Laura Bates in the UK. It now gives women a platform to chart and discuss every form of discrimination, indignity and abuse internationally. The not-for-profit Women's Media Centre Women Under Siege programme has harnessed the unique capabilities of the internet to map and document the numerous incidences of sexual assault which suggest rape is being used systematically as a weapon of war by government and government-aligned forces in Syria. There are numerous other fine examples of everyone from activists, journalists, politicians, musicians and actors using their experience, skills and profile to highlight the women's cause online. So the internet can clearly be a vital tool in raising awareness and even organising against both casual and extreme sexism and misogyny on a local, national and international scale. And given the potential speed and scale of campaigning in this new world, it can even be harnessed to campaign for greater responsibility and protection from those who provide and profit from individual platforms themselves.

Yet the dark side is equal and opposite and has spawned a whole new hell of misogynistic abuse often laced with racism, menaces and direct intimidation. It goes well beyond the grey and disputed borderline of hate speech and deep into the land of threats to rape, maim and kill. It seems an irony to me now, that when I was young, typing seemed a predominantly female accomplishment. 1950s cinema depictions of the 'typing pool' featured well turned-out young women gently tapping away hundreds of words a minute to a jolly rhythm punctuated by the satisfying ring of the end of a line of correspondence. In my mind at least, this image is now replaced with the notion of armies of online woman-haters bashing away at their computers in the dark, punching the keyboard as if punching their female targets and the more high-profile or political a woman the greater a target for this new brand of pure bile.

Why does social media lead to abuse?

Why should this be so? Why do some people feel so much more free to hate, insult and threaten on social media than in person, via traditional post or even by email? Is it the speed of the medium which shortens the distance and blurs the distinction between the thought and its communication? Is it online anonymity that makes the difference? Is it something about the brevity of the form or the blizzard of other users which encourages the bluntest, most shocking and sometimes cruelest expression rather than anything more reasoned, courteous or nuanced? Or is it that Twitter in particular turns communication into broadcasting or even into a constant online riot that is as exhilarating to some men as an old-style bar-room brawl?

Is it the medium merely exposing what was always locked away or is there something about its design or operation which actively inspires the hatred of women? What is it about these new so apparently democratic spaces that so readily lends them to the lynch mob?

The case of Diane Abbott

My friend Diane Abbott is a senior UK politician and a case in point. She entered the House of Commons as Britain's first black woman Member of Parliament in 1987 and has never been a stranger to political, personal and media attack on account of her strong and articulate socialist, anti-racist and human rights voice. Never comfortable residing anywhere near that sad place called victimhood, she only spoke out against personal abuse in February 2017. This was after a particularly harrowing flurry of online hatred directed against her caused by what she described as the 'perfect storm' of Brexit legislation and a Conservative cabinet minister putting his arm around her in a House of Commons bar, only to text demeaning remarks (leaked late to a tabloid newspaper) about her appearance to another male Conservative colleague.

The newspaper response was predictable and telling, revelling in the intrigue, but inevitably not focusing on the white male Conservative veteran's bad behaviour and instead on her instant expletive response. This appeared to give licence or encouragement to an online free-for-all that led to the suspension of a Conservative local councillor for tweeting an image of Abbott as an ape with lipstick.

A great deal worse was to follow in the subsequent days and months leading up to the 2017 General Election campaign in which an ultimately resilient Abbott became the deliberate target of orchestrated right-wing derision and abuse. A great communicator but nonetheless unaccustomed to taking to the page, rally, despatch box or microphone on her own behalf, the Shadow Home Secretary wrote a piece in The Guardian newspaper which was all the more poignant and shocking for the fact she had remained silent about the campaigns of targeted racist misogyny against her for so long. She had received abuse concentrating on her race and appearance, likening her to various animals and the rape and death threats that have become all too common against women in any form of public life. This she described as 'the politics of personal destruction', an amplified and publicly broadcast version of the kind of emotional and threatened physical violence women have been more used to experiencing in the cage of domestic abuse. It is as if the age-old reactionary attacks on equality and social progress begin to see women campaigners in general, but those of the left in particular, as the individual personification of all they are ideologically opposed to. So they become fair game for annihilation, by any means necessary or momentarily satisfying.

She said: "Suppose someone had told me back then that 30 years on I would be receiving stuff like this: 'Pathetic useless fat black piece of shit Abbott. Just a piece of pig shit pond slime who should be fucking hung (if they could find a tree big enough to take the fat bitch's weight)'. I think even the young, fearless Diane Abbott might have paused for thought."

And that is surely the point, the Wild West of the internet is capable of giving a platform to the voiceless for good or ill. It empowers hate certainly as much as love and solidarity, some would argue more. And it creates a series of dilemmas relating to how to respond.

The fight back

One option is to fight back, tweet for tweet in handset to handset combat in the moment. There might be some satisfaction in this. But surely there is also some danger for the victim of the abuse. Is she subjecting herself to greater mental and emotional torment and arguably even encouraging or rewarding the abuser with attention from the person with whom he has already demonstrated an altogether unhealthy interest? I know this may be a controversial view and I am in no way suggesting women should be chased away from the internet any more than they should be chased off the nighttime streets. Feminist campaigner Caroline Criado-Perez writes movingly of being hurt and patronised by well-meaning women who she felt unsupported by with their advice to turn off the machine and ignore the abuse. It is certainly not a policy that stands up to scrutiny when the analogy is made with the real or offline world. Yet I worry nonetheless about the greater potential for psychological intrusion of these new media. And they are continually accessed with a small personal device that is also the means of contacting friends and loved ones.

Another option must be to enlist online support from other users of the platform in question. This might level the playing field. But one can imagine witnesses to the worst abuse might feel reluctant to become its objects themselves. This leaves the option of calling out the sheriff in the form of whatever regulation and enforcement the corporate provides, or indeed the police where the nature of the abuse passes into the realms of criminal law.

Problems prosecuting online abuse

One highly sympathetic and experienced police officer spoke to me of his frustrations in trying to engage law enforcement in general, and prosecutors in particular. He told me stories of tweets which seemed to be way beyond insult and abuse and on the cusp of incitement to violence. He told me of taking up complaints from online witnesses armed with screen-shots of the offending tweets. Then police officers in different parts of the country would knock on suspects' doors, interviewing and even arresting them.

It was at this point, in his view, the system seemed to break down. A file was sent to a distant prosecutor who the police officer would never be able to meet and talk to. A decision on an almost tick-box pro-forma might indicate no further action or action for the low-hanging fruit of a minor 'malicious communication' offence, rather than one of threat or violence. And this with little by way of explanation with which the police officer might comfort a victim or witness that they had at least been taken seriously.

Further, in cases where the malicious or dangerously inciting tweet had not actually been seen by its target, he was being asked to interview her and thus cause her distress, even though her evidence was unnecessary and irrelevant to proving the offence. He was worried about such a practice turning the police into reluctant agents of abuse rather than defenders against it. His tale was reminiscent of the way sex crime and domestic abuse used to be treated; not that serious, or not really a criminal matter, or even somehow the victim's fault.

He described the typical suspect of this kind of online abuse as a white man in his middle or older years. The suspect is often disgruntled with his lot in life and often from a place left behind both politically and economically by ruling elites. By contrast, a great many of the targets are apparently strong women in public life. They are predominantly but by no means exclusively, women of the left. This life-long professional police officer spoke as if personally upset by his experience and all the more concerned given our meeting came only months after the brutal hate-fuelled murder of Jo Cox in June 2016.

This was the first killing of a British Member of Parliament since the Conservative Ian Gow was murdered by the Provisional IRA in 1990. Cox, an impressive 41-year-old Labour woman MP, had represented Batley and Spen in West Yorkshire for less than a year after many years working in international development. Her 52 year-old constituent Thomas Mair was convicted of her murder perpetrated by stabbing, then shooting and then stabbing her again. Mair was a regular user of the internet at his local library. He used the resource to search on various far-right and homicide-related topics and is said to have singled out Cox for her pro-European and immigration views. Perhaps the internet is the new frontier for a male conservative fight-back against such social progress as has been made in recent years – at least in relation to the consensus around the worth of human life – if not yet respect for all people.

Real world vs virtual world abuse

If a woman were subject to the kind of shouted abuse on a town or village street that women, high profile women in particular, constantly receive online, it would be taken far more seriously by existing social and legal structures. Yet as in so many other ways, society, politics and law seem slow to catch up with and respond to the new online world. I have never been a fan of criminalising hate speech and widely cast criminal offences such as incitement to hatred as opposed to the incitement to actual sexual or violent offences. Nor do I think a host of extremely broad public order offences should necessarily be replicated in the digital sphere. Many of these have been used and abused as a means of political control which would be especially dangerous in the present context.

However, campaigns of online abuse constituting harassment, and threats to rape and kill are criminal in both the real and virtual world. If anything, there is the greater danger of their prevalence when the not-so-brave misogynistic bullies need not look their prey or anyone else in the eye. Police and prosecutorial authorities should be better equipped and more able to deal with complaints of online criminal behaviour. I am not advocating the kind of blanket surveillance they have sought licence for, and yet which do not seem to have helped the cause of women. I am talking about the authorities having a greater understanding of this new world and its consequences, so as to be able to take specific criminal complaints seriously and then to act upon them with sufficient resources.

Further if we continue with the analogy with the real world, given the corporate and monetised nature of most social media platforms, it is highly arguable that my public square or street metaphor is not the right one. Some of these social media platforms and spaces are closer in kind to a customer entering a bar, club or restaurant where the landlord is legally entitled and perhaps even morally obliged, to regulate behaviour to a higher standard than the understandably lower threshold of the criminal law. If a man might be thrown out of McDonald's for calling a woman a pig or a bitch or a dog (without going further and actually threatening her safety), why should he not be ejected or barred from Facebook or Twitter if such global corporate brands want to demonstrate their respect for half the human race? Or is it that in a world where the President of the United States is arguably an internet troll himself, the direction is towards normalising this kind of behaviour instead of tackling it?

Note on the contributor

Shami, Baroness Chakrabarti, is a Labour peer and Shadow Attorney General in Jeremy Corbyn's Shadow Cabinet. Previously she was Director of the civil liberties advocacy organisation Liberty from 2003 to 2016. This chapter is an edited version of chapter 2 of her recent book *Of Women: In the Twenty-First Century*, published by Penguin in October 2017.

The remoaner queen under attack: the trolling of Gina Miller

What happens when a private individual takes on a very public cause? Amy Binns and John Mair examine how the case of Gina Miller demonstrates how fast social media can whip up a storm of abuse

Gina Miller shot to fame after taking the British government to court for attempting to force through Article 50, the mechanism which started the Brexit process. It was a case that, like the 2016 Referendum itself, polarised Britain. While Leavers were outraged that their vote to exit the EU was not the final word, Remainers watched with bated breath in hope that their disaster could turn to triumph.

In the middle was the previously unknown financier Gina Miller. Articulate, photogenic and unafraid to comment on a controversial issue, she might have been made for the media. Widespread coverage led to her becoming a hate figure online, with two men arrested for making threats to kill her.

In her own words, in her book Rise (Miller, 2018), she outlines the hate her campaign had generated:

> "Over the past two years I've been the target of extreme bullying and racist abuse. Ever since I took the UK government to court for attempting to force through Article 50, the mechanism for starting Brexit which would have led to the nation leaving the European union without Parliamentary consent, I live in fear of attacks.

> "I receive anonymous death threats almost every day. Strangers have informed me graphically that they want to gang rape me and slit the throats of my children, how the colour of my skin means I am nothing more than an ape, a whore, a piece of shit that deserves to be trodden into the gutter."

This study analyses 18,036 tweets, which include the username @thatginamiller, from October 1, 2016 to February 27, 2017, from just before the opening of her High Court case to beyond the Supreme Court ruling on January 26 . It uses the same methods and sentiment analysis software described in the chapter 'What makes a target?', (P 201) built by Dr Martin Bateman at the University of Central Lancashire.[1]

The beginning

The first few days of October 2016 show the @thatginamiller account functioning as any active, private account. It received as few as four mentions a day, rising to 45 when Ms Miller promoted a charity concert. Very few mentioned the upcoming court case.

The initial spike in tweets came on October 13, the date of the opening of her High Court case. This was largely news driven. As the lead litigant, several news sites ran profiles of Gina Miller. The Guardian described her as having a 'long history of taking on powerful establishments' (Topping, 2016). It referenced an interview in the Financial Times, in which she mentioned her nickname of 'black widow spider', due to her lobbying for more transparency in the City of London. (Racism and Fees Fire up Gina Miller, 2016). This is a term that came back to bite her.

These are heavily retweeted: 4,668 tweets mention @thatginamiller on the opening day. But although this is a huge increase of activity for a private account, there was relatively little hostility at slightly less than three per cent of all mentions.

Though newspapers ran stories on the four-day case, it did not capture public interest, at least in cyberspace. There was very little further traffic directed at Ms Miller's account until the High Court judges gave their decision on November 3, traffic then continued through the Court of Appeal case and finally to the Supreme Court itself, which pronounced on January 26, 2017.

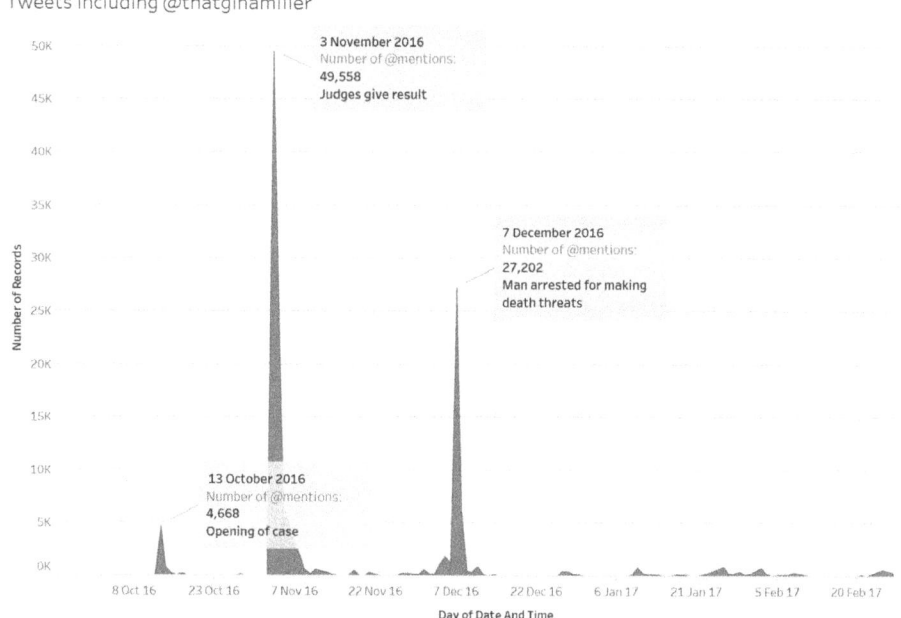

Tweets including @thatginamiller

3 November 2016
Number of @mentions:
49,558
Judges give result

7 December 2016
Number of @mentions:
27,202
Man arrested for making death threats

13 October 2016
Number of @mentions:
4,668
Opening of case

The plot of sum of Number of Records for Date And Time Day.

The Trigger

On November 3, the High Court judges ruled that the Government was obliged to go to Parliament with any Brexit deal. It was the end of Leavers' and Theresa May's hopes for a swift, hassle-free Brexit. Cameras were not permitted in this hearing, so although the judges received much hostility in the press, it was Gina Miller, speaking on the steps of the court, who became the face of the result. It was at this point that Ms Miller became a hate figure for a section of Brexit supporters.

Spikes in hostility online are often driven by broadcast appearances (Committee on Standards in Public Life, 2017). The spike in traffic was enormous, mostly driven by retweets from news organisations across Europe but also comments from individuals. Over November 3 and 4, 79,040 tweets mentioned her account. This is a volume of traffic far greater than any individual can deal with. It included 9,908 hostile tweets, a jump in hostility to 13 per cent, compared to the three per cent at the opening of the case.

These include tweets such as:

> *I despise interfering busybodies like @thatginamiller. Wonder who picked up the legal costs?*

> *Jew Alan Miller and his pet monkey try to torpedo Brexit via lawsuit. Jew judges sided with jew racial comrade.*

> *Examples of scum I want out of my country. They are baying for if you were wondering.*

> *cin her face after made me vomit profusely Seems no end 2 wot the wealthy elite can do. Enuf is enuf.*

> *#Eurogirl @thatginamiller is the new Guy Fawkes and needs to be thrown on the nearest bonfire.*

> *@thatginamiller is a disgrace she wears a poppy to remember those died fighting for our freedom at the same time she attempts to take it away!*

> *#ginamiller who the fuck is this slag V 17.4 million voters. Fuck the judges. YOU WILL LOSE.*

However, this outpouring of anger was not entirely directed at Ms Miller. She had become a lightning rod for the Brexit issue. People on both sides were fighting across her, flooding her Twitter feed with hostility. For example:

> *@thatginamiller seems to be labelled both a traitor and a foreigner. She can't be both. Make your minds up Nazis.*

> *Obviously white men in the UK have found a convenient vehicle for their pent-up sexism and racism in @thatginamiller. Disgraceful.*

Many others were straightforwardly positive. Across the whole dataset, 388 tweets used the phrase *"thank you"*, and 168 said *"well done"*. Other examples include:

> @thatginamiller *da god! Give this woman a throne. a dragon. whatever she wants.*

> @thatginamiller *Should get a medal.!*

> *As an antidote to the hate. I love you xxx* @thatginamiller

Stoking the fire

Leaver news sites went to town on Gina Miller, turning her into a target for their readers. A Daily Mail profile on November 4 (Sunderland, 2016) painted her as an ageing trollop, resurrected the 'black widow spider ' insult, described her as cougarish, implied she lies about her charity work and finished:

> *"Today the balding, bespectacled financier [Alan Miller] is worth nearer £30m. Some have wondered why a livewire like Mrs Miller is married to him. Cynics may say she has about thirty million good reasons."*

The Sun's front page on November 4 emphasised Ms Miller's origins, asking: 'Who do EU think you are? Loaded foreign elite defy will of Brit voters'. All these served to generate more traffic to her account.

Another major spike occurs on December 7, when there was Europe-wide coverage of the arrest of a man for making death threats against her. He was later released without charge. The day of the first arrest resulted in 1,719 hostile tweets in a total of 27,202 which mention her @username.

Over the following weeks, there were further smaller spikes as the legal process continues. On December 11 a Labour amendment in parliament called on the government to publish its timetable before triggering Article 50. Ms Miller said the motion was irrelevant, and this story triggered another spike of 818 tweets, of which 147 were hostile.

Further spikes occurred on January 10, when she appeared on radio station LBC; and on January 26 when the Supreme Court gave its verdict in her favour and a second man was arrested. This was Viscount Philipps, who was later jailed for 12 weeks.

Ms Miller remembered (Miller, Rise, 2018):

> *"Four days after I won my Brexit challenge Viscount Philipps offered a bounty on Facebook of £5000 for the 'first person to 'accidentally' run over this troublesome first generation immigrant'. Describing me a 'boat jumper he added 'if this is what we should expect from immigrants send them back to their stinking jungle'."*

Another spike occurred on February 2, the day after MPs voted in favour of triggering Article 50 by a huge majority. After this victory for Leavers, commentator Katie Hopkins called her a snake-in-the-grass in the Daily Mail:

"Gina darling, I wouldn't ask for your help if I had just wet myself after a nasty sneezing episode (stranger things have happened). We don't need your help with anything. We never did. You are a walking irrelevance. Run along and play with someone equally impotent – Nicola Sturgeon perhaps?

"Despite your powerful connections and your cash, we won – with the power of a little pencil on a piece of string and a tick in a box."

Katie Hopkins lost her LBC contract after calling for a 'final solution' in relation to the Manchester Arena bombings. She has since left the Daily Mail and MailOnline too and is writing for alt-right sites in the US.

What drives the haters?

Perhaps surprisingly, there is little overt racism around her colour: words such as nigger and coon never appear in the entire dataset of 18,036 tweets. The word black in reference to her is used only 50 times. Some are hostile:

Who is @thatginamiller? Another Anti White Black Bitch That should be deported. Like Abbott The Black Labour MP

but most use the word positively or to reply to racism:

@thatginamiller is a black woman from Guyana who brought the case against Brexit. I just love irony. Also she's my new hero.

However, there is significant debate and hostility around her perceived status as an immigrant. The word foreign/foreigner appears 115 times, Guyana appears 98 times, migrant/immigrant 53 times, deport 36 times. Again, some of these comments are from her supporters, but many are hostile.

Gotta love how a foreigner like is trying to stop #Brexit if you dont like it fuck off back to Guyana. The people have spoken!!!

@thatginamiller U need to go bk to where ever it is u came from stop shagging rich folks u sket . #deporther

In fact, Ms Miller was born in the then British Guiana (now called Guyana after independence in 1966) and came to Britain as a child to boarding school. Her father, a lawyer, worried about his children's safety. The money ran out and the government banned export of foreign currency. She then had to do menial jobs in the morning to keep her and her brother at school. She has never returned to Guyana to live.

Some tweeters made these points positively in tweets such as:

Guyana was a British colony when was born there in 1965 – she qualifies for British citizenship.

Others called out media critics:

> *The Sun owned by a loaded foreigner lambasts @thatginamiller for being 'a loaded foreigner.*

Apart from her origins, there are two more major focal points of hostility: her wealth and her perceived treachery. The words *traitor/traitorous/treachery* appear 117 times. Many tweets refer to this, including death threats such as:

> *treasonous fool. she should be dragged on hurdles to the tower and given a traitors death.*

> *November already has Guy Fawkes' Night. In history what date will be remembered as #GinaMiller night. @thatginamiller*

In terms of her status, *wealth/wealthy* appear 51 times, rich 87 times (not including partial words such as *richard*), *millionaire* 82 times. These tweets are almost entirely negative. Her status is also seen as making her out of touch with ordinary people, and lacking any right to represent them. The words *arrogant/arrogance* appear 69 times, and smug 17 times. Examples include:

> *@thatginamiller Father an attorney-general. Rodean girl. Married to multi-millionaire financier. The voice of authentic Britain apparently.*

> *Obviously then as a millionaire is far more intelligent and her views are more important than that of us plebs Arrogant bitch*

> *@skynews Don't be so naïve – rich bitch was just protecting her financial interests*

> *Guyanese just used her husband's millions to attempt to overrule a democratic vote by the majority of the British people*

> *@thatginamiller needs to spend some of her capitalist millions on neck surgery what a wrinkly mess it is #TheAgenda*

> *Another kick in the crack for you and the millionaire whore*

> *I've never wanted to slap a woman as much as I want to slap that smug b*tch*

Conclusion

Although Ms Miller was certainly aware that the case would generate enormous publicity, she was taken by surprise by the level and virulence of the online comments. She said in her book:

> "Social media, email and other platforms create breeding grounds for hate that are terrifying. I've watched as perpetrators have discovered a new boldness.... they no longer linger alone in their rooms or at the end of some bar in a pub; social media has amplified their destructive voices and created echo chambers that echo their views."

Gina Miller is a case study in the echo chamber of anonymous hate that exists in not-so-dark corners of social media. The 140-character comments are aimed at hurting and destroying her. Few would be made face to face. Many governments, including the UK and the US, are losing patience with social media companies' inability to control the users on their platforms. This case adds weight to the arguments of those calling for stronger regulation.

Notes

[1] The data in What Makes a Target? was captured in real time, but this dataset was collected in 2018. This means that some seriously abusive tweets may be missing, having been deleted by the users or by Twitter in the interim. This dataset may therefore slightly under-represent hostility.

References

Committee on Standards in Public Life. (2017). Intimidation in Public Life. London. Retrieved from https://www.gov.uk/government/publications/intimidation-in-public-life-a-review-by-the-committee-on-standards-in-public-life

Miller, G. (2018). Rise. Life Lesson in Speaking out,Standing Tall and leading the Way Edinburgh: Canongate.

Racism and Fees Fire up Gina Miller. (2016, April 24). Financial Times. Retrieved August 7, 2018, from https://www.ft.com/content/a9ee95cc-0711-11e6-9b51-0fb5e65703ce

Sunderland, R. (2016, November 4). Mrs Hedge Fund worth £30million and the Brazilian crimper. Daily Mail. Retrieved August 7, 2018, from http://www.dailymail.co.uk/news/article-3903812/Mrs-Hedge-Fund-won-5m-divorce-payout-Brazilian-crimper-started-millionaire-backer-Bentley-Trio-launched-action-halt-Brexit.html

Topping, A. (2016, October 13). Gina Miller: the woman taking on Theresa May over article 50. The Guardian. Retrieved August 7, 2018, from https://www.theguardian.com/politics/2016/oct/13/gina-miller-theresa-may-article-50-brexit-parliament-legal-challenge

Note on the contributors

Dr Amy Binns spent ten years as a newspaper reporter before entering academia. She teaches print and digital journalism at the University of Central Lancashire. Her research is largely around finding practical solutions for difficult behaviour online, which involves working with a wide range of people including media industry professionals. She still loves a good story, and is currently working on a biography of science fiction author John Wyndham.

The sentiment analysis software used in this research was developed by Dr Martin Bateman, senior lecturer at the University of Central Lancashire. His research interests are, networks and distributed systems, network based computer forensics, protocol analysis, video identification and cloud systems.

John Mair is the lead editor on this book as he has been on the previous 24 Abramis 'Hackademic' volumes. He is a former BBC television producer and university lecturer. To declare an interest, he too was born in British Guiana, knew Gina's father Doodnauth Singh SC, and has put Gina speaking on three platforms in the UK.

Trolling the messenger

Social media has liberated journalists from many of the constraints of the past – but also made them uniquely vulnerable to vicious abuse and online threats. Richard Tait looks at what needs to be done to stop it

In the current climate of criticism of many aspects of social media, it is easy to forget the huge benefits it can bring to journalism as a profession – the ability to break stories instantly in video or text to a worldwide audience, the ease of research and the opportunity to put uncensored journalism at the centre of the global conversation. Above all, social media turns journalism into a two-way process – journalists can no longer almost 'fire and forget' their stories into a newspaper or a bulletin. Feedback and reactions are often instantaneous and can often take the story on.

But although no journalist should object to criticism or challenge (it's never been a profession for the thin-skinned or over-sensitive) the abuse and threats which too many currently receive just for doing their job have got to a level where concerted effort is required by everyone involved – journalists, their employers and the social media platforms which publish this abuse – to deal with a problem which if left unchecked will threaten freedom of expression.

In the UK, the worst examples have been around reporting politics where coverage of three bitterly divisive votes – Scottish independence, the EU Referendum and the 2017 general election - on social media seems to have been accompanied by unprecedented polarisation and personal attacks on individual journalists. Nick Robinson, who as BBC political editor was targeted by some Scottish nationalists for his coverage of the independence campaign in 2015, put it succinctly in his 2017 Steve Hewlett lecture: the social media 'echo-chambers' of like-minded political enthusiasts now regarded the mainstream media (MSM) as the enemy and legitimate targets:

> 'Their most shared and liked stories are attacks on the MSM and the BBC in particular for ignoring their stories or giving too much coverage to the other side. They share a certainty fuelled by living in a social media bubble that we reporters and presenters are, at best, craven – obeying some dictat from our bosses or the government - and, at worst, nakedly biased' (Robinson, 2017).

When does abuse become a crime?

The problem is where does sincerely held criticism become intimidation, trolling or hate speech? When does abuse become a crime? In the 2017 general election Jeremy Corbyn's appearance on the BBC's Woman's Hour went awry as he embarrassingly forgot the cost of Labour's child care proposals. It was one of those 'gaffes' which seemed for 24 hours much more important than it really was – the Labour leader went on to a much better result than the polls and the pundits had predicted. But his interviewer, Emma Barnett, was subjected to anti-Semitic abuse on social media for the (highly professional) way she handled the situation. Mr Corbyn said he condemned all abuse directed towards a journalist doing her job, but the combination of racism and misogyny in some of the attacks on her were, sadly, only too familiar to journalism organisations which have become increasingly aware of the issue.

What is now happening to many journalists, particularly women journalists, on social media goes far beyond disagreeing with their coverage. A recent piece of research by the International News Safety Institute (INSI) and the International Women's Media Foundation (IWMF) found in a survey of nearly 1000 women journalists from around the world that two thirds of them reported they had experienced some form of intimidation, threats or abuse in relation to their work, ranging in severity from name-calling to death threats – 25 per cent of it online (Barton, Storm, 2014).

A Moroccan journalist reported 'the threat of murder, rape and publish[ed] photos of me to the internet and Facebook with the discredit of lies.' A Canadian journalist said "primarily the threats/ insults come from anonymous online commenters. I've had people threaten to assault me repeatedly; one threatened to 'human flesh hunt' me" (Barton, Storm, 2014).

'...a bloody migrant whore, a Jewish whore, a Muslim whore, a Gipsy whore'

When the issues were discussed at the November 2017 NewsXchange conference in Amsterdam, one of the panelists, the Swedish journalist Alexandra Pascalidou, said 'everything I do I receive threats'. One of the first prominent Swedish journalists from a migrant background she was called ' a bloody migrant whore, a Jewish whore, a Muslim whore, a Gipsy whore'. While in the studio presenting a live current affairs programme on Swedish Television, she got online death threats to her daughter who was at school at the time. She described her professional life as 'like a low intensity war' (NewsXchange, 2017).

As Pascalidou pointed out, the scale of abuse could lead to self-censorship and would scarcely encourage efforts to make journalism as a profession more diverse and more representative of the societies it serves. One third of the delegates in the audience (representing many of the world's leading broadcasters, newspapers and news agencies) put up their hands when asked if they too had experienced online abuse.

Representatives of the social media companies at the conference accepted their share of responsibility for the situation. Peter Greenberger, Twitter global director of news partnerships, said "we've been behind on this…and it's something that is our top priority right now. We are actioning a lot more than we used to – we clearly need to take action on more." Fares Akkad, Facebook head of media partnerships for the Middle East and Africa, said "this is absolutely a very personal issue for a lot of us… journalism safety is monumental. Unfortunately I have heard a lot of similar stories and it is something we take very, very seriously." (NewsXchange, 2017)

Spreading best practice in online safety

It was also clear that this was a shared responsibility – there were very varying levels of support for journalists from their employers and publishers in cases of online harassment and cyber-bullying. When INSI was set up in 2003 as a network of leading media organisations to promote journalism safety, we faced the same issues when trying to protect journalists in conflict zones and those working on potentially dangerous investigations. The best employers and organisations already had good guidelines and policies and were already taking care of their staff and freelance contributors – the challenge was to spread that best practice throughout the media industries worldwide.

Since NewsXchange, INSI has brought together representatives of Twitter and Facebook with colleagues from 20 major international news organisations to a series of meetings on online harassment. We have discussed the tools that currently existed to report abuse and support those who are being abused, and shared ideas for how to plug the gaps in these areas, including what the platforms could do and what news organisations might also do. The first meeting in London in February 2018 was the best attended safety group event in our history, evidence of the fact that this often overlooked issue is now causing a significant threat to journalists' ability to work safely.

And INSI is planning a project to establish best practice in this field. For individual journalists this will include advice on how to manage their own social media profiles to minimise risk and how to report and deal with online harassment. For employers and managers there will be guidelines on anticipating campaigns of abuse and mitigating the risks, and supporting journalists before, during and after an event of harassment.

Are journalists different?

Do journalists deserve special treatment? No one should have to face death or rape threats for expressing a point of view, whether a professional journalist or an individual participant in an online discussion group. And there are other groups that are targeted to an unacceptable level and equally need far more effective protection. The British MP Jess Phillips recently revealed she had received 600 online rape threats in one night (Snowdon, 2017). But we believe journalists also deserve some extra consideration. As a profession, journalists have always put themselves in harm's way in the public interest – whether reporting conflict or investigating corruption, still the two most dangerous sorts of assignment. In the world of social media, they have no alternative but to engage with the platforms which now carry so much of the world's news – and that currently makes them particularly vulnerable.

Without journalists making their material available online the social media platforms, which are now many people's first source of news, would never have grown as fast as they have and, after years of not taking this issue sufficiently seriously, there are encouraging signs that the platforms themselves increasingly recognise their responsibilities. Facebook chairman and CEO Mark Zuckerberg, in his evidence to the US Congress on April 10th 2018, crossed an important line when he accepted, for the first time, that Facebook was responsible for its content.

Although he pointed out that Facebook did not make the content and said he still saw Facebook as tech company not a media company, he accepted it had a responsibility to its users. "It's not enough just to build tools. We need to make sure that they're used for good." He also accepted the need for regulation: "I think the real question, as the internet becomes more important in people's lives, is what is the right regulation, not whether there should be or not" (Zuckerberg, 2017).

The social media platforms have a long way to go before they can offer anything approaching the same protections and remedies as traditional media such as newspapers and broadcasters – clear definitions of what is and what is not acceptable; sufficient resources to deal with complaints in a timely and decisive way; and some form of independent assessment of how effective their regulation (whether statutory or self –regulation) is (Tait, 2017).

Of course, social media will never and should never be regulated as tightly as some traditional media. Dealing with online harassment effectively may look like a big move for an industry, which has up to now benefited from the argument that it is in the platform rather than the publishing business (when it reality is has always been in both) and is not responsible for the content. But as far as the protection of journalists is concerned, that argument has run out of road. Both social and traditional media now need to play their part in ensuring that the current level of online abuse of journalists has to come to an end.

References

Barton, Alana, Storm, Hannah (2014) Violence and Harassment Against Women in the News Media: A Global Picture, IWMM/INSI. Available online at https://newssafety.org/research-projects/survey-violence-against-women-journalists/. Accessed on June 27, 2018

NewsXchange (2017). Session: Journalist Safety, Cyberbullying and Online Harassment. Available online at https://vimeo.com/245150651. Accessed on June 27, 2018

Robinson, Nick, Steve Hewlett Memorial Lecture, 29 September 2017. Available online at http://www.bbc.co.uk/news/uk-politics-41439172. Accessed on June 27, 2018

Sherwin, Adam (2017) Emma Barnett slams abuse from Corbyn supporters after 'car-crash' BBC Woman's Hour Interview. iNews, May 30, 2017. Available online at https://inews.co.uk/essentials/emma-barnett-slams-abuse-corbyn-supporters-car-crash-bbc-womans-hour-interview/. Accessed on June 27, 2018

Snowdon, Kathryn (2017) Labour MP Jess Phil Phillips Received More Than 600 Rape Threats In One night, Huffington Post, June 12, 2018. Available online at https://guce.oath.com/collectConsent?brandType=eu&.done=https%3A%2F%2Fwww.huffingtonpost.co.uk%2Fentry%2Flabour-mp-jess-phillips-600-rape-threats_uk_5b1f894be4b0bbb7a0e1147b%3Fguccounter%3D1&sessionId=3_cc-session_9f528f4c-a3a4-4874-9982-77f2a9b9dabd&lang=en-gb&inline=false. Accessed on June 27, 2018

Tait, Richard (2017) Evidence to House of Lords Select Committee on Communications: The Internet: to Regulate or not to Regulate? Available online at http://data.parliament.uk/writtenevidence/committeeevidence.svc/evidencedocument/communications-committee/the-internet-to-regulate-or-not-to-regulate/written/82667.html. Accessed on June 27, 2018

Zuckerberg, Mark (2017) Transcript of Mark Zuckerberg's Senate Hearing, April 10, 2017, The Washington Post. Available online at https://www.washingtonpost.com/news/the-switch/wp/2018/04/10/transcript-of-mark-zuckerbergs-senate-hearing/?noredirect=on&utm_term=.680c32ba84da. Accessed on June 27, 2018

Note on the contributor

Richard Tait is Professor of Journalism at the School of Journalism, Media and Culture, Cardiff. From 2003 to 2012 he was Director of the School's Centre for Journalism (where Emma Barnett was one of his students). He was Editor of Newsnight from 1985 to 1987, Editor of Channel 4 News from 1987 to 1995 and Editor-in-Chief of ITN from 1995 to 2002. He was a BBC Governor and chair of the Governors' Programme Complaints Committee from 2004 to 2006, and a BBC Trustee and chair of the Trust's Editorial Standards Committee from 2006 to 2010. He is a fellow of the Society of Editors and the Royal Television Society and a board member (and former Treasurer) of the International News Safety Institute.

Democracy under threat? Journalists need help in handling Internet Trolls

The nature of journalism puts reporters in the firing line of internet trolls. Claire Wolfe argues that without being properly trained in how to deal with attacks journalists could self-censor their comments online and dilute their role as guardians of freedom of speech and the exchange of ideas

Journalists in the firing line

Journalists have become figures of hate in many quarters where they previously enjoyed something approaching respect. Derided for poking their noses into other people's affairs, irrespective of what dens of iniquity they may unmask, and seen as pariahs at disaster scenes and parasites at public events, the plight of the hack continues to nosedive. With the Internet oozing disinformation, uploaded by mischief makers and naïve DIY news-gathers, journalists are also seen as being sloppy and sensational online, not helped by the pressure for huge eyeball rates to drive up revenues and replace dwindling hard copy sales.

But journalists are not just operating to line their own and their bosses' pockets, or are they? There may be some conflict here, but the pure concept of journalism as a bridge between what's happening in the world – embracing both the foul and the fabulous – and the public could not be more fraught. Putting aside the many theories on objectivity, there appears to be an increasing lack of tolerance when views are expressed that don't chime with the reader, and journalists are regularly in the firing line.

Journalism in democratic societies involves the discussion of concepts, decision-making and all the factors which help people to understand world dynamics and to play a part in the progress of 'civilisation' (McQuail 2009: 283). Journalists have a duty to challenge and question those in power, a role anchored in concepts of the media as the fourth estate and should cover a wide range of political opinions and positions' (Keene 1992 in Newton: 155 Pyper and Linton 1995). But for some individuals, this ever widening panorama, made possible through the Internet and other technological advances, has had the opposite effect. They are looking through the wrong end of the telescope and completely missing the big picture. This has manifested itself with a growing army of Internet trolls.

The trolling psyche

There are plenty of 'troll' definitions. Hiding behind fake profiles gives them the courage to be more vindictive over sensitive topics (King 1996). Some infiltrate groups posing as like-minded members and then strike from within causing mayhem, embarrassing and insulting people for their own amusement (Hardaker 2010: 237, Donath 1999, Morrissey 2010). What they come out with isn't necessarily their honestly-held belief either. They generate false or incorrect utterances to encourage negative or aggressive responses (Morrissey 2010). They are attention-seeking and like to smash people's confidence (King 1996 and Bishop 2013). Perhaps one of the worst things for journalists is that an encounter will take time to sort out. As Cunningham in Gillmor, 2004, states: "A troll is a time thief… That is what makes trolling heinous."

Media owners generate controversy

To a large extent media owners have orchestrated a high level of engagement with their audiences. With falling hard-copy revenues they turned to the Internet with varying success to lure advertisers onto their webpages. The use of search engine optimisation to draw in readers was quickly harnessed by some outlets, for instance Mail Online. Employing controversial columnists, like Katie Hopkins, helped to develop the audience, although she was let go after tweeting of the need for a 'final solution' after the 2017 Manchester arena bombing (Gore 2017). She likewise overstepped the mark at The Sun and the LBC radio network. Tryyg 2012 noted: "Trolling and other negative behaviour on magazine websites is widespread, ranging from subtly provocative behaviour to outright abuse. Publishers have sought to develop lively online communities, with high levels of user-generated content. Methods of building sites have developed quickly, but methods of managing them have lagged behind."

Media outlets seeking to boost audiences through titillation and controversy have effectively built troll-baiting and troll-feeding into their business models. With the thought of any kind of censorship making journalists' 'skin crawl' (Singer 2009). There was reluctance to police the area too heavily, but gradually, and largely for legal reasons, moderation became a staple. The costs grew along with the flood of comments as more people engaged online. But then came a key moment. Respected online journal PopularScience.com switched off the comments section in 2013. Online Content Director Suzanne LaBarre posted: "Comments can be bad for science. That's why, here at PopularScience.com, we're shutting them off" (LaBarre 2013). They were as committed to fostering lively, intellectual debate as they were to spreading the word of science far and wide, but: "The problem is when trolls and spambots overwhelm the former, they diminish their ability to do the latter… even a fractious minority wields enough power to skew a reader's perception of a story."

A steady stream of media organisations then began to close down or restrict the comments section, arguing it was too costly to effectively police. But media owners still wanted online discussion so the responsibility fell more to individual journalists responding via social media. Incidentally, they were also expected to promote stories and upcoming issues of their papers. What training did they have for dealing with trolls? None. What incentives did they have? Well, keeping in with the editor, and for freelancers, further work.

Case studies – toughen up, tone it down or quit

Journalists have been left to fend for themselves. For instance, shortly after troll attacks on BBC Political Editor Laura Kuenssberg, Deputy Director of News Fran Unsworth said their female stars needed to learn to 'disassociate' themselves from online abuse (Foster, 2016).

Well-known British journalist Julie Burchill is well documented for her hard-hitting stance following a number of high profile spats. There are some unhappy endings, however. In February 2014 the Australian model turned television presenter Charlotte Dawson committed suicide (Webb 2014). She had survived one suicide attempt and waged a public war against trolls, but Twitter comments such as: 'please hang yourself promptly' and 'neck yourself you filthy s***' intensified (Webb, 2014).

Attracting less attention was an incident in 2013 when Emma Barnett, Women's Editor at The Telegraph, Guardian columnist Hadley Freeman and Independent columnist Grace Dent, were sent a bomb threat tweet. Barnett had ignored it and gone to the pub. But police took the issue seriously and the man, who thought he was untraceable, was tracked down and cautioned. Barnett said: "More people don't want to provoke others, so they start to self-censor what they say if they are trolled. But if you're a journalist, your job is to provoke" (Ridley 2014).

Journalist Linda Grant quit the Guardian after being targeted (Thorpe and Rogers 2011). A Women in Media survey of 1054 Australian journalists found 41 per cent of staff journalists and 18 per cent of freelancers were attacked by trolls (O'Brien 2016). According to a Demos report, around five per cent of the tweets a female journalist receives are derogatory or abusive, compared to under two per cent for male journalists (Edge 2014). A survey by the National Union of Journalists and University of Strathclyde showed reporters had received death threats and 'feared for their safety' with more than 80 per cent saying cyber-bullying extended beyond working hours. More than 80 per cent had not reported the abuse to police, more than half said it had affected how they worked and more than 40 per cent did not tell their employer (Addicot 2016).

Journalists' experiences

My research involved interviews with 20 journalists and 40 journalism undergraduates. Many of the journalists had similar stories and the abuse was not restricted to women. An experienced national journalist, who vowed not to be intimidated, said his Facebook page was destroyed after he infiltrated and exposed a Fascist party. "If we gave in to threats and intimidation from people like that, they would continue to advance their cause unchecked which wouldn't do at all. We're asked to make a story as good as we can and as controversial as possible and to drive the agenda for the next day. I'm sure that's a lot to do with driving traffic to online and social media."

A seasoned male journalist received abuse and threats over a blog about the political astuteness of Pussy Riot. He said: "There's so much hypocrisy going on the part of online newspapers. Of course the abuse is part of their business model because it creates clicks, which create advertising revenue… This will only change if the advertising model changes, when advertisers realise having their ad next to a lot of bile doesn't do them any good and they stop measuring attention in terms of mere clicks. But I'm not holding my breath."

Journalists new to the industry were generally more guarded. One said: "I think it is best to stay away (from heated debates online) and avoid confrontation as everyone is entitled to their opinion and it says more about the commenter than you." Another said following online abuse they now "have to think very carefully about wording." Three other newcomers said bad experiences affected what they wrote and their ability to freely express themselves. One incident involved a 'troll-fest', a coordinated attack from a group troll Facebook account. This involved 'hundreds and hundreds of Instant Messages and comments'.

Another incident involved a reader being upset about a comment. "The blog editor decided to remove the section that had outraged the reader. Afterwards, I decided to dilute my opinions and observations down so as to avoid such moments in the future."

The reporters only sought information on how to deal with attacks during and after the event.

A BBC news editor said they had restricted their below the line comments to two or three due to the high cost of moderating sites after stories were being 'hijacked' by extremists, including fascists, homophobes and people with sexist views. "When you spend too much of the licence fee money on external moderators weeding out extremist views then the ends don't justify the means," he said.

Employers had done nothing, or very little, to prepare staff for the inevitable flak generated via their online profiles. Support was minimal. Journalists and students alike felt more should be done to prepare them. The biggest danger areas, unsurprisingly were gender (especially feminism and looks for women), politics, race, religion, disability and, in sports, stating a football allegiance.

Implications and solutions

Clearly some journalists were moderating their own comments to avoid a backlash. Women, often faced with rape and death threats, are particularly vulnerable. Some of the best tactics for thwarting trolls were devised by feminist groups. Disturbingly, my research showed some journalism undergraduates were already experiencing some of this vitriol online. Learning to 'button up' at such a tender age could have repercussions when embarking on a career in journalism. A subconscious fear of generating abuse could lead to a more sanitised approach to thorny topics. There have been some moves to combat online thugs. Recent high profile cases have prompted action from social media giants and the Government to protect the young and outlaw anonymous trolls. This includes setting up a new national police hub to crack down on online hate crime (Roberts 2017) enabling the monitoring of social media posts and unmasking of anonymous users posting hateful material. This has, however, generated concerns from some free speech groups and even the former European Commissioner for Human Rights, Thomas Hammarberg, who said: "People are at a loss to know how to apply rules for the traditional media to the new media" (Roberts 2017).

In response to demand from my research sample, I devised a survival guide, an evolving process, for our students and for newcomers to the industry. There are perils online and a duty for journalists to safeguard the open channels of communication. Being prepared and knowing who to go to for help is important. You wouldn't let anyone loose on the road until they've passed their driving test, so why allow young journalists to enter the shark-infested water of online journalism without adequate training. It is critical that new generations of journalists maintain the principles of freedom of the press. They should feel confident and safe about expressing themselves online, and be both prepared and equipped to deal with situations if targeted.

References

Addicot, Ruth (2016) Taking on The Trolls? National Union of Journalists and University of Strathclyde, The Journalist February/March 2016 NUJ: London

Bishop, Jonathan (2013) Examining the Concepts, Issues, and Implications of Internet Trolling ,Centre for Research into Online Communities and E-Learning Systems, UK, Scopus: US

Donath, Judith, S. (1999) Identity and Deception in the Virtual Community In Kollock, P. and Smith M. (eds). Communities in Cyberspace, London: Routledge Available at http://smg.media.mit.edu/people/Judith/Identity/IdentityDeception.html , accessed on 22 February 2015

Edge, Abigail (2014) Beyond the Block-Button Advice for dealing with Online Abuse, Journalism.co.uk 12 December. Available at https://www.journalism.co.uk/news/beyond-the-block-button-advice-for-dealing-with-online-abuse/s2/a563447/ ,accessed 8 February 2015.

Foster, Patrick (2016) BBC News chief: Female reporters need to 'harden up' and ignore web trolls. Telegraph 16 May. Available online at https://www.telegraph.co.uk/news/2016/05/19/bbc-news-chief-female-reporters-need-to-harden-up-and-ignore-web/ , accessed on 22 June 2016.

Gillmor, Dan (2004) We the media: Grassroots journalism by the people for the people, O'Reilly Media Inc., Sebastopol, CA.

Gore, Will (2017) What's the truth behind Katie Hopkins ending her contract by "mutual consent" with Mail Online? Independent 28 November. Available online at https://www.independent.co.uk/voices/katie-hopkins-daily-mail-why-did-she-end-her-contract-a8079816.html ,accessed on 6 December 2017

Hardaker, Claire (2010) Trolling in asynchronous computer-mediated communication: From user discussions to academic definitions Journal of Politeness Research. Available online at https://clok.uclan.ac.uk/4980/2/Hardaker,%20C.%202010.%20Trolling%20in%20ACMC.pdf accessed on 25 September 2013)

King, Storm (1996) Researching Internet communities: Proposed ethical guidelines for the reporting of results. *The Information Society 12*:119-127.

LaBarre, Suzanne (2013) Why We're Shutting Off Our Comments, Popular Science 24 September 24. Available at https://www.popsci.com/science/article/2013-09/why-were-shutting-our-comments, accessed on 6 February 2014.

Book Rogers, Simon (2013) Facts are Sacred: The Power of Data, London: Faber and Faber

McQuail, Denis (2010) McQuail's Mass Communication Theory 6th ed., London: Sage

Morrissey, Lochlan. (2010) Trolling is an art: Towards a schematic classification of intention in Internet trolling. Griffith Working Papers in Pragmatics and Intercultural Communications, 3(2), 75-82.

Newton, Kenneth (1995) The Mass Media: Fourth Estate or Fifth Column? Pyper, Robert & Robins, Lynton (1995) Governing the UK in the 1990's Palgrave: London pp 155-176

O'Brien, Natalie (2016) Social media trolling of female journalists is insidious, The Sydney Morning Herald. 6 March. Available at http://www.smh.com.au/nsw/social-media-trolling-of-female-journalists-is-insidious-report-shows-20160305-gnba81.html#ixzz49rwsjlDS, accessed on 12 March 2016.

Ridley, (2014) Why Female Journalists Are A Major Target For Internet Trolls (Sexism Has Something To Do With It) Huffington Post 8 October 2014, updated 9 October 2014.
https://www.huffingtonpost.co.uk/2014/10/07/female-journalists-women-trolled-feminism-sexism_n_5946346.html?guccounter=1, accessed on 15 February 2016.

Roberts, Rachel (2017) Online hate crime to be tackled by new national police hub, Home Secretary says, Independent, 8 October
Available online at https://www.independent.co.uk/news/uk/politics/online-hate-crime-amber-rudd-home-office-national-police-hub-facebook-twitter-trolls-a7988411.html, accessed on 16 October 2017

Singer, Jane B (2009) Moderation in Moderating Comments: Media Ethics Magazine Spring 2009, Vol. 20, No. 2 Accessible online at: http://www.mediaethicsmagazine. com/index.php/analysis-commentary/3746269-moderation-in-moderating-comments ,accessed on 15 September 2014.

Thorpe, Vanessa and Rogers, Richard (2011) Women bloggers call for a stop to 'hateful' trolling by misogynist men Guardian 6 November. Available online at

https://www.theguardian.com/world/2011/nov/05/women-bloggers-hateful-trolling, accessed 21 March 2014

Tryyg, Sanna (2012) Is Comment Free? Ethical, editorial and political problems of moderating online news. POLIS, London School of Economics and Political Science, London, UK. Previously available at http://blogs.lse.ac.uk/polis/files/2012/01/ IsCommentFree_PolisLSETrygg.pdf ,accessed 24 August 2014.Now available at http:// eprints.lse.ac.uk/59870/

Webb, Sam (2014) Trolled to death: Model Charlotte Dawson bombarded with vile messages over Twitter, Daily Mail, 23 February. Available at http://www.dailymail.co.uk/ tvshowbiz/article-2565903/Trolled-death-Model-Charlotte-Dawson-bombarded-vile-messages-Twitter-just-hours-death.html#ixzz4AJ7Xd6Ho ,accessed on 24 August 2014.

Note on the contributor

Claire Wolfe is Principal Lecturer in Journalism at the University of Worcester and a Senior Fellow of the Higher Education Academy. She is a former Daily News news editor and night editor and Birmingham Mail reporter. She has been on the Association for Journalism Education Executive committee six years and is a Royal Television Society member. Her interests cover developing media partnerships and work-based learning. Research areas also include law and ethics, social media and gender issues. Presented at World Journalism Education Congress, New Zealand, 2016. Email c.wolfe@worc.ac.uk

Digital weapons in a post-conflict society

Faith Gordon and Paul Reilly examine how social media is being used by all sides in current-day Northern Ireland where paramilitary style assaults remain endemic

Anti-social behaviour remains high on the community agenda in Northern Ireland, as demonstrated by media headlines in 2018 such as 'Residents 'at the end of tether' over anti-social behaviour in North Belfast' (Irish News, May 28).

Media coverage typically positions children and young people as the main perpetrators of anti-social behaviour within these communities (Gordon 2018). This is congruent with official youth justice policies directed towards children and young people, which frame this social group as being primarily responsible for anti-social behaviour, social disruption and low-level intercommunal violence near sectarian interfaces (Jarman and O'Halloran 2001; Gordon 2018).

Such stereotyping has often been linked to the suspicion that surrounds groups of young people hanging around on street corners in these areas (Hamilton et al. 2003: 13). This often distracts policymakers and audiences from the paramilitary violence perpetrated against children and young people within these communities; indeed, there is a long history of young people being exiled or subjected to so-called paramilitary 'punishment attacks' for alleged anti-social behaviour (Hillyard et al. 2005: 190).

This chapter will explore the relatively under-researched issue of how social media is used in relation to paramilitary style assaults in Northern Ireland. Drawing on the preliminary findings from an ongoing study by the authors, it will explore how social media platforms such as Facebook and Twitter are being monitored by the police in order to identify such incidents and to encourage citizens to report them to the authorities. The chapter concludes by assessing the impact of the #stopattacks campaign and the role of community-based organisations and youth workers in establishing an alternative discourse in this area.

Research context: post-conflict society

Northern Ireland has the youngest population of any jurisdiction in the UK and is also one of the poorest regions in the European Union (EU), with 25 per cent of children said to be living in poverty in 2016 (Barnard, 2018). Its communities continue to suffer from 'conflict-related trauma', after more than 30 years of violence, 'pervasive sectarianism, hard-line policing, military operations and paramilitary punishments' (Scraton 2007: 148). As previous research demonstrates, paramilitary violence against children and young people remains endemic within communities (Gordon 2018). For example, the 'Above the Law' report by The Detail found that 4,336 paramilitary style assaults were reported to the police in Northern Ireland between January 1990 and the end of October 2014 (Torney et al. 2015). As a social group, it is children and young people in particular who are at the receiving end of such violence.

Paramilitaries' use of social media in the digital age

Contemporary research such as Gordon's (2015; 2018) has explored the impact of naming and shaming and media intrusion upon children and young people. In this research, children, adolescents and their advocates provided examples of how paramilitary style assaults and vigilante assaults, followed sustained negative media coverage. Significantly, the research found that when they were also subjected to abuse and bullying (and in some instances paramilitary style assaults) after creating social media content that challenged negative stereotypes of young people living in working class communities (Gordon 2018). This was congruent with previous research which found that police and community workers expressed concerns about the use of these platforms to facilitate new forms of anti-social behaviour that had the potential to exacerbate tensions in contested interface areas within Belfast (Reilly 2011; 2012).

One underexplored issue is the use of social media by paramilitary groups in Northern Ireland, to police children and young people. Historically, these groups would punish young people deemed to be engaging in anti-social behaviour using methods such as displaying posters in public spaces, tar- and-feathering attacks, and banning them from using local community-based services.

In the digital age, there have been some reports that Facebook has been used by paramilitaries to post the names and photographs of individuals accused of anti-social behaviour. Such posts were said to be published online before or after a series of paramilitary style assaults in communities (see BBC Newsline, January 19, 2017). In one such incident, a republican paramilitary style assault on a 17-year-old man in West Belfast was linked to a hit list that contained the details of 50 people accused of crimes such as drug dealing and burglary and that had been circulated on social media (Rutherford 2017).

Yet, preliminary research by the authors into newspaper coverage of paramilitary style assaults suggests that few of them involve social media. While it is likely that such incidents are under-reported, our study of the three main Northern Irish daily newspapers (Belfast Telegraph, Irish News and News Letter) found that there were few other examples; the aforementioned hit list story was the only one of 144 articles focusing on paramilitary style assaults in these publications to mention social media being used in this way.

While the scale of the use of social media by paramilitaries to threaten young people has yet to be established, evidence has emerged suggesting the police are monitoring social media with a view to prosecuting individuals involved in organising or instigating violence.

During the public disorder seen during the union flag protests (December 2012-March 2013), the then Justice Minister, David Ford, confirmed that the Police Service of Northern Ireland (PSNI) was monitoring social media for messages which amounted to incitement to hatred or to commit criminal offences such as arson (The Guardian 6 December 2012). Statistics obtained from the PSNI under the Freedom of Information Act showed that 2,111 social media-related incidents had been reported to the police between January and May 2013, compared to 2,887 reported incidents during the calendar year of 2012. A total of 229 of these cases were reported in relation to the content posted during the peak of the flag protest movement in January and February 2013 (Spencer, 2012).

Yet, PSNI Operations Superintendent Ken Pennington pointed to the problem of verification of social media content, when asked about why the police had not done more to address the sectarianism and threatening behaviour on social media (Nolan et al., 2014: 40). Moreover, this emphasis on policing the role of social media in inciting violence has often been at the expense of investigating whether platforms such as Facebook have been used to organise and promote paramilitary style assaults within working-class loyalist and republican communities.

Tools for campaigns and as a means of resistance

There is a growing body of literature exploring the use of social media as a tool for social activism that challenges power relations (see Meikle 2018 for an overview). In contrast, there has been relatively little research investigating how children and young people, as well as their advocates, utilise social media as a tool of resistance in calling for social change in a post-conflict society. In such contexts, children and young people may benefit significantly from the ability to use social media to challenge the aforementioned negative stereotyping of this social group as being folk devils who are primarily responsible for anti-social behaviour and other societal problems (Gordon 2018).

Active resistance towards paramilitary violence and intimidation has emerged in the form of the #stopattacks campaign, first launched in 2009 by social enterprise Public Achievement under the guise of its Where is my Public Servant project (WIMPS). Led by Public Achievement's Chief Executive Paul Smyth, #stopattacks has used sought to hold the PSNI Chief Constable to account for the poor clearance rates of paramilitary style assaults, which are reportedly below four per cent (Smyth, 2017). What started off as a campaign that provided a voice to the families and victims affected by paramilitary style assaults, has evolved into a highly sophisticated social media campaign involving the sharing of video content on Facebook, Twitter and YouTube.

A key strategic objective of #stopattacks has been to improve media reporting of these attacks, which have tended to downplay the consequences for the victims and their families. Most recently, the campaign has commissioned a short film in which young people from Belfast interview families, victims and the emergency services who respond to such incidents. This has been shared on Facebook, Twitter and YouTube with the stated intention of the content being used by schools and youth groups in Northern Ireland to facilitate discussion on this issue. Future work should focus on the efficacy of this campaign in challenging the media stereotyping of young people and paramilitary style assaults in the context of a deeply divided society.

What now?

There remain many questions as to the role of social media in paramilitary style assaults in Northern Ireland. As discussed above, it is clear that platforms such as Facebook and Twitter are being used by loyalist and republican paramilitaries to threaten and intimidate children and young people, particularly in working-class communities in sectarian interfaces. Yet, the scale of such activity is difficult to estimate due to the low reporting rate of such incidents and media coverage that tends to either overlook or misrepresent such attacks.

Nevertheless, social media does appear to have potential as a tool to resist such practices, as demonstrated by its use by the police and other key stakeholders to gather data on paramilitary style assaults. Future work should focus on the efficacy of such campaigns to increase the reporting of these attacks within these communities and to improve the discourse that surrounds these issues in policy circles.

References

Barnard, H. (2018) Poverty in Northern Ireland, Joseph Rowntree Foundation, available at: https://www.jrf.org.uk/report/poverty-northern-ireland-2018 (accessed June 10, 2018).

Gordon, F. (2018) Children, Young People and the Press in a Transitioning Society: Representations, Reactions and Criminalisation, Palgrave Macmillan, Socio-Legal Series: London.

Gordon, F., McAlister, S. and Scraton, P. (2015) 'Behind the Headlines: Research Report', Childhood, Transition and Social Justice Initiative, Queen's University Belfast.

Hamilton, J., Radford, K. and Jarman, N. (2003) Policing, Accountability and Young People, Belfast: Institute for Conflict Research.

Hillyard, P., Rolston, B., Tomlinson, M. (2005) 'Poverty and Conflict in Ireland: An International Perspective', Issue 36 of Research Report Series, Belfast: Combat Poverty Agency.

Jarman, N. and O'Halloran, C. (2001) 'Recreational Rioting: Young People, Interface Areas and Violence', Child Care in Practice, Volume 7, Number 1, pages 2-16.

McAlister, S., Scraton, P. and Haydon D. (2009) 'Childhood in Transition: Experiencing Marginalisation and Conflict in Northern Ireland', Belfast: Queen's University Belfast, Save the Children and Prince's Trust Northern Ireland.

McRobbie, A. and Thornton, S. (1995) 'Rethinking "Moral Panic" for Multi- Mediated Social Worlds', British Journal of Sociology, Volume 46, pages 559–574.

Meikle, G. (ed.) (2018) The Routledge Companion to Media and Activism. London Routledge.

Nolan, P., Bryan, D., Dwyer, C., Hayward, K., Radford, K., & Shirlow, P. (2014) The Flag Dispute: Anatomy of a Protest, Supported by the Community Relations Council & the Department of Foreign Affairs and Trade (Ireland)

'Northern Ireland: paramilitaries playing role in violence, say police', The Guardian, December 6, 2012, accessible online here: https://www.theguardian.com/uk/2012/dec/06/northern-ireland-loyalist-paramilitaries-violence (accessed on December 6, 2012)

'People on 'anti-social' behaviour list shot, says Sinn Fein, BBC Newsline, January 19, 2017, Accessible online here: https://www.bbc.co.uk/news/uk-northern-ireland-38674687 (accessed on January 19, 2017)

Reilly, P. (2012) Community worker perspectives on the use of new media to promote conflict transformation in Belfast. Urban Studies, 49(15): 3385-3401, DOI: 10.1177/0042098012440464.

Reilly, P (2011) 'Anti-social' networking in Northern Ireland: policy responses to young people's use of social media for organising anti-social behaviour, Policy and Internet, Volume 3, Issue 1, Article 7.

'Residents 'at the end of tether' over anti-social behaviour in North Belfast', Irish News, May 28, 2018, Accessible online here: http://www.irishnews.com/news/northernirelandnews/2018/05/28/news/residents-at-end-of-tether-over-anti-social-behaviour-in-north-belfast-1340315/ (accessed on May 28, 2018)

Rutherford, A. (2017) Teenager shot in legs one of 50 named on social media 'hit list', Belfast Telegraph, July 15, 2017, p6.

Scraton, P. (2007) Power, Conflict and Criminalisation, London: Routledge.

Smyth, P. (2017) Stop Attacks- Beyond the Societal Shrug: Addressing Paramilitary Attacks on Young People in Northern Ireland, available at: https://wiseabap.files.wordpress.com/2017/08/beyond-the-societal-shrug.pdf (accessed May 10, 2018)

Spencer, B.J. (2014) Social media offences reported to PSNI in 2012, available at: http://www.brianjohnspencer.com/2887-social-media-offences-reported-to-psni-in- 2012/ (accessed on August 10, 2014)

Torney, K. et al. (2015) 'Above The Law: paramilitary 'punishment' attacks in Northern Ireland', The Detail. Accessible Online here: http://www.thedetail.tv/articles/above-the-law-paramilitary-punishment-attacks-in-northern-ireland (accessed on August 20, 2016)

Note on the contributors

Dr Faith Gordon is Lecturer in Criminology at Monash University in Melbourne. Faith has more than ten years' experience researching in the area of children, young people and the media and is Director of the interdisciplinary Youth Justice Network; a Research Associate of the Information Law & Policy Centre, Institute of Advanced Legal Studies; and a Senior Research Fellow of the Centre for the Study of Democracy, University of Westminster. Faith has written a sole-authored monograph for Palgrave Macmillan's Socio-Legal Series entitled 'Children, Young People and the Press in a Transitioning Society: Representations, Reactions and Criminalisation'. Faith's research findings and recommendations have been cited by the UN and her expertise continues to be utilised by legal practitioners in Northern Ireland.

Dr Paul Reilly is Senior Lecturer in Social Media & Digital Society at the University of Sheffield. He specialises in the study of online political communication, with a specific interest in how social media is used to promote better community relations in divided societies. He has written one book on the role of the internet in conflict transformation in Northern Ireland ('Framing the Troubles Online: Northern Irish Groups and Website Strategy,' Manchester University Press 2011) and is currently finishing his second on the role of social media in contentious politics in the region (due 2019). His work has been published in a number of journals including First Monday, Information, Communication & Society, New Media & Society, Policy and Internet and Urban Studies. This research has been funded by a number of organisations including the British Academy, EU 7th Framework Programme for Research (FP7), EU Horizon 2020, and the Northern Ireland Community Relations Council.

Social media and adolescents' mental health: Is the moral panic justified?

Social media, it has been argued, has had a negative impact on the mental health of the young. Discourses of fear and danger have become endemic in contemporary society, as parents, schools and policy-makers grapple with the cyberworld embedded in the lives of children and adolescents, but how true are these concerns, asks Dr Michelle O'Reilly

Traditional media has undoubtedly played an important role in the social creation of a moral panic regarding social media use. The sensationalist reporting of the impact of social media on the identities, behaviours, and wellbeing of young people is a widely spread phenomenon.

Young people and digital technology in the news

Journalists frequently report on the negative effects of social media on child and adolescent mental health. Headlines are often severe in tone and point to a disconnected youth who are at risk in the age of digital technology. Such sensationalised discourses point to the dangers we are placing young people in, not only in terms of 'attack' from external sources through cyberbullying, trolling, and sinister paedophile rings looking to groom the innocent, but also in terms of self-imposed impact such as sleep deprivation, limited social skills and connection, addiction, and failure to engage in the 'real' world. For example:

> Paedophiles using clash of the clans and Instagram to groom children as young as seven
>
> (Source: Scheerhout, 2016: The Mirror)

> Social media sites are damaging children's mental health, headteachers warn
>
> (Source: Busby, 2018: The Independent)

> Teen suicide rate suddenly rises with heavy use of smartphones, social media
>
> (Source: Kelly, 2017: Washington Times)

Although the adverse discourses embedded through traditional media are interesting and do reflect some real risk to the safety of younger populations, arguably this is disproportionate to the reality. Notably in any given year there are thousands of news articles reporting different issues related to mental health and social media, warning adults to protect the young from its effects. What is especially interesting is how these media dimensions have co-constructed and contributed to a moral panic and a negative discourse around the very existence of social media in young people's lives.

Adolescents, mental health and social media use

Interestingly these media-proposed perspectives are reflected by young people themselves as they adopt the dystopian discourse of social media and its reported negative impact on their wellbeing as a group. They buy into the need for better digital literacy, greater levels of education about social media use, and the idea they are a generation plagued by digital risks to their health.

Adolescence is a particularly significant developmental period for susceptibility of the influence of both social media, and traditional media reporting of it. Developmentally these young people go through a phase of psychological, biological and social change as they develop new skills, responsibilities and intimate relationships (Christie and Viner, 2005; Erikson, 1968).

It is recognised that the modern generations of adolescents are under increasing pressure with considerable emphasis on academic attainment and exam stress, the broader influence of technology, and a new modern world far removed from that of previous generations. This is a developmental period marked by a high level of mental health conditions (Burns, Durkin and Nichols, 2009), and globally between 10-20% of adolescents are diagnosed with a disorder (Kieling, Baker-Henningham, Belfer et al., 2011).

Of course, it is also the period of the lifespan with a marked social media usage, with figures showing 97 per cent of adolescents using it regularly (Woods and Scott, 2016). A recent Ofcom report showed even younger children are extensive users of technology, with 23 per cent of 8-11-year-olds having a social media profile and 81 per cent using YouTube (Ofcom, 2017).

Negative impact

There is a significant body of literature which points to the negative consequences for children and adolescents. This includes social media addiction (Jiang, 2014), inappropriate sexual messaging (Livingstone and Görzig, 2014), privacy violations, (O'Keeffe and Clarke-Pearson, 2011), cyberbullying (Cowie, 2013), trolling (Griffiths, 2014), and grooming (Davidson, 2012), to name but a few. Indeed, research has indicated that 28 per cent of 11-16-year olds report having an upsetting experience on social media (Lilley, Ball and Vernon, 2014).

However, susceptibility to risk is arguably not universal (Piortowski and Valkenberg, 2015) and exposure to risk may not necessarily result in harm (Livingstone and Gőrzig, 2014). The so called 'risk society' (Beck, 1992) is one that must be navigated by adolescents as they learn to carve out their identities and manage their social worlds and social networks. Indeed, it could be the case that some risk exposure is necessary for them to learn how to stay safe online.

Tension in the argument

Recent research has begun to illustrate the tensions in the dystopian perspective (see Wajcman, 2014; Gregg, 2013) as challenges to the populist accounts about the social consequences for youth are put under the microscope. Social media can be a source of information (Burns et al., 2009), and an opportunity for mental health promotion (O'Reilly, Dogra, Hughes et al., forthcoming, 2018, a), and thus there are possibilities for a more positive discourse around its usage.

Digital media creates opportunities for youth engagement, and could boost self-esteem (Valkenburg and Peter, 2009), provide a pathway for learning (Ito, Horst, and Bittani, 2013), and allow community-building (Jenkins, Shresthova, Gamber-Thompson et al., 2016). Furthermore, young people themselves promote the value of social media as a mechanism for learning coping strategies and to learn about their mental health (Bone, Duggard, Vostanis and Dogra, 2015).

The dilemma then is the possible anti-social nature of social media, which raises questions about the actual impact on young people's mental health. The negative discourse and the sensationalist headlines have generated a fear culture around social media, presenting the dangers hiding behind the screen, and yet there are some useful opportunities to use social media in a more positive way.

Adolescents' perspectives

The moral panic of social media has heightened perspectives and attitudes regarding the possible hazards associated with it as connected to the suspension of meaningful social relationships. As noted, what is of special interest is the reconfiguration, that is, the reification of sensationalised negative perspectives of social media by its most avid users, the adolescents themselves.

In a recent qualitative focus group study involving 54 adolescents aged 12-18, the perspectives of social media were consistently negative (see O'Reilly, Dogra, Whiteman et al, forthcoming, 2018 b). Predominantly and frequently, social media was constructed as 'dangerous', and a hazard to their mental wellbeing.

For example, consider the following from O'Reilly et al. (forthcoming, 2018, b):

> *"It's a dangerous place social media and I think some people don't actually know how dangerous it is."*

P7 Leicester yr11(aged 15-16yrs)

Anonymity, trolling and the monster lurking in cyberspace

A specific and pervasive view amongst the adolescents in the study was the tension of anonymity. They recognised how stigmatising the experience of mental disorders were for young people and saw the anonymous social media help-seeking channels as a positive way for support, information and guidance to be sought. However, they also noted the darker side of anonymity, constructing cyberbullying and trolling an inevitable aspect of modern adolescence.

Research has indicated trolling is a significant social media issue. In a study of 2000 14-18-year-olds, a third reported victimisation of trolling, with a quarter suffering regular attacks, and one-in-ten confessing to instigating such behaviour (Rice, 2013). The adolescents in our study accepted this was part of adolescent life. For example, consider the following from O'Reilly et al. (forthcoming, 2018, b):

> *"There's always going to be people like that, especially on social media where you can be like no-one will know who you are cos you're completely hidden."*
>
> P2 Leicester yr10 (aged 14-15yrs)

> *"There are a lot of people who are nasty on social media or say things are actually too scared to say it to their face and it's an easy way out really."*
>
> P4 Leicester yr11 (aged 15-16yrs)

These perspectives indicate young people themselves perpetuate the media discourses of social media's negative impact on wellbeing. Notably, they rarely referenced their own lives or experiences, and instead considered their population more generally, and this reflects a broad acceptance of the dominant rhetoric without a critical questioning of its personal meaning or ascription (O'Reilly et al., forthcoming, 2018, b).

Adolescents, mental health promotion and the need for information

Conversely, while confessing to frequent and considerable social media use, and reiterating the moral panic around social media, the adolescents also presented its positive impact. For example, adolescents recognised they increasingly relied on social media for psychoeducation and for relaxation or coping with stress (O'Reilly et al., forthcoming, 2018, a). Thus it is a plausible and cost-effective tool for mental health promotion (Betton, Borschmann, Docherty et al., 2015).

Indeed, the adolescents felt education about mental health was important and social media was valuable for this because of its social networking aspect, its educational possibilities, and where required, its anonymity. For example, consider the following from O'Reilly et al. (forthcoming, 2018, a):

> *"It was like, it was a few months back when I was quite depressed and I needed to talk to someone and I didn't want to go down to the doctors or whatever because*

that's just, I just find that awkward talking to someone in person, so I just did it on social media instead."

P5–Leicester year-group11

"Social media's definitely like an amazing platform for like advertisement. You could really like, as we were saying that mental illness is kind of taboo, I think through social media there is definitely a way to get it out of the taboo and into everyday life"

P4-Leicester year-group13

Conclusions

Children and young people need more education about both social media and mental health, as well as how the two are connected. While there has been a drive to provide information about the risks faced on the internet (Livingstone, 2008) research illustrates they want more information about how to use social media correctly (Rice, 2013). Although social media is a useful channel for mental health education, they want this to be juxtaposed and integrated with school activity (O'Reilly, Adams, Whiteman et al., forthcoming, 2018, c).

Social media could have a positive impact on mental health and wellbeing, and the news rhetoric dampened or challenged. Social media may extend social networks and provide information, presenting a tension in accepting what is arguably a false dichotomy between the 'real' and the 'virtual' (Jurgenson, 2014). The dystopian position needs to be defied, which is reflected in the dilemmatic thinking and behaviour of adolescents as they navigate the perceived online danger versus the opportunities to become better educated and supported in the so-called digital age.

Evidently, young people are becoming increasingly aware of their digital footprint, as they seek to offset their use of social media as a source information and support, while being aware of the risks of participating in a cyber-society. Indeed, for some the assumptions of adults that they are irresponsible with the information, networks and content of their social media lives can be frustrating for those young people engaged in it (boyd, 2014). Perhaps unsurprisingly, young people continually develop new strategies to manage social media and the blurred boundaries between their public and private worlds (Marwick and boyd, 2014).

For journalists therefore, questions must be raised about their moral duty in reporting the 'epidemic' of mental health problems in society's youth, and positioning the role of social media at the heart of this social difficulty, against the tensions and questions that this moral panic creates. We must wonder at how 'real' the problem is, and the extent to which it is peddled by sensationalist headlines and the contribution that this has on the societal fear of social media, for an adult generation often less technologically savvy than their children.

References

Beck, U. (1992). *Risk society: Towards a new modernity.* London: Sage.

Betton, V., Borschmann, R., Docherty, M., Coleman, S., Brown, M., and Henderson, C. (2015). The role of social media in reducing stigma and discrimination. *The British Journal of Psychiatry, 206,* 443-444

boyd, d., (2014). *It's complicated: The social lives of networked teens.* USA: Yale University Press.

Bone, C., Dugard, P., Vostanis, P., & Dogra, N. (2015). Students' understandings of mental health and their preferred learning platforms. *Journal of Public Mental Health, 14(4),* 185-195

Burns, J., Durkin, L., and Nicholas, J. (2009). Mental health of young people in the United States: What role can the internet play in reducing stigma and promoting help seeking? *Journal of Adolescent Health, 45,* 95-97

Busby, E. (2018). Social media sites are damaging children's mental health, headteachers warn. As retrieved on 21st May from: https://www.independent.co.uk/news/education/education-news/headteachers-social-media-children-mental-health-school-association-college-a8246456.html

Christie, D., and Viner, R. (2005). ABC of adolescence: Adolescent development. *British Medical Journal, 330,* 301-304

Cowie, H. (2013). Cyberbullying and its impact on young people's emotional health and well-being. *The Psychiatrist, 37,* 167-170

Davidson, J. (2012). Online grooming and the targeting of vulnerable children: Findings from the EC Online Groomers study, in Livingstone, S., and Palmer, T. (Eds.), *Identifying vulnerable children online and what strategies can help them (pp: 18-20).* London: UK Safer Internet Centre

Erikson, E. (1968). *Identity: youth and crisis.* New York: Norton.

Gregg, M. (2013). *Work's intimacy.* New Jersey: John Wiley and Sons.

Griffiths, M. (2014). Adolescent trolling in online environments: A brief overview. *Education and Health, 32(3),* 85-87

Ito, M., Horst, H., and Bittani, M. (2008). *Living and learning with new media: Summary of findings from the digital youth project.* Chicago, IL: John D and Catherine MacArthur Foundation Reports on Digital Media and Learning

Jenkins, H., Shresthova, S., Gamber-Thompson, L., Kligler-Vilenchik, N., and Zimmerman, A. (2016). *By any media necessary: The new youth activist.* NY: New York University Press.

Jiang, Q (2014). Internet addiction among young people in China: Internet connectedness, online gaming, and academic performance decrement. *Internet Research, 24 (1),* 2-20

Jurgenson, N. (2012). When atoms meet bits: Social media, the mobile web and augmented revolution. *Future Internet, 4(1),* 83-91.

Kelly, L. (2017). Teen suicide rate suddenly rises with heavy use of smartphones, social media. As retrieved 21st May 2018 from: https://www.washingtontimes.com/news/2017/nov/14/teen-suicides-rise-with-smartphone-social-media-us/

Kieling, C., Baker-Henningham, H., Belfer, M., Conti, G., et al. (2011). Child and adolescent mental health worldwide: Evidence for action. *Lancet, 378,* 1515-1525.

Lilley, C., Ball, R., & Vernon, H. (2014). *The experiences of 11-16-year olds on social networking sites.* London: NSPCC report.

Livingstone, S. (2008). Taking risky opportunities in youthful content creation: Teenagers' use of social networking sites for intimacy, privacy and self-expression. *New Media & Society, 10(3),* 393-411.

Livingstone, S., and Gőrzig, A., (2014). When adolescents receive sexual messages on the internet: explaining experiences of risk and harm. *Computers in Human Behavior, 33,* 8-15

Marwick, A., and boyd, d. (2014). Networked privacy: How teenagers negotiate context in social media, *New Media & Society, 16(7),* 1051-1067.

Ofcom (2017) 'Children and Parents: Media Use and Attitudes Report', As retrieved 11th March 2017 from; https://www.ofcom.org.uk/data/assets/pdf_file/0020/108182/children-parents-media-use-attitudes-2017.pdf

O'Keeffe, G., and Clarke-Pearson, K. (2011). Clinical report – The impact of social media on children, adolescents, and families. *Pediatrics, 127(4),* 800-804.

O'Reilly, M., Adams, S., Whiteman, N., Hughes, J., Reilly, P., and Dogra, N. (forthcoming, 2018, c). Whose responsibility is adolescent mental health in the UK? The perspectives of key stakeholders. *School Mental Health*

O'Reilly, M., Dogra, N., Hughes, J., Reilly, P., George, R., and Whiteman, N. (forthcoming, 2018 a). Potential of social media in promoting mental health in adolescents. *Health Promotion International*

O'Reilly, M., Dogra, N., Whiteman, N., Hughes, J., Eruyar, S., and Reilly, P. (forthcoming, 2018, b). Is social media bad for mental health and wellbeing? Exploring the perspectives of adolescents. *Clinical Child Psychology and Psychiatry*

Piotrowski, J., and Valkenburg, P. (2015). Finding orchids in a field of dandelions: Understanding children's differential susceptibility to media effects. *American Behavioral Scientist, 59(14),* 1776-1789

Rice, L. (2013). *It's time for more Lolz NOT trolls.* Vinspitred, January, 13

Scheerhout, J. (2016). Paedophiles using clash of the clans and Instagram to groom children as young as seven; as retrieved on 21st May 2018 from: https://www.mirror.co.uk/news/uk-news/paedophiles-using-clash-clans-instagram-7117707

Valkenburg, P., and Peter, J. (2009). Social consequences of the Internet for adolescents: A decade of research. *Current Directions in Psychological Science, 18(1),* 1-5

Wajcman, J. (2014). *Pressed for time: The acceleration of life in digital capitalism.* University of Chicago Press.

Woods, H., and Scott, H. (2016). #Sleepyteens: Social media use in adolescence is associated with poor sleep quality, anxiety, depression and low self-esteem. *Journal of Adolescence, 51,* 41-49

Note on the contributor

Dr Michelle O'Reilly is Associate Professor in the School of Media, Communication and Sociology and the School of Psychology at the Greenwood Institute of Child Health, University of Leicester, and is a Research Consultant for Leicestershire Partnership NHS Trust. Michelle's research expertise is broadly in the areas of child mental health, family therapy, qualitative health research and research ethics. She is interested in language and mental health and has recently co-authored a book on social constructionism and mental health, and one on applied conversation analysis. She is also the editor of the book series 'the language of mental health'.

Hate's coming home: the rise of football-related abuse on social media

The beautiful game may have vast support across continents and classes but, John Price says, it has an ugly side that it seems few are really willing to tackle

In many ways the 2018 World Cup in Russia was a joyous celebration of the game – but it was also a reminder of one of the sport's current major problems.

The Brazil midfielder Fernandinho scored an own goal, which meant his nation was knocked out of the tournament at the quarter-final stage. In the hours and days that followed, a stream of racist abuse was directed at the player via social media. Even the footballer's wife and mother received such abuse, forcing the latter to close her Instagram account.

The Brazil Football Union came to the defence of its player, posting on social media: "Football represents the union of colours, genres, cultures and people. We are with you. Racists will not pass!" The case provides a stark example of how the racism that was once so often heard on the terraces of football grounds has found a new home online.

This chapter examines the rise of football-related discrimination and abuse on social media. It begins with an examination of the scale of the problem before discussing some examples and the reasons behind them. It finishes by critically assessing how the game of football has responded to this relatively new outlet for hate in the game.

The rise of social media abuse in football

In the 2012/13 season, Kick It Out – football's main anti-discrimination organisation in the UK – began to receive complaints about racism and other forms of hate speech on social media. That year they received 19 reports of such abuse. The following season this figure had risen to 142, and by the following year social media was the most common source of complaints about discrimination in football (Bennett and Jonsson 2017). The charity knew the number of complaints received was a tiny fraction of the abuse happening online, but one thing was clear – football-related racism had most definitely moved from the stands to online spaces.

In response, Kick It Out commissioned social analytics company Brandwatch (2015) to conduct research into the social media abuse of Premier League teams and players. The study estimated that almost 135,000 discriminatory posts were made across the 2014/15 football season. More than 95,000 discriminatory posts were directed at Premier League teams, with approximately 39,000 such posts aimed at Premier League players.

Chelsea was the most abused club (approximately 20,000 posts) closely followed by Liverpool (19,000) and Arsenal (12,000). Former Liverpool striker Mario Balotelli was the most targeted individual, receiving more than 8,000 discriminatory posts. Racism was the most common form of discrimination identified, comprising 28 per cent of the abuse. Gender was the next most common grounds for abuse (25 per cent), followed by discrimination in terms of sexual orientation (19 per cent), disability (11 per cent) and antisemitism (9 per cent). The research was repeated again the following season with very similar results and approximately 134,000 discriminatory posts identified.

Roisin Wood, Kick It Out's chief executive, said: "This is a huge amount of awful abuse. A lot of it is vile, and something needs to be done" (Conn, 2015).

Despite the huge number of abusive posts being aimed at footballers on social media, a relatively small number of perpetrators have ended up facing criminal charges. In June 2011, a Norwich fan became the first to be banned for life by a football club following a racist tweet aimed at his club's new signing, James Vaughan.

Luke O'Donoughoe, then 23, was charged under the Communications Act 2003; he pleaded guilty, and was sentenced to a 12-month community order and 120 hours of unpaid work (Farrington et al 2014). The following year, in another notable exception, then university student Liam Stacey, was jailed for the racist tweets he published as Bolton footballer Fabrice Muamba lay fighting for his life on the pitch at Tottenham. Stacey had posted:

"LOL. F*ckMuamba. He's dead!!! #haha."

He then sent a string of racist messages in response to other Twitter users challenging this original post. The day after his abusive tweets, the 21-year-old was charged under the Racially Aggravated Public Order Act 1986 s4A. He pleaded guilty and was ordered to serve to 56 days in prison, eventually serving half of that sentence. Passing sentence, District Judge John Charles told Stacey:

"It was racist abuse via a social networking site instigated as a result of a vile and abhorrent comment about a young footballer who was fighting for his life. At that moment, not just the footballer's family, not just the footballing world but also the whole world were literally praying for his life. Your comments aggravated this situation. I have no choice but to impose an immediate custodial sentence to reflect the public outrage at what you have done" (Morris, March 2012).

Stacey was drunk at the time he published his racist tweets and later said he did not know why he had done it. Interestingly, his Twitter handle included his surname and so there was no clear sense of anonymity encouraging him to act in the way he did. This points to a subtler explanation of why some people feel emboldened to publish material on social media that they would not say or shout in someone's face.

Suler's Online Disinhibition Effect (ODE) provides a useful model for thinking about how this might occur (2004). He identifies six factors that, although they interact variously with different people and contexts, generally tend to promote ODE – in other words, they increase the chances of someone expressing prejudice or hate speech being online. These factors include:

- dissociative anonymity – the idea that people are able to either hide their identity online or separate their online and offline identities;
- invisibility – even when someone's identity is known, the fact they cannot be seen or heard by another can change their behaviour;
- asynchronicity – the tempo of online activity means people can send something and then forget about it, leaving the consequences for another time;
- dissociative imagination – the idea that we are able to create imagined identities for ourselves with different sets of rules;
- minimisation of status and authority – the absence of visible signs of authority online, leading to a sense of freedom to speak out and misbehave.

For Suler, these factors mean that Liam Stacey, and many others, can feel empowered and dissociated enough to behave in ways online that they would not countenance in their offline encounters. Goffman (1990) has previously drawn the distinction between people's backstage and frontstage behaviour – the idea that people will project different versions of themselves depending on whether they are in public (frontstage) or private (backstage) contexts.

Typically, expressions of hate speech and socially abhorrent behaviour have been more likely to occur backstage. The power of social media though, as explained by Suler's ODE, is that it provides football supporters and others with a sense of being backstage, while their comments are very much frontstage and on full view for all to see.

Football's response

The response from the game of football to the growing problem of online racism and abuse has been slow, poorly co-ordinated, and largely ineffective.

To be fair, the game is not alone in struggling to cope with online abuse, and its work has been hampered by the failure of others – including social media tech giants largely unwilling to take responsibility for the content produced on their platforms; a disjointed and poorly resourced police effort; and recent legal guidelines making prosecutions for online behaviour less likely (Farrington et al 2014).

Kick It Out now has a reporting mechanism allowing fans and players to quickly, and anonymously, report online abuse, while the Football Association (FA) does have some guidelines for players and their use of social media. However, these guidelines largely ignore the crucial issue of what players should do in the event of receiving abuse or hate speech. As Bennett and Jonsson (2017: 212) have assessed: "The lack of guidelines and consistency primarily makes dealing with online discrimination in football complex. This is especially challenging for Kick It Out who have limited resources to tackle this issue alone."

There are also major weaknesses in the effectiveness of the social media training given to players across different levels of the game. For example, there are no consistent, mandatory levels of training and advice provided for players on this issue. Part of the reason for this is a lack of co-ordination between the relevant authorities and an absence of decisive, pro-active leadership from the FA.

Another problem is a general lack of co-operation from the clubs themselves. Education officials from the Professional Footballers Association (PFA) report having difficulties in gaining access to players. One said: "We have to go through the player liaison officer, or the manager or the PFA delegate to say, 'Look, can we have a meeting with the players? There's certain channels you've got to go through whereas in the past I could go down to Chelsea or Tottenham and go in and no problems at all, it's totally changed. The players aren't as accessible as they used to be" (Kilvington and Price 2017).

Even club officials themselves report being frustrated by their own employers in attempting to help and advise players about how to be safe online. For example, the Head of Safeguarding at one Premier League club said:

> "Currently first-team players are almost considered untouchable and no support is in place for all kinds of difficulties they may face. I could deliver online training, but the main barrier is access to the players as this is seen as a distraction from their football activities." (Kilvington and Price 2017)

The problem is further exacerbated by a lack of engagement from players. When Kick It Out attempted to conduct its own survey with footballers, about their experiences of discrimination, it attempted to contact 4,000 players via their clubs – and received only 200 responses. Many clubs failed to pass on the survey to their players and, in cases where they did, many players simply chose to ignore it. For Kick It Out officials, this is because some players have hardened to the abuse that often accompanies the game. One said:

> "It's too much hassle. They haven't got time. It's not a big deal. Players are a different breed because they've lived in the criticism business since they were

8 or 9, so they've developed a way of dealing with things which is a no fuss way" (Kilvington and Price 2017).

Another factor is that many players now use social media to develop their personal brands and make money through sponsorship and advertising; even employing companies to control social media feeds on their behalf (Sanderson 2018). For some, perhaps the abuse is just the downside that comes with such benefits.

Conclusion

Football cannot be blamed for racism and other forms of hate speech. These problems are deeply ingrained in society. But while overt acts of racism within and around football matches have – to some extent – been managed, these expressions of hate have found another home online. The feeling of being backstage while using social media, combined with the tribal and emotional nature of football, means that people are posting hundreds of discriminatory posts each day. The vast majority of these posts go unreported and unpunished – thereby encouraging the problem to grow.

The world of football appears bemused at what to do, with players largely left to fend for themselves online. The response to the problem has lacked clarity, resources and commitment from the game's governing bodies, from the clubs and from the players themselves. Hate has found a home – and nobody seems to know what to do about it.

References

Bennett H and Jonsson A (2017) Kick It Out: Tackling online discrimination in football, in D Kilvington and J Price (eds) Sport and Discrimination. London: Routledge.

Brandwatch (2015) 'Case Study: Tackling unprecedented levels of social media abuse'. Available at https://www.brandwatch.com/2015/05/case-study-uncovering-and-tackling-shocking-abuse-in-football/

Conn D (2015) Kick It Out calls for collective action on social media abuse towards players. *Guardian Online*, April 16. Available at http://www.theguardian.com/football/2015/apr/16/kick-it-out-social-media-abuse-to-players-clubs

Farrington N, Kilvington D, Price J and Saeed A (2014) *Sport, Racism and Social Media*. London: Routledge.

Goffman, E. (1990). The presentation of self in everyday life. London, England: Penguin Books.

Kilvington and Price (2017) Tackling Social Media Abuse? Critically assessing English football's response to online racism. Communication and Sport. DOI: 10.1177/2167479517745300

Morris S (2012) Student jailed for racist FabriceMuamba tweets. Guardian, March 27. Available at www.guardian.co.uk/uk/2012/mar/27/student-jailed-fabrice-muamba-tweets.

Sanderson, J (2018) Identity and Speech in Sports in the Social Media Era, in MA

McCann (ed) The Oxford Handbook of American Sports Law. Oxford University Press: Oxford.

Suler J (2004) The online disinhibition effect. CyberPsychology & Behavior 7 (3): 321–326.

Note on the contributor

Dr John Price is Senior Lecturer in Journalism at the Centre for Research in Media and Cultural Studies, University of Sunderland.

Section Six

Regulating social media:
inevitable or Mission Impossible?

* * *

We need a decision, and we need it now

Richard Tait

For the last 20 years social media has had things very much its own way. Its success has not just been due to the brilliance of its technology and the business acumen of its architects. Two factors above all added rocket fuel to the growth of the social media titans – the mistakes of the competition and the failure of politicians and regulators to understand that, even in a casino, there have to be rules. Allowing social media to operate and grow with minimal regulation for so long was always going to end in tears.

The failure of the traditional media industries, in the main, to compete effectively has been well chronicled elsewhere in this book. In the UK, an obsession with consolidation, cost reduction and short-term profits meant that by the time newspapers and commercial television invested in digital platforms it was in many cases too little too late.

There was precious little strategic thinking – I can still remember (though I have been trying to forget) the enthusiasm with which some of ITN's own customers/ shareholders set out to cripple ITN's initial forays into online and digital news, helping ensure that the ITN brand, which had been one of the best known and respected news brands in the UK, has now all but disappeared from the online space. The last time I looked, ITN's Twitter feed had 3,000 followers. BBC News has 9.49m and CNN 40.3m.

Politicians and regulators must also take responsibility for what has happened. For all their research departments and impressive evidence-based analysis, regulators know that the politicians make the weather – and for most of the last two decades, in the UK and the US at least, the prevailing political view has been that regulation should fall away and let the market and technology determine the direction of travel.

On one of the rare occasions in the UK where regulators did take a hard line, they got it farcically wrong. In 2009 the UK competition authorities blocked Project Kangaroo – a BBC/ITV/Channel 4 proposal to launch a video-on-demand service. This terrible decision left the field open to Netflix and Amazon. The US giants now dominate the market and video streaming has more subscribers than pay TV. Ofcom, the current media regulator, has recently recognised that decision was 'a tragedy' and is encouraging the three broadcasters to try again a decade later. It is hard to know whether to laugh or cry.

But we are where we are and, in the light of the recent scandals and public concern about social media, the political climate has changed. Mark Zuckerberg, the founder of Facebook, told the US Congress in April 2018 that the regulation of social media was 'inevitable'. It was a huge concession – up to that point the supporters of the social media giants had argued they were platforms, not publishers, and that regulating social media was, like regulating the internet, Mission Impossible.

The chapters in this section analyse what can be done, even at this late stage, to achieve that mission. Leighton Andrews has had remarkable career across broadcasting and politics – he has been the BBC's Head of Public Affairs and education minister in the Welsh government. He is now professor of practice in public service leadership and innovation at Cardiff Business School.

He sees a dramatic turnaround in political attitudes to social media. The motives of those who argued for the lightest of regulation varied – the fear of stifling the economic growth of a new technology, journalistic concern for freedom of speech, neo-liberal opposition to regulation on principle and the idealism of those who believed social media would of itself create a better word. But until 2017 they were winning the argument – social media companies were shielded from legal responsibility for what they published and their spectacular emergence as some of the biggest companies on the planet went unchallenged on grounds of monopoly or fair trading.

He believes it is not too late to take action, but it needs to be much better coordinated than at present. There are different initiatives at EU level, for example, but he writes "it is questionable whether they add up to a coherent package of reforms." His solution is to create a new category of information utilities for search and social media, which would be licensed by a regulator. They would have reporting responsibilities; the regulator would have strong backstop intervention powers. "Today, the regulation of social media is no longer a media issue but a social issue," he says.

As well as arguments for greater regulation of what the social media companies do, there have also been calls to break them up, as US anti-trust laws dismantled the Standard Oil monopoly in 1911. Others argue that the market itself will create effective competition in the sector. Neither view gets much encouragement from

Patrick Barwise, emeritus professor of management and marketing at London Business School and one of the media industry's most respected economic analysts. Tech markets are 'winner-take-all' and the current market leaders will be almost impossible to displace or break up. He quotes the view of one the co-founders of Paypal – 'competition is for losers'.

What is needed, he argues, is a new approach to regulation to deal with a unique situation. "Developing such an approach will require economic regulators to tackle a number of somewhat unfamiliar sources of market power – such as big data, habitual usage, switching costs, lock-in, and tax avoidance – without discouraging innovation or significantly reducing the manifold benefits of digital technology."

Winning political and public support for a tougher regulatory regime may be easier said than done – the scandals have scarcely put the brakes on the social media companies' continued growth. They offer the consumer amazing tools, which have become an essential part of modern life, often at little or no direct cost. And for most of the last 20 years they have also been able to rely on the argument, even from media rivals, that state intervention in the media is potentially so dangerous a threat to freedom of expression (and/or an obstacle to economic growth and innovation) that it is much better to leave the internet alone.

But that proposition seems to be losing sway. Paul Connew is one the UK's most experienced newspaper executives, having edited the Sunday Mirror and been deputy editor of both the Mirror and the News of the World. He has always argued that social media's positives significantly outweighed its negatives. Now he admits "I have (nervously) changed my mind."

He has been convinced by the scandals around the election of Donald Trump in the US and the House of Commons Culture Media and Sport committee's conclusion "that the UK faced a democratic crisis sparked by the manipulation of personal data and the spread of fake news and pernicious views." He is far from confident that politicians in the US really have the appetite to confront companies, which are seen as great American success stories, but he does see a tough battle ahead between the social media companies and European regulators.

And what in this should be the role of UK regulators? Christopher Graham knows where many of the regulatory bodies are buried from his career as a BBC producer, then Secretary to the BBC Board, Director General of the Advertising Standards Authority and finally Information Commissioner from 2009 to 2016. He thinks, with the exception of John Birt's BBC, which clearly did recognise the transformative potential of digital technology, industry and politicians in the UK have been behind the curve of developments for most of the last two decades: "in a business where the leading players are consistently several jumps ahead, both of the competition and of the authorities, the contribution of Whitehall and Westminster has consistently been several steps off the pace."

But the Information Commissioner's Office (ICO) has been taking on the social media companies in the last year and the politicians, after years of foot-dragging, are beginning to give the ICO the powers it will need. "I hope the experience of Facebook and Cambridge Analytica will persuade government and parliament to get on with delivering what is necessary if digital media are to be a blessing and not a curse," he writes.

Assuming the political will is there, what would regulation of social media look like in practice? Phil Harding is a former Editor of the Today Programme and Controller of Editorial Policy at the BBC. He believes regulation of social media content need not be complicated but is certainly in the public interest. He proposes a model with different layers of regulation, "some statutory backed up by legislation; some voluntary run by the industry itself."

His model is very much in synch with developments in data protection and media regulation across the EU. But he points out the contrast between this and the more laissez-faire approach of the US, where effective media regulation has virtually disappeared. He sees the EU as determined to set an international standard for regulation, encouraging its trading partners to align with Europe. If the UK wants to pursue effective regulation of social media, it would seem to make sense to work closely with the EU.

But where the UK positions itself on data protection and content and advertising regulation as Brexit approaches is a key choice. Mark Zuckerberg's appearances in 2018 before the US Congress and the European Parliament and his non-appearance in Westminster tells you all you need to know about the geo-politics of social media regulation. There are, in reality, only two games in town – align with the US or stay close to the EU. In social media, as in many other things, some very big decisions need to be made very soon.

The regulatory moment is upon us

Threats from governments and European institutions are bringing about changes in the attitudes of tech businesses, says Leighton Andrews, but this may not go far enough. Social media firms may need to be designated as information utilities – with all the increased oversight that utilities around the world work under

Let me start with two quotes, six months and a continent apart. The first is from the chief executive of Ofcom, Sharon White, who told the Cambridge RTS Conference in September 2017 that while she believed that Facebook and Google were media companies, she didn't "think regulation is the answer because I think it is really hard to navigate the boundary between regulation and censorship of the internet" (Andrews, 2017b). Six months later, in an interview with CNN, Facebook's founder Mark Zuckerberg said, "I'm not sure we shouldn't be regulated," (Kantrowitz, 2018).

Had we moved in a relatively short period to a regulatory moment? Or do the two quotes themselves prolong and recycle the oft-repeated error that the internet isn't and has never been regulated, reinforcing the fatalism of those who would urge caution, restraint and ultimately obsequious hand-wringing, rather than confronting the power of what a House of Lords Select Committee called 'the data monopolies' (House of Lords, 2018b)?

There are good grounds for believing that we have witnessed a regulatory turn; that this has moved well beyond media policy; that European regulatory proposals may become the 'gold standard' for global regulation; and that there are signs that, even if Brexit happens, the UK will not be immune from the regulatory tide.

The 2017 Conservative Manifesto, being implemented as I write through the Digital Charter, the Green Paper on Internet Safety and other measures, contained a series of proposals, including establishment of the regulatory framework in law. The manifesto was explicit in its emphasis:

> Some people say that it is not for government to regulate when it comes to technology and the internet. We disagree (Conservative Party, 2017).

Indeed, by July 2018, even Ofcom had arguably changed its position to support regulation (White, 2018).

Of course, the roots of the suggestion that regulation 'of the internet' amounts to censorship are manifold. There is a long tradition on the wilder shores of cyber-libertarianism that the internet is a free zone that challenges governments and regulatory systems and is ultimately unregulable (Barlow, 1996).

There is a neo-liberal logic to the opposition to regulation of all kinds in order to maximise profit under platform capitalism (Srnicek, 2017). There is also the simple, more benign narrative of the emergence of the internet and the World Wide Web as popular means of communication and connection in the mid 1990s, when governments in the US and Europe were genuinely concerned not to stifle new and innovative forms of services of the Information Superhighway or Information Society (Collins, 2009).

Then there is the long-standing tradition of journalistic opposition to state censorship and restraints on freedom of speech. Finally, the Snowden revelations have increased suspicion about the role of state security agencies and reinforced libertarian criticism of government regulation from a different libertarian perspective – that of the civil libertarian, data rights or privacy activist, arguably temporarily elevating concerns about the surveillance state or society (Gandy, 1989) even above those of surveillance capitalism (Zuboff, 2016).

The media industry's fight-back against Facebook and Google

The legacy legislation of the Information Society era of is of course the US Communications Decency Act of 1996, the EU's Electronic Commerce Directive of 2000, and the UK's 2003 Communications Act. The first two limited the liability of internet platforms as carriers of information akin to USPs (Kohl, 2016). The UK legislation created Ofcom without a remit for regulation of the Internet (Lunt and Livingstone, 2012), meaning that Ofcom might be left with responsibility for regulating only a smaller area of the overall media market (Andrews, 2017a).

Over recent years, because of the impact of the information intermediaries on the economics of the media, including their dominance of advertising revenue in the smartphone era (Enders, 2016; Baron, 2017) and news publishers' dependence on them for distribution (Ganter and Nielsen, 2017; Bell, 2017), it has been from within media policy that some of the most developed policy and regulatory responses have emerged (for example, Helberger et al, 2015; Helberger, 2018; Tambini and Labo 2016).

Media companies, such as News Corporation (Thomson, 2018), the Guardian Media Group (2017) and the New York Times (Thompson, 2018), have been at the forefront of the recent fightback against Facebook and Google. In the UK, the Press Gazette launched a well-supported 'duopoly' campaign about the power of the two tech titans (Ponsford, 2017). The News Media Association in the UK called for a Competition and Markets Authority examination of the digital advertising market and a review of the status of Facebook and Google in terms of media law. The News Media Alliance in the United States is pressing for special anti-trust exemption to allow news organisations to band together to negotiate collectively on technology advertising and revenue-sharing (Stangel, 2017).

Early 2017 saw the entry of large advertisers into the fray, with Proctor and Gamble particularly reducing its digital advertising spend and demanding more rigorous accountability (Neff, 2017). A wide range of advertisers soon after withdrew advertising from YouTube following an expose that programmatic (algorithmically-driven) advertising was placing advertisements next to terrorist or other illegal content (Mostrous and Dean, 2017; Solon, 2017; Vizard, 2017).

The debate has moved beyond the media

Arguably, however, today, the debate over the role of information intermediaries such as Facebook, following the Cambridge Analytica controversy and the revelations of abundant Russian election and referendum interference, revealed by painstaking investigative journalism (Cadwalladr, 2017, 2018) and detailed academic research (Albright, 2017) has moved well beyond the media industry and now encompasses a far wider range of issues that fundamentally raise the role of state sovereignty and the political sphere of regulation.

They include electoral laws and the functioning of democracy (Tambini et al, 2017); state security and the role played by hostile actors in the spread of disinformation (Geddes, 2017); also human rights issues, crime including terrorism, child abuse, hate speech, and discrimination (House of Commons, 2017); the regulation of advertising (House of Lords, 2018a), data protection and privacy issues; algorithmic transparency and artificial intelligence (Royal Society/ British Academy, 2017; House of Commons, 2018; House of Lords, 2018b); and competition policy (OECD, 2016).

The European Union has emerged as one of the major territories in which the 'functional sovereignty' (Pasquale, 2018) of the internet intermediaries is being challenged on a broad front, although individual states, including Germany, France and the UK, are also re-asserting their technological sovereignty, with laws against hate speech removal (BBC, 2018), fake news dissemination (Assemblee Nationale, 2018) and a code of practice for social media companies, potentially underpinned by legislation (DCMS, 2018). Facebook has also been under investigation by regulators in these jurisdictions (Rankin, 2018; ICO, 2018) – and in July 2018, the UK's Information Commissioner announced that she was levying the maximum fine on Facebook (Hern and Pegg, 2018).

Facebook and Google may be media companies or publishers, but they are more than media companies. They are advertising engines, data controllers, information service providers and algorithm developers and they are moving into a variety of new fields such as artificial intelligence, virtual or augmented reality, leveraging the revenues they are earning from advertising.

Their corporate power is unprecedented. They have purchased early-stage ventures, which might have turned out to threaten their position, and their dominance risks damaging innovation. In their main fields, they are arguably now natural monopolies.

The role of network effects and economies of scale driven by big data consolidates and concentrates their power as first-movers. The entry costs for new suppliers are so high as to be prohibitive. Their ability to imitate and replicate at low cost the new services offered by competitors reduces the effects of competition. It is difficult for consumers to switch or exit when in the case of Facebook, most of their friends may be on the platform, and in the case of Google, its dominance of data makes it difficult for any other search engine to approach the quality of service it provides. Cross-platform sharing of data within a group of companies such as Facebook, Instagram and WhatsApp, intensifies their dominance.

Regulation has always been a factor

It was always a myth to suggest that the internet was exempt from regulation. Its underlying technology was regulated. States have remained the primary actors in regulation (Drezner, 2004). Recent EU action has proved that American ownership of the platforms is no barrier to regulatory action (EC, 2017a and b). A debate has opened on the adequacy of existing regulatory tools, such as competition policy, where online dominance gained through network effects is hard to measure in traditional competition policy terms as consumers are paying with their attention, and their data, rather than through traditional forms of pricing (OECD, 2016; Coyle, 2016 and 2018; Graef, 2018).

Data, and the role of algorithmic sorting, is clearly on the agenda of competition authorities in the European Union (Vestager, 2018a and 2018b). EU moves to tax the revenues of intermediaries and other technology companies, given the size of the EU market, have considerable potential (Guarascio, 2018); the EU's General Data Protection Regulation is already forcing technology companies to consider it as a global standard, although Facebook has moved 1.5bn users out of its jurisdiction by switching responsibility for them from Ireland to California (Hern, 2018).

The European Commission (EC) produced guidelines for 'online platforms' to increase the proactive prevention, detection and removal of illegal content inciting hatred, violence and terrorism online (EC, 2017c). In terms of fake news, the EU's high-level group (EC, 2018) has produced a series of recommendations, which offer proposals for countering fake news and disinformation without introducing content censorship (EU, 2018). New copyright proposals currently under discussion, though contested, illustrate further moves away from the established Information Society-era consensus (Sweney, 2018).

All of these proposals, however, emanate from a variety of policy domains. It is questionable whether they add up to a coherent package of reforms. I suggest creating a new category of information utilities for specific markets such as search and social media, drawing on proposals for the 'statutory underpinning' of a new regulatory framework suggested by a former Ofcom regulator (Foster, 2012).

Information utilities would be licensed as such and they would have specific reporting regulations in respect of the regulator, which would be granted strong back-stop intervention powers. Dominant information utilities – whose dominance might be measured in terms of their significant market power, possibly according to, for example, their share of the online or mobile advertising markets – would have the most stringent reporting duties. These proposals would be compatible with the imposition of a 'duty of care' on social media companies being proposed by others (Woods and Perrin, 2018).

In the case of Facebook, its founder has regularly referred to it as 'a social utility' (Reagan, 2009) or, simply, 'a utility' (Kirkpatrick, 2010) and in his 6000-word manifesto last year, referred to it as 'social infrastructure' (Zuckerberg, 2017) on several occasions. Perhaps we should take Zuckerberg at his word and accept that Facebook is a social utility and a form of social infrastructure. Utilities, after all, are regulated (Boyd, 2010) – and so is critical infrastructure (Picard and Pickard, 2017).

In the past, Parliament has regulated to control monopoly power. For example, the 1984 Telecommunications Act, introduced when BT was privatised, recognised the danger of such a dominant player being able to exert anti-competitive power and put in place a strong regulatory framework. The situation of Facebook and Google is different, but they are dominant in their spheres and have significant market power. Their potential for exploitation by hostile state actors, as we have seen in both the US presidential election and in the UK's EU referendum, means that they should be seen as critical social infrastructure. There would need to be a lead regulator – possibly Ofcom, possibly the ICO – in respect of this new framework for information utilities, which should additionally be charged formally with convening regular meetings with other relevant regulators.

We know that regulatory interest can 'nudge' dominant players to modify behaviours, as the outgoing former Ofcom chief executive, Ed Richards, told the House of Lords in November 2014 (House of Lords, 2014). The ability to 'nudge' behaviour away from what society would regard as undesirable is inevitably more effective if transgressing companies are aware that back-stop powers are available to regulators. Today, the regulation of social media is no longer a media issue but a social issue.

References

Albright, J 2017. Who Hacked the Election? Ad Tech did. Through "Fake News," Identity Resolution and Hyper-Personalization, 31 July
https://medium.com/tow-center/who-hacked-the-election-43d4019f705f

Andrews, L. (2017a). Fake News and the threat to real news. A submission to the House of Commons Select Committee on Culture, Media and Sport.

Andrews, L. (2017b, 25 September). Why regulators like Ofcom are dropping the ball on 'Fake News', dark advertising and extremism. Retrieved from https://www.opendemocracy.net/uk/leighton-andrews/why-regulators-like-ofcom-are-dropping-ball-on-fake-news-dark-advertising-and-ex

Assemblee Nationale, Proposition de Loi relative à la lutte contre les fausses informations, 21 March, retrieved from http://www.assemblee-nationale.fr/15/propositions/pion0799.asp

Barlow, J.P., 1996. A Declaration of the Independence of Cyberspace https://www.eff.org/cyberspace-independence

Baron, E. (2017, May 31). Mary Meeker's internet trends: Google, Facebook dominate as ads move to web from TV. Retrieved from http://www.mercurynews.com/2017/05/31/mary-meekers-internet-trends-google-facebook-dominate-as-ads-move-to-web-from-tv

BBC, 2018. Germany starts enforcing hate speech law. January 1, Retrieved from http://www.bbc.co.uk/news/technology-42510868

Bell, E. 2017. How Mark Zuckerberg could really fix journalism, Columbia Journalism Review 21. Retrieved from https://www.cjr.org/tow_center/mark-zuckerberg-facebook-fix-journalism.php

Boyd, D. (2010). Social network sites as networked publics: Affordances, dynamics, and implications. In Z. Papacharissi (Ed.), Networked self: Identity, community, and culture on social network sites (pp. 39-58). New York & London: Routledge.

Cadwalladr, C. 2017. The great British Brexit robbery: how our democracy was hijacked. Observer, 7 May

Cadwalladr, C. 2018, 'We're waiting for answers': Facebook, Brexit and 40 questions, Observer, 12 May

Collins, R. (2009). Three myths of internet governance. Bristol: Intellect.

Conservative Party (2017) The Conservative Party Manifesto https://www.conservatives.com/manifesto

Coyle, D. 2016. Making the most of platforms: a policy research agenda. Toulouse School of Economics Working Paper. Retrieved from http://bruegel.org/wp-content/uploads/2016/10/platforms_dcoyle2.pdf

Coyle, D. 2018.'Platform dominance: the shortcomings of Antitrust policy' in Moore, M. and Tambini, D. (eds) Digital Dominance, Oxford: OUP.

DCMS, 2018 Government response to the Internet Safety Strategy Green Paper, 7 June, retrieved from https://www.gov.uk/government/consultations/internet-safety-strategy-green-paper

Drezner, D. 2004 'The Global Governance of the Internet: Bringing the State back in' Political Science Quarterly, 119 (3) 477-498

Enders Analysis (2016). UK digital ad forecast 2016-2018: Strong but uneven growth. Report, (November). Retrieved from http://www.endersanalysis.com/content/publication/uk-digital-ad-forecast-2016-2018-strong-uneven-growth

European Commission 2017a. Mergers: Commission fines Facebook €110 million for providing misleading information about WhatsApp takeover. Retrieved from http://europa.eu/rapid/press-release_IP-17-1369_en.htm

European Commission 2017b. Antitrust: Commission fines Google €2.42 billion for abusing dominance as search engine by giving illegal advantage to own comparison shopping service. Retrieved from http://europa.eu/rapid/press-release_IP-17-1784_en.htm

European Commission 2017c, Security Union: Commission steps up efforts to tackle illegal content online, 28 September, retrieved from
http://europa.eu/rapid/press-release_IP-17-3493_en.htm

European Commission, 2018. Final report of the High Level Expert Group on Fake News and Online Disinformation, 12 March, retrieved from
https://ec.europa.eu/digital-single-market/en/news/final-report-high-level-expert-group-fake-news-and-online-disinformation

Foster, R. (2012). News Plurality in a Digital World, Reuters Institute for the Study of Journalism. July.

Gandy, O.H. 1989. The Surveillance Society: Information Technology and Bureaucratic Social Control Journal of Communication, 39 (30) 61-76

Ganter, S.A. & Neilsen, R.K. (2017). Dealing with digital intermediaries: A case study of the relations between publishers and platforms. New Media and Society. Advance online publication. Retrieved from http://journals.sagepub.com/eprint/dxNzFHygAIRHviKP9MFg/full

Geddes, D., 2017 Web giants too slow to combat fake news, says former GCHQ chief Robert Hannigan, 21 October, retrieved from https://www.thetimes.co.uk/article/web-giants-too-slow-to-combat-fake-news-says-former-gchq-chief-robert-hannigan-hzj38nn8b

Graef, I. 'When data evolves into market power – data concentration and data abuse under competition law' in Moore, M. and Tambini, D. (eds) Digital Dominance, Oxford:OUP.

Guarascio F, 2018. 'EU tells tech firms it wants to tax profit, not revenue' 7 March, retrieved from https://www.reuters.com/article/us-eu-tax-digital/eu-tells-tech-firms-it-wants-to-tax-profit-not-revenue-idUSKCN1GJ2QX

Guardian, 2017. The Guardian view on digital giants: they farm us for the data. Retrieved from https://www.theguardian.com/commentisfree/2017/jun/18/the-guardian-view-on-digital-giants-they-farm-us-for-the-data

Helberger N Kleinen-von Königslöw K and van der Noll R (2015) Regulating the new information intermediaries as gatekeepers of information diversity Info 17 (6): 50-71.

Hern, A. 2018. Facebook moves 1.5bn users out of reach of new European privacy law, Guardian 19 April retrieved from https://www.theguardian.com/technology/2018/apr/19/facebook-moves-15bn-users-out-of-reach-of-new-european-privacy-law

Hern, A. and Pegg, D. 2018 Facebook fined for data breaches in Cambridge Analytica scandal. 11 July https://www.theguardian.com/technology/2018/jul/11/facebook-fined-for-data-breaches-in-cambridge-analytica-scandal

House of Commons, 2017. Home Affairs Select Committee: Hate crime: abuse, hate and extremism online, 14th Report of Session 2016-17, 25 April HC 609

House of Commons, 2018 Select Committee on Science and Technology, 'Algorithms in decision-making inquiry', Oral Evidence 23 January. http://data.parliament.uk/writtenevidence/committeeevidence.svc/evidencedocument/science-and-technology-committee/algorithms-in-decisionmaking/oral/77536.html

House of Lords, 2014. 'Exit' interview with Ed Richards, 18 November, retrieved from https://www.parliament.uk/business/committees/committees-a-z/lords-select/communications-committee/publications/?type=&session=26&sort=false&inquiry=all

House of Lords, 2018a House of Lords Select Committee on Communications, UK advertising in a digital age, 11 April retrieved from https://www.parliament.uk/business/committees/committees-a-z/lords-select/communications-committee/inquiries/parliament-2017/advertising-industry/

House of Lords, 2018b. 'AI in the UK: ready, willing and able?', House of Lords Select Committee on Artificial Intelligence. HL Paper 100, 16 April retrieved from https://publications.parliament.uk/pa/ld201719/ldselect/ldai/100/10002.htm

Information Commissioner's Office, 2018. Blog: A win for the data protection of UK consumers, retrieved from https://ico.org.uk/about-the-ico/news-and-events/blog-a-win-for-the-data-protection-of-uk-consumers/

Kantrowitz, A. (2018). Mark Zuckerberg: 'I'm not sure we shouldn't be regulated', Buzzfeed, 22 March https://www.buzzfeed.com/alexkantrowitz/mark-zuckerberg-im-not-sure-we-shouldnt-be-regulated?utm_term=.ngMRV3aKo#.lwAo9lAkx

Kirkpatrick, D, 2010. The Facebook Effect. London: Random House.

Kohl, U. 2016. Intermediaries within Online Regulation, in Rowland, D. Kohl, U. Charlesworth, A. (eds) Information Technology Law (5th Edition), London: Taylor and Francis

Lunt, P. and Livingstone, S. 2012. Media Regulation. London: Sage.

Mostrous, A. & Dean, J. (2017, March 23). Top brands pull Google adverts in protest at hate video links. The Times.

Neff, J. (2017, January 29). P&G tells digital to clean up, lays down new rules for agencies and ad tech to get paid. Advertising Age. Retrieved from http://adage.com/article/media/p-g-s-pritchard-calls-digital-grow-up-new-rules/307742/

OECD (2016); Big Data – bringing competition policy to the digital era, Background note by the Secretariat, 29-30 November.

Pasquale, F. 2018. Digital Capitalism – how to tame the platform juggernauts, Friedrich-Ebert Stiftung, Bonn, ISBN 978-3-96250-091-7

Picard, R.G., & Pickard, V. (2017). Essential principles for communications and media policymaking. Reuters Institute for the Study of Journalism. Retrieved from https://reutersinstitute.politics.ox.ac.uk/our-research/essential-principles-contemporary-media-and-communications-policymaking

Ponsford, D. (2017, April 10). Press Gazette launches 'Duopoly' campaign to stop Google and Facebook destroying journalism. Press Gazette. Retrieved from http://www.pressgazette.co.uk/press-gazette-launches-duopoly-campaign-to-stop-google-and-facebook-destroying-journalism/

Rankin, J. 2018. EU tech czar Margrethe Vestager: 'Social media could deactivate democracy' retrieved from https://www.theguardian.com/world/2018/jun/08/margrethe-vestager-eu-tech-regulator-i-fear-social-media-will-deactivate-democracy

Reagan, G. (2009, July 13). The evolution of Facebook's mission statement. Observer.com. retrieved from http://observer.com/2009/07/the-evolution-of-facebooks-mission-statement/

Royal Society and British Academy, 2017. Data management and use: governance in the 21st century. A joint report by the British Academy and the Royal Society. Retrieved from https://royalsociety.org/~/media/policy/projects/data-governance/data-management-governance.pdf

Srnicek, N. (2017). Platform capitalism. Cambridge: Polity Press.

Solon, O. (2017). Google's bad week: YouTube loses millions as advertising row reaches US. Observer. Retrieved from https://www.reddit.com/r/technology/comments/61hhxt/googles_bad_week_youtube_loses_millions_as/

Stangel, L. (2017). Newspapers will lobby for antitrust exemption to band against Facebook and Google. Retrieved from https://www.bizjournals.com/sanjose/news/2017/07/10/newspapers-lobby-antitrust-facebook-fb-google-goog.html

Sweney, M. 2018 YouTube faces paying billions to music stars after copyright vote, 20 June, retrieved from https://www.theguardian.com/technology/2018/jun/20/music-industry-wins-key-vote-in-youtube-copyright-battle?utm_source=dlvr.it&utm_medium=twitter

Tambini D, Labo S, Goodman E, Moore M (2017) The new political campaigning, LSE Media Policy Project, Media Policy Brief 19. http://eprints.lse.ac.uk/71945/7/LSE%20MPP%20Policy%20Brief%2019%20-%20The%20new%20political%20campaigning_final.pdf

Vestager M 2018a Competition and a fair deal for consumers online, 26 April, retrieved from http://ec.europa.eu/competition/speeches/index_2018.html

Vestager M. 2018b When technology serves people 1 June, retrieved from http://ec.europa.eu/competition/speeches/index_2018.html

Vizard, S. 2017. Vodafone blocks ads from appearing on sites that promote hate speech or fake news. Marketing Week.

White, S. 2018. It's time to regulate social media sites that publish news. July 13.https://www.thetimes.co.uk/article/it-s-time-to-regulate-social-media-sites-that-publish-news-pxsg9t3fv

Woods, L and Perrin, W., 2018. Written evidence (IRN0047), House of Lords Communications Select Committee, retrieved from https://www.parliament.uk/business/committees/committees-a-z/lords-select/communications-committee/inquiries/parliament-2017/the-internet-to-regulate-or-not-to-regulate/publications/

Zuboff, S. (2016). Big other: Surveillance capitalism and the prospects of an information civilization. Journal of Information Technology, 30, 75-89.

Zuckerberg, M. (2017, February 16). Building global community. Retrieved from https://www.facebook.com/notes/mark-zuckerberg/building-global-community/10154544292806634

Note on the contributor

Leighton Andrews is Professor of Practice in Public Service Leadership and Innovation at Cardiff Business School. He was Minister for Education and Skills (2009-13) and Minister for Public Services (2014-16) in the Welsh Government and elected Assembly Member for the Rhondda from 2003-16 in the National Assembly for Wales. He was BBC Head of Public Affairs in the mid 1990s, responsible for UK and EU public affairs.

Why Tech Markets Are Winner-Take-All[1]

Once a company dominates a technology market, it is almost impossible to displace, says Professor Patrick Barwise

'Competition is for losers. If you want to create and capture lasting value, look to build a monopoly'- Peter Thiel, cofounder of PayPal and Palantir

In the 1960s, IBM dominated the mainframe computer market. It still does. In the 1980s, Microsoft and Intel dominated the PC software and processor markets. They still do. From the 1990s, with the World Wide Web, the winners were Google in search, Amazon in e-commerce and Facebook in social networking. They still dominate those markets. Since 2007, Apple and Google (Android) have dominated the market for mobile internet operating systems.

Dominant tech companies can be 'eclipsed but not displaced'

The pattern is clear. New tech markets are volatile and highly competitive, but once a company achieves clear market leadership – usually as a fast follower with better execution than the pioneer – it soon attains complete dominance and is then almost impossible to displace. Instead, the threat is that, at some point, a newer, bigger, adjacent market emerges, dominated by another player, as mainframes and PCs have been overshadowed by online, mobile and cloud-based technologies. In the words of industry analyst Ben Thompson (2014), dominant tech companies can be 'eclipsed but not displaced'.

In this chapter, I discuss nine mutually reinforcing factors driving this phenomenon – nine reasons why tech markets are 'winner-take-all' and market leaders such as GAFA (Google, Apple, Facebook and Amazon) and Microsoft, once established, are so hard to displace. The first four factors reflect economics and technology.

Four economics and technology factors

1. Traditional economies of scale, scope and learning
   Much of the tech giants' dominance comes down to traditional economic factors. Digital products and services have high fixed costs and low-to-zero marginal costs, leading to marked economies of scale, reinforced by significant

economies of scope and learning. For instance, AI and cloud-based resources can support a wide range of diverse activities and get better and more efficient the more they are used.

2. Direct (within-market) network effects

The value of a communications network increases disproportionately as it expands, bringing in more other people for each user to connect with (Rohlf 1974). This is a 'direct network externality' ('externality' because it involves third parties in addition to the individual customer and firm). Obviously, it is especially important for social media such as Facebook.

3. Indirect (cross-market) network effects – or 'platform economics'

Most tech companies are, at least to a degree, 'platform' businesses: they create value by matching customers with complementary needs, such as software developers and users (Microsoft's MS-DOS and Apple's App Store), suppliers and customers (Amazon), drivers and potential passengers (Uber) or advertisers and consumers (Google and Facebook). These 'two-sided market' network effects are 'indirect' because – unlike with direct, within-market, externalities – the value to participants in each market (e.g. diners) depends on the number of participants in the *other* market (e.g. restaurants) and *vice versa* (Rochet and Tirole 2003). Once a platform dominates both markets, indirect network effects become self-sustaining as users on each side help generate users on the other.

New platform businesses face the chicken-and-egg challenge of achieving critical mass in both or all[2] the key markets simultaneously. This is why the failure rate is high, and tech start-ups such as Twitter, LinkedIn, Uber, Pinterest and Snapchat may sustain many loss-making years – and may never achieve profitability as standalone businesses.

4. Big data and machine learning

Digital businesses gather data relentlessly, cheaply and efficiently. To exploit it, they use analytics, increasingly automated ('machine learning'), mainly to drive continuous improvement in products and services, pricing, personalisation and advertising targeting. They often add free or subsidised services to generate more data, producing a recursive relationship between adoption and usage, product and service quality, and further adoption and usage. Amazon, for example, constantly evaluates and refines its services and communications, doubling up on what works and reinforcing its dominance. The combination of big data and machine learning amplifies network effects and returns to scale, again strengthening tech market leaders' dominance and deterring others from entering.

Five behavioural factors

These four widely recognised economic and technology factors are reinforced by five less widely recognised behavioural factors. Two of these are on the demand side:

1. Strong user brands and habitual usage

   In November 2017, WPP ranked Google, Apple, Amazon, Microsoft and Facebook – in that order – as the five most valuable brands in the world, worth a total of just over a trillion dollars, nearly 30 per cent of the companies $3.6 trillion combined market capitalisation (Kantar Millward Brown 2017). Digital products are 'experience goods': users need to try them and learn about them (from their own or trusted others' usage experience) to judge their quality. Well-known, trusted brands are essential in online markets to encourage trial and discourage switching to a competitor. Usage becomes habitual or even addictive, reinforcing the incumbents' dominance.

2. Switching costs and lock-in

   Tech companies also deploy a range of strategies to lock users in by making it difficult or costly to switch to a rival (Klemperer 1987). Incompatibility between providers ('walled gardens' – for example, where iOS apps do not work on Android), non-portable data, time invested in learning a particular system, service customisation, and accruing content such as playlists that cannot be migrated, all discourage switching (Katz and Shapiro 1985, Ratchford 2001, Huang 2018).

   Finally, at least as important as these demand-side factors are three supply-side behavioural factors:

3. Attractiveness to talent

   The brand valuations mentioned above relate to *consumer* brand equity – the brand associations in consumers' long-term memory that make them more likely to buy or use the brand in the future. Tech giants also have significant *employee* brand equity, the equivalent in the talent market. This enables them to attract the best technical, managerial and commercial staff, further reinforcing their product-market dominance.

4. Powerful founders and hard-driving corporate culture

   All the tech giants have, or had, strong, capable, hard-driving, hands-on founders such as Jeff Bezos, Steve Jobs and Mark Zuckerberg. The resulting corporate culture is epitomised by Intel cofounder Andy Grove's (1998) 'Only the paranoid survive' and Facebook's former motto, 'Move fast and break things'. At Amazon, Bezos famously insists that every day is still treated as 'Day One for the internet'. This obsessive, relentlessly active, innovative corporate culture is a significant strength, further reinforcing the tech giants' continuing market dominance. Arguably, it also drives their hyper-aggressive tax and acquisition policies, further adding to their competitive advantage.

5. Geography - or 'cluster economics'
Despite earlier expectations (Cairncross 1997) and the claims of Brexit enthusiasts, geography still matters. Innovative, creative clusters like Silicon Valley, Hollywood and the City of London combine talent, social capital (informal networks and a shared culture) and a range of support services (Bell 2005). Google (Alphabet), Apple and Facebook are all located in Silicon Valley – the archetypal innovation cluster – as are Oracle, Intel and Cisco. Amazon and Microsoft are based in Seattle, a two-hour plane ride to the north. These eight companies account for more than half of the 14 tech companies in the global top 100 public companies by market capitalisation. Apart from China (whose big tech companies are still largely focused on their highly protected home market), no other *country* has more than one. Silicon Valley is also home to many recent tech start-ups. If one of these starts to be a significant threat – or opportunity – the incumbent will surely know about it soon enough to acquire it or attack its business model with new service features. The incumbent's early-warning system will be especially acute if it provides the start-up with cloud-based or other services.

Winners take all – and keep it

Will 'creative destruction' – capitalism's ability to innovate, destroy and reinvent itself (Schumpeter 2010) – eventually take care of the tech giants' market dominance? This seems unlikely because in most cases the combination of winner-take-all factors is so powerful. For example, a challenger to Google in search would have to offer an incentive or a noticeably better experience to attract users, over a period long enough to break their Googling habit. This would take years and cost many billions, with no guarantee of success at the end of it. In 2013, Microsoft's estimated cumulative losses in search were $11 billion (Reed 2013).

It is therefore hard to see the titans losing control of their core markets anytime soon. The partial exception is Apple. Still the most profitable company in the world, Apple now faces challenges as it is increasingly forced to include Google services in its ecosystem and its price premium over high-end Android devices is eroded. The other tech giants also face some competition at the margin of their core markets. For Google, the main direct threat is Amazon's growing search business, as consumers looking for a product increasingly go direct to Amazon, possibly using its Echo smart speaker (and microphone!) and Alexa voice assistant. Similarly, in social media, users can 'multi-home' – engage with more than one platform – enabling competitors to co-exist with Facebook. Nevertheless, following the pattern described earlier, there seems little chance of Google, Amazon, Facebook or Microsoft being pushed out of their global core market dominance in the foreseeable future.

Eclipse by a rival with a dominant share of a new and potentially bigger market is always a possibility, however. To head off this threat, the big tech firms invest heavily in emerging products and technologies, whether through their own R&D, by acquiring promising start-ups, or by replicating those they cannot buy. Self-driving technology is a good example, with companies such as Tesla, Google and Apple jostling to capture the leading position in a high-stakes new market.

Is there a problem?

Google users pay nothing for an excellent search service, while search advertisers have a highly effective tool that did not exist 20 years ago, for which they pay a competitive, auction-based market price. This situation creates a new challenge for regulators: extreme market concentration which nonetheless offers customers great value for money.

Responses to date differ between Europe and the US. European antitrust legislation focuses on ensuring fair competition, reflected in the Commission's June 2017 2.42bn euro fine on Google for 'systematically' prioritising its own shopping service over rivals in searches. US legislation focuses more narrowly on whether market dominance leads to demonstrable consumer harm. Because the dominant tech platforms are all US-based, this is likely to be an area of growing transatlantic conflict in the future.

The tech giants' market dominance is unlikely to be resolved by market forces ('creative destruction') alone, because the multiple factors driving it, discussed in this chapter, are so powerful. We need a new regulatory approach to encourage competition and counter the abuse of market power in these winner-take-all markets. Developing such an approach will require economic regulators to tackle a number of somewhat unfamiliar sources of market power – such as big data, habitual usage, switching costs, lock-in, and tax avoidance - without discouraging innovation or significantly reducing the manifold benefits of digital technology. The financial stakes are high and the intellectual and (geo-) political challenges will be severe. Beyond the realm of economic regulation, there are also many broader social and political challenges associated with Big Tech, such as data privacy and security, fake news, cyberbullying, and election tampering (Moore and Tambini 2018). These fall outside the scope of this chapter.

Notes

[1] This chapter is based on Patrick Barwise and Leo Watkins, 'The Evolution of Digital Dominance: How and Why We Got to GAFA' in Moore and Tambini, 2018: 21-49 https://lbsresearch.london.edu/914/ .

[2] Some platforms operate in 'multisided' markets because they facilitate interaction between several types of user. For instance, Facebook connects six: friends as message senders, friends as message receivers, advertisers, app developers, and businesses as both message senders and receivers (Evans and Schmalensee 2016: 110).

References

Bell, Geoffrey G. (2005) Clusters, networks and firm innovativeness, Strategic Management Journal Vol. 26, No. 3 (March) pp 287-95

Cairncross, Frances (1997) The Death of Distance: How the Communications Revolution Will Change Our Lives and Our Work, Boston MA: Harvard Business School Press

Evans, David S. and Richard Schmalensee (2016) Matchmakers: The New Economics of Multisided Markets, Boston, MA: Harvard Business Review Press

Grove, Andy (1998) Only the Paranoid Survive, London: Profile Books

Huang, Yufeng (2018) Learning by doing and the demand for advanced products, Marketing Science, in press

Kantar Millwood Brown (2017) Brandz Top 100 Most Valuable Global Brands 2017, London: WPP

Katz, Michael L. and Carl Shapiro (1985) Network externalities, competition and compatibility, American Economic Review Vol. 75, No. 3 (June) pp 424-40

Klemperer, Paul (1987) Markets with consumer switching costs, Quarterly Journal of Economics Vol. 102, No. 2 (May) pp 375-94

Moore, Martin and Damian Tambini, eds. (2018) Digital Dominance: The Power of Google, Amazon, Facebook, and Amazon, New York: Oxford University Press

Ratchford, Brian T (2001) The economics of consumer knowledge, Journal of Consumer Research Vol. 27, No. 4 pp 397-411

Reed, Brad (2013) Microsoft has lost $11 billion trying to compete with Google, BGR.com, 9 July

Rochet, Jean-Charles and Jean Tirole (2003) Platform competition in two-sided markets, Journal of the European Economic Association Vol. 1, No. 4 pp 990-1029

Rohlf, Jeffrey (1974) A theory of interdependent demand for a communications service, Bell Journal of Economics and Management Science Vol. 5, No. 1 (Spring) pp 16-37

Schumpeter, Joseph A. (2010) [1942] Capitalism, Socialism and Democracy, London: Routledge Classics

Thompson, Ben (2014) Peak Google, www.stratechery.com, October 22.

Note on the contributor

Patrick Barwise www.patrickbarwise.com is Emeritus Professor of Management and Marketing at London Business School. He joined the School in 1976 after an early career at IBM and has published widely on management, marketing and media. His latest book, The 12 Powers of a Marketing Leader, co-authored with former McKinsey partner Thomas Barta, was published in October 2016. He is also former chairman of Which?, an experienced expert witness in international commercial, tax and competition cases, and has been involved as an advisor and early investor in three online market research start-ups.

A reluctant Damascene conversion on the road to regulation

An unlikely pairing of Donald Trump and Mark Zuckerberg combined to change the mind of a vocal opponent of state social media regulation. Paul Connew charts his uneasy journey from a free-for-all advocate to a cautious supporter of a measure of governmental control

Things move fast in the world of social media. Just ask Mark Zuckerberg, the founder of Facebook (original corporate slogan: 'Move Fast and Break Things').

It was only back in the summer of April 2017 that Zuckerberg seemed to be switching his image from the supreme 'nerd's nerd' to a master plan to run for the presidency of the United States in 2020.

There was the whistlestop tour of the US, with Zuckerberg's personal Facebook profile expounding the updated Zuckerberg/Facebook mantra, 'Bring The World Closer Together', with The Great Nerd himself being pictured meeting politicians, military top brass, multi-ethnic church and community leaders, sporting icons, showbiz royalty, et al.

The message appeared clear: If a septuagenarian uber-conservative Manhattan property tycoon, worth merely a few billion dollars, like Donald Trump, could become President of the United States (Potus) then what was to stop a 'liberal' *real* modern Master of the Digital Universe, aged just 34 and worth a cool $75bn-plus, aspiring to replace him?

After all, Trump had transferred his TV 'Apprentice' celebrity to electoral triumph, so surely Zuckerberg could trade his techie 'hero' status from the Oscar-nominated, $240m-grossing, 2010-movie 'The Social Network' (in which Jesse Eisenberg portrayed the Facebook creator) to matching effect?

The great data harvesting scandal

But that was before Facebook became embroiled in the Cambridge Analytica data harvesting scandal and the revelation that the world's most powerful social media company had, wittingly or otherwise, allowed itself to become the weapon by which Russia sought to swing the 2016 election in favour of Trump and against Hillary Clinton. And the mind-boggling scale of how Facebook ruthlessly uses its data-harvesting capabilities for commercial exploitation of its users came under unprecedented public scrutiny.

If Twitter was Trump's personal platform for attack, denigrating Clinton, obsessively accusing the American MSM of spreading fake news, Brad Parscale, the social media guru who ran the digital side of the Trump campaign, told me: "Donald Trump won…but Facebook was the method". Parscale, who denies any collusion with Russia, is now heading up Trump's re-election campaign and has recruited some former Cambridge Analytica operatives to the team.

Zuckerberg faces the heat

Whatever the final outcome of the various investigations taking place on both sides of the Atlantic into sinister Russian interference in the US presidential election, Brexit and other elections across Europe, the Trump/Facebook connection has spectacularly deleted Mark Zuckerberg's credibility as a White House candidate and might yet demolish Donald Trump's second term ambitions. It even led to calls from a number of investors for Zuckerberg to step down and investor pressure did result in him diluting, to some degree, his overarching personal control, proving that even a high-tech Colossus isn't immune to the diktats of the traditional corporate world.

Instead 2018 witnessed the spectacle of the social media wunderkind making a very different journey to Washington from Silicon Valley, to appear before both houses of Congress as they probed the mass data harvesting scandal and its implications. It saw Zuckerberg recast from the Teflon-coated Titan of social media's brave new world to just another embattled CEO forced to eat humble pie, serving up faltering apologies and unconvincing mitigation, and vows to crackdown on illicit political ads, in equal measure. YES, Zuckerberg acknowledged a 'betrayal of trust' to Facebook's users en masse, but, NO, he failed to win the trust that his creation genuinely has the will, or the wherewithal, to effectively self-regulate.

A similarly uncomfortable encounter followed in May 2018 before EU lawmakers in Brussels, although — at the time of writing — Zuckerberg is resisting repeated requests to appear before British parliamentarians.

How much that is down to the leading role played by my friend the Observer journalist Carole Cadwalladr (a worthy winner of the 2018 Orwell Prize for Journalism) in exposing how the Trump-connected operation had improperly obtained the Facebook data of up to 87m people (including several million in the UK ahead of the EU referendum) remains an intriguing question.

But if Zuckerberg needed a further reminder that he certainly wasn't omnipotent it came with the immediate 20 per cent stock price plunge that followed Facebook's 2018 second quarter report in July when growth figures didn't match Wall Street's expectations and the company conceded it 'would continue to decelerate' throughout the year. Although monthly active user figures were up by 11 per cent year over year, and the company still made $13.2bn, the first quarter decline in the US and Europe was a serious blow and privately senior executives acknowledged that the Cambridge Analytica data harvesting scandal was a highly significant factor.

In terms of perspective, however, it is worth noting that Facebook's $120bn July 2018 stock market slump alone was greater than the entire value of a global giant like Nike and several sizeable nations' entire economies, while Zuckerberg's creation was still, at the time of writing, worth more than Coca-Cola, PepsiCo and McDonald's combined.

From hero to zero?

While Mark Zuckerberg may have gone from hero to zero in some quarters, with all thoughts of a potential Potus role shelved for the foreseeable future, the zeros on the end of his personal fortune won't be too badly hurt; even though Facebook lost more than $100bn in market capitalisation in the immediate fallout from the data harvesting maelstrom. That said, the company remains worth well over $400bn, with more than two billion global users (outnumbering the reach of the Roman Catholic church and totting up to almost a third of the Earth's total population) and is one of the five largest companies in the world, just 14 years after Zuckerberg launched it from his Harvard student dorm. The nerd's nerd indeed!

As it happens, I've met and interviewed Donald Trump several times in the past and spoken to Mark Zuckerberg just once. Very different characters, true enough, but together they've managed to send me on the road to a personal digital Damascene conversion of sorts. For his part Zuckerberg gave me his long-past-its-sell-by-date mantra that he isn't the world's most powerful editor/publisher, just a platform provider. (A pitch made more ludicrous still with Facebook's June 2018 UK launch of a print, *repeat* print, magazine, Grow, aimed at high-end business leaders, which the company insisted wasn't really a magazine at all but 'a business marketing programme'.) A semantic contortion of Trumpian proportions.

Positives v negatives

For years I've argued that social media's positives significantly outweighed its negatives. Even as I defended the vital importance of legacy media, especially newspapers, as the bulwark of democracy and lamented how they were being ravaged and all too often wiped out by the advertising-gorging tech behemoths. Somehow, though, it seemed that any form of state regulation of social media represented censorship and as much a threat to freedom of expression as the post-Leveson, Royal Charter political frenzy had to the press.

But thanks to the fake news Twitter-ranting president of the United States and the CEO/founder of Facebook, and the data harvesting/Russian meddling stench, among others, I've (nervously) changed my mind.

My cautious conversion was reinforced again by the initial House of Commons' Digital, Culture, Media and Sport (DCMS) Committee report on fake news and disinformation published in July 2018 and triggered by the Cambridge Analytics data scandal. Although occasionally overly-apocalyptic, its broad conclusion that the UK faced a democratic crisis sparked by the manipulation of personal data and the spread of fake news and pernicious views was hard to argue with, along with its call for tighter regulation of social media giants and that they should be classified somewhere between platform and publisher.

Likewise, the DCMS report made sense in arguing that Facebook, Google and co should have 'clear legal liability to act against harmful and illegal content on their platforms', although establishing that in law could well prove a protracted trip across a legal minefield. But the report's call for the social media giants to face a hefty fine based on a percentage of their annual turnover, rather than the current £20k maximum fine for involvement in electoral fraud, represented a realistic step in defence of democracy.

My regulatory conversion was reinforced further by the Associated Press's valuable investigation in the summer of 2018, which exposed Google's deceit in still recording users' movements even when they had explicitly withdrawn consent by disabling their location history setting. It was another signal that the big tech giants saw themselves as the new 'Masters of the Universe' impervious to moral, ethical or even legal restraints.

It is worth noting that Google's Code of Conduct has now dropped any mention of its original company slogan 'Don't Be Evil'. And the infamously arrogant and presumptious quote of its former CEO, Eric Schmidt – "If you have something you don't want anyone to know, maybe you shouldn't be doing it in the first place" – still encapsulates the social media world behemoths conviction that privacy is ancient history in Silicon Valley's pursuit of global dominance and still greater profit, without effective, balancing international regulation.

For me, the issue isn't the use of social media for political advertising per se. It's a legitimate, modern day platform with the essential proviso that it's not based on subliminal and illicitly-obtained data targeting, and that the source and affiliation of the advertiser is totally transparent.

At the end of July 2018, Facebook did take the initiative in blocking and publicly flagging up fresh attempts to interfere in America's November 2018 mid-term elections. That was welcome, even if it had the primary whiff of a PR move to counter the company's record share slump amid the date harvesting backlash.

Shortly afterwards Mark Thompson, the former BBC Director General, by now New York Times' CEO, floated the idea that Facebook should consider removing news from users' feeds unless they could develop an effective system for removing 'low grade news' and fake news. It was hard to disagree with Thompson's view that it was terrifying that Facebook was relying on algorithms – 'a machine behind closed doors' – to rank the world's news sources and that 'publications would only be ranked at the top for as long as they remain in Facebook's good books.'

Fake news at warp speed

While I'm cognisant of those voices, such as Paul Levinson, the distinguished Professor of Communications and Media Studies at America's Fordham University, who argues passionately that 'Government regulation of social media would be a cure far worse than the disease' and threaten the First Amendment. Rightly, he flags up that fake news didn't start with the internet and that, centuries ago, for example, anti-Semitic publications spread lies about Jews murdering Christian children and drinking their blood. The difference now is that social media enables such vile, vicious and incendiary black propaganda to spread like cyber wildfire among millions within nano seconds.

For me, it was significant when on April 11, 2018 Sir Tim Berners-Lee, British inventor of the world wide web marked its 29tth anniversary by calling for its regulation to combat its 'weaponisation' and declared the big tech giants couldn't be trusted to do the job themselves against the bad actors exploiting it. It was also recognition that smart phones and mobile apps had revolutionised the internet revolution.

In the UK, hopefully, a balanced alliance of political commonsense, public opinion and mainstream media vigilance would counter zealot voices seeking dangerously draconian restraints on social media.

In another revealing UK study, conducted by the youth charity Plan International UK, which helped forge my cautious Damascene conversion, 50 per cent of girls and 40 per cent of boys who were surveyed reported being victims of online bullying. Add to the mix, the ample evidence compiled around hate speech, revenge porn, child sexual abuse imagery, grooming, rape and murder threats and terrorist propaganda and the dark side of the social media revolution can't simply be tolerated as an inescapable downside price to pay in return for its undoubted upsides.

Will GDPR make the difference?

But Facebook, Google and the rest of the social media marketeers have, of course, been confronted by a major challenge to their business models since May 2018 with the EU's introduction of GDPR (General Data Protection Regulation) legislation. The stringent privacy rules strike at the heart of Facebook and others' ability to sell advertising based on targeted user data information. Initial estimates suggested that around 73 per cent of Facebook's user ad-targeting could be illegal under the new legislation, which outlaws processing data based on race, ethnicity, political opinions, religious belief, trade union membership or sexual orientation without users' active consent.

American lawmakers are set to agonise much longer, with an uncertain outcome, over similar regulation, while its Twitter-devotee Potus has already hinted it wouldn't get his support. Polls also show that, despite users' concern over data harvesting and Russian election meddling, the majority of Americans oppose state regulation of social media. American reluctance was underscored by President Trump's vitriolic July 2018 attack on the EU over its imposition of a record $5bn fine on Google for breaching European anti-trust laws.

Linking it to his portrayal of the EU as a 'greater foe' to US trade interests than Russia, Trump called the fine an 'attack on one of America's greatest companies'. It's somewhat unfortunate, too, that in the US the Capitol Hill debate about regulation has developed (partly due to Presidential pressure) into a partisan argument over whether it favours liberal over conservative voices rather than the far wider issues of social media giants' societal power and influence.

Long term, across Europe, GDPR could change the face of Facebook and reshape the social media landscape....although the court of public opinion appeared confused, or even ambivalent, as the regulation took shape. By the same token, optimism among European lawmakers that it could signal a radical reduction in the influence and prominence of fake news online is, alas, likely to be a long-term test and a tough, continuing battle to promote the virtues of legitimate media news sources rather than a rapid victory.

In his excellent book What's The Future And Why It's Up To Us, Tim O'Reilly, the leading thinker on information technology renowned as 'The Oracle of Silicon Valley' points out that such is the warp speed of today's social media traffic that human fact checkers cannot be the solution to the fake news crisis.

If nothing else, however, it might force Mark Zuckerberg to revert to the 6,000-word treatise he wrote while flirting with a presidential run and setting out his vision for Facebook's future. "The important thing is to develop the social infrastructure—to give people the power to build a community that works for all of us."

YES, and not just for the multi-billionaire, data-harvesting, power-broking Titans of Silicon Valley, Mr Zuckerberg.

References

Pew Research Center-Social Media Use 2018.

The New York University Center for Business and Human Rights: 'The Role of Internet Platform Companies in Fighting Terrorist Incitement and Politically Motivated Disinformation', 2018.

The Four: The Hidden DNA of Amazon, Apple Facebook and Google by Scott Galloway, Bantam Press 2017.

What's The Future and Why It's Up To Us by Tim O'Reilly, Penguin 2017.

Reuters Institute Digital News Report 2018.

Why Facebook Faces a Foggy Future, Scott Denning, Forbes Magazine, March 2018.

Tow Center for Digital Journalism: 'Platforms and Publishers' 2018.

'Government regulation of social media would be a cure for worse than the disease',

Professor Paul Levinson, Fordham University, New York, Salon, February 2018.

Mark Zuckerberg: Evidence to US Congressional inquiry, 2018.

Note on the contributor

Paul Connew is a media commentator and consultant, broadcaster, author and PR advisor. He is currently a columnist for The New European and The Drum and regularly commentates on media issues for the BBC, Sky, CNN, al-Jazeera and Talk Radio. He is a former editor of the Sunday Mirror, deputy editor of the Daily Mirror and the News of The World and a former US bureau chief for the Mirror Group. He is also a long-standing judge of the British Press Awards and the Royal Television Society Awards.

On the side of the angels – how to keep digital a blessing, and not a curse

The UK has had 25 years to prepare for the power of digitally-driven media, says Christopher Graham, but the country has been lagging behind

Sometimes, the perspective of a non-combatant – an old soldier, even – can add something to the debate. I am one such, having been retired for more than two years now from my seven-year stint as Information Commissioner. Long before my appointment as Commissioner, I had been deeply involved in media, running the Advertising Standards Authority and, before that, at the BBC, first as a journalist and a producer in both radio and TV, and then, in management, as a deputy editor and managing editor, and finally as BBC Secretary.

So I have at least a 25-year perspective on digital and its impact on media, news, and Westminster – and, these days, I don't have to toe anybody's line. So, for what it's worth, here is my take on part of how we got to where we are in the use and abuse of personal information in the digital space.

Trust and confidence, surely, are the essentials for both honest journalism and effective marketing – and for sensible politics too. I first learned this from my father, who, for more than 30 years, worked for the BBC's External Services at Bush House. Dad told me tales of his wartime service, broadcasting to occupied France and to Germany. And my school days were accompanied by discussions about the Cold War, Sino-Soviet tensions, and Euro-Communism. Dad stressed the impact (and, thence, the importance) of telling it straight, especially when the news was unwelcome, in order for good news to be believed.

Years later, as a news trainee, I did my best to follow in that tradition, working with such giants as William Hardcastle and Brian Redhead. Eventually, I found myself at the corporate centre in the Secretary's Office, running between the Director General, John Birt, and the Chairman, Marmaduke Hussey. Among my responsibilities were taking the minutes at meetings of the Board of Governors and the Board of Management (BOG and BOM), and liaising with Whitehall and Westminster.

And then came digital

I remember I was taking the minutes at the first meeting of Board of Management after the summer break, in September 1995. Ignoring my carefully prepared agenda, the DG started talking about what he'd seen on a recent visit to the West Coast. Oh John, not 'what I did in the summer hols' please, I thought.

John Birt said something on the lines of 'this is going to be the third broadcasting medium'. So likely, I thought. 'I want you', John said, looking around the assembled directors of this and that round the Board Room table, 'to play with digital, and understand its potential and its impact'. Play! I thought. John, we've got a really packed agenda with, top of the list, that lease we have to agree for that building in Langham Street. No time for play.

Marmaduke Hussey was not convinced either. And yet he was wonderfully impressed when later I was able to advise him on some computer glitch or other which he had encountered while working on his memoirs. 'Try, Control-Alt-Delete, Dukey,' I offered. It was about the only thing I knew about computers, but it worked.

Of course, John Birt and, later, the next Chairman, Christopher Bland, were able to manoeuvre the BBC into pole position for digital media. And all that Birtism of the 1990s has been vindicated.

By the time I arrived at the Advertising Standards Authority in 2000, as a Director General myself, I was a good deal more digitally aware. But I found an industry, the value of whose products depended absolutely on trust and confidence, even more conservative and resistant to change than had been the old BBC. I spent four years getting the industry – advertisers, agencies, and media – to see the advantage of extending effective self-regulation from print media to TV and radio. And even when we had achieved that, the advertisers didn't want to know about digital. Instead, we wasted yet more time trying to achieve consistency of interpretation and application of the non-broadcast and broadcast codes.

When the industry finally got round to the regulation of digital advertising, it was for advertising in paid-for space only. Not websites, and not email advertising. Getting even to the foothills of the digital mountain took far too long. On a good day, the ad industry wanted to fight current battles rather than think about the future. On a bad day, time was wasted on battles that had been lost long ago. If I'd been able to spend half the time I had to devote to considering advertising claims about Penelope Cruz's eyelashes to working on the potential of real digital marketing we could have saved a lot of angst.

Today's ASA has caught up brilliantly, but progress was hard won in the teeth of opposition from those who did not want any regulator telling them what to do.

In the crossfire

Then at the Information Commissioner's Office, we were caught in the crossfire between privacy campaigners who thought the ICO was useless and politicians who saw us as at best irrelevant and at worst bureaucratic busybodies.

I kept on my office desk in Wilmslow an illustration from a childhood history book showing King Canute and the incoming tide. It was to teach me humility, but also spoke of the need for realism, both as to the ICO's potential role and our existing powers.

The response of privacy campaigners to Google Streetview, over my first summer in 2009, was hysterical. And I found similar Luddite attitudes on the Article 29 Working Party in Brussels, with very little practical thinking about how the new media might actually be sensibly regulated in the public interest.

In Whitehall and Westminster, there was constant foot dragging under administrations of every stripe – Labour, Coalition, and Conservative – reluctant to give the Commissioner either the powers or the resources necessary to regulate information rights in the digital age. Indeed, I was frequently having to fight rearguard actions to preserve the modest arsenal I had inherited from my predecessors.

I remember having to deal with the campaign by one cabinet minister to exempt local government councillors from the requirement to notify as data controllers. His minister of state made it all too clear to me that, so far as he was concerned, I was part of the bureaucratic burden he was in politics to remove. Another minister told me that making company directors personally liable in cases of data misuse would place an unreasonable burden on business.

As the clock ticked towards the implementation of the EU's General Data Protection Regulation, I tried to free the ICO from the public sector pay policy in order to address the uncompetitive pay structure which rendered the regulator all too vulnerable to having our expert staff poached. In the midst of austerity, Whitehall simply did not want to know.

My 'keep calm and carry on' message about GDPR, posted on the ICO website the day after the EU referendum, met with a furious response from Whitehall. In my final few days as Commissioner, I was able to point out that GDPR would happen in May 2018, whether the UK was in or out of the EU, and we would anyway have to implement something very similar in order to continue sharing data across EU borders. My advice was not well received. Some months later, the Government caught up. But the UK had lost more preparation time. Late again.

Reluctance and protectionism

The suspicion of the ICO, born no doubt of the part played by the Freedom of Information Act in the MPs' expenses scandal, was shared, if for other reasons, by the print media who were passionately opposed to the introduction of a custodial penalty for the most serious data breaches. The same titles that today inveigh against invasions of privacy by Facebook *et al* were determined to protect their own access to personal information – in the name of press freedom. And the reluctance of both the politicians and the press over many years to grasp the digital nettle is one of the reasons why we in the UK find ourselves with our current crisis of confidence in digital media, way behind events and running to catch up.

It seems to me that the digital world is a classic case of a field where regulation needs to keep up with fast-moving developments to be effective and so that trust and confidence are preserved. But, in a business where the leading players are consistently several jumps ahead, both of the competition and of the authorities, the contribution of Whitehall and Westminster has consistently been several steps off the pace.

Despite all this, the ICO in my time as Commissioner, succeeded in producing media guidance in response to Leveson, guidance that was respected by both media and campaigners. And, following the Right to be Forgotten judgment of the EU Court of Justice in 2014, the ICO developed an approach to complaints that respected both privacy rights and freedom of expression. Many in the media said it would never work – but it's working. I remember the response when I accused the media lobbyists of crying wolf: 'But there is a wolf!' Well, it turned out there wasn't.

Perhaps I should be more optimistic. After all, it's been today's ICO that has been taking on the social media companies (Facebook and Cambridge Analytica, WhatsApp and, again, Facebook) over the past year. Indeed, the UK and the ICO are now seen as leaders in this space by data protection authorities globally. And the Government has moved to give the ICO the powers needed to be an effective digital regulator. Digital Preservation Orders, No Notice inspection powers, access to data held by cloud providers – these are powers that very few, if any, other DPAs enjoy, whether in Europe or internationally.

But as we mark the centenary of the 1918 armistice, I am reminded of a First World War newspaper cartoon about the Asquith coalition, entitled *The Hymn of Too Late*. The various rival personalities, including Asquith and Lloyd George, Bonar Law and Curzon are singing:

> *We are too late! We are too late!*
> *It's really most unfortunate,*
> *I, I alone am worth my salt*
> *I never, never hesitate*
> *When managing affairs of state*
> *It's all the other fellow's fault*
> *HE – makes – US – late*

I hope the experience of Facebook and Cambridge Analytica will persuade government and parliament to get on with delivering what is necessary if digital media are to be a blessing and not a curse.

I remember John Birt dismissing some of his BBC critics as 'old soldiers polishing their muskets'. The passage of time has proved Birt right and his critics wrong. But old soldiers aren't invariably wrong.

In my case, however, a word from Harold Macmillan may be more appropriate: 'Old actors shouldn't hang around the Green Room'. So I don't, and I won't. I am very admiring of what Elizabeth Denham and her ICO team are achieving; and I hope she doesn't have to experience the carping and foot-dragging I had to put up with in the face of the digital challenge. After all, we have all had more than 25 years to begin to get this right.

Note on the contributor

Christopher Graham is Chair of Public Services Lab LLP (www.capacitylab.co.uk) and Vice-President of the Council of Liverpool University. He was UK Information Commissioner from 2009 until 2016.

Tackling the impossible, doing the essential – the road to regulation

Once the regulation of content on social media was thought of as unnecessary and impossible. Now in the wake of a series of scandals and a sharp change in public opinion, politicians are promising action. Phil Harding examines the arguments and outlines a model of regulation that could work

"[Internet companies] only ever take action when the threat of regulation is real." Damian Collins, chair Culture, Media and Sport Select Committee.

"Some people say that it is not for government to regulate when it comes to technology and the internet. We disagree." Conservative Party election manifesto 2017.

The social web promised us a digital utopia: a free exchange of ideas and views, free of governance or regulation. The trouble is it hasn't worked out that way.

The sharp change in mood has been driven by the growing list of social ills that have been laid at social media's door: fake news, endangering democracy, plundering and selling personal data, shielding criminality and corruption, hate speech, terrorism, child pornography, cyber-bullying – not to mention tax avoidance and abuse of monopoly market power.

The end result of this growing disenchantment with social media has been that the debate about content regulation has now moved on from whether or not we should do it to the practicalities of where and how. Regulation won't be easy but for the first time the political will to enforce it is there.

The political seesaw

For many years politicians were in awe of technology and the big technology companies. World leaders were anxious to be seen to be keeping up with the new trends. The promises of the companies were beguiling: Facebook would foster friendships; Google would enable us to search the world's information; Twitter would democratize free speech; Amazon would take the fuss out of shopping. Why would anyone want to stand in the way of progress, much less regulate it?

Generous funding of political campaigns in the US and intensive lobbying everywhere helped reinforce the tech companies' case.

Now the political seesaw has jumped the other way. Where once there was a feeling that the capitalism and tech ideas coming from Silicon Valley were good for society, there is now an increasingly hostile mood.

Why regulation?

Why do societies have regulation at all? Some form of regulation is essential for the proper functioning of economies and societies. It underpins markets, protects the rights and safety of citizens and ensures the delivery of public goods and services. The foundation of good regulation is to avoid exploitation and to prevent harm, especially to those who are most vulnerable. At the same, regulation is rarely costless. Businesses often complain that red tape holds them back while citizens may complain about the time they waste filling out paperwork.

Striking the right balance between the cost, bureaucracy and restriction of freedom caused by regulation and the prevention of potential harm likely without it is hard at the best of times, with social media it is devilishly difficult.

Social media and the law

It is not true of course that social media content is totally unregulated at the moment. There has always been regulation of the internet in terms of copyright, intellectual property, data protection and so on. Internet law is closely related to the laws that relate to other similar areas of broadcasting, retail, and information handling. While there is no specific regulator for the internet in the UK as yet, a number of statutory and non-governmental organisations, such as the Information Commissioner and the Advertising Standards Authority, cover some aspects.

The big difference between regulation of the internet and other media at the moment is that there are no specific laws in the UK governing internet content as such as there are for other types of publishing. That is the nub of the current debate. Should there be some form of regulation governing what is published on the web? It has been given extra urgency by the increasing blurring of content over the various platforms. In the moment it takes to push a button or to instruct Alexa you can switch your phone or your big screen from say a tightly regulated ITV programme to a totally unregulated YouTube video. Same screen, same format, same potential audience, should it be the same sort of regulation?

What others have done

The United States and Europe have always had sharply contrasting political attitudes to regulation. The US favours a laissez-faire approach to protect the free market. Europe goes for a much tougher, more interventionist approach. Politicians across Europe have started to question the role of the tech giants.

The EU seems determined to cement its role as the world's foremost tech watchdog. Some see Europe's recent measures on data protection as a model for future international content regulation. EU officials, when negotiating possible trade deals, are now encouraging other countries to follow Europe's lead on data protection, arguing that a unified global approach is the only way to curb Silicon Valley's power.

In Germany platforms with more than two million users, such as Facebook and Twitter, are now required by law to remove potentially illegal material within 24 hours of being notified or face a fine of up to €50m. In Italy, Facebook has been fined €3m, in France €150,000, both over abuses of personal data. The German move was particularly significant. For the first time it showed that governments could and would act to regulate content.

Publisher or platform

If the balance of debate between regulation and non-regulation has switched in the last couple of years so too has the debate about whether social media companies are publishers or merely technocratic providers of platforms with no editorial function.

This debate matters because if companies are deemed to be publishers then they also have some ethical and legal responsibility for the content uploaded and shared on their networks. It's been a complicated debate exemplified perhaps by the conflicting statements made by Mark Zuckerberg on the topic. In August 2016 he argued that Facebook was a 'tech company, not a media company'. By the time he gave evidence to the US Congress in April 2018 he had modified that statement to "I agree that we're responsible for the content, but we don't produce the content". In the UK the outgoing chair of Ofcom, Dame Patricia Hodgson, told the Commons CMS Select Committee that she personally believed companies like Facebook, Twitter and Google should be reclassified as publishers of content.

Recently the Select Committee in its interim report on fake news recommended that a new hybrid category be created for social media companies. The substantial risk with this is that it becomes too complicated, too difficult to define and falls between the two stools.

Fake news and the thought police

One of the thorniest issues facing social media regulation is how to deal with fake news: whether social media should be regulated to deal with accuracy and hyper-partisan content.

In the recent French Presidential election, President Macron's campaign was targeted online by fake news rumours alleging that he was gay and that he had a secret bank account in the Bahamas. Now the French government has proposed a draft law which in the run up to elections would allow political parties to complain about widely spread assertions they deemed to be false or implausible and go to a judge who could immediately move to stop publication. The difficulties such a law can provoke were soon illustrated by the row that ensued with both right and left wing opponents accusing the government of trying to create a form of thought police and institute state censorship. What happens for example when every candidate in an election decides hostile press coverage is fake news?

Too big, too important

One of the arguments that has been raised against any form of social media regulation is that it is impossible. Critics say the tech companies are too big to be within the reach of any meaningful form of regulation.

Certainly they are big: Facebook has 2.07bn monthly active users, more than a quarter of the world's population, who create 4.3bn posts per day. Some 1.17bn people use Google Search. WhatsApp has 1.2bn users, Instagram 700m monthly active accounts. The sheer scale of social media has created the impression of an unstoppable behemoth trampling over governments and across borders. But the recent switch in public and political opinion has radically changed that. Mark Zuckerberg may have ignored the invitation from the British parliament but he did turn up to be questioned by the US Congress and the European Parliament.

Moves to self-regulation

The very threat of some form of legislative regulation has brought about a radical change in the attitude and behaviour of Silicon Valley, which has announced an increasing number of moves towards self-regulation. The EU has told social media companies to take urgent steps to tackle fake news and abuse of personal data before the European elections in 2019 or face regulation by legislation.

The platforms have responded by bringing in new measures to tackle some of the worst problems. Facebook has hired hundreds of moderators in Germany alone. Tens of thousands of accounts and pages have been closed. Twitter is hiring new 'independent' advisors. Facebook says it will hire up to 4,000 people to enforce new rules on political advertising in the US.

Google and Facebook are both introducing measures to up-rank more trusted content. Both have brought in fact-checking agencies and are collaborating with mainstream newsrooms to help filter out misinformation, especially around elections. These actions have gone some way to allay concerns but because the companies have always been playing catch-up the remedies offered often appear as no more than reactive attempts to head off more serious action.

The role of artificial intelligence (AI) in weeding out illegal content is already significant and will grow further. Though the tech companies are reluctant to talk about how they are doing this, the use of AI is likely to involve video and audio recognition and text screening.

The threat of regulation has also meant that the companies have been pressurised into publishing many of their hitherto secret sets of codes, principles and guidelines to which they have been working. Facebook has published what it calls a set of community standards covering topics such as violence and criminal behaviour, the use of false names, nudity and fake news. But when it comes to the details, Facebook's guidelines are decidedly sketchy.

On fake news it merely says: *Reducing the spread of false news on Facebook is a responsibility that we take seriously. We also recognise that this is a challenging and sensitive issue. We want to help people stay informed without stifling productive public discourse. There is also a fine line between false news and satire or opinion. For these reasons, we don't remove false news from Facebook, but instead significantly reduce its distribution by showing it lower in the News Feed.*

What of course this paragraph dodges is how Facebook determines what is false in the first place. In the UK, politicians are unconvinced that the companies are doing enough. When the then Culture Secretary Matt Hancock invited 14 tech companies to talks only four showed up. He cited that as evidence that self-policing had not worked. Legislation was needed.

A future model

It seems almost certain that in the UK we are now moving towards some form of regulation of internet content. There have been too many instances of abuse. Public and political opinion has swung quite sharply. From the policy debates that are happening we can begin to piece together the first outlines of how that regulation might work. It's an emerging picture and is likely to change and develop in the light of practical experience and the pace of technological change. This is what a possible model could look like:

- Initially there could be different layers of regulation: some statutory backed up by legislation; some voluntary run by the industry itself. There could be three layers.

- Firstly, there would be statutory legislation introduced by the government and which would give certain powers to a media regulator, such as Ofcom, to enforce.

- This would be based on the principle of social media having a duty of care to its users.

- The legislation would lay out the fundamental principles; the regulator would then turn those into working definitions. This route offers the greatest flexibility for future change.

- The regulator would have a range of powers including enforcement notices, fines and powers of direction.

- Another area for legislation could be a move towards greater transparency for political advertising with all electronic campaigning required to have an easily accessible digital imprint including information on the publishing organisation similar to that required for election literature on paper.

- A second layer of regulation could entail a looser set of overall guiding principles, which firms would be invited to sign up to but which would be externally monitored, perhaps by the regulator. This might be how fake news is tackled, at least to start off with.

- The third and final layer would be those areas where the social media companies set their own rules and guidelines, and police them themselves.

- On statutory legislation, the government has said it will produce a White Paper in the autumn. The government has clearly grown tired of waiting for the tech companies to institute their own system of voluntary self-regulation especially on areas of greatest public concern. New legislation is likely to concentrate on the areas of greatest harm to the most vulnerable: on the safety of children online; on cyber-bullying; intimidating or humiliating online content and on the use of the internet by criminals.

- Very small media companies could be exempt from legislation, at least at first, to protect start-ups. This will also deal with some of the freedom of speech arguments. The law will be tightened to ensure that what is illegal offline is also illegal online. Loopholes will be closed.

- Internet service providers (ISPs) may be obliged to offer a content blocking feature for parents.

- In order to fend off more draconian legislation the bigger social media companies may be persuaded to offer to put more money into a major co-ordinated digital literacy programme in schools. This could be extended to a programme of civic literacy too.

- The role of AI in filtering out undesirable material, already significant, will grow.

Social media can be a huge force for good, but it's becoming more and more important that we temper and reduce its harmful effects. That's the purpose of regulation. Thoughtful regulation needn't be complicated. It is in the interests of the technology companies, it's certainly in the public interest.

Note on the contributor

Phil Harding is a journalist and broadcaster. He has written extensively on the media and media regulation. For many years he was a senior executive and editor at the BBC. Among the jobs he held there were Controller of Editorial Policy and Editor of the Today programme. E: phil@hardingmedia.com

Postscript

Where quantity, most definitely, does not mean quality

Gina Miller knows more than most of the awesome power that social media can wield. Here she asks for some civilisation to be brought to its jungle-like laws

Social media has taken us back in time to ancient Sparta where decisions all too often got to be made on the basis of who shouted the loudest. Certainly, few, if any, would claim the biggest stars it has created – and I'm afraid Donald Trump comes to mind – are softly-spoken and contemplative men (and yes, they always tend to be men) who are known for choosing their words with the utmost care.

Some years ago, I opened a Twitter account because I took the view that lies, bullying and intimidation should be called out, and I saw no reason why people like myself, on the progressive left, should surrender this enormously influential platform to the hard, regressive right. I wanted, too, to take forward arguments on a number of issues – not least Brexit – by introducing new information into the public domain. Still, my early hopes this might be a place for reasoned and informed debate have proved to be sadly misplaced.

In our courts, major boardrooms and academic establishments – and still, to a very large extent, in Parliament – arguments are conducted in a logical and mostly courteous way, on the basis of the facts. I found on Twitter, they are almost always conducted on the basis of raw emotion. What is more, you often find yourself arguing not with a recognisable individual, but, all too often, someone hiding behind a mask, if indeed it is someone at all and not a bot programmed to spew out venom from a Russian troll factory.

If Tony Blair makes an intervention on Brexit – always well argued in his lawyerly way – the shrill cry that always goes up on social media is simply Iraq. When Sir Vince Cable addresses the same issue, arguing his case just as carefully, it's tuition fees. I don't dispute these issues are embarrassing for both these men, but these responses are simply not rational or relevant in the context of Brexit. The normal rules of sensible debate do not, alas, apply in this new forum of debate.

I doubt anyone, when they consider how social media has become more and more a part of our lives since the beginning of this millennium, would say it has made our politics, our journalism and our society – and let's be clear these estates are all inter-related – any better. Indeed, I sometimes wonder if Sir Tim Berners-Lee – the creator of the World Wide Web – hasn't given us something every bit as threatening to our peaceful existence as Robert Oppenheimer, the father of the atomic bomb.

Even in the late 1990s, I recall how it was not uncommon to read in our broadsheet newspapers authoritative pieces of around 3,000 words by seasoned foreign correspondents reporting from overseas capitals. Even then, that degree of analysis was, however, starting to go out of fashion. The clickbait culture of videos of cats stuck up trees was taking hold, and the effect the internet had had on newspaper economics meant by the time Blair ordered British troops into Iraq in 2003, no major newspaper in this country had a full-time correspondent on their staff who was still based in Baghdad. As a result, there was no grizzled old foreign correspondent who could have written what now seems a very obvious piece along the lines of 'any fool can win this war – but then what?'

By 2005, when a young man named Jean-Charles de Menezes was shot dead by British police officers on the London Underground, I recall a number of supposedly respectable figures in our public life tweeting in the immediate aftermath such comments as 'got the bastard'. Had they only waited a few hours, it would have become clear that so far from being a Middle Eastern terrorist, as they had all assumed, he was in fact a blameless young Brazilian. The problem with social media, I was beginning to realise, was it requires situations to be assessed too quickly and all too often on minimal information. The catchphrase of Margaret Thatcher's Aids campaign of the 1980s was starting to haunt me: '*don't die of ignorance*'.

We are, however, where we are and we need to recognise the dangers social media now confronts us with, and, more than that, how we must not allow its rules – to all intents and purposes, the law of the jungle – to dominate our politics, our mainstream media and our national discourse.

Twitter rules mean if you make a grotesquely insulting remark about, say, Muslims, you get, as a direct result, more followers. You might even in due course get to be invited on to Question Time or the Today programme and begin to lay the foundations to a political career and your brand – albeit a very nasty and incendiary one – will incrementally increase in value. I know for a fact that bookers to major media shows will say in their defence, if you challenge them about why they had this or that racist bully on the programme, that you need only look at their online followers to see they have popular support.

This is not of course itself a healthy argument for allowing anyone what Margaret Thatcher used to call 'the oxygen of publicity'. The respected and eloquent actor Sir Patrick Stewart spoke compellingly in the summer of 2018 of how the BBC – and indeed the entire media industry – responded half a century ago to Enoch Powell's Rivers of Blood speech, which so wickedly and recklessly sought to stir up racial hatred in our country. Powell's incendiary comments garnered, of course, sensational headlines the following day, but, after that, it was interesting how media stardom was denied to Powell.

Powell would, of course, have loved to have been invited on to current affairs shows on television and radio and to have given interviews to newspapers, but it didn't happen. On the relatively rare occasions it did, the politician was subjected to vigorous and informed questioning.

News executives had in those kinder and gentler days a greater sense of restraint – if not simply good taste – which meant they wanted as little to do with Powell as humanly possible. Above all, that is what we now need to reclaim and the bookers on current affairs shows need to understand the number of followers someone has on Twitter has nothing whatsoever to do with whether they have anything useful to offer to our public life. All too often, I would say it means quite the opposite. The effect social media has on our politics, our media and our society must therefore not only be recognised, but urgently addressed.

Note on the contributor

Gina Miller is a British-Guyanese businesswoman who won a court action when she challenged the British government over its right to implement Brexit without parliamentary authority.

Other titles in the abramis 'Hackademic' series:

Oct. 2008

Beyond Trust: Hype and Hope in the British Media
ISBN: 978-1-84549-341-7

Sept. 2009

Playing Footsie With the FTSE?: The Great Crash of 2008
ISBN: 978-1-84549-397-4

Aug. 2010

Afghanistan, War and the Media: Deadlines and Frontlines
ISBN: 978-1-84549-444-5

Mar. 2011

Face The Future: Tools for the Modern Media Age
ISBN: 978-1-84549-483-4

Aug. 2011

Investigative Journalism; Dead or Alive?
ISBN: 978-1-84549-490-2

Sept. 2011

Mirage In The Desert? Reporting The 'Arab Spring'
ISBN: 978-1-84549-514-5

Jan. 2012

The Phone Hacking Scandal: Journalism on Trial
ISBN: 978-1-84549-533-6

Mar. 2012

What Do We Mean By Local?: Grass-Roots Journalism - Its Death and Rebirth
ISBN: 978-184549-540-4

Sept. 2012

The Phone Hacking Scandal: Journalism on Trial (Revised Edition)
ISBN: 978-1-84549-556-5

Feb. 2013

After Leveson?: The Future for British Journalism
ISBN: 978-184549-576-3

Aug. 2013
What Do We Mean By Local?(2nd Edition): The Rise, Fall
- and Possible Rise Again - of Local Journalism
ISBN: 978-1-84549-593-0

Jan. 2014
Data Journalism: Mapping the Future
ISBN: 978-1-84549-616-6

Feb. 2014
Is The BBC In Crisis?
ISBN: 978-1-84549-621-0

Jan. 2015
FOI 10 years on: Freedom Fighting or Lazy Journalism?
ISBN: 978-1-84549-646-3

Aug. 2015
The BBC Today: Future Uncertain
ISBN: 978-1-84549-656-2

Oct. 2015
Data Journalism: Inside the global future
ISBN: 978-1-84549-663-0

May 2016
What Price Channel 4?: Would Privatisation be a Disaster,
an opportunity or a Rebirth?
ISBN: 978-1-84549-680-7

Dec. 2016
Last Words?: How can journalism survive the decline of print?
ISBN: 978-1-84549-696-8

Jun. 2017
Brexit, Trump and the Media
ISBN: 978-1-84549-709-5

Oct. 2017
Data Journalism: Past, Present and Future
ISBN: 978-1-84549-714-9

Lightning Source UK Ltd.
Milton Keynes UK
UKHW020906021118
331647UK00005B/353/P